Disarming the Allies of Imperialism

Disarming the Allies of Imperialism
Agitation, Manipulation, and the State during China's Nationalist Revolution, 1922-1929

Michael G. Murdock

East Asia Program
Cornell University
Ithaca, New York 14853

The Cornell East Asia Series is published by the Cornell University East Asia Program (distinct from Cornell University Press). We publish affordably priced books on a variety of scholarly topics relating to East Asia as a service to the academic community and the general public. Standing orders, which provide for automatic notification and invoicing of each title in the series upon publication, are accepted.

If after review by internal and external readers a manuscript is accepted for publication, it is published on the basis of camera-ready copy provided by the volume author. Each author is thus responsible for any necessary copy-editing and for manuscript formatting. Address submission inquiries to CEAS Editorial Board, East Asia Program, Cornell University, Ithaca, New York 14853-7601.

Cover design Evangeline Ray

Number 131 in the Cornell East Asia Series
Copyright © 2006 by Michael G. Murdock. All rights reserved
ISSN 1050-2955
ISBN-13: 978-1-885445-32-2 hc / ISBN-10: 1-885445-32-6 hc
ISBN-13: 978-1-885445-31-5 pb / ISBN-10: 1-885445-31-8 pb
Library of Congress Control Number: 2006925210
Printed in the United States of America
23 22 21 20 19 18 17 16 15 14 13 12 11 10 09 08 06   9 8 7 6 5 4 3 2 1

⊗ The paper in this book meets the requirements for permanence of ISO 9706:1994.

To my beloved wife and companion. Thank you Setsu . . . .

Contents

Acknowledgements

It takes a village to write a book, and rare it is that the process will not exact a full tax on the kindness of others. This project began in 1991 as a short paper for Albert Feuerwerker. At the time I never could have guessed that a modest essay of fifteen pages would expand and eventually consume the valued time of so many. Special thanks goes to Ernest P. Young for his unfailing willingness to read long, unwieldy drafts, offer incisive and insightful commentary, and head my dissertation in the right direction. I am also indebted to Rhoads Murphey, C. S. Chang, Ralph Williams, Raymond Grew, and Roger Hackett for their lofty expectations and timely encouragement during the course of my graduate studies at the University of Michigan.

Time in Ann Arbor helped immensely for there I enjoyed the company of an unusually talented community of friends, faculty, and peers. I am particularly indebted to Terry Bodenhorn, Rob Culp, Rich Pult, Jonathan Skaff, Beth Notar, Andrew Chittick, Noriko Kamachi, the late Steve Averill, Li Dangke, Seth Harter, Bill Londo, Kathy Lopez, Yili Wu, Michael Harvey, and many others whose names my porous memory cannot seem to summon. Other locales and interactions contributed as well. Guy Alitto imparted penetrating critique in Eugene, Oregon. In Boston, John Fitzgerald helped clarify my understanding of GMD dynamics. At a conference in Tallahassee, Leslie Chen shared unique perspectives on warlordism. Marilyn Levine offered input in Provo while Joseph T. H. Lee, Tom Buoye, and Laura Stevens gave encouragement in Seattle. I am also grateful to Greg Lewis and Parks Coble, who graciously entertained my interpretations at a meeting in Weber, Utah, and to Eddy U and Rob Culp who endured more of the same in Pittsburgh. I learned from every encounter and am thankful to those who shared their time and expertise.

Others contributed assistance from a greater distance. Michael Tsin, Keith Schoppa, Ernest Young, Rob Culp, Daniel Bays, Parks Coble, and Joseph T. H. Lee very generously read chapter drafts. Shen Zhijia offered feedback while the book was still just a series of papers. I would also like to acknowledge Leslie Chen, in particular, for making available a collection of valuable sources involving his remarkable father Chen Jiongming. Colleagues at Brigham Young University also invested themselves. Rod Bohac, J. Michael Farmer, Ignacio Garcia, Gail King, Lani Britsch, and Arnold Green read early drafts or offered assistance in other ways. Clayne Pope, Frank Fox, and Neil York dug deep into institutional pockets when travel and funding were required. I must also express special appreciation to my friend and colleague Lee Butler for his unselfish help in pushing my manuscript to reach its potential.

The staff at the Academia Sinica and the Nationalist Party archives in Taipei, especially Lin Tsung-chieh, proved immensely patient. Colin Green and his wife Show-ling Hsieh made my time there much more productive and pleasurable than it otherwise might have been. I would also like to thank Evangeline Ray at CEAS for her cheerful, professional, and eager assistance each and every time—no matter how often—I encountered an obstacle. While they remain anonymous, the CEAS reviewers provided remarkably incisive comments in their thoughtful critiques for which I will always be grateful.

Lastly, I must thank those closest to me. The project benefited from the shared efforts of several gifted research assistants, including Nate Smith, Matt Real, Jjana Morrill, Debbie Romney, Jen Myers, Katy Cao, Victoria Liu, and Eve Johnson. Special kudos goes to Niu Yue, whose Herculean energy, vision, intelligence, and goodness taught me much about nobility in the world. Among the many who contributed, however, the most selfless was Setsu. Not only did she endure this project's many requisite sacrifices, she also spent weeks in the Nationalist archives painstakingly transcribing hand-written documents when we were not allowed to photocopy them. Thank you Setsu.

This book became a reality thanks to the collective aid of many gracious individuals. Be they factual, mechanical, or conceptual, however, all errors are exclusively mine.

M.G.M.

Abbreviations

CCP	Chinese Communist Party
CEC	Central Executive Committee (GMD)
Congress Declaration	*The First National Congress Declaration*
Doctrine	*The Doctrine of Sun Yat-sen*
GMD	Nationalist Party *(Guomindang)*
GSC	Guangzhou Strike Committee
NRA	National Revolutionary Army
ROC	Republic of China
PRC	People's Republic of China

The following abbreviations appear in the references list and the footnotes:

BCCM Leslie H. Dingyan Chen, comp. *A Collection of Historiographical Materials for a Biography of Chen Chiung-ming (1878-1933).*

CWR *China Weekly Review.*

FO British Foreign Office, Confidential Prints, China.

GHGZ Guangzhou he Hankou guomin zhengfu 廣州和漢口國民政府. Fifteen microfilm reels. Zhongguo dier lishi dang'an guan. 中國第二歷史檔案館. Nanjing, China.

GZD Guomin zhengfu dang'an 國民政府檔案. Guoshiguan 國史館. Taipei, Taiwan.

HGLW *Hubei geming lishi wenjian huiji* 湖北革命歷史文件彙集.

J3QD Zhongguo Guomindang Jiangxi disanci quansheng daibiao dahui jueyian 中國國民黨江西第三次全省代表大會決議案.

2QDD Zhongguo Guomindang dierci quanguo daibiao dahui huiyi jilu 中國國民黨第二次全國代表大會會議記錄.

QWBD Zhongyang qian wubu dang'an 中央前五部檔案. Zhongguo Guomindang zhongyang weiyuanhui dangshi weiyuanhui 中國國民黨中央委員會黨史委員會. Taipei, Taiwan.

USDS	U.S. Department of State, Records of the Department of State Relating to the Internal Affairs of China, 1910-1929.
ZGLH	Zhongguo Guomindang zhongyang zhixing weiyuanhui Guomin Zhengfu weiyuanhui linshi lianxi huiyi jilu 中國國民黨中央執行委員會國民政府委員會臨時聯席會議記錄.
2-ZLQ	Zhongguo Guomindang dierjie zhongyang zhixing weiyuan linshi quanti huiyi jilu 中國國民黨第二屆中央執行委員臨時全體會議紀錄.
ZWDL-QC	Zhongguo Guomindang zhongyang weiyuan gesheng getebie qushi haiwai gezong zhibu daibiao lianxi huiyi yian qicao weiyuan tanhua hui jilu 中國國民黨中央委員各省各特別區市海外各總支部代表聯席會議議案起草委員談話會紀錄.
ZWDL-XJ	Zhongguo Guomindang zhongyang weiyuan gesheng getebie qushi haiwai gezong zhibu daibiao lianxi huiyi xuanyan ji jueyian 中國國民黨中央委員各省各特別區市海外各總支部代表聯席會議宣言及決議案.
ZWDL-YS	Zhongguo Guomindang zhongyang weiyuan gesheng getebie qushi haiwai gezong zhibu daibiao lianxi huiyi yishilu 中國國民黨中央委員各省各特別區市海外各總支部代表聯席會議議事錄.
1-ZWQH	Zhongguo Guomindang diyijie zhongyang zhixing weiyuanhui disanci quanti weiyuanhui huiyi jilu 中國國民黨第一屆中央執行委員會第三次全體委員會會議紀錄.
2-ZWQH	Zhongguo Guomindang dierjie zhongyang zhixing weiyuanhui disanci quanti huiyi xuanyan ji jueyian 中國國民黨第二屆中央執行委員會第三次全體會議宣言及決議案.
ZXWD	Zhongyang diyi-erjie zhixing weiyuanhui dang'an 中央第一, 二屆執行委員會檔案. Zhongguo Guomindang zhongyang weiyuanhui dangshi weiyuanhui 中國國民黨中央委員會黨史委員會. Taipei, Taiwan.
1-ZXWH	Zhongguo Guomindang diyijie zhongyang zhixing weiyuanhui huiyi jilu 中國國民黨第一屆中央執行委員會會議紀錄.
2-ZXWH	Zhongguo Guomindang dierjie zhongyang zhixing weiyuanhui changwu weiyuanhui huiyi jilu 中國國民黨第二屆中央執行委員會常務委員會會議紀錄.

Maps

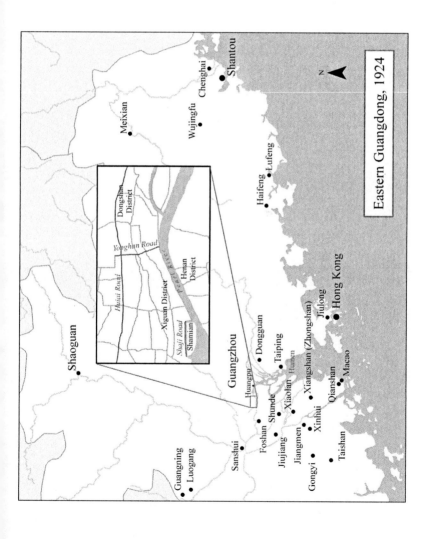

Eastern Guangdong, 1924

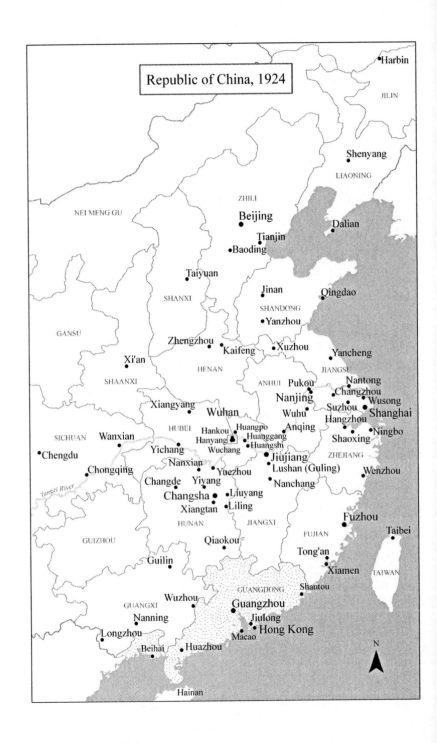

Republic of China, 1924

1. Failed Revolutions
—Discovering the Obstacles to National Unity

There is a tendency on the part of foreigners to attach political labels to Chinese politicians and to classify them individually as moderate or extremist, right or left, Communist or Conservative, etc., and the same foreigners are constantly being puzzled and disconcerted because the people so labeled do not run true to form. The truth is that the Chinese who now fill the political stage are actuated in their grouping much more by personal attraction or animosity than by political ideas and are quite ready to be either extreme or moderate as may suit their purpose for the time being.[1]
—*J. F. Brenan, British Acting Consul-General, Guangzhou, March 21, 1927*

In March 1927, Britain's acting consul-general in Guangzhou filed a report on recent developments so His Majesty's Government could respond with appropriate policy. Rather than analyze the political dynamics of China's burgeoning revolution, however, J. F. Brenan chose to relay random personal observations about its leaders: "Sun Fo [Sun Ke] is an unscrupulous windbag . . . and C. C. Wu [Wu Chaogang] is another. . . . T. V. Soong [Song Ziwen] has feathered his nest pretty well since becoming Finance Minister, and Kung [Kong Xiangxi] is already a wealthy man, whose wife . . . has social ambitions and likes entertaining on a large scale." More trivia followed: Chiang Kai-shek had adopted a son born to a concubine and Dai Jitao; Song and Kong were both Christians of bourgeois stock; Wu undermined other GMD leaders from Shanghai's French concession; and so forth.[2]

Perhaps it was arrogance, perhaps frustration, that led Brenan to conclusions uncharacteristic of the piercing analyses expected from consular authorities. More likely, as the quote opening this chapter implies, efforts to formulate a coherent picture simply failed, leading him to relay prattle because the "political labels" to which he referred and their concomitant analytical explanations offered little insight.

---

1. *FO* 405/253 [F4170/2/10], p. 114, Enclosure, Brenan to Lampson, Guangzhou, March 21, 1927. Sun Yat-sen, Chiang Kai-shek, and Taipei will be identified by the Romanization most recognizable to English readers. Other Chinese names and terms will follow pinyin conventions.
2. *FO* 405/253 [F4170/2/10], p. 114, Enclosure, Brenan to Lampson, Guangzhou, March 21, 1927.

Brenan's report about the Nationalist (*Guomindang* or GMD) base, a slippery realm where political actors slid in and out of character depending on circumstances, betrays discomfort and bewilderment. Assessments sought clear distinctions and predictability but then struggled to typologize even major revolutionary participants. The problem, however, was not unique to Brenan. Before April 1927, reports on GMD politics shared little consensus and disagreed about even "left" and "right" designations. Shanghai observers, for example, identified the "right-wing" or "liberals" with Sun Yat-sen's disaffected associates operating shadow Nationalist systems in Shanghai or Beijing and defined the "left-wing" or "radicals" as Guangdong revolutionaries aligned with the Soviets.[3] Hong Kong analysts juxtaposed Chen Jiongming "moderates" to Sun Yat-sen's "radicals" or distinguished between Chen's "Cantonese" and Sun's "Soviet" interests.[4] Beijing reports portrayed anyone opposed to northern militarists Wu Peifu or Zhang Zuolin as "red."[5] In Guangdong, some divided Sun's party between "moderates" opposed to anti-foreignism and "radicals" steeped in it. Some claimed that all party members were "left" while others reserved that designation for Soviet or CCP leaders only.[6] Still others called all revolutionaries "red," but then distinguished between "lukewarm reds" and "extremist reds."[7] One adroit assessment segmented revolutionary interests into "moderate," "moderate extremist," and "extremist extremist" camps.[8] Brenan's predecessor James Jamieson went further, calling Chiang Kai-shek a "moderate," Liao Zhongkai an "extreme radical," and Hu Hanmin a "radical conservative." Unable to place Wang Jingwei, Jamieson conjured up the appellation "60 percent radical."[9]

Label schemes varied with geography and political perspective. As Brenan's quote above indicates, however, they also fluctuated because revolutionary behavior defied preconceived categories. Some figures, such as Liao Zhongkai, almost always ended up at the left end of the political spectrum with a red, extremist, radical, or Bolshevist label, but others, such as Chiang Kai-shek, shifted back and forth. The foreign press called him the

---

3. *FO* 405/252 [F1353/2/10], p. 212, Tilley to Chamberlain, Tokyo, January 12, 1927; *FO* 405/248 [F3250/194/10], p. 43, Enclosure, extract from *Peking Leader*, May 22, 1925.

4. *FO* 405/253 [F3553/2/10], p. 50, Enclosure 3, political assessment, January 18, 1927.

5. *FO* 405/251 [F2124/10/10], p. 193, Macleay to Chamberlain, Beijing, April 1, 1926.

6. The Hong Kong branch manager of the Bank of China went as far as to claim that there was no such thing as a right wing in the GMD regime; everyone holding power belonged to the so-called left-wing because they all relied on labor agitation. *FO* 405/252 [F1199/2/10], p. 156, Enclosure, Tsuyee Pei statement, December 30, 1926.

7. *CWR* 34 (September 12, 1925): 44; *CWR* 34 (October 17, 1926): 174.

8. "Extremist extremists" allegedly sought "complete destruction" of British trade. *FO* 405/252 [F2145/67/10], pp. 346-347, General Macdonogh memorandum, March 4, 1927.

9. *FO* 405/253 [F3553/2/10], p. 50, Enclosure 3, political assessment, January 18, 1927. See *FO* 405/248 [F3817/2/10], p. 154, Enclosure, Jamieson to Palairet, Guangzhou, July 2, 1925.

"ultra-red general" for his hot tongue but could also refer to him as "moderate"—depending on the content of his latest speech.[10] Labels only confused. Indeed, as Jamieson put it, "Whatever their divisions on matters of domestic policy, so far as their outlook on foreign affairs in general, and their relationship with the British Empire in particular, are concerned, there is, perhaps, little difference in practice between the two factions, which are both strongly Nationalist."[11] Individual revolutionary leaders engaged in a broad range of activities that bled from one category into another.[12] Only in April 1927, after Chiang attacked the communists and readily identifiable battle lines appeared, did political labels begin to enjoy anything close to a general consensus.

In sharp contrast to the wildly varied reports by Brenan and his contemporaries, official historical accounts—the product of regime-sponsored research institutions and presses—encountered little struggle with typologies. After April 1927, classifications became virtually standardized. What arose as a confusing and inconsistent array of categorizations before 1927 was replaced after 1927 by certainty and conformity about what was meant by the revolution's "left" and "right" and what distinguished the two.[13] The shift was significant. For decades afterwards, these divisions became the focus of regime-sponsored historiography that clumped studies around the two factions and promoted a narrative strictly defined by their interactions. Studies fixated on Soviet involvement, the CCP role, GMD interests, and the tensions between all three groups. Standardized understandings of left/right distinctions had a long reach. Library classification systems in Taiwan and the People's Republic of China, for example, base their periodization of Chinese history on pillar events from the faction-centered narrative of GMD/CCP competition.[14]

---

10. *FO* 405/252 [F934/934/10], p. 138, Enclosure 3, Major Johnson memorandum. Also see *FO* 405/252 [F989/2/10], p. 143, Enclosure 2, Asiatic Petroleum Oil Company letter, Changsha, December 17, 1926.

11. Jamieson praised Borodin's "uncommunist" features and condemned so-called "moderates" for their anti-foreignism. *FO* 405/252a [F2790/1/10], p. 17, Anti-British Boycott negotiations memorandum, Guangzhou, July 13, 1926.

12. *FO* 405/252a [F2790/1/10], pp. 17-32, Anti-British Boycott negotiations memorandum, Guangzhou, July 13, 1926. As late as March 1927, yet another classification scheme emerged when the British identified as "moderate" all those seeking reconciliation with Chiang Kai-shek and called "extremist" anyone using popular agitation to put the military in its place. *FO* 405/253 [F4290/2/10], p. 120, Teichman to Lampson, Hankou, March 15, 1927.

13. The "left" generally referred to the Soviets, Chinese Communist Party (CCP) members, and Nationalist Party (Guomindang or GMD) members who supported communist involvement in the revolution. The "right" included those of the GMD who opposed the communists.

14. One major Chinese cataloging system, for example, distinguishes between CCP-centered periods such as "After the May Fourth Movement and the Founding of the Chinese Communist Party (1919-1924)," "The First Revolutionary Civil War Period (1924-1927)," and "The Second Revolutionary Civil War (Agrarian Revolutionary War) period (1927-1937)." See *Zhongguo tushuguan shufenlei fa*, pp. 129-130. In contrast, system in Taiwan use Republican China's presidents and major warlord conflicts. See He, ed., *Zhongguo tushu shijin fenleifa*, pp. 386-389.

Regime interest in left/right rivalry needs little explanation. Segmenting history into clean factional divisions served political interests. Both the Chinese Communist Party (*Gongchandang* or CCP) and the GMD trace their pedigree to the Nationalist Revolution and the legacy of Sun Yat-sen's revolution.[15] Both established regimes that claimed to be China's only legitimate government. Thus, each employed history to validate its own position and condemn that of its rival.[16] Left/right designations distinguished friends from enemies and justified international and domestic efforts to confront the latter. Politics impacted historical memory, framed historical debate, and narrowed historical inquiry. In the words of Prasenjit Duara,

> The history of China . . . must attend to the politics of narratives—whether these be the rhetorical schemas we deploy for our own understanding or those of the historical actors who give us their world. . . . From the first years of the twentieth-century [sic], many of the historical actors we study themselves sought to narrate their history in the linear, teleological mode and thus performatively propel Chinese history into the progress of universal History.[17]

According to identity and nationalism scholarship of the last two decades, revolutionary China's official history *had* to be written that way. Partha Chatterjee's work on Indian nationalism, for example, demonstrates how the process of defining the Indian nation translated directly into revolutionary power.[18] Since no preeminent cultural, social, or political identity existed, the first task of nineteenth-century Indian revolutionaries was to create one—to invent a national identity that could then be liberated from British control.[19]

---

15. Sun Yat-sen has been enshrined as a revolutionary icon by both parties.

16. Examples are too numerous to list. One highlight is Chiang Kai-shek's *Sue zai Zhongguo*, which was translated and widely disseminated throughout the West as *Soviet Russia in China*. Here and elsewhere, official histories have contended wildly over specifics. For example, Sun's alleged Three Great Policies *(sanda zhengce)*—alignment with the Soviets, cooperation with the CCP, and aid to peasants and workers—have been strongly discredited by ROC scholars while cited in the PRC with mantra-like repetition. (See Jiang, "Lun beifa shiqi de yige kouhao: 'Sanda zhengce'.") The wide use of terms such as *gongfei* ("communist bandits") or *Jiangzei* ("the traitor Chiang Kai-shek") in studies also stands as a simple but often-encountered reminder of the unabashed politicization of official historiography.

17. Duara, *Rescuing History from the Nation*, pp. 26-27.

18. Common usage often randomly transposes the English terms "country," "state," and "nation." In this study, the term "state" will exclusively refer to government or regime power, glossed from the Chinese terms *zhengfu* or *zhengquan*. The term "nation," glossed from the Chinese terms *guo* or *guojia*, will connote the imagined community defined by Benedict Anderson and other theorists of national identity. (See Anderson, *Imagined Communities.*) Although the Chinese terms *guo* or *guojia*, have meant many things over the centuries, by the 1920s or so they had come to closely resemble "nation" in the imagined community sense.

19. Benedict Anderson's work infused new life into the old idea that "nations are created" by describing how nationalism in South America followed on the heels of cultural identification. Finding avenues of political and social power blocked by others born in Europe, Spaniards born

With Britain dominating all political and economic means of power, revolutionaries turned to culture as the foundation of this new identity. Once articulated, this "Indian national culture" served as a base of operations for nationalists who utilized their monopoly on socializing literature, music, theater, folk art, language, *and historical memory* to assail Britain's economic and political systems. Cultural norms denounced enemies of the nation, popularized its agenda, publicized national movements and events, and prepared individuals to be good citizens of the nation. By manipulating culture to build mass support, shape it into an anti-British symbol, and employ it as a means of activism, Indian nationalists garnered revolutionary power.[20] With time, national culture—what Chatterjee calls the "inner sphere"—produced a new Indian nation under the nose of British imperialists fixated on "outer sphere" political and economic power.

The dynamics of the Indian case—one colonial power, one revolutionary party, British disinterest in culture, and an unwritten history free of expectations or preconceptions—allowed Indian revolutionaries to define national culture and from it build sociocultural power. China's situation, however, was never so simple. National culture may have been "inner sphere" in India, but it was recognized as an extension of state control and was thus clearly "outer sphere" in China. Chinese traditionally thought of themselves in terms of dynasty *and culture* because the state so often defined itself in sociocultural terms through institutions such as the Confucian exams.[21] Thus loyalties to the state often rested on cultural institutions rather than an imagined or independent abstraction known as "China."[22] Because Chinese identity

---

in America (or creoles) resented their second-class station and desired change. As they collectively shared experience through the mechanism of print capitalism, they identified with others and the "nation" was born in their minds. Anderson, *Imagined Communities*, pp. 37-83.

20. Until the twentieth century, "India" did not exist as an entity recognizable to the peoples of the South Asian sub-continent. Bengal, Gujarat, Kashmir, and so forth, were occasionally unified under historical regimes such as the Mughals, but never long enough to engender an identity of "India." See Chatterjee, *The Nation and Its Fragments*.

21. Chinese references to their collective self, i.e., *Da Mingguo* (the Great Ming), *Da Qingguo* (the Great Qing), *Hanren* (the people of the Han dynasty) and *Tangren* (the people of the Tang dynasty), imply a historical or cultural identity rather than one formed around the state because such references could be found long after the respective Han and Tang states had disappeared. These identities were often subsumed by incoming regimes but then became independent again when state power declined. See Fitzgerald, "The Nationless State," p. 86.

22. While the state can also be described as an abstraction, it at least enjoyed concrete manifestations of its existence (examinations, magistrates, police, government buildings, and so forth). The abstraction of a Chinese "nation," had no symbols because it was not even defined in the minds of Chinese. Fitzgerald cites Liang Qichao's dismay at the observation that, "Hundreds of millions of people have maintained this country in the world for several thousand years and yet to this day they have not got a name for their country." Sun Yat-sen took a more positive view, noting that the Chinese inability to distinguish the nation from the state was a direct result of the strong correlation between the Chinese race and the Chinese state. Fitzgerald, "The Nationless State," p. 86.

coalesced around the state, the periodic collapse of state power meant the collapse of the nation until a successful political movement could assert another dominant identity. Modern experience proved no different. As John Fitzgerald notes,

> The assertion of *national* continuity rests uneasily alongside the distinctive and often competing definitions of the nation which have been put forward by each state-building movement in its turn. . . . Put simply, each of the major state movements of the past century has advocated a distinctive and mutually exclusive definition of the national self: Confucian reformers associated the collective self with a distinctive civilization, liberal republicans conceived of the nation as a body of citizens, Nationalist (Kuomintang [Guomindang]) revolutionaries thought of a Chinese race, and China's Marxist-Leninists have qualified citizen and race by reference to social class.[23]

Regime change brought a reconceptualization of the nation and thus new sociocultural assumptions and norms. In this context, the relationship between sociocultural dabbling, nation defining, and politics was intimate; action involving one inherently affected the others. Naturally, each new definition aimed to serve regime interests by prescribing who would be included or excluded, how people would be organized, and how they would act collectively. Because national definitions sought to induce society's most powerful interests—be they peasant, capitalist, or racist anti-Manchu—to align with the regime or defining movement, they had to avoid broad definitions of generic appeal or universal inclusion. Such a definition would only engender a weak identity incapable of eliciting unity or power. Thus the state was empowered by advancing certain groups and restraining others, shaping the relationship of the state to those groups, promoting state-sanctioned cultural and social norms, identifying orthodox versus heterodox behavior, and so forth.[24]

According to Homi Bhabha, however, this process also produces cracks in a nation. Any attempt to sharply delineate the boundaries of a nation by specifying which people, behavior, and attitudes are included, automatically excludes all people, behavior, and attitudes not fitting that description. Asserting a national definition—even with the explicit goal of unifying a people—cannot but divide since each attempt to include one particular group automatically alienates another. In other words, through prescriptions and proscriptions, inclusion and exclusion, any national identity sufficiently strong to produce useful unity and social influence also creates an excluded other, not just outside the geographical boundaries of the nation but within

---

23. Fitzgerald, "The Nationless State," p. 76.
24. Fitzgerald, "The Nationless State," pp. 87, 90.

them as well. Healing this breach, again, is national culture—not as Chatterjee's weapon of nation defining and revolutionary attack, but as a silencing, comforting blanket of oneness. By promoting all the unifying elements of national culture—including a state-sanctioned official history or master narrative, national drama, literature, and music, a national language, and so forth—a regime can subsume ill-fitting minorities when they accept this new national culture as their own. Although national culture and unifying history might not erase segmentation, their application can ensure that unity can at least be imagined for a time and thus provide some degree of social control.[25]

Thus, in the realm of nation-building, at least, national culture plays two distinct roles. It functions as an instrument of sociopolitical power against external "others" (as Chatterjee describes) and as a pacifying, unifying force capable of subsuming internal "others" (*a la* Bhabha). The former carves out space for the new nation's institutions while the latter preserves illusions of national sociocultural uniformity. It is in this latter sense—also called universalizing history—that China's revolutionary regimes pressed historical memory into a mold of left/right dynamics. Regimes generally try to bleach out internal tensions or inconsistencies and highlight quieting images of popular unity. Most universalizing history, therefore, portrays conflict as arising between revolutionaries and their foes. China's official histories of the twentieth century, however, employed a different strategy. Anxious to generate and preserve images of predestined uniformity, legitimacy, and stability, China's revolutionary regimes channeled attention toward left/right factional tensions emerging *within* the revolutionary movement itself. By emphasizing the jagged line separating left/right ideological and political differences, ideologues obscured *other* tensions that were even more damaging to imagined unity. Official national culture and historical memory of both the Republic of China (ROC) and the People's Republic of China (PRC), in short, captured both Chatterjee's and Bhabha's definitions of national culture at the same time: an imagined unity based on a national culture defined in stark contrast to its internal (factional) opposite. National culture, politics, and historical memory thus all became part of a grand universalizing function that showcased left/right tensions rather than obscured them and built socio-cultural unity on fear of the dreaded "other" party. It is no accident, therefore, that Chiang Kai-shek prefaced his historical reproof of communism with an oath to liberate China that he might avoid becoming "unworthy of [his mother's] upbringing." Nor is it odd that Mao Zedong would inaugurate the Cultural Revolution by condemning what was "'left' in form but 'right' in essence."[26]

---

25. Bhabha, "DissemiNation," p. 299.
26. In Chiang's own words, "As a solemn token of our determination not to fail in the end, I hereby dedicate today the manuscript of my book SOVIET RUSSIA IN CHINA to the sacred memory of our dearly beloved mothers. . . . By this token my wife and I dedicate ourselves once

While China's competing regimes sought to universalize the history of the Nationalist Revolution, independent Chinese, Western, and Japanese scholars tried to explicate it, using a variety of analytical approaches. Different objectives and methods notwithstanding, however, they often arrived at the same ultimate destination: historiography dominated by the tale of left/right revolutionary strife. For decades after 1927, non-regime scholarship mirrored regime-sanctioned history by clumping studies around the key topics of Soviet, CCP, and GMD interests. Adopting the assumptions and direction of regime-sanctioned research, independent studies routinely highlighted Soviet involvement—as indicated by Conrad Brandt's *Stalin's Failure in China, 1924-1927;* Dan Jacobs' *Borodin;* Anthony Saich's *The Origins of the First United Front in China;* Robert C. North's *Moscow and Chinese Communists;* Jiang Yongjing's *Borodin and the Wuhan Government;* and C. Martin Wilbur and Julie Lien-ying How's *Missionaries of Revolution.* Other works concentrated on the CCP, including Maurice Meisner's *Li Ta-chao and the Origins of Chinese Marxism,* Arif Dirlik's *The Origins of Chinese Communism,* and Lee Feigon's *Chen Duxiu.* Still others examined the Nationalist Revolution through the lens of the GMD right-wing, such as Li Yunhan's *Cong Ronggong dao Qingdang.* A variety of studies by Eto Shinkichi, Ishikawa Tadao, Tanaka Tadao, and a host of Western scholars focused on major incidents of left/right interaction: the Zhongshan gunboat incident, CCP-led peasant mobilization in Haifeng, rivalry between Wuhan and Nanjing, the anti-communist coup of April 1927, and so forth. Independent Chinese, Western, and Japanese scholars arrived at very different conclusions. Nevertheless, their foci and interpretations were often the same. Even studies interested in parallel historical topics—such as Jean Chesneaux's *The Chinese Labor Movement, 1919-1927,* Robert B. Marks' *Rural Revolution in South China,* and Donald Jordan's *The Northern Expedition*—were heavily influenced by fundamental assumptions based around left/right factional divisions.

Independent research often stemmed from immediate political issues of the post-1927 era. Duara writes of the Western need to write history in the linear, progressive (or digressive) mode associated with Enlightenment philosophy. Eager to find "progress" (or at least "blame" so progress might better occur in the future), Western and Japanese scholars tended to examine the 1920s in terms of subsequent looming events. The GMD/CCP Second United Front, China's civil war, and the Cold War standoff inspired scholars to view the Nationalist Revolution as the inauguration of grander succeeding struggles between the Nationalists and Communists. Seeking to determine:

---

more, as it were, to the supreme task to which we are called and thus strive to be not unworthy of our upbringing." Chiang, *Soviet Russia in China,* p. vii. For Mao's quote see Robinson, *The Cultural Revolution in China,* p. 81.

Who really lost China? Will global capitalism prevail? Is Vietnam a just war? What threat does Asian communism pose? and *Can Taiwan hold out indefinitely?* scholars unearthed early evidence of "communist plots" or "reactionary backlash" during the Nationalist Revolution. Independent scholarship may have differed in its motivations, but it ultimately addressed the same questions and adopted the same assumptions about left/right distinctions laid down by party ideologues and doyens. Cut deep in the historiographical road after decades of accumulated scholarship, left/right factional ruts were difficult to avoid.[27] Even efforts to defy strong political currents by supporting contrary historical trends often accomplished little more than prompting scholars to switch sides—i.e., from a GMD-sympathetic stance to a pro-CCP one, for example, ensuring that variation simply toggled between dichotomized options.

Accounts emphasizing GMD/CCP/Soviet competition—here called the "faction-centered paradigm"—have enhanced historical understanding. They cut cleanly through thick historical knots and streamline the complex drama of China's Nationalist Revolution. By emphasizing the tensions, plots, and coups seething along the loose-knit juncture between the Nationalists and the Communists, scholars could explain dynamics with just three primary actors: revolutionaries (of both parties), the "people" who rallied to the revolutionary flag, and "enemies" who opposed it. Nevertheless, in choosing this path the paradigm also ignored others. By presenting Chinese nationalism as a magical balm that healed division and unified China—because by definition that is what nationalism does—faction-centered studies sterilized and shielded it from investigation. By emphasizing the "awakening" trope—a theme of propaganda that divided China's interests between the "awakened" *(juewu or juexing)* and "non-awakened" *(wujuewu)*—complexities in Chinese society were reduced to simple binary code. By focusing on GMD/CCP dynamics, official narratives pushed non-revolutionary interests and the revolution itself to the margins. This should not be surprising. As long as universalizing histories helped national culture cement a national identity and support their respective political orders in Taiwan and China, other historical analyses, especially those that might sully or complicate the memory of revolutionary China's proud march into modernity, either had to kowtow to the prevailing paradigm or take a back seat.

In the post-Cold War era, a time when competition between the CCP and GMD enjoys less immediate relevance, however, the faction-centered paradigm has proven dissatisfying. It ignores the Nationalist Revolution's primary purpose: to unify China under a strong centralized administration. By definition, the revolution's primary line of friction, competition, and activity

---

27. Access to archival materials often required some degree of political conformity, compelling even independent historical institutes to follow the lead of China's respective regimes.

should have been the boundary separating revolutionaries from China's non-revolutionary interests. Nevertheless, until the Cold War ended, questions addressing this arena were overshadowed by faction-centered inquiries. The relationship between the revolution and the Chinese people, organizations, and interests it sought to unify was not ignored. It was, however, often portrayed as little more than confirmation of factional differences, if not a mere backdrop to inter-party fighting.[28] The result divided revolutionary actors into cleanly segmented left/right, people/enemy dichotomies and cleared official history of confusing anomalies. The result was a revolutionary narrative that featured a movement predestined to succeed and vulnerable only to internal sabotage by reactionary party leaders or scheming communist insurrectionists. The result embalmed the inner workings of Chinese nationalism and the Nationalist Revolution in lead-crystal cases while historical studies debated: *Which of the two parties should legitimately hold power?*

While these results may have satisfied the political demands of decades past, they also produced grave distortions. For example, studies of the Nationalist Revolution often assume a natural anti-Christian bias among left-wing revolutionaries.[29] Kenneth S. Latourette, Jonathan Chao, and others attribute Christianity's troubles to "nationalism," "communists," "radicals," or "leftists" as if incompatibility were self-evident.[30] Certainly, evidence of leftist involvement in the Anti-Christian Movement abounds. Anti-Christian rhetoric denounced Christianity for sapping revolutionary vigor, cloaking imperialist penetration, and stunting Chinese nationalism. Propaganda portrayed missionaries as imperialist agents who pacified Chinese with promises of material or heavenly rewards. CCP national congresses, leftist dominance in anti-Christian organizations, leftist newspapers and journals, discovered

---

28. Claims that the CCP directed propaganda and mass organizations while the "right-wing" GMD dominated military force may be posited, for example, but suggest that the two factions worked in opposing directions rather than in tandem.

29. For example, the Anti-Christian Movement illuminated Protestantism's urban secondary and post-secondary institutions, which faced intense disruption, as opposed to Catholicism's rural elementary schools, which better resisted agitation. See Yip, *Religion, Nationalism, and Chinese Students*, p. 53. Also, anti-Christian terminology subtly suggests that Catholics might not have been involved at all. The Anti-Christian Federation *(Fan Jidujiao tongmeng)* used the term *Jidujiao* to denote things "Christian." To actual Christians, however, the same term is translated as "Protestant" and stands in contrast to "Catholic" (or *Tianzhujiao*). (Here, because anti-Christian forces did not distinguish between Catholics and Protestants, and since there is no Chinese term that includes both, the term *fandui Jidujiao* will be translated as "anti-Christian.")

30. Latourette, *A History of Christian Missions in China*, pp. 724, 794; Chao, "The Chinese Indigenous Church Movement," p. 271; *FO* 405/248 [F3250/194/10], p. 43, Enclosure, extract from *Peking Leader*, May 22, 1925; *FO* 405/247 [F1260/194/10], p. 203, Palairet to Chamberlain, Beijing, February 25, 1925. Indicating an assumed conntection, British reports highlighting CCP involvement in anti-Christian activity often enough began with the phrase, "As might be expected."

Soviet documents, and so forth collectively linked leftists to anti-Christianity. One such "leftist" report, allegedly seized from the Russian embassy by warlord troops, clearly betrays an anti-Christian bias:

> On the one hand, the Church acts as [an] espionage agent for imperialism, investigating conditions in the interior of China: politics, economics, popular sentiment, and customs. On the other hand, it uses such high-sounding words as "peace" and "universal love" and occasionally even spends money to buy the people's confidence. The Church wishes to deceive all oppressed peoples and lead them to forget their own actual sufferings in order to insure a strong and lasting foundation for imperialist oppression.[31]

In sum, it is hard to avoid the conclusion that "radicals" deserve much of the credit (or blame) for revolutionary anti-Christian activity.

Nevertheless, while this observation seems innocent enough, corollary assumptions produce untenable conclusions. They imply a clean vertical break between the anti-Christian left and not-so-anti-Christian right, perpetuating the notion that the left pursued anti-Christian objectives while right-wing leaders sought moderate or less-than-anti-Christian policies. They also infer that "superstitious" or "imperialistic" missionaries could expect little or no cooperation from left-wing leaders.

A closer look at how revolutionaries actually engaged Christian enterprises, however, shows factional ties to be a poor indicator of relations. Mikhail Borodin, chief Soviet advisor to the GMD and clearly of the left, often defended Christian interests. Zhou Enlai, a high-ranking CCP officer, enjoyed close ties to foreign missionaries. Meanwhile, right-wing leaders, such as Wu Zhihui, Zou Lu, and Dai Jitao, were instrumental in advancing the Anti-Christian Movement.[32] Liao Zhongkai, a left-wing leader and principle founder of the Anti-Christian Federation, enrolled his son at a Christian middle school, sent his son and a daughter to Lingnan University, and engaged in industrial ventures with the YMCA.[33] Several left-wing/radical leaders, including Xu Qian and Song Qingling (Madame Sun Yat-sen), were devout Christians and kept close ties with foreign missionaries while

---

31. "Resolutions on the Peasant Movement," in Wilbur and How, *Missionaries of Revolution*, pp. 745-749.

32. Fanny and Mikhail Borodin enrolled their children in Shanghai mission schools because they provided the best education for English speakers. Holubnychy, *Michael Borodin and the Chinese Revolution*, p. 265. Borodin often came to the aid of foreign missionaries. *FO* 405/253 [F4454/2/10], p. 19, extract from the *Manchester Guardian*, May 2, 1927; Rea, ed., *Canton in Revolution*, p. 65; Lutz, *Chinese Politics and Christian Missions*, pp. 231-255. Zhou penned versus from a famous Chinese poem about world peace in the diary of Bishop Logan Roots when he retired from work in China. "World Brotherhood," *Chinese Recorder* 70:4 (April 1939): 214.

33. Snow, *The Chinese Communists*, pp. 23-25; *USDS* 893.00/5994, Jenkins to Department of State, Guangzhou, January 7, 1925.

right-wing/moderates such as Chiang Kai-shek and Sun Ke (Sun Yat-sen's son) could berate missionaries with anti-Christian rhetoric as well as anyone. Other inconsistencies defy standard assumptions. Anti-Christian mobs often bypassed supposedly "superstitious" churches and mission homes to target Christianity's most modern institutions: its schools and hospitals. Left-wing leaders not only refused to nationalize missionary schools and hospitals, as anti-Christian demonstrators desired, they actually sent Nationalist police and troops to protect besieged institutions from disruption. Christian party heads could be more anti-Christian in their behavior than even the Soviets. In short, when placed side-by-side with actual events, general assumptions about the link between anti-Christianity and alleged "leftists" do not stick.

One reason faction-centered assumptions do not consistently align with revolutionary realities is that they rely on political label schemes that, as Brenan noted above, proved useless. Indeed, actual behavior could vary wildly from label-derived expectations. In official history, faction-centered typologies, analyses, and narratives fit together beautifully. Within both the Beijing and Taipei versions, revolutionary action matches ideology, revolutionary heroes engage "reactionary" or "communist" villains, revolutionary processes follow rational, predictable routes toward revolutionary objectives, revolution naturally wrests unity from chaos, and so forth. Left/right typologies work because they are based on the factional affiliation of individual actors and—since the studies themselves often aim to explain left/right interaction—demonstrate little discrepancy between classification labels and behavior; communists and GMD left-wing figures generally acted in the best interests of the left while right-wing GMD members advanced the agenda of the right. However, in the larger context of revolutionary interactions with non-revolutionary forces, left/right typologies and their derivative assumptions collapse. Brenan failed to classify the relationship between major revolutionary figures and British interests because those on the Nationalist side refused to stay in character and act as their particular political label demanded. When he and his contemporaries found inconsistencies between labels and realities, they were compelled to create odd *ad hoc* classifications (i.e., "60 percent radical") or abandon them entirely.

In the context of left/right infighting, revolutionary labels and behavior match. Outside that narrow range, however, they do not. Despite this poor fit the faction-centered paradigm has thrived while scholarly analyses that might challenge it have struggled—and not just because it enjoyed the favor of powerful regimes. Faction-centered views are persuasive, even if they do spring from portrayals of a deterministic and omnipotent nationalism that obscures its own inner-workings. The Nationalist Revolution hosted so many contradictions and featured such an irrational mix of incompatible visions and objectives that faction-centered views were the only ones that made any sense. Inconsistencies defy interpretation and the Nationalist Revolution was full of them. For example, while popular revolutionary agitators savaged imperialists and their institutions, top revolutionary leaders cultivated warm relations with the powers, namely, Britain, Japan, and the United States. Although Guomindang leaders maintained a powerful centralizing agenda, they relied on decentralized popular movements to bring it about. Even as party ideologues promised a democratic system, they set up a dictatorship to institute it. Commenting on yet another comparable paradox, John Fitzgerald explains, "The juxtaposition of divisive class struggle and cohesive nation-building *confounds attempts to theorize Chinese nationalism.*"[34] [Emphasis added.] In short, while efforts to universalize China's history advanced, largely by simplifying revolutionary dynamics, efforts to "theorize," rationalize, or otherwise analyze it have not.

Embracing the Nationalist Revolution's paradoxical qualities, this study argues that inconsistency—more than culture, symbols, ideology, geography, or any other factor—gave revolutionary nationalism its distinctive edge. Indeed, the very features that obscure analytical explanations of Chinese nationalism during the Nationalist Revolution are what enabled its success. China's particularly forbidding sociopolitical climate meant that no single nationalistic approach could produce sufficient power to unify the country. Guomindang leaders, therefore, were forced to employ two opposing strains of nationalism at the same time. The result was a unique revolutionary blend. Although fraught with tension and contradiction, its resulting synergy opened valuable opportunities to Nationalist leaders as they strove to unify China's diverse interests.

Contradiction: Readying a People, 1912-1918

The Nationalist Revolution's particular variety of nationalism rose from the confluence of two currents: Sun Yat-sen's vision of Chinese modernity and the challenges of China's broader sociopolitical landscape. (Actually, the relationship looked more like a car crash.) The two streams shared little in common and flowed in opposite directions. Nevertheless, their tumultuous interactions eventually produced the environment in which Chinese nationalism evolved and the conditions to which it would have to adapt.

Sun Yat-sen was China's foremost revolutionary leader, founder of the Guomindang, and credited father of Chinese nationalism. Toppling the Qing dynasty in late 1911, Sun made ready to transform his new Republic of China into a modern power. In August 1912, GMD pronouncements identified his basic objectives:

(1) to preserve political unity in a unitary state *and to follow a centralized system so as to carry out the task of reconstruction*; (2) to develop

---

34. Fitzgerald, *Awakening China*, p. 316.

local self-government so as to teach the people to exercise their political power and build up the local foundations of the Republic as a complement to the central government; (3) to enforce racial integration so that the various cultures within the Republic can be developed to become one enjoyed by all; (4) to implement the policy of the people's livelihood through national socialism and to foster the livelihood of the citizens by the power of the state in order to bring about a speedy and balanced economic development; and (5) to maintain international peace through good faith in diplomacy and respect for the *status quo*, and to devote ourselves exclusively to domestic reconstruction.[35]

Sun's plan was straightforward enough. However, all efforts to implement it met setback after incapacitating setback. In crude terms, Sun could not overcome the paradoxical conditions imposed by China's sociopolitical context. Scholarship since 1989 has illuminated key components. Fitzgerald's seminal study shows how Sun's party labored to "awaken" China's people to nationalism. Michael Tsin portrays Nationalist struggles to win control over the revolutionary base in Guangzhou. C. Martin Wilbur's work fleshes out international and domestic pressures. Prasenjit Duara addresses the cultural demands—such as universalizing history—that went into nation-building. Leslie Chen shows that revolutionaries did not necessarily monopolize revolutionary activity.[36] Collectively, these and other studies unveil the mutually exclusive prerequisites that Republican China's order imposed on all incipient nationalisms. Domestic and international forces fiercely competed for political, economic, military, social, and cultural influence in a plastic sociopolitical landscape that shifted constantly with each war and regime change. It was not the strength of his opponents that plagued Sun, however, as much as the eerie way in which the demands of his own vision and those of the post-Qing order conspired against him. Threats came frequently, not in lock-step succession but in powerful combinations. Only the most flexible nationalistic approach had any hope of success. Although no one was more adaptable than Sun, no matter how he defined the Chinese nation and structured his revolutionary approach, he could not simultaneously cover all the requisite bases and free his movement from ensnaring contradictions.

The root of the problem was centrifugal energy within China's sociopolitical ecosystem. Since the late Qing, momentum had favored disintegration, not unification or centralization. Immediately after the Republic was

35. Shieh, *The Kuomintang*, p. 38.
36. Fitzgerald, *Awakening China*; Tsin, *Nation, Governance, and Modernity in China*; Wilbur and How, *Missionaries of Revolution*; Wilbur, *Sun Yat-sen*; Wilbur, *The Nationalist Revolution in China*; Duara, *Rescuing History from the Nation*, pp. 17-50; Chen, *Chen Jiongming and the Federalist Movement*.

founded in 1912, Sun's loosely organized Revolutionary Alliance (Tong-menghui) broke apart as various interests pushed to validate their visions and shape China's emerging modernity. Proposals for the new order varied widely. Some argued for a federation of Chinese provinces based on the U. S. model.[37] Others called for a larger pan-Asian alliance arrayed against white-race imperialism. Still others, like Sun, advocated a strong, centralized, democratic system.

To preserve what unity remained, Sun gave up the presidency to military strongman Yuan Shikai who promised to safeguard the Republic while democratization proceeded. Provincial elites expanded local self-governing institutions and political parties proliferated, including Sun's newly formed Guomindang.[38] When Yuan used his executive power to crush his rivals in March 1913, however, Sun was forced to modify his priorities. First, he vowed to bring down Yuan's presidency. Second, he promised to restore the Republic and continue the march toward democracy. Last, he swore never again to entrust China's fate to another. He would direct all transformation himself.[39]

These objectives, however, placed Sun face-to-face with the first of several sticky conundrums. As Bhabha might have predicted, Sun had to choose between a narrow movement guaranteeing his own personal control and a broader movement aimed at attracting widespread support. Trusting no one, he initially chose the former. On June 23, 1914, while exiled in Tokyo he formed the Revolutionary Party (Gemingdang) from loyal remnants of the Guomindang and proceeded to fortify his authority. He snubbed invitations to ally with other anti-Yuan groups and instituted secret society conven-tions—i.e., mandatory fingerprinting, sworn oaths of loyalty, strict disci-

---

37. Young, *The Presidency of Yuan Shih-k'ai*, p. 20. Federalists argued that following the U.S. system, allegedly comparable to ancient China's experience with decentralized authority *(fengjian)*, could provide strength where centralism *(junxian)* had failed. *(Fengjian* and local self-government were linked long before concepts of modernity and reform entered the scene.) Min, *National Polity and Local Power*, pp. 90-136. In short, federalism did not emerge as an alternative to nationalism, but a variant form of it. Centralists and provincialists both sought to strengthen China; they simply disagreed on how to proceed.

38. See McCord, *The Power of the Gun*.

39. Sun retaliated with the Second Revolution, but it collapsed in August. (For details see Young, *The Presidency of Yuan Shih-k'ai*, pp. 120-137.) In response, Sun asserted, "This time I shall conduct the whole affair personally. . . . The first Revolution [against the Qing] broke out before I could reach China. . . . In the Second Revolution [against Yuan] I did not take part, for I thought that many there were quite competent to carry out the work to a successful conclusion . . . but too many cooks spoiled the broth!" Cited in Schiffren, *Sun Yat-sen*, p. 177. Sun's comment is somewhat disingenuous for he did participate in the Second Revolution, albeit ineffectively. The key point is that Sun's views had changed. As Friedman describes, "Political and intellectual evolution in China changed the ephemeral views of Sun Yat-sen into a concentrated vision. . . . Sun found himself right in all his political instincts except the one of not imposing his will. Wiser now, Sun would insist on his way as the way." Friedman, *Backward Toward Revolution*, pp. 35-36.

pline—to keep his following deferential. Rejecting an earlier plan to democratize over nine years, a new charter promised indefinite Gemingdang rule and guaranteed Sun the coveted presidency if and when the revolution succeeded. This obsession with power, however, alienated many of his supporters, including his closest associate Huang Xing.[40] Others left after May 1915 when Sun offered to give Manchuria and Mongolia to Japan and accept the infamous Twenty-One Demands in exchange for aid.[41]

Unified but stunted, the Gemingdang struggled. When Yunnan allies of Liang Qichao, leader of another anti-Yuan organization, spearheaded a coalition movement in December 1915, Sun found himself on the sidelines. The following April he left for Shanghai, abandoned his exclusivity, and invited other revolutionary forces to ally under his command, but it was too late.[42] Few responded. Only Yuan's sudden decline and death in 1916 spared Sun further isolation and embarrassment.

With Yuan out of the picture, Sun assumed a low profile, content that the Republic's original parliament had been restored. The following year, however, when Beijing's new chief Duan Qirui decided to dissolve it outright and central authority disintegrated into warlordism, Sun returned to making revolution.[43] Again facing Bhabha's paradox, he this time chose the other option: an inclusive movement of broad appeal. Noting that both Yuan and Duan had derived much of their political strength from foreign aid and recognition, Sun formed an opposition government designed to draw foreign attention away from the Beijing regime and bind together China's disconnected parts. In July 1917, amid legitimizing rhetoric about "protecting the constitution," the Guangzhou regime rose, building on a foundation of two million Chinese dollars (allegedly) from Germany, a portion of the Chinese navy, a handful of friendly warlords, and some 250 former members of China's parliament. Sun bolstered his marketability on September 1, 1917 by having the southern parliament elect him Generalissimo *(dayuanshuai)*.[44]

---

40. Huang had sought cooperation with other anti-Yuan groups, but Sun refused, countering that a coalition-based revolution would only fail—as it did in 1911. Friedman, *Backward Toward Revolution*, pp. 56-63. Writing of Huang later, Sun insisted that others not "mix with Huang and his men too much, for they did not join me yet in the new organization which I formed since the failure of the second revolution. Until he swear [sic] his loyalty to me and obey [sic] my order implicitly, I would have nothing to do with him and his men." See Wilbur, *Sun Yat-sen*, p. 89.

41. Wilbur, *Sun Yat-sen*, pp. 83-91; Schiffren, *Sun Yat-sen*, pp. 182-83; Chang and Gordon, *All Under Heaven*, p. 58. The audacious Twenty-One Demands sought to extend Japanese influence over China's military and political institutions, among other things.

42. Schiffren, *Sun Yat-sen*, pp. 185-187; Friedman, *Backward Toward Revolution*, pp. 190-195, 199.

43. After Yuan, President Li Yuanhong restored the original 1912 parliament, but he could not contain militarism. In June 1917, militarist Premier Duan Qirui dissolved the parliament in favor of a pliable parliament that he "restored" on August 14. See Chang and Gordon, *All Under Heaven*, p. 59.

44. Sun left the presidency open for Li Yuanhong in the hope he would join the Guangzhou

Enthusiasm and trappings notwithstanding, Sun could not remain astride his new administration. Warlord and politician allies found him convenient for their own purposes. Rivalry between Guangxi leaders and Sun's "Triumvirate" rent solidarity.[45] Extensive negotiations with the Germans and Americans failed to impress or secure recognition from either. Sensing disintegration, Sun redoubled efforts to win foreign aid but with no success.[46] In April 1918, other leaders of the southern coalition reduced the Generalissimo's status to one of seven committee members. Demoted by his supporters and frustrated by his ineffectiveness, Sun abandoned Guangdong for the foreign concessions of Shanghai.

Failure did offer one bonus; it showed how far Sun's nationalism would have to stretch to unify all Chinese under a centralized democratic system enjoying economic development and stable international relations. It also clarified one set of prerequisites his movement would have to satisfy. Defining revolutionary organizations in narrow exclusive terms preserved his status and cemented control, but engendered little broad-based support. Conversely, defining his movement in broad inclusive terms garnered support but fragmented integrity and undermined his influence. Unable to attract support and maintain unity at the same time, Sun's revolution either stagnated or splintered.

Returning to Shanghai and pondering his predicament, Sun decided to lobby a different constituency. Eschewing his earlier practice of focusing on revolutionary and political elites, Sun appealed directly to his countrymen. In late 1918, he unveiled his latest program of social reform and constitutional democracy in an essay entitled *The Doctrine of Sun Yat-sen* (hereafter *Doctrine*).

Although *Doctrine* ostensibly outlined a vision of China's modern future, it tried to win Chinese sympathy by employing extensive and explicit references to China's traditional past. [47] Sun attacked the ancient adage "knowledge is easy, action is difficult" *(yizhi nanxing)* and reversed the couplet, pledging "knowledge is difficult, action is easy" *(yixing nanzhi)*. Declaring that he alone possessed the knowledge to save China—the requisite "difficult" part—Sun assumed the role of a sage philosopher king. To his party he gave the tasks of transmitting this special understanding, rooting out enemies, and preparing China's people for democracy and constitutional rule.[48] Lower in this presumed hierarchy, below himself and his party, sat all

---

regime. Sharman, *Sun Yat-sen*, p. 212.

45. The Triumvirate included Guangdong's Wu Tingfang, Tang Shaoyi, and Sun himself. See Sharman, *Sun Yat-sen*, p. 212.

46. Wilbur, *Sun Yat-sen*, pp. 91-96.

47. Schiffren argues that Sun's passion for traditional culture grew from his limited exposure to it. Schiffren, *Sun Yat-sen*, p. 210. Also see Chang and Gordon, *All Under Heaven*, pp. 62-63.

48. Sun, *Memoirs of a Chinese Revolutionary*, p. 91. Sharman explains, "As regards China's

other Chinese whose duty was to "carry out what they receive from the . . . first two groups without doubting and without hesitating."[49]

Asking his countrymen to assume their "proper" place, Sun turned to other traditional conventions. He paraphrased Confucius' preface to the *Great Learning (Daxue)*, asking all to begin "cultivating self" *(xiushen)*, and "ordering family" *(qijia)*, so the loftier goals of "governing the country" *(zhiguo)*, and "pacifying the world" *(pingtianxia)* could follow.[50] Appealing to traditional notions of ritualistic duty *(li)*, he argued:

> We must begin with the oath, which serves as the starting point for making the "heart straight" *(zhengxin)* and the "mind sincere" *(chengyi)*. . . . At the beginning of the Republic, my party comrades considered the oath an unimportant matter, wanting to abolish it, and said that many of the ideals I advocated were shallow and easy things. . . . This ceremony, which is at the root of the rule of law, was abolished with the founding of the Republic. This is the major reason for the failure of our revolutionary reconstruction.[51]

If others would just follow his lead, Sun pledged, saving China would "be just as easy as turning a hand or breaking a twig."[52]

Despite Sun Yat-sen's claims to sagacious vision, few Chinese responded. One problem, of course, was that there were few universal notions of national culture because it had yet to be defined in China's new order and it was evolving in a number of new directions all at once, diluting the salience of any particular strain, especially one so steeped in a fading tradition. Not many Chinese were inspired to act on Confucian-esque arguments and notions alone.

---

problem, Sun] felt that the thinking had already been done. Had not he himself drafted sound plans for China's reconstruction? Nothing remained but to put the plans into effect." Sharman, *Sun Yat-sen*, p. 234.

49. Sun, *Memoirs of a Chinese Revolutionary*, p. 84. In Schiffren's words, "It was common practice [Sun] pointed out to identify individuals with the religions, theories or doctrines they originated. Buddha, Confucius, Jesus, Darwin and Monroe were well-known examples. Thus, obeying Sun Yat-sen, he said, simply meant pledging allegiance to his Three Principles and five-power constitution: personal and ideological obedience were inseparable." Schiffren, *Sun Yat-sen*, p. 212.

50. Sun, *Memoirs of a Chinese Revolutionary*, p. viii.

51. Sun, "The Doctrine of Sun Yat-sen," in Wei, et al., eds., *Prescriptions for Saving China*, pp. 211-212. Sun referenced verse 4 from the Text of Confucius, the preface to the *Great Learning (Daxue)*: "The ancients who wished to illustrate illustrious virtue throughout the kingdom, first ordered well their own States. Wishing to order well their States, they first regulated their families. Wishing to regulate their families, they first cultivated their persons. Wishing to cultivate their persons, they first rectified their hearts. Wishing to rectify their hearts, they first sought to be sincere in their thoughts. Wishing to be sincere in their thoughts, they first extended to the utmost their knowledge. Such extension of knowledge lay in the investigation of things." See Legge, *The Four Books*, vol. 1, pp. 357-358.

52. Sun, *Memoirs of a Chinese Revolutionary*, p. viii.

A bigger problem, however, stemmed from the way Confucian ideals of "all under heaven" *(tianxia)* were reflected in Sun's democratic idealism. Sun wanted *all* Chinese to participate in the construction of his vision and, therefore, defined the "people" in broad terms of race; no Chinese would be left behind.[53] That meant, however, that each one also had to share his views. As defined in *Doctrine*, all who understood his doctrines as prescribed in *Three Principles of the People (Sanmin zhuyi)* and demonstrated "loyalty to the Republic" counted as the "people"—those in whom national sovereignty was vested. In *Doctrine*, Sun swore an oath to serve the Republic and called on all concerned Chinese to do the same, claiming that, "Everyone who has passed through this oath-taking ceremony will then have performed his moral and legal duty to qualify as a citizen of the Republic of China."[54]

While this standard may have fit his idealist vision, because he refused to narrow the national definition enough to advantage certain specific interests, Sun could not attract the support of any. Indeed, given the number of certifiably loyal Chinese who took Sun's oath, the "people" of China was a very small group.

Sun could not have been too disappointed, however, because technically the "people" and the national culture binding them as one were both still in the making. His party had not yet begun to create or shape either. Besides its duties as "transmitter" of sagely knowledge, Sun's revolutionary party was also charged with helping Chinese "cultivate self," "order families," and make "hearts straight" and "minds sincere." Until that process was well underway, one could only expect that few would subscribe to Sun's oath. Only after the party began injecting his version of national culture into the minds of Chinese everywhere would the "people" emerge ready to support their new nation.[55]

Shaping national culture and generating his own "people"—the approach described by Chatterjee for India—offered Sun a chance to maintain control and attract support at the same time. Unfortunately for him, however, shaping hearts and minds was already a crowded and busy enterprise in China. Almost all of China's proliferating educational institutions harbored some particular vision of the future. Private schools founded by gentry interests promoted traditional values. Established by Western-educated elites, others emphasized modern science, mathematics, Western culture, and

---

53. Fitzgerald explained it best: "To the makers of Nationalist China any concession that yielded the fundamental integrity of the race was not an alternative to national extinction but a form of national extinction." Fitzgerald, "The Nationless State," p. 98.
54. To Sun, this was the best way to prevent despotism. Sun, "The Doctrine of Sun Yat-sen," in Wei, et al., eds., *Prescriptions for Saving China*, p. 214; Sun, "The Foundation for Building the Republic of China," in Wei, et al., eds., *Prescriptions for Saving China*, p. 248.
55. Sun, "The Doctrine of Sun Yat-sen," in Wei, et al., eds., *Prescriptions for Saving China*, p. 214; Sun, *Memoirs of a Chinese Revolutionary*, p. 101.

philosophy.[56] Rural reformers, such as Yan Yangchu (James Yen), tailored education to peasant needs while foreign-trained educators such as Hu Shi and Tao Xingzhi promoted curricula more suited to urban settings. Institutions ranged from tiny traditional one-room academies *(sishu)*, where students still memorized the ancient classics, to medical universities teaching modern surgical techniques. Collectively, public schools generally belonged to a regional and/or national system, but most private schools refused, preferring unfettered autonomy in order to protect their sociocultural influence.[57] Movements big and small, such as John Dewey's Progressive Education or Liang Shuming's anti-iconoclasm, competed for educator and institutional loyalty.[58] Newer revolutionary schools displaced gentry reformist institutions which, in turn, had overshadowed westernizing schools set up during the late Qing.[59]

Competition was fueled by the common belief that education would shape China's future political order. Don Munro notes that, "One basic assumption in Chinese thought is that a change in educational techniques is a key to changing human behavior, and thus by implication a key to solving urgent political and social problems."[60] Liberal intellectuals, such as Hu Shi, claimed that education could save China by fostering "right" beliefs.[61] Chen Qitian, the editor of the *Chinese Educational Review (Jiaoyu zazhi)*, insisted that education be geared to reconstitute the nation. Prominent educator Fan Yuanlian claimed that China needed "not educational internationalism, localism, or socialism, but educational nationalism."[62]

Different notions about what constituted "right," "proper," or even "national" action, however, spawned intense rivalries between competing philosophies, thrust education into heated debates over national salvation, and obstructed efforts to unify China's numerous institutions. For good or ill, China's educational world reflected the country's political realm—both were highly competitive and fragmented.

With so much at stake, foreign schools run by Western, Russian, and Japanese educators engaged this debate of national direction with great

---

56. Bastid, *Educational Reform in Early Twentieth Century China.*
57. Even general policy of Beijing's Minister of Education "scarcely reached beyond regions of the North near to the capital where the Beijing government was able to exercise some authority." Bastid, "Servitude or Liberation," pp. 13, 291.
58. Liang denounced western education, complaining that it created a class committed only to itself and transformed intellectuals into a "decadent, parasitic aristocracy unjustifiably supported by society." Alitto, *The Last Confucian*, pp. 142-143.
59. Bastid, *Educational Reform in Early Twentieth-Century China*, pp. 86-87.
60. Munro, *The Concept of Man in Early China*, p. 163. "Orthodox" education that legitimized Qing authority was rewarded as its students gained access to political power, cementing the bond between education and politics. Education outside regime blessing was persecuted as "heterodox." Chang and Chang, *Crisis and Transformation*, pp. 334-345.
61. Munro, *The Concept of Man in Early China*, p. 165.
62. Peake, *Nationalism and Education in Modern China*, pp. 125-127.

enthusiasm. Of these, Christian schools stood out. Enjoying a head start of several decades, Christian missionaries directed the grandest foreign educational enterprise. In the nineteenth century, missionaries focused on saving souls, believing that China would modernize as it became Christian. By the 1890s, however, that view reversed when low conversion rates spawned evangelistic theories claiming that social problems "blinded" China's millions to Christian truths, thus preventing wide-scale conversion. [63] Denouncing the "evils" of concubinage, footbinding, infanticide, child brides, poverty, opium use, corruption, and so forth, missionaries who prized social reform over direct evangelism established thousands of institutions designed to transform China's sociocultural world in order to prepare Chinese for Christianity.

The Christianizing drive started small and was opposed by advocates of traditional proselytizing, but it quickly grew after the turn of the century and eventually claimed as much as 80 percent of the personnel operating in British missions. [64] When China's political order crumbled into warlordism, these missionaries were well positioned to take advantage. Paul A. Varg explains what they intended to do:

> What . . . missionaries hoped for was a mass movement of Christians in favor of reconstruction along lines compatible with the ethical teachings of Christianity. Just as the Communists sought to capitalize on the rise of Chinese nationalism and social unrest for the purpose of fixing on China the soviet system, so did these Christian leaders hope to link up the social-ethical teachings of Christianity with the aspirations of the Chinese people so that Christianity might become an integral part of the new nation that was emerging. [65]

In short, missionaries came to view Christian education not just as a tool of sociocultural change but as a means of political transformation as well, thus binding Christian sociocultural objectives to larger political goals. Advocates of this "social gospel" saw themselves as revolutionary in their own right, destined to shape a new China by educating impressionable, young Chinese and socializing a generation of future leaders sympathetic to a modernity defined in pro-Western, liberal-democratic, Christian terms. [66]

Unable to compete in the brutal realm of warlord politics, missionaries emphasized education and sociocultural change, which, as Chatterjee's study

---

63. The turning point came when Rev. James S. Dennis published his widely influential *Christian Missions and Social Progress*. An excellent account of the theological and historical roots of the "social gospel" movement can be found in Cui, *The Cultural Contribution of British Protestant Missionaries*, pp. 8-14.

64. Cui, *The Cultural Contribution of British Protestant Missionaries*, p. 20.

65. Varg, "A Survey of Changing Mission Goals and Methods," p. 6.

66. Cui, *The Cultural Contribution of British Protestant Missionaries*, pp. 207-334.

implies, was safer than political or military activity but could be equally effective at defining a nation. Even U.S. President Woodrow Wilson endorsed the plan, claiming that an infusion of democratic and Christian virtues would bring about the stability and progress necessary to transform China into a modern country.[67] Energized by this Christianizing agenda, missionaries trained in social and cultural transformation represented a powerful and well-endowed voice in the debate over China's national direction.[68] With time, hundreds of thousands of Chinese were exposed to the religion through its hospitals, orphanages, schools, universities, clubs, and other facilities, and forecasts predicted only growth.

Within this volatile educational realm, where Chinese and foreign systems battled to define national culture and win hearts and minds, Sun could not compete. In 1918, his *First Steps Toward Democracy* was used as a text by some like-minded educators.[69] In 1920, he asked supporters to incorporate his doctrines into popular textbooks.[70] However, beyond these modest steps, Sun had no schools and little influence. Without institutional parity, he could not engage the struggle, garner resources, or capture popular attention. China was no India. In China, the political value of national culture was well understood, ensuring that the sociocultural sphere hosted an exceptionally energetic array of interests all trying to mold China's development by promoting their own pet agendas via an enormous range of institutions. Few willingly conceded sociocultural space to rivals, keeping the spectrum of possible national identities and versions of national culture broad, diverse, and packed. As long as no single vision rose to dominate, individual Chinese had a wide selection from which to choose. In this buyer's market, Sun's attempt to sell sacred knowledge and ritualistic oath-taking must have appeared quaint indeed. It was certainly ill-equipped to compete with other purveyors of culture. Without better means to shape national culture and construct a "people" that would follow him, Sun's movement was fated to remain interminably stuck between stagnation and fragmentation.

---

67. Trani, "Woodrow Wilson, China, and the Missionaries," p. 332. Wilson reportedly announced to a group of ministers, "This is the most amazing and inspiring vision—this vision of that great sleeping nation suddenly awakened by the voice of Christ. Could there be any greater contribution to the future momentum of the moral forces of the world than could be made by quickening this force which is being set afoot in China?" Varg, *Missionaries, Chinese, and Diplomats,* pp. 80-81.

68. By 1926, Protestants alone directed sixteen major universities and colleges, ten professional schools, four theological schools, and six medical campuses, in addition to hundreds of middle and primary schools. Total property investments amounted to some US$19 million. Varg, "A Survey of Changing Mission Goals and Methods," p. 6. Fundamentalist missionaries criticized such efforts as "humanistic" distractions to Christianity's "true" purposemovement.

69. Fitzgerald, *Awakening China,* p. 268.

70. Chan, "Sun Yat-sen and the Origins of the Kuomintang Reorganization," p. 19.

Irony: Securing State Power, 1919-1923

According to Sun, the surest solution to this revolutionary quandary was power at the top of China's political pyramid. Like emperors of old, influence through a state apparatus would quickly enable him to concurrently define national culture, construct a "people," and formulate his particular variety of the Chinese "nation." Unfortunately for him, a few major obstacles blocked the way. First, of course, was the stupendous task of seizing power. Second, the infrastructure on which central government authority once rested had to be rebuilt. Finally, militarism had to be supplanted by civilian rule.[71] Unable to accomplish any of these objectives on his own, Sun turned to the foreigners. A second essay entitled *The International Development of China* (completed in late 1918), promised solid returns to any power willing to support China's development and help Sun become China's next president. As usual, however, Sun could not arouse foreign interest.

Frustration gave way to encouragement the following spring when China's poor treatment at the Versailles peace talks unleashed a torrent of popular demonstrations that collectively came to be known as the May Fourth Movement. Hoping to capitalize on its energies, Sun reversed his pleading tactics by denouncing foreign imperialism. On June 13, he threw himself into the national spotlight by blasting his former Japanese allies for imperialist misconduct and their Twenty-One Demands. Patriotic Chinese responded and soon contributed enough funds to underwrite yet another party restructuring. In October 1920, Sun revived his party's old name—the Nationalist Party (Guomindang or GMD)—and on November 20 introduced a new constitution based on his doctrines of the Three Principles of the People, the Five Power constitution, and single-party tutelage. For himself, Sun took the lofty title of president *(zongli)*.

At first glance, a strident anti-imperialist and anti-warlord platform looked like the magic bullet Sun needed to convert Chinese into his "people." It enjoyed wide appeal among May Fourth students, intellectuals, workers, and merchants longing for national unification.[72] Nevertheless, Sun still had

---

71. Yuan Shikai's reign had undermined civilian rule by dismantling the "provincial regimes" (of Jiangxi, Jiangsu and Anhui), replacing provincial leaders (i.e., Tan Yankai [Hunan] and Li Yuanhong [Hubei]) with central appointees, dissolving provincial and county assemblies, disbanding provincial armies in favor of "guest army" *(kejun)* troops loyal to the center, recommissioning law-of-avoidance laws, implementing a new exam system, and subordinating provincial finances to the center. Because they were easier to control, Yuan had tried to strengthen provincial civil leaders and gave centrally appointed military governors only loose authority over their armies. His efforts failed, however, largely because he otherwise relied so heavily on military rather than political measures. McCord, *The Power of the Gun*, pp. 172-194.
72. The May Fourth Movement enhanced interest in centralism. Although warlordism did not reflect what provincialist federalists envisioned for China, its control and manipulation of provincial institutions soured their perceived worth. As McDonald explains, warlordism's rise meant "all civilian-based reforms were doomed." McDonald, *The Urban Origins of Rural*

reservations. Despite his own rhetoric, he still saw more potential in the northern militarists, provincial federalists, and foreign imperialists than in China's excited urbanites. He wanted and needed popular support but not necessarily popular involvement. The people worried Sun. Mass demonstrators struck him as unruly and impulsive. Iconoclastic intellectuals scoffed at his claims to transcendent knowledge. Anti-imperialist students aroused disruptive peasant and worker activism.[73] Once in motion, popular forces were hard to control. More important, approval among the masses did not automatically translate into state power. Few could deny that national power still flowed through the fingers of foreigners and militarists and thus had to be acquired from them. Sun could not envision how China's people could construct a state, but he could easily foresee how a state might formulate a "people." Since only militarist and foreign interests offered access to state power, their support had to be achieved if his vision was going to succeed. As a result, Sun dove headfirst into scheming and dealing with China's power brokers like any other ambitious politician. In the best-case scenario, a successful arrangement could secure militarist and foreign backing, propel him into Beijing's halls of power, and offer the influence he needed to implement his vision.[74]

Anything less than instant and total success, however, threatened to tear Sun's movement asunder by imposing on it two more irreconcilable demands. The first of these pitted provincial/localist loyalties against Sun's national vision, quickly leading to his undoing. Problems first appeared in November 1920, when militarist Chen Jiongming—a reform-minded provincialist and supporter of Sun Yat-sen—captured Guangzhou and invited him to return. Setting up office in Guangzhou a second time, Sun quickly instituted another opposition regime and persuaded over two hundred former members of parliament to elect him "Extraordinary President" *(feichang da zongtong)* of the Republic of China in April 1921.[75]

Sun's interest in Guangdong drew primarily from its utility as a means to national power. Without a base, he could never be more than an embellished pawn in Beijing even *if* invited to form a cabinet there. As the head of an

---

Revolution, p. 58. Provincialists were also losing the semantic battle. They advocated decentralized authority *(fengjian)* as opposed to centralized authority *(junxian)*, but when Marxists glossed "feudalism" as *"fengjian,"* the Chinese term became tainted with the negative connotations tied to Marx's typology. Min, *National Polity and Local Power*, pp. 112-136. With time, provincialists such as Tang Dezhang and Zhang Taiyan had to completely drop *fengjian* rhetoric because of its communist connotations. Duara, *Rescuing History from the Nation*, pp. 153-175.
73. Schiffren, *Sun Yat-sen*, p. 210. Also see Chang and Gordon, *All Under Heaven*, pp. 62-63.
74. Sun convinced himself that international assistance was all he needed. Speaking of relations between the north and south, he once told U.S. businessman Thomas W. Lamont, "Peace between South and North? Why yes. Just you give me $25,000,000, Mr. Lamont, and I'll equip a couple of army corps. Then we'll have peace in short order." Wilbur, *Sun Yat-sen*, p. 99.
75. Chan, "Sun Yat-sen and the Origins of the Kuomintang Reorganization," pp. 21-22.

important province, however, he was qualified to engage in national-level talks and schemes with other regional authorities such as Zhang Zuolin and Wu Peifu. National prominence, in short, required regional dominance—or at least the appearance of such since actual power in Guangdong was not as important as whether other players in north and central China perceived it. Therefore, Sun did not view the province as much more than a convenient source of revenue and legitimacy for his northern politicking and as temporary housing for his opposition government—itself simply bait to attract foreign recognition and aid. Anxious to enhance his marketability, Sun pressured Chen Jiongming to conquer Guangxi in the summer of 1921. By year's end, Sun had accumulated enough status and clout as a regional leader that he could enter into plans with Zhang Zuolin and Duan Qirui to defeat Wu Peifu and seize the coveted Beijing presidency.

Unfortunately for Sun, this kind of plotting infuriated his supporters in Guangdong. Those idealizing a centralist vision of China were upset that he would pander to "enemy" northern warlords. Followers of Chen, who had painstakingly cultivated strong provincial identities, meanwhile, were horrified at Sun's wanton neglect of their province.

Provincial loyalties in Guangdong were strong. In 1920, just before Chen drove Guangxi and Yunnan forces from Guangzhou, he had publicly promised that his aptly named Guangdong Army would liberate its "native home" *(laojia)* from "foreign" (non-Guangdongese) invaders. Entering Guangzhou in November, he addressed locals as his "elders and brothers" *(fulao xiongdi)*, stressed his own Guangdong origins, and announced, "From this day forward, Guangdong will be collectively possessed by the Guangdongese, collectively governed by the Guangdongese, and collectively enjoyed by the Guangdongese."[76] Moving beyond rhetoric, Chen promoted a program of national salvation that sought China's unification through a federation of independent provinces.[77] Since the federalist vision rested on independent and self-sustaining provinces, Chen heavily emphasized development in and for Guangdong. He announced a period of "rest and savings" *(xiuyang shengxi)*, renounced war, and began repairing Guangdong's war-damaged infrastructure. His regime banned gambling and opium use, built an iron bridge over the Pearl River, constructed a public library, and tore down Guangzhou's city walls to build paved, electric-lit thoroughfares.[78]

---

76. "Gao yue fulao xiongdi shu," in *Chen Jiongming ji*, eds. Duan and Ni, p. 504. Also see "Anmin gaoshi," in *Chen Jiongming ji*, eds. Duan and Ni, p. 500. Since 1916, Guangxi and Yunnan forces had controlled Guangdong.

77. The model often cited was that of the United States of America. Duara, *Rescuing History from the Nation*, p. 187. Mao Zedong promoted provincialism at this time but vacillated between Hunan independence and a larger federation of provincial regimes. See McDonald, "Mao Tse-tung and the Hunan Self-Government Movement," pp. 751-777.

78. Chen, *Chen Jiongming and the Federalist Movement*, pp. 101, 133, 141; "Guangdong dubo zhanxing zhizui zhangcheng," in *Chen Jiongming ji*, eds. Duan and Ni, p. 521; "Jindu bugao," in

To ensure that democratization could proceed unencumbered, Chen empowered civilian leaders vis-à-vis military authority, disbanded more than two-thirds of his army (to Sun's dismay), and restored self-governing institutions.[79] Cities were encouraged to form municipal charters and, in December 1920, Chen unveiled the Provisional Charter of Guangzhou. Popular elections selected members of the Municipal Executive Committee, the Municipal Advisory Committee, and other offices, including the mayorship. Comprised of elected and appointed officials, advisory committees made decisions on issues submitted by their respective executive committees, giving Guangzhou—on paper at least—the most democratic system in China. In November 1921, Chen instructed newly elected county officials: "Is an elected magistrate better than an appointed one? This election is intended to be an experiment. . . . In sum, the success or failure of the system of elective magistrates rests on the shoulders of you gentlemen."[80]

By December 1921, the restored Guangdong Provincial Assembly ratified a new Provisional Constitution for Guangdong, identified the rights of Guangdong citizens, and asserted Guangdong's rights vis-à-vis Beijing. Civilian-led administrations set the province apart and imbued its citizens with a strong sense of loyalty. Its populace enjoyed more rights and freedoms than Chinese anywhere else in the country. Even newspapers critical of Chen operated without repression or restriction.[81] The new Provincial Education Commission ordered the formation of a compulsory education system and established the University of Guangdong in mid-1921.[82] According to many, Guangdong was well on its way to becoming China's model province, a feature proudly noted by local Guangdongese.

Provincialist interests committed to the federalist model directly competed with Sun's centralist vision, but even they represented only a portion of his opposition. Beneath budding provincialist institutions sat an even broader spectrum of localist interests: groups and organizations maintaining economic or social influence at the local level. In rural areas, endemic competition between peasants, bandits, landlords, and secret societies was

---

Chen Jiongming ji, eds. Duan and Ni, p. 522.

79. The desire to improve civilian rule is one reason why Chen invited to Guangzhou reputable political figures such as Sun Yat-sen, Wu Tingfang, and Tang Shaoyi—three of Guanzhou's original seven-man administration in 1918—as well as the cultural modernizers Wu Zhihui, Dai Jitao, and Chen Duxiu. Chen, *Chen Jiongming and the Federalist Movement*, pp. 101.

80. Provisional regulations for selecting county magistrates appeared in December 1920, just one month after Chen assumed the governorship. "Xiansheng dui xin xianzhang zhi xunshi," *Huazi ribao* (November 17, 1921).

81. Chen, *Chen Jiongming and the Federalist Movement*, pp. 141-142, 154-156.

82. The Provincial Education Commission was founded on February 14, 1921. Most accounts explain that Guangdong University was established in November 1924, the date that Sun Yat-sen ordered its formation. Chen Jiongming actually set up a predecessor University of Guangdong in 1921, but this contribution has been virtually erased from institutional memory. See *Zhongshan Daxue gaikuang*, frontispiece.

exacerbated by warlord armies canvassing the countryside for conscripts and loot. To guard against predation, many villages set up armed militias or "people's corps" *(mintuan)* which operated as local police units and took fees for protective services. Larger defense corps trained locals or hired mercenaries from the outside. Some gentry leaders maintained personal *mintuan*, although they, often enough, were merely gangs of toughs used to dominate irrigation, operate gambling, or run smuggling enterprises. Secret societies, such as the Red Flags, Black Flags, or Big Sword Society, hosted their own armed forces while self-governing societies, merchant associations, guilds, reformist agricultural associations, credit societies, and lineage organizations could band together in a variety of ways when common interests were challenged. Several organizations, such as mutual protection alliances, were extensive and could span several townships *(xiang)*.[83] Some were old and had long shaped local politics.[84] Others were relatively new and inexperienced. Most, however, stood poised to exploit opportunities and parry threats.

In urban areas, the sweep and variety of localist organizations was even more pronounced. Owners of private railroads, such as the Guang-zhou-Jiulong line and sections of the developing Guangzhou-Hankou Railroad, pursued narrow interests. Organized labor unions *(gonghui)* pushed their own causes while student organizations demonstrated for a range of reasons. Private enterprises abounded, including chambers of commerce, banks, hotels, department stores, companies, factories, charitable organizations, hospitals, urban committees, and merchant associations.[85] Courts, independent of any government, expanded throughout Guangdong while county police organizations defended against bandits and other lawless elements. Business community interests were advanced by extensive networks and umbrella organizations such as Guangzhou's four chambers of commerce.[86] Mirroring Shanghai's commercial associations, these organizations routinely appeared on the political stage. Extensive guild and market society militias helped to avert militarist and brigand plunder. Guangzhou's wealthy commercial district, Xiguan, commanded thousands of armed merchant corpsmen.[87] Armed volunteers and paid mercenaries helped police

---

83. Wilbur and How, *Missionaries of Revolution*, pp. 108-109.
84. Sun's Revolutionary Alliance (Tongmenghui), which predated the GMD, utilized sojourner associations in Shanghai even long before 1911. Goodman, "The Locality as Microcosm of the Nation?" pp. 405-408. Similarly, in 1916, Sun recruited localist interests in Shandong to help against Yuan Shikai. Friedman, *Backward Toward Revolution*, pp. 197-198. In both cases, involvement proved unstable.
85. Tsin's *Nation, Governance, and Modernity in China* is the definitive account of localist interests in Guangzhou and their interactions with the GMD.
86. The four included the General Chamber of Commerce, the Associated Chamber of Commerce, the Guangzhou Merchants Association, and the Guangzhou City Traders League. *CWR* 32 (March 7, 1925): 21.
87. Wei Yan, pseud., ed., *Guangdong kouxie chao*, juan 1, p. 1.

and supervise traffic. Stockades and ramparts protected markets and shops during the day while systems of gates and palisades sealed commercial areas at night. Some of the larger and more sophisticated militias even bought weapons on the international market and established training programs for their volunteer corpsmen.[88] When government authority failed to maintain peace and order, merchant corps took up the slack, quelling unrest and securing stability. Other communities followed Guangzhou's example and, by 1925, merchant corps thrived in all of Guangdong's 138 greatest cities and towns.[89]

Set up to safeguard and expand control over precious social, political, and economic resources, many—if not most—provincialist and localist organizations opposed Sun's habit of "squandering" Guangdong's resources on politicking schemes with northern militarists. Provincialist and localist—not centralist—interests dominated Guangdong's organizational and institutional spectrum, thus better serving Chen's federalist vision than Sun's centralist one.[90] Despite their alliance with Sun, Guangdong provincialists found his northern escapades galling and counter-productive. Convinced that national power was finally within reach nonetheless, Sun ignored complaints, forcefully promoted his own agenda, and launched preparations for yet another scheme: a military campaign toward Jiangxi to support Zhang Zuolin and Duan Qirui—Sun's new friends. Chen went a different direction, opening negotiations to form a consortium of southwest China's provincial regimes committed to federalism.

Although tensions rose as a result, Sun refused to bypass a chance at national power. In April 1922, therefore, he dismissed Chen for half-hearted support of his military campaign and declared himself commander over the Guangdong Army. Chen patiently accepted Sun's demands but lost little actual influence since he still retained the loyalty of his troops. Ignoring a host of menacing portents, Sun enthusiastically pressed ahead with plans for a northern expedition.

All prospects collapsed, however, when Wu Peifu defeated Sun's allies, restored the parliament, and gave the Beijing presidency to Li Yuanhong on June 11. Many advised Sun to resign as China's southern president lest his continued posturing imperil Beijing's delicate *status quo* and jeopardize the stability of China, but he refused and continued to issue presidential proclamations despite complaints that the Republic of China's constitution no longer needed his protection. On June 16, however, the charade ended when troops loyal to Chen Jiongming launched a *coup d'état*, driving Sun out of

---

88. Li, *Student Nationalism in China*, p. 24.
89. *CWR* 35 (February 6, 1926): 291.
90. Under the right conditions, national and provincialist/localist interests are not antithetical. See Goodman, *Native Place, City, and Nation*. In 1924 Guangdong, however, competition over scarce resources ensured that they were.

Guangzhou and bombarding his presidential palace in the process.[91] Once again betrayed by his own alleged supporters and friends, Sun's second Guangzhou regime came to an end.

As long as nationalist and provincialist loyalties competed over the same resources, represented by the province of Guangdong itself, Sun's schemes to secure national power inevitably split his movement. This was just the beginning, however, for a second unavoidable paradox—this time juxtaposing popular anti-imperialism and Sun's quest for foreign aid—proved equally divisive.

Sun had long sought foreign aid. Believing that it sustained Beijing's corrupt administration and could quickly usher him into power, he tirelessly advertised himself, his party, and his southern regime as a better investment.[92] From 1920 to mid-1922, he attracted some foreign interest. Prominent individuals from Britain and the U.S., including John Dewey, Bertrand Russell, Ernest Price (U. S. vice-consul in Guangzhou), Jacob Gould Schurman (U.S. minister to China), and several Christian missionaries urged sympathy, if not outright recognition, for Sun's government.[93]

Nevertheless, for a variety of reasons foreign heads of state withheld support. U. S. firms interested in Sun's regime found their overtures torpedoed by State Department authorities unwilling to aid Guangzhou as long as it opposed the Beijing government—China's recognized regime. The British Foreign Office was only slightly more diplomatic, refusing aid allegedly because of "neutrality," but also because it feared that Sun "coquetted with communism and Indian sedition."[94]

To pique foreign attention, Sun feverishly embellished his legitimacy by claiming to speak for the Chinese people. Since the May Fourth Movement, however, few messages could capture public sympathies like strident anti-imperialism. Sun fully recognized its power in attracting Chinese acclaim and gained significantly whenever he employed it (even if slow to raise his voice). The problem, of course, was that while anti-imperialism enhanced his status, visibility, and legitimacy as the spokesman of the Chinese nation, it also estranged the powers from which he sought assistance. Thus, when

---

91. Chang and Gordon, *All Under Heaven*, p. 71.

92. Schiffren, *Sun Yat-sen*, pp. 214-215; Chang and Gordon, *All Under Heaven*, p. 68.

93. Price called Sun the "only hope for China" and lobbied for U.S. support in 1920. DeAngelis, "Jacob Gould Schurman, Sun Yat-sen, and the Canton Customs Crisis," pp. 268, 290-293; Schiffren, *Sun Yat-sen*, p. 216; Chang and Gordon, *All Under Heaven*, p. 68.

94. Sun refused to conduct business with American firms except as a representative of the Republic of China in order to legitimize his regime when the State Department ratified any resulting contracts. Anxious to avoid being cornered into *de facto* dealings with Sun's regime, foreign diplomats circumvented even the most innocent of Sun's requests. Wilbur, *Sun Yat-sen*, pp. 104-108. Some, however, simply opposed Sun; Britain's Sir Ronald Macleay, for example, long argued against offering British assistance. Wilbur, *Sun Yat-sen*, p. 147.

hotly pursuing foreign aid, Sun stifled anti-imperialist outbursts, offering instead foreign privileges, profits, and treaty rights. Unfortunately for him, however, this, in turn, enraged the same patriotic Chinese whose support he needed to maintain claims of legitimacy. Foreign attention required evidence of popular support which required anti-imperialist rhetoric which, then, diminished foreign interest. Once again, Sun was stuck in a bind that juxtaposed two elements necessary to gain state power: popular acclaim and foreign recognition.

In early 1922, labor strikes helped Sun extricate himself from this quagmire (as explored in chapter 2), but only temporarily. His sudden banishment from Guangzhou in June killed all forward momentum. Without a base, he lost what political capital he had accumulated as a regional leader. At the same time, prospects he had been courting in Beijing dried up thanks to Wu Peifu's victory. Finally, documents from Sun's bombed-out presidential palace revealed secret plans involving international pariahs Russia and Germany, undermining his foreign opportunities. A few regional militarists continued to court the GMD leader, but without status as a regional commander he had lost most of his bargaining power.[95] Out of options, Sun looked elsewhere.

The Russians had been courting Sun since 1920, but he politely kept their overtures at arm's length to avoid burning bridges with the other powers.[96] By late 1922, however, dead ends and another round of U. S., British, and Japanese rejections prompted him to reconsider. In January 1923, Sun opened negotiations with Russian agents in the hope that other powers, eager to preempt expanding Soviet influence, would intervene with counter offers. As soon as he secured an agreement with Soviet agent Adolf Joffe, therefore, Sun flaunted it in front of British and U.S. diplomats, sure that it would win him their notice if not sympathy.[97] His hopes were misguided, however. Instead of opening opportunities vis-à-vis the other powers, Sun's new pact slammed them shut by casting him as a threat to U.S., Japanese, and British interests. The powers were already suspicious of Sun's opposition to Beijing,

---

95. Wilbur, *Sun Yat-sen*, pp. 127-129.

96. Moscow hoped a bourgeois revolution would mute growing British and Japanese dominance in China and therefore sent a series of agents to contact Sun. Voitinsky invited him to meet Soviet leaders in Moscow but was politely refused. In December 1921, agent Maring (J. F. M. Sneevliet) advised him to build a popular movement, but Sun expressed preference for his own "tightly controlled party with himself wielding dictatorial power." Chan, "Sun Yat-sen and the Origins of the Kuomintang Reorganization," p. 30. Despite his hesitancy, Sun kept communication lines open. In January 1922, he complimented Russia and later held a series of meetings with Comintern agent Dalin before being forced to flee Chen Jiongming's revolt.

97. In a newspaper editorial, Chen Youren (Eugene Chen) chided the powers, asserting that "continued hostility to Russia, and what appears like hostility to Sun Yat-sen on the part of certain great powers might force an alliance between Russia and China." Wilbur, *Sun Yat-sen*, p. 140; Schiffrin, *Sun Yat-sen*, p. 235.

anti-imperialism, ties to Germany, and a host of other issues. The Sun/Joffe agreement only confirmed imperialist beliefs that Sun was trouble.[98] He later tried to tempt Japan into a pan-Asian alliance with Russia to challenge Anglo-American dominance but was politely refused.[99] U.S. authorities lost interest while the British received him in Hong Kong but ultimately maintained their neutrality.[100]

In Sun's mind, nothing could help him avoid the problems of stagnation or fragmentation like securing state power at the national level, but, by the end of 1922, his best efforts had been deeply disappointing. He needed state authority to prepare a "people" that could constitute and ultimately inherit his "nation," but all negotiations, deals, and schemes with northern militarists and politicians aimed at securing that power had only turned Guangdong's provincialist and localist interests against him. To earn a place at the national politicking table, Sun needed regional influence, but the moment he took a seat, control over his base in Guangdong began to slip. It was no accident, therefore, that Wu Peifu's victory in north China disrupted Sun's efforts to seize national power, but the *coup de grace* came at the hand of provincialists in Guangzhou.

Efforts to augment his legitimacy by building popular support fared no better. Nothing raised Sun's popularity, solidified his reputation as China's most noteworthy spokesman, and aroused followers like strident anti-imperialism. At the same time, however, such rhetoric estranged foreign diplomats and closed international opportunities. Toning down outbursts to win foreign sympathy, on the other hand, irritated his followers, mystified popular patriotric associations, and lowered his legitimacy.

Sadly for him, in order to succeed in his pursuit of state power, Sun could not just opt for one side of either equation. He had to maintain regional dominance *and* pursue his national agenda. At the same time, he needed the legitimacy of popular acclaim *and* foreign aid. The harder Sun pushed in one direction, the stronger the backlash from another.

---

98. Aware of Soviet intentions, the powers tried not to dash Sun's hopes while keeping their distance and isolating him by encouraging his enemies. Conrad Brandt misquotes Sharman by claiming that U.S. Minister Jacob Gould Schurman approached Sun with a proposal of Western assistance. Brandt, *Stalin's Failure in China*, p. 33. Actually it was Sun who approached Schurman. In early 1924, after meeting Sun again, Schurman promised the foreign community that the U.S. would offer neither assistance nor recognition. "America's Policy: Dr. Schurman's Interview with Sun Yat-sen," *Peking and Tientsin Times* (18 January 1924); "Dr. Schurman and Canton," *Peking and Tientsin Times* (18 January 1924); Sharman, *Sun Yat-sen*, p. 250.

99. Sun justified his Russian ties by claiming that they too had Asian blood. Schiffren, *Sun Yat-sen*, pp. 232-233. Holubnychy contextualizes Sun's letter by portraying it as a desperate plea written during the early morning hours of Chen Jiongming's attack against his palace. Holubnychy, *Michael Borodin and the Chinese Revolution*, p. 299. (Sun's pan-Asian call generated little support in Japan, just as Japan's World War II version of pan-Asianism failed to capture interest in China.)

100. Wilbur, *Sun Yat-sen*, p. 147.

Paradox: Bifurcated Nationalism as the Solution?

In the fall of 1922, Sun Yat-sen was back in Shanghai engaging the same tired schemes. To defend against further "betrayal" by supposed followers, he ordered another party restructuring and adopted yet another constitution on January 2.[101] Shorn of his base and slighted by most foreigners and militarists alike, Sun turned to anti-imperialism and anti-warlordism. As it often did, the move aroused Chinese interest and attracted donations from Hong Kong and overseas patriots. Putting the funds to immediate use, Sun's followers purchased the aid of Yunnan and Guangxi mercenaries who routed Chen Jiongming's army. Sun returned to Guangzhou and, on January 15, 1923, set up his third regime in six years. By March 2, he had again proclaimed himself Generalissimo of the southern government and had again entered another round of northern politicking, certain that state power lay just beyond his fingertips.

Predictably, Sun's movement continued to flounder. Nevertheless, difficulties in securing national power were only the beginning. Sun had once naively assumed that Chinese would embrace the Three Principles, gravitate to his party, and accept "proper" training before eagerly democratizing China. Sun initially sought, as Fitzgerald explains, *"a pedagogical state structure* that would relate to its citizens as a teacher might relate to a pupil, or, as Sun liked to think, as the imperial tutor once instructed the emperor."[102] [Emphasis added.] By 1923, however, it was clear that most Chinese would not join Sun's "nation" unless dragged into it. He argued passionately that nothing should lie between loyalty to family/clan and loyalty to the nation, but he quickly discovered that countless provincialist and localist loyalties did indeed fill the gap.[103] Competing programs—liberal, socialist, federalist, centralist, Christian, traditional, and so forth—added further division.

As a result, Sun's envisioned role resembled that of the imperial tutor only when pedagogy encountered the eager and enthusiastic. When it engaged the hesitant, unconvinced, or defiant, Sun looked more like the firm-handed emperor. Reluctant to share sovereignty with anyone but those of tested loyalty, he suspended his irenic vision of sage-like authority peacefully guiding Chinese toward a democratic modernity in favor of a *realpolitik* struggle to construct and impose a national identity from a position of towering and uncontestable state power.

Viewing China's segmented identities and rival programs as obstacles to national unification and democratization, Sun refined his plans for state

---

101. Schiffren, *Sun Yat-sen*, p. 233; Sun, "Zongli jiaoyi: zuzhi guomin zhengfu zhi biyao an," *Geming wenxian*, vol. 76, pp. 18-22.

102. Fitzgerald, *Awakening China*, p. 20.

103. In Sun's words, "In the relation between the citizens of China and their state, there must first be family loyalty, then clan loyalty, and finally national loyalty." Sun, *San Min Chu I*, pp. 115, 124.

power by prescribing three phases through which his desired national government would have to pass: military dictatorship, party tutelage, and popular sovereignty. The third stage represented Sun's end democratic ideal in full bloom. The first two would bring it about, even though they represented its antithesis. To Sun, there was nothing irrational about this formula. Something had to bend China's divisions and diverse identities into a single, national identity. If that something happened to be a dictatorship, then the ends justified the means.

Seizing national power and Beijing's coveted presidency, therefore, became an obsession—the only way to implement his vision of China's future. Nevertheless, even if he had managed to land himself an important position in Beijing and secure foreign support, Sun still would have struggled. According to C. Martin Wilbur, neither would have made a difference:

> Every major faction attempted to utilize these, yet none had been able to accumulate enough preponderance to break the system of regional separatism, not even Yuan Shih-k'ai [Yuan Shikai] with the Peiyang Army [Beiyang Army] and foreign financial support. Some additional power was necessary. *This power was ideology.*[104] [Emphasis added.]

Wilbur highlights the primacy of ideology but does not specify how it worked. Ideology had earned Sun regional status and control over Guangdong three times, but it could not buoy him up when he tried to extend influence to the national level. Either it remained insufficiently developed or he did not yet know how to use it. Indeed, for the eleven-year period preceding 1923, one can easily reverse Wilbur's assessment: despite militarist support, control of Guangzhou, an opposition government, *and a nationalistic ideology*, Sun still could not control even his own supporters, let alone acquire national influence. Yuan's failures showed the limits of state power. Sun's failures revealed shortcomings of nationalistic ideology. Something else was needed if Sun's movement was to ever overcome its challenges.

As indicated above, the biggest impediment to success was not the might of Sun's competitors but their positioning on China's sociopolitical chess board. Any movement in one direction opened vulnerabilities in another because all rival game pieces were interconnected. In short, the strength of Sun's opposition was greater than the sum of its parts. Rival interests did not act independently, to be defeated one-by-one, but formed intended and unintended combinations that cornered Sun by juxtaposing certain fundamental revolutionary needs with other ones. Like a fly in a spider's web, Sun found that struggling against one strand only entangled his movement with others. To gain legitimacy for northern politicking and its promise of national

---

104. Wilbur, "Military Separatism and the Process of Reunification under the Nationalist Regime," p. 221.

power, Sun needed a regional base, yet, the very act of dealing with northerners then undermined control in that same base. To gain foreign support and its promise of national power, Sun required acclaim among his countrymen, yet, seeking it through popular anti-imperialism only weakened foreign ties. When he solidified his position through disciplinary oaths and systems, Sun maintained control over his revolutionary party, but alienated potential allies. Conversely, if he pursued inclusive coalitions, he won broad support but lost control.

What Sun needed was a way to maintain control and unity within the party, create and expand the Chinese "people," and secure state power without provoking China's militarist or foreign powers—all at the same time. As Bhabha might have predicted, however, attention to any one of these three areas automatically generated alienation in the other two. Somehow Sun had to find a nationalistic approach that could negotiate this mine field of paradoxes before the pattern of revolutionary self-destruction could be broken. Without a way to account for all variables and progress in all areas simultaneously, even landing the Beijing presidency and heading China's state apparatus would only put Sun in the awkward position once occupied by Yuan Shikai whose dictatorial ways could barely maintain the *status quo*. Unfortunately for Sun and his revolutionary vision, no single nationalistic program could remotely satisfy all the contradictory demands of the party, people, and powers. Every revolutionary approach he had tried since 1912 had generated progress in one area but also precipitated party insurrection, public apathy/anger, or militarist/foreign intervention in the other two.

As this study will show, Sun's party eventually found an answer, but it was not the introduction of Chinese "nationalism" as the faction-centered paradigm claims. Rather, the solution lay in the exploitation of a creative cocktail of *nationalisms*, each with its own distinct revolutionary approach. Rejecting static, consistent, or monolithic conceptualizations of the "nation," Guomindang leaders employed instead a range of views dominated by two mutually exclusive programs with dramatically different objectives, tactics, and visions. The first, here called the "state-building" approach, sought to strengthen China via domestic stability, economic development, alliances with localist and provincial interests, and warm foreign diplomatic arrangements. Top revolutionary leaders associated with the party's Central Executive Committee (CEC) drove most state-building efforts. The second, here called the "agitative" approach, pursued social upheaval, class struggle for mass interests, economic disruption, and popular agitation aimed at destroying imperialism and warlordism. Agitation thrived at the local level and is best represented by popular mass-organization upheaval.

Significantly, both approaches were directed by high Nationalist officials at the same time, resulting in a bifurcated revolutionary approach or "bifurcated nationalism" that combined into a single movement two mutually exclusive nationalistic agendas. The state-building and agitative approaches existed independent of each other but did not act independent of each other. Under the right conditions, the two could be carefully synchronized to maximize political opportunity. Coordinating activities high and low, revolutionary leaders enjoyed options, flexibility, and power sufficient to concurrently unify the party, expand the "people," and manipulate militarist/foreign interests all at the same time. Hosting mutually exclusive visions of China's future "nation," the Nationalist Revolution thrived on irony, contradiction, and misdirection. It confounded attempts to explain it because labels and classification systems could not predict whether a revolutionary leader might play the state-builder part or shift to an agitative role. From the perspective of those confronting it, the revolution swept forward as a mishmash of warlord allies, mercenaries, radical students, Soviet advisors, communists, labor organizers, strike pickets, Nationalist officers, and every other claimant to revolutionary legitimacy. Defining "revolutionary," the "people," and the "nation" was impossible. No clear boundary distinguished any of them. Instead, each resembled a blurred and indistinct membrane through which individuals and interests could be passed back and forth, included or excluded, embraced or rejected, depending on revolutionary need. Fluid and amorphous, the revolution outmaneuvered much stronger foes and gradually wore down even powerful imperialist institutions as it consolidated power. While Chatterjee's Indian nationalists painstakingly identified and defined the fine details of national culture, China's revolutionaries were doing the opposite—obscuring national culture with inconsistency, contradiction, and multiplicity. While individual revolutionary participants may have held in their own imaginations a clear idea of what the revolution sought, where it was going, and what would come of it, interests and groups outside the revolution could not be sure. Cloaked in ambiguity and exploiting the cover it provided, Sun's revolutionaries pressed forward.

How bifurcated nationalism produced flexibility and power is the primary focus of this study. Analytically, faction-centered interpretations segment the revolution vertically into left and right factional halves. Fixed on intra-revolutionary dynamics, official memory has nimbly ignored embarrassing conundrums that might spoil the pristine images sought by universalizing history. It has swept aside inconsistencies and ironies: revolutionary manipulation of popular and foreign interests, contradictions between word (propaganda) and deed (policy), regime designs behind "spontaneous" popular agitation, hazy notions of "revolutionary" and the "people," the utility of betrayal, and so forth. It has allowed generations to imagine that the revolution's primary rivalries existed within revolutionary ranks rather than within the larger matrix of Chinese society. It has exalted Chinese nationalism's ability to convert, persuade, awaken, and include to myth-like proportions.

The success of faction-centered universalizing history in each of these areas, however, has also obscured how nationalism actually worked. To avoid doing the same, this analysis will eschew the path carved by decades of work on CCP/GMD relations. Here, revolutionary ranks will be divided horizontally, between top-level state-building efforts and low-level mass-driven agitative activity to reveal the symbiosis between the two. The following eight chapters will illuminate the evolution of this bifurcated nationalism by segmenting the Nationalist Revolution (1924-1928) into three time periods. The first, covered in chapters 2 through 4, explores Sun's revolutionary approach as it developed from 1922 through June 1925. Chapter 2 tracks its conceptual beginnings, the growth of its institutions as outlined at the First National Congress, and its ability to enhance revolutionary options. Chapters 3 and 4 demonstrate its value against localist merchants and Christian educational interests, respectively. Even in the face of overpowering military and political challenges, this bifurcated system allowed the Nationalists to expand revolutionary influence.

The second period, spanning June 1925 through June 1926, is covered in chapter 5. During these twelve months, bifurcated nationalism and its concomitant strategies helped weaken revolutionary rivals in Guangdong and solidify Guomindang power. The Nationalist defeat of key allies of imperialism—military foes, domestic enemies, and foreign rivals—cemented base-area strength and stability, allowing revolutionary leaders to shift emphasis from recruitment to assimilation as they systematically extended centralized control. The last period reaches from June 1926 through 1928, and is covered by chapters 6 through 9. They explore the seesaw events of the Northern Expedition. As revolutionary forces spread through south China, flaws in the bifurcated approach compromised party control at the top. Ironically, British and warlord authorities, which had become familiar with Nationalist strategies, began to play the ambiguities of bifurcated nationalism to their own advantage. Manipulated by their own system, top revolutionary leaders found themselves forced to abandon their divided tactics in favor of a single revolutionary vision.

2. Decentralized Centralism
—Constructing the Infrastructure of Change, January 1924 - June 1925

The population of Kwangtung [Guangdong] has begun to show a sharply negative attitude toward Sun's government. The workers, who along with the artisans number up to 350 thous. [sic] in Canton [Guangzhou] and who had met with enthusiasm Sun's return from Shanghai, at the present have begun to show a complete indifference to the fate of his government and have completely ceased taking an interest in his defeats or victories. The petty municipal bourgeoisie, which has severely suffered from the anarchy resulting from the changes of fortunes at the fronts and from constant expectations of intrusions by the enemy, with every alarming rumor was either closing the doors of its shops or was hiding under the flag of foreign powers. The coolies have been arrested by the batches and dispatched to the fronts as forced labor. . . . Unsystematic collections of taxes have caused more misunderstandings and bitterness than the profits they have brought into the treasury. As for peasants, they regard Sun's struggle with Ch'en [Chen] . . . as a calamity which has fallen exclusively upon them. They have stopped paying their taxes and sell their products to the army, and, in final account, they have been rising with arms in their hands in one or another place, thus striking at the rear of the armies.[1]
—Mikhail Borodin, Soviet advisor to the Nationalist Party, 1923

On October 6, 1923, Comintern agent Mikhail Borodin set foot in Guangzhou for the first time. His trip from Shanghai had been harrowing. To avoid Hong Kong police he had bypassed larger commercial steamers in favor of a smaller vessel directly bound for Guangzhou. Despite precautions, however, the voyage still threatened life and limb. A seasonally late typhoon drowned two hundred sheep on the deck and nearly sank the ship before it reached shelter in Taiwan. Terse and understated, Borodin's own account betrays a confidence that no police or storm threat could shake. As Soviet Russia's chief political advisor to the GMD, he enjoyed unequaled status, combining authority from the Soviet Government, the Russian Communist Party, and the Comintern. Contemporaries described him as self-assured, tall and

---

1. Cited in Holubnychy, *Michael Borodin and the Chinese Revolution*, p. 291.

37

broad-shouldered with dark, wavy hair, deep-set eyes and a great black handle-bar mustache—a striking contrast to the "diminutive and graying" Sun.[2] Nevertheless, the two shared much in common. Both had spent years abroad as émigrés in the U.S., both spoke fluent English, and both fiercely hungered for a free and independent China.[3]

Borodin's enthusiasm quickly waned, however, when crude assessments demonstrated just how fragile the Guomindang's position in Guangzhou really was. As the passage above indicates, he blamed the party for failing to strengthen ties with the local population and for allowing corruption to proliferate.[4] Borodin's criticisms likely struck a tender nerve in Sun Yat-sen, conjuring up past disappointments and their ultimate cause: failure to secure unity, loyalty, and support. In the past, Sun had always responded to these types of problems by surrounding himself with the trappings of power. Borodin, however, suggested a new direction, one that would do more than simply borrow power from militarists, foreigners, and politicians. According to the Soviet advisor, the party needed to intentionally generate power from society's lower orders.

Despite some opposition, Borodin's blueprint eventually won support, precipitating plans for another party reorganization. Animated, Sun enthusiastically told his followers that they would convert Guangzhou into a revolutionary base, export revolutionary spirit, and eventually seize national power as the Bolsheviks had done.[5] At the party's First National Congress, held through January 1924, GMD leaders unveiled the nuts and bolts of their new revolutionary approach. Delegates ratified a declaration of purpose welding new revolutionary elements, including a role for China's masses and popular ideology, with older party objectives, such as centralized authority and the restoration of Chinese sovereignty. Outlining the general plan, the *First National Congress Declaration* (*Congress Declaration* hereafter) asserted:

> After reorganization, party organization will be founded on a spirit of strict discipline. Employing a variety of appropriate measures, party members are to be educated and trained as revolutionary figures capable of propagating ideology, mobilizing the masses, and organizing political power. At the same time . . . they are to spread universal propaganda to all the people, inducing them to join the revolution, seize political power, and defeat the enemies of the people. Once the party has seized power and established a government, it will forcefully end reactionary movements . . . and imperialist plots . . . in order to eradicate anything ob-

---

2. Holubnychy, *Michael Borodin and the Chinese Revolution*, pp. 250, 259-260.
3. Vishnyakova-Akimova, *Two Years in Revolutionary China*, p. 179.
4. T'ang, *The Inner History of the Chinese Revolution*, pp. 159-160.
5. *Guofu quanji*, vol. 2, section 8, p. 187.

structing the implementation of GMD ideology. Furthermore, the party will be equipped with political power as [China's] central authority. *As the only one with organization and authority*, this party . . . can then fulfill its ambitious work for all of China.[6] [Emphasis added.]

Abandoning the muted timbre of earlier GMD manifestos, the *Congress Declaration* vigorously affirmed GMD intentions: to mobilize, organize, and induce the people to defeat their enemies and seize national power. Unlike Sun's 1918 *Doctrine of Sun Yat-sen*, which doled out democracy to those deemed worthy, the party now aimed to organize and compel Chinese to help it gain control. Sweeping "universal propaganda" *(pubian de xuanchuan)* aimed at the people replaced vaguely defined and softly peddled notions of their "education and training" *(jiaoyu ji xunlian)* as featured in Sun's 1918 declaration.[7] Proposals to "eradicate" *(shanchu)* obstacles invigorated tepid 1918 descriptions about defeating China's enemies. In short, with the First National Congress of 1924, the Nationalists abandoned their earlier role as a passive, paternalistic authority waiting for social progress to evolve in favor of an active influence, energetically directing China's populace as it wrested order from the jaws of chaos.

Enthusiastic positivism notwithstanding, beyond these general terms, the *Congress Declaration* failed to explain how the party would institute revolutionary change. It promised to break the cycle of failure entrapping Sun's movement, generate revolutionary power, and secure influence at the national level, but offered little more than vague images of a revolutionary movement carried forward by China's masses. Nevertheless, while the details about this revolutionary transformation remained unexplained, a few important components did emerge.

Central Party Command: Sun Yat-sen

Before any other reforms, the party had to be reorganized. Shifting back and forth between inclusive and exclusive models of party organization, Sun had tasted the bitterness of both and the sweet success of neither. One aim of Congress leaders and Borodin, therefore, was to fortify the GMD's internal integrity using Leninist structures as a general framework and to stabilize Sun's position by centralizing power within a rigid hierarchical administration that jealously limited power to a few key officials. To make sure Sun could remain astride his own movement, Congress delegates prescribed a cult of personality around his person and thought. Sun did not resist. Belief in his personal destiny had made him quite comfortable speaking for China. When once asked, for example, how foreign governments could possibly know

---

6. "Zhongguo Guomindang diyici quanguo daibiao dahui xuanyan," *Geming wenxian*, vol. 69, pp. 91-92.
7. See Sun, *Memoirs of a Chinese Revolutionary*, p. 101.

what China *really* desired given its divided condition, Sun quickly replied, "Ask me. What I think, China thinks."[8] He even claimed to be the personification of China's commercial advancements, wealth, education, civilization, and progress.[9] Echoing Sun's earlier statements of self-proclaimed sagacity, Congress delegates honored his ideological contributions by describing the Three Principles as the "heart of party essence" *(dang zhi jingshen de zhongxin)* and enshrined Sun himself as the "exemplary model" *(renge de mofan)* and the "master/sage of party ideology" *(dang zhuyi zhi daoshi).* Delegates granted Sun organizational immortality by handing him the presidency with the qualifying statement, "beyond Sun Yat-sen, the Presidential system cannot exist."[10] No one, in short, could succeed Sun—the "father of the nation" *(guofu).* GMD ideologue and long-time supporter Dai Jitao described the relationship:

> Because of Sun we have a President; the President produced the "Three Principles of the People" and the "Three Principles of the People" produced the President. Because of the first we now have the second and because of the second we now have the first. The two cannot be separated. As a result, the existence of the Presidential system *(zongli zhi)* in our party is a manifestation of this special spirit; it is the *personification of principle.*[11] [Emphasis added.]

Ideologically and institutionally reinforcing Sun's semi-sacred status also meant that Congress architects could justify centralizing power in a top-heavy Leninist system while maintaining the ideals of a democratic committee system. Power resided in the National Congress, comprised of selected delegates. However, since it convened only every year as prescribed by the constitution, between sessions it defaulted to its representative Central Executive Committee (CEC). This body organized and directed subordinate party organs, headed committees, appointed officers, controlled finances, and represented the party in external affairs. The CEC also administered the national government, as well as special ministries overseeing propaganda, labor, peasants, youth, women, internal investigation, and so forth. A smaller Standing Committee comprised of core CEC members oversaw routine affairs between CEC meetings. Key members of this Standing Committee and chief ministers of the Nationalist Government combined to form the Central Political Council, which considered problems raised by the various

---

8. *USDS* 893.00/5348, Enclosure, Brownall, Sun at Canton Christian College, Guangzhou, December 21, 1923.

9. *USDS* 893.00/5348, Enclosure, Hainer, Sun's Remarks at Canton Christian College, Guangzhou.

10. "Zhongguo Guomindang zongzhang zhiding an," *Geming wenxian*, vol. 76, p. 10.

11. "Zhongguo Guomindang zongzhang zhiding an," *Geming wenxian*, vol. 76, pp. 9-10.

ministers.[12] From his constitutionally guaranteed position atop this central-ized system, Sun enjoyed considerable power. Article 19 of the GMD con-stitution identified him specifically as the party's president *(zongli)*; article 20 ordered all GMD members to follow his direction; articles 21 and 22 appointed him chair of all National Congresses and CECs; article 23 gave him veto power over all National Congress resolutions; and article 24 granted him authority of final decision in all CEC actions.[13]

Central power extended down through provincial, county, district, and sub-district units organized to mirror central structures.[14] Decisions flowed downward. Despite repeated references to its democratic ideals, the Leninist system left lower units little voice regarding party policy. Rather, their first order of business was to execute instructions from higher bodies. Even National Congress elections could not reverse the downward orientation of power. Ostensibly, party assemblies elected delegates who then converged at the National Congress to elect the CEC. However, because the party con-stitution nowhere specified who could be delegates, because their term of office ended once the CEC was selected, and because the CEC itself deter-mined how many delegates were chosen and how they were to be elected, it was relatively easy for an entrenched CEC to pack a Congress and maintain the *status quo*. Bolstered by constitutional privilege (and barring a *coup* or death), CEC members could retain power almost indefinitely.[15]

To preserve hierarchical control, Congress leaders prescribed strict party discipline as "the foremost of all important issues involved in the party reorganization." [16] Regulations emphasized traditional Chinese ideals of subordinating individual ambitions to group-held objectives while nurturing expectations of unquestioning loyalty and self-sacrifice. In his opening address to Congress delegates, Sun strongly argued,

> There is one thing of the greatest importance in a political party, that is, all members of the party must possess spiritual unity. In order that all the members may be united spiritually, the first thing is to sacrifice freedom,

12. "Diyici quanguo daibiao dahui tongguo Zhongguo Guomindang zongzhang," *Geming wenxian*, vol. 70, pp. 47-48. Also see Sharman, *Sun Yat-sen*, pp. 259-260. The minutes of all Standing Committee meetings were declared "secret" unless specifically slated for public release. (Discussion item #6), *1-ZXWH*, vol. 2 (June 2, 1924).

13. "Diyici quanguo daibiao dahui tongguo Zhongguo Guomindang zongzhang," *Geming wenxian*, vol. 70, pp. 46-47. Also see "Zhongguo Guomindang zongzhang zhiding an," *Geming wenxian*, vol. 76, p. 10.

14. Lower level units were headed by executive committees selected by their own respective congresses. "Zhongguo Guomindang zongzhang zhiding an," *Geming wenxian*, vol. 76, pp. 6-7.

15. Sharman, *Sun Yat-sen*, pp. 259-261. Temporarily abandoning her usual stinging criticism, Sharman claims that Congress reforms helped protect against "wreckage from internal disinte-gration" by concentrating power in small groups rather than larger "unwieldy legislatures and quarreling factions." Sharman, *Sun Yat-sen*, p. 262.

16. Sun, "Zongli jiaoyi: jilü wenti jueyian," *Geming wenxian*, vol. 76, p. 11.

the second is to offer ability. If the individual can sacrifice his freedom, then the whole party will have freedom. If the individual can offer his ability, then the whole party will possess ability. . . . The past failures of the party were due to the fact that while the individual member had freedom, the party as a whole had none, and that while the individual member had ability, the party as a whole was powerless. Herein lies exactly the failure of the Kuomintang [Guomindang] of China. Our re-organization today is to get rid of this shortcoming.[17]

Party discipline, long a pillar of Sun's organizational mind-set, was fitted with new institutions. Party Investigation Committees watched individuals and bureaus for improprieties. Given broad responsibilities, they held party rank commensurate with the executive committees they investigated, and maintained scrutiny, censorship, discipline, and impeachment powers.[18] From the Bolsheviks, the Nationalists also borrowed a system of political commissars to encourage party members and troops, sanction party orders, spread propaganda, and maintain discipline. The Investigation Ministry, which operated under CEC supervision, added an additional layer of scrutiny (although it was later dropped for a time).[19] To deal with the unscrupulous or disloyal, Congress resolutions described punishments, sanctions, and compulsory measures. GMD members were ordered to watch each other before being ominously warned, "Should any party member break party regulations or defy party ideology, they will be treated with the most serious sanctions."[20] Sun had long expelled the disloyal. Now, however, discipline became a regular function of GMD organization, offering the promise (if not the realization) of greater efficiency.

Ideological Flexibility: "Nation" and "People"

The prospects of heading a disciplined, centralized party, united in purpose and committed to revolutionary objectives, must have tantalized Sun indeed, especially after his symbolic and political status were raised to towering, unassailable heights. Nevertheless, iron discipline he had wielded before. After centralizing decision-making power within the party and tightening the party's internal hierarchy, therefore, Borodin and Congress delegates moved to shape another key pillar of revolutionary power: ideological understandings of what was meant by the Chinese "nation" and its "people."

---

17. Cited in Sharman, *Sun Yat-sen*, pp. 257-258.
18. Party Investigation Committees reported findings to local administrative offices or directly to the CEC. "Guanyu jiancha weiyuanhui zhi jueyian," *Geming wenxian*, vol. 79, p. 3; Sharman, *Sun Yat-sen*, p. 261.
19. Wilbur, *The Nationalist Revolution in China, 1923-1928*, p. 12.
20. Sun, "Zongli jiaoyi: jilü wenti jueyian," *Geming wenxian*, vol. 76, p. 12. More detail can be found in section 11 of the party regulations *(dangzhang)*. See "Diyici quanguo daibiao dahui tongguo Zhongguo Guomindang zongzhang," *Geming wenxian*, vol. 70, pp. 53-54.

Defining the Chinese nation required considerable attention. Sun had long claimed that the party should direct the dealings of the nation. In January 1924, however, he expanded this assumption, asserting that the Congress must both reorganize the party and "establish the nation" *(jianshe guojia)*. Explaining the link, he continued, "We will reorganize the party and place the party above the nation *[ba dang fangzai guoshang]*. . . . We must use the party to create a nation. . . . The party has power and with it we can build a nation."[21] As thus conceived, since the "nation" was created by the party, the latter enjoyed higher status; and, since the party had not yet created the "nation," no nation technically existed. For many, this was hard to swallow. Even before the May Fourth Movement, Chinese everywhere had acted on behalf of imagined understandings of the Chinese nation. In contrast to these various visions, the First National Congress defined the Nationalist version—a "nation" distinguished by its ties to the party itself. As Sun explained, "in places where the GMD has not obtained political power, *the party and the nation are different*," implying, of course, that in areas where the GMD *did* possess political power, the party and the "nation" were the same or at least very tightly connected.[22] In short, Congress leaders recognized two distinct definitions of the Chinese nation: a "nation" permeated by party influence in areas where the GMD possessed influence and a non-GMD nation awaiting the party's unifying input and, therefore, imagined in a variety of ways in the minds of other Chinese.

Assumptions about the Chinese people *(guomin)* were also refined. The Guomindang allegedly represented the people, and from them borrowed legitimacy and even its name.[23] Those not of the people were deemed enemies. Since most Chinese felt deeply about the Chinese nation, but not necessarily the GMD version of it, the party had a hard time distinguishing the two groups before January 1924. First National Congress adjustments simplified the equation, however, by reversing the relationship and defining the "people" in terms of their proximity to the party. Enemies were distant; the "people" were close. As described by Fitzgerald, "Any institution or group of people reluctant to take up the invitation to attack feudalism and imperialism, or perhaps *bold enough to challenge the right of the revolutionaries to define the friends and enemies of the nation* on their behalf, could with good reason be counted an ancillary of feudal interests or a lackey of imperialism."[24] [Emphasis added.]

---

21. Sun wanted to establish a national government, in part, because he knew the powers would never recognize his regime otherwise. Sun, "Zongli jiaoyi: zuzhi guomin zhengfu zhi biyao an," *Geming wenxian*, vol. 76, pp. 19-22.

22. Sun, "Zongli jiaoyi: jilü wenti jueyian," *Geming wenxian*, vol. 76, p. 12.

23. In 1922, Sun noted that sovereignty resided in the people. Sun, "The Foundation for Building the Republic of China," in Wei, et al., eds., *Prescriptions for Saving China*, pp. 250-251.

24. Fitzgerald, "The Nationless State," p. 96.

Definitions of both nation and people did not occupy a point in a continuum as much as a range of points, some specific and some general. This range and party willingness to select whichever single point on it worked best, in turn, meant that the revolutionary leaders could employ any number of approaches. When dealing with alleged enemies such as imperialists, for example, the *Congress Declaration* employed two distinct and contradictory voices. On one hand, it denounced imperialist powers as a "raging tide" *(nuchao)* that used "military robbery and economic oppression" *(wuli de lueduo yu jingji de yapo)* to steal China's independence and impose "a state of semi-colonization" *(ban zhimindi zhi diwei)*. Potent exclusive prose excoriated the imperialists and proclaimed that the Guomindang would harness popular nationalism, hone it into an anti-imperialist movement, and use it to bring about "true freedom and independence" *(zhenzheng de ziyou yu duli)*.[25] Shoring up his commitment to popular anti-imperialism, Sun criticized past dealings with the powers, proclaiming, "We absolutely cannot tread the same tracks as in the past, stopping in the middle and once again compromising. From now on, we should, without exception, give up on compromising and harmonizing means. Moreover, we must recognize that compromise is a huge mistake in our efforts to carry the revolution out to the end."[26]

On the other hand, the same *Congress Declaration* also offered precisely what Sun disparaged—compromise via coaxing overtures to warm reciprocal relations with the powers. Inclusive and accommodating tones called for deepening diplomatic and cooperative ties with the powers, expressing hope for new equal treaties based on principles of "mutual respect" *(huzun)* and promising to recognize and repay all (harmless) foreign debts via imposts on commercial and social organizations. Congress declarations even vowed that any power retracting its imperialist privileges would be considered by China to be a "most-favored nation" *(zuihui guo)*.[27]

Oddly enough, Congress delegates offered foreign imperialists the same choice held out to China's own people. Eschewing the intolerance characterizing most other nationalistic programs of the twentieth century, GMD revolutionaries extended a welcoming hand to even the foreign powers. Chinese and foreigners alike faced the same two voices, one offering inclusion and the other threatening exclusion. As long as they abandoned imperialist activities, foreigners, while unable to enter the ranks of the Chinese "people," could at least enjoy close association with China and honored positions of friendship.

---

25. "Zhongguo Guomindang diyici quanguo daibiao dahui xuanyan," *Geming wenxian*, vol. 69, pp. 84, 89.
26. Sun, "Zongli jiaoyi: Zhongguo Guomindang diyici quanguo daibiao dahui xuanyan an," *Geming wenxian*, vol. 76, p. 2.
27. "Zhongguo Guomindang diyici quanguo daibiao dahui xuanyan," *Geming wenxian*, vol. 69, pp. 92-93.

Throughout proclamations made by First National Congress delegates, and indeed throughout the entire Nationalist Revolutionary period, these two voices sounded side-by-side.[28] Their coexistence was neither accidental nor a reflection of crude factional differences, but arose as a function of blurry and subjective criteria about who belonged in the "people" and "enemy" categories. Most important were not the categories themselves, but the intimation that movement could occur between them. Three points explain. First, the two voices implied multiple definitions of the *guomin*. The ideal, of course, involved fully revolutionized "people" co-creating the "nation" by actively aligning with the GMD and struggling toward its ends—those Sun had longed for since 1912. In contrast were Chinese who remained passive heirs, destined to inherit the GMD "nation" and enjoy its fruits, but offering little aid in its formation. Those in the latter category possessed revolutionary *potential* while those in the ideal group generated *actual* revolutionary power. To Sun, the *guomin* included those who actively allied with the revolutionary movement as well as those who would ally *if* they could just "awaken" to their true calling.[29] In sum, the "people" represented a continuum of meanings: the revolutionary, the inert, and everything in between.

Second, since the *guomin* comprised a range of attitudes, behaviors, and organizations, Congress leaders could easily include non-party groups and organizations within the revolutionary movement. As long as they did not jeopardize Nationalist plans, non-party and even non-revolutionary groups could be considered part of the *guomin*. Even so-called enemies, by hearkening to the party's accommodating voice, could be recategorized and included as part of the "people" if they abandoned self-interest for the revolutionary path. In pragmatic terms, Sun's movement enjoyed a clean and unencumbered way to woo defectors and incorporate defeated enemies into the GMD nation. As individuals and groups joined the ranks of the "people," the enemy would disappear.

Third, and most important, the GMD's two voices provided a means for the party to impel passive *guomin* and enemies alike toward the revolutionized end of the spectrum. Depending on circumstances, GMD leaders could invite inclusion, threaten exclusion, or employ any other technique to coax and push different groups toward the desired response. The *Congress Declaration* specifically invited the Constitutionalists *(Lixian pai)*, the Provincial Federationists *(Liansheng zizhi pai)*, the Conference of Harmony Faction

---

28. The two voices are reflected in CEC foreign policy. Leaders instituted an anti-imperialist propaganda program aimed at the *guomin*, but then prescribed a committee staffed by "experts" and Nationalist cadres to deal with foreigners. "Bendang ge zhixingbu difang dangbu duiwai taidu wenti an," *Geming wenxian*, vol. 79, pp. 14-15. A more detailed rendition of GMD foreign policy objectives can be found in "Diyici quanguo daibiao dahui xuanyanzhong zhi Guomindang zhenggang," *Geming wenxian*, vol. 70, p. 383.
29. Fitzgerald's *Awakening China* is the definitive study of this process.

(Heping huiyi pai), and the Businessmen Government Faction *(Shangren zhengfu pai)*—all powerful, patriotic but non-GMD organizations—to participate in the Nationalists' drive against warlordism.[30] Party leaders enticed others by pledging specific benefits. Women's suffrage groups, for example, were promised equal rights if they would support the GMD, while class economic interests were also, in the words of Su Qiming, "bound . . . together with the political objectives of the Nationalist Revolution."[31] As Sun explained,

> On the one hand, the people's revolution can achieve victory only when the peasants and workers of the country give it their whole-hearted support. On the other hand, the Guomindang will do its best to help peasant and labor movements in order to strengthen the people's revolution. Both the peasants and the workers are asked to join the Guomindang and to give their continuous devotion and efforts to promoting the People's Revolution. Inasmuch as the Guomindang is opposed to the imperialists and the militarists, who are the most dangerous enemies of the workers and peasants, *participation in the struggle of the party is to struggle also for their own interests.*[32] [Emphasis added.]

Various non-party interests were presented with the same offer: support the Nationalist Revolution and your specialized goals will reach fruition. As a result, GMD interest in social reform shifted from a means for improving living standards to a tool for enticing popular support.

Using a range of definitions of the nation and *guomin*, while also speaking with two voices to non-party interests, gave GMD leaders remarkable flexibility. In crude terms, they could employ carrot-and-stick incentives by offering inclusive benefits or applying exclusive compulsion. Power extended far beyond this simple dynamic, however. Because the party determined who warranted inclusion and who deserved exclusion, it could shape the playing field to its own advantage. An "enemy" or "people" label, in short, was not permanent but dependent on subjective measurements of relative defiance or conformity to revolutionary objectives. Equipped with a broad definition of the "people," the party could justify alliances or negotiations with almost any interest—even heinous Yunnan and Guangxi mercenaries. At the same time, interests once considered part of the "people" could easily lose that status. What separated enemies from people, in short, was not class, race, or group—or even affiliation with any particular ideological,

---

30. "Zhongguo Guomindang diyici quanguo daibiao dahui xuanyan," *Geming wenxian*, vol. 69, pp. 86-88.

31. Liang, "Beifa qijian Guomindang lingdaoxia de funü yundong," pp. 492-493; Su, "Beifa shiqi de nonggong yundong," p. 519.

32. "Zhongguo Guomindang diyici quanguo daibiao dahui xuanyan," *Geming wenxian*, vol. 69, pp. 84-94; Sharman, *Sun Yat-sen*, p. 264.

behavioral, or organizational group—but simply whatever party leaders felt best served their interests. Since they alone differentiated enemies from non-enemies, GMD officials could prioritize battles by confronting rivals one by one or bypassing them altogether if necessary. At any given time, "enemies" could comprise a distinct group close at hand (such as Chen Jiongming's Guangdong Army) or a generalized and amorphous entity farther away (such as warlordism in general). By controlling that definition and selectively identifying its targets, the revolution could better manage its challenges. According to Sun, "China formerly did not know that she was in decline and so perished; if she had seen ahead, she might not have perished. The ancient sayings 'the nation without foreign foes and outside dangers will always be ruined,' and 'many adversities will revive a state' are altogether psychological truisms."[33] If possessing external threats was valuable, the ability to determine who they were and when to meet them was doubly so.

First National Congress flexibility was not new. Sun had long been willing to do almost anything to gain power. Bending, reversing, and flip-flopping came to him naturally. What the Congress added was ideological explanation of what had been seen as arbitrary vacillations. It also defended against dilution of the revolutionary agenda by introducing a simple but strict prioritization of revolutionary goals: *first* establish a centralized system, *then* meet special interest, class, or localist objectives. As further defense against division, the First National Congress also ensured that inclusion in the revolutionary movement did not mean revolutionary equality as much as assimilative processing. Peasants and workers, thus, were urged to join the GMD and struggle for revolution, subjecting themselves to the ideological constraints of Sun adoration, party discipline, command and control, and so forth.

Fluid conceptualizations of enemies and the "people" provided flexibility, but they required more to transform *guomin* potential into revolutionized *guomin*. Since so few made the transition on their own, Borodin and Congress architects outlined specific ways to change popular attitudes—systems Fitzgerald calls the "pedagogical state structures" behind "awakening."[34] One such structure was a vast propaganda enterprise copied largely from the Leninist model and mandated to carry GMD ideology into the nethermost reaches of Chinese society. Like other components defined at the First National Congress, propaganda networks mirrored the party's hierarchical administration. The Propaganda Ministry was placed directly under the CEC to assure effective coordination and retain control within the party's upper echelons.[35] Under CEC direction, party branches in Shanghai, Beijing,

---

33. Sun, *San Min Chu I*, p. 102.
34. Fitzgerald, *Awakening China*, p. 20.
35. "Zhongyang zhixing weiyuanhui gebu zuzhi wenti an," *Geming wenxian*, vol. 79, pp. 1-2.

Hankou, Sichuan, and Harbin oversaw propaganda work in their respective areas.[36] Lower-tiered provincial and local GMD offices followed the direction of their superiors.[37] As mandated, the Propaganda Ministry identified propaganda targets and coordinated efforts throughout all China by networking through branch propaganda bureaus outside the base area and down through local cells. Ancillary organs, such as local youth or labor bureaus, served the needs of top propaganda officials by investigating current events, anticipating opportunities, and calculating future responses before submitting findings to the CEC.[38]

In February 1924, CEC leaders outlined the Propaganda Ministry's basic responsibilities: produce propaganda materials, distribute propaganda to other government departments, establish party schools *(dang xuexiao)* and set up curriculum, administer subordinate propaganda bureaus to ensure uniformity, and scrutinize against errors related to GMD principles or policy. Every two weeks, all other CEC ministries were required to submit reports to the Propaganda Ministry so it could incorporate new information into its message.[39] Field reports included accounts of propaganda activities for the same purpose. By mid-1924, the list of Propaganda Ministry responsibilities had grown considerably, revealing a distinct sensitivity to media and cultural institutions. Charges to watch newspapers were expanded to include magazines, communication companies, movie production firms, theaters, and performing arts groups. In addition, the CEC ordered the Ministry to expand its reach, ordering that "cultural institutions established by the party or managed by party comrades . . . (such as newspapers, magazines, communications companies, schools, educational associations, lecture societies, performance and movie theaters, musical organizations, etc.) should retain close relations with the Propaganda Ministry."[40]

Competition and inexperience meant some setbacks. Just when Shanghai's daily paper Wanguo Daily *(Wanguo ribao)* became an effective GMD organ, *Republican Daily (Minguo ribao)* fell away from CEC control. Upper

---

36. "Zhongyang zhixing weiyuan fenpei gedi wenti an," *Geming wenxian*, vol. 79, pp. 4-5.

37. "Gesheng dangwu jinxing jihua jueyian," *Geming wenxian*, vol. 79, pp. 7-8.

38. Between the central and five regional offices, all Chinese—even those overseas—were covered. "Zhongyang zhixing weiyuanhui ji gedi zhixingbu zhijie guanxia quyu wenti jueyian," *Geming wenxian*, vol. 79, pp. 2-3. The CEC hired readers to search foreign newspapers for reactions to party activities in order to provide GMD propaganda leaders with intelligence. "Zhongyang zhixing weiyuanhui ji Shanghai Beijing Haerbin deng zhixingbu zuzhi ji yusuan an," *Geming wenxian*, vol. 79, p. 11. Also see "Linshi Zhongyang zhixing weiyuanhui baogao gaiyao," *Geming wenxian*, vol. 76, p. 32.

39. "Zhongyang zhixing weiyuanhui gebu zhiwu gaiyao," *1-ZXWH*, vol. 1 (February 20, 1924).

40. Other new duties included: providing political training for the GMD military; collecting and publishing all speeches and writings by Sun Yat-sen and other leaders; establishing propaganda schools; and gathering information on international relations, economics, national, and political developments from non-GMD media. "Zhongguo Guomindang zhongyang zhixing weiyuanhui xuanchuanbu banshi zhangcheng," *1-ZXWH*, vol. 1 (April 24, 1924).

party levels were responsible for keeping lower levels trained and functioning at peak effectiveness. Nevertheless, difficulties continually vexed Nationalist administrators. "Sloppy" *(sanman)* performance and unfamiliarity with propaganda principles and organization frustrated the Shanghai Executive Committee, which responded by dispatching twenty trainers to straighten up scruffy organization in local propaganda bureaus.[41] In July 1924, propaganda training accelerated with the establishment of a GMD Propagandist Development Institute. Arguing that greater talent was needed, CEC member Wang Jingwei presented a proposal for training students (eighteen years or older with middle school educations) over a period of three months. Curriculum included everything from Sun Yat-sen ideology to speech-making and social psychology. At the end of the three-month term, successful graduates were assigned to work with various GMD offices *(dangbu)* up and down the party's chain of command.[42] Gradually, the propaganda network strengthened.

Another "pedagogical" pillar was education, headed this time by both the Propaganda and the Youth Ministries. Education had long enjoyed a special place in Sun's vision. In 1918, he had described it as the means for preparing Chinese for democracy and blamed the early Republic's failure on its neglect.[43] On March 1, 1920, he went further, describing schools as the "font of civilization and progress."[44] At the First National Congress, however, education—like everything else—was restructured to meet practical revolutionary needs. Noting education's matchless propaganda, training, and political potential, and inspired by Borodin's Leninist designs, GMD leaders outlined four distinct educational mandates.

The first involved specialty schools for training party cadres in specific fields. Highlights included propaganda institutes and officer training schools (fashioned after the famous Military Academy at Huangpu). Other schools followed. Proposed in June 1924, the Peasant Movement Lecture Institute emerged to train roving teams of peasant association *(nongmin xiehui)* organizers. Young party members—selected for their vigor and interest—studied peasant conditions and mastered practical skills such as distance walking, horseback riding, and militia formation.[45] Within the Institute's first three months, 175 graduates had been distributed throughout south China to set up similar institutions in their home counties.[46]

---

41. "Shanghai zhixingbu qingqiu zengjia yusuan an," *1-ZXWH*, vol. 2 (June 16, 1924).
42. "Zhongguo Guomindang dangli xuanchuanyuan yangchengsuo zhangcheng," *1-ZXWH*, vol. 5 (July 7, 1925).
43. Sharman, *Sun Yat-sen*, pp. 216-217.
44. Sun, "The Means of Introducing Local Self-Government," in Wei, et al., eds., *Prescriptions for Saving China*, pp. 244-245.
45. "Nongmin yundong diyibu shishi fang'an," *1-ZXWH*, vol. 2 (June 30, 1924); "Nongmin yundong jiangxisuo zuzhi jianzhang," *1-ZXWH*, vol. 2 (June 30, 1924).
46. Wilbur, *The Nationalist Revolution in China*, p. 16. Peng Pai was the Institute's first director.

In July 1925, the GMD Commerce Ministry—a late addition to the CEC's array of administrative organs—proposed a Merchant Movement Lecture Institute for the purpose of "cultivating talent for the merchant movement," "guiding merchants to better oppose imperialism and warlordism," and "helping merchants better understand the party's position and collectively follow the correct path of the Nationalist Revolution."[47] As planned, the Institute would recruit forty students, train them for three months, and send them out to organize merchant associations in Foshan, Jiangmen, Shunde, and so forth. Classes included standard Sun Yat-sen ideology and revolutionary history but added special courses such as *Methods of Propagandizing Merchants*, *China's Commercial Conditions*, and *The True Condition of Merchant Groups*.[48]

A second mandate was mass education. Most Chinese had little or no schooling, presenting the GMD with ample opportunity to predispose China's masses to party thought. Discussing mass education's value as propaganda, Dai Jitao proposed,

> If the Guomindang establishes schools in the countryside and induces all the children of the poor rural peoples to attend, then all would know of the GMD! After one or two years, [we could] ensure that they all studied books on the Three Principles of the People. Many would follow and better understand party ideology. At that point, propaganda would . . . be more effective.[49]

Shortly after the First National Congress, the Youth Ministry promised to "universalize party principles" *(dangyi puji)* by forming "commoner" *(pingmin)* schools taught by party member educators using existing Guangzhou school facilities after regular hours. As outlined, the schools would focus on non-traditional students or those denied other opportunities. By May's end, eleven *pingmin* schools were instructing some 1,318 students between the ages of fourteen and twenty. Girls outnumbered boys by a ratio of nearly two to one.[50] By June, the lower Yangzi also hosted a thriving *pingmin* educational system that, due to warlord reactions against other efforts, enjoyed the distinction of being the revolution's primary means of exercising influence in Shanghai, Jiangxi, and Anhui.[51] By the end of 1925,

See Galbiati, *P'eng P'ai and the Hai-Lu-feng Soviet*, pp. 176-177.

47. "Chouban shangmin yundong jiangxisuo yijianshu," *1-ZXWH*, vol. 5 (July 23, 1925). Although an alleged "radical," it was Wang Jingwei who proposed a Commerce Ministry so merchants would not feel abandoned by the party.

48. "Zhongguo Guomindang dangli shangren yundong jiangxisuo zhangcheng," *1-ZXWH*, vol. 5 (July 23, 1925).

49. "Chuban ji xuanchuan wenti an," *Geming wenxian*, vol. 76, pp. 13-14.

50. "Qingnianbu baogao pingmin xuexiao qingxing," *1-ZXWH*, vol. 2 (June 2, 1924); "Qingnianbu baogao pingmin xuexiao qingxing," May 31, 1924.

51. "Shanghai zhixingbu qingqiu zengjia yusuan an," *1-ZXWH*, vol. 2 (June 16, 1924).

even far away Xi'an hosted twenty *pingmin* schools headed by teachers who, as local party leaders bragged, were all "pure comrades of our party" *(chunxi wudang tongzhi).*[52] In July 1925, the Youth Ministry proposed a summer school system to educate older workers. Running from late July to late August during early morning and late night hours, the twenty proposed schools promised to teach over four hundred workers in courses entitled *Sun Yat-sen Ideology, Revolutionary History, General Knowledge of the People,* and *Letters and Math.* Anyone could sign up—excepting those with communicable diseases.[53] *Pingmin* education specifically targeted students between the ages of fourteen and twenty-one because, it was believed, this cohort most readily accepted "the party platform and party principles" *(danggang dangyi).* Viewed as an important means to "universalize party principles," *pingmin* education expanded, particularly outside GMD territories.[54]

The third educational mandate aimed to convert public schools within Nationalist territory into "party schools" *(dang xuexiao).* As will be fully explained in chapter 5, once GMD authorities took over a school, they altered curricula, changed faculty and administrators, and revolutionized school culture. The fourth mandate, which will also be illuminated in subsequent chapters, covered party efforts to curtail the educational might of rival programs. Dai Jitao explained the CEC's general position regarding non-party education to First National Congress delegates:

Not only should party schools use [party] books, but party-edited curricula should be disseminated to all other schools so that, at a minimum, over one-third of a school's curricula will be party texts. In this way, in the future, other schools will all become party schools. In addition, the introduction and recommendation of teaching personnel is very important because recommending a party member to enter a school then gives the party a portion of power within that school. At present, Nanyang or other foreign schools seeking teachers repeatedly request recommendations from the Jiangsu Provincial Educational Association or a similar organization, all of which are reactionary. Thus all those that are introduced and go are reactionary. Therefore their influence expands daily while that of our party weakens daily.[55]

Throughout 1924 and 1925, schools run by foreigners and those headed by "education tyrants" *(xuefa)*—such as the Jiangsu Provincial Educational Association—attracted keen Guomindang attention. Field reports routinely complained about Christian educators who "stupefied" *(hunmi)* young stu-

52. "Linshi Shaanxisheng dangbu baogao diyihao," *1-ZXWH*, vol. 5 (December 25, 1925).
53. "Shuqi gongren xuexiao jihua," *1-ZXWH*, vol. 5 (July 23, 1925).
54. "Qingnianbu baogao pingmin xuexiao qingxing," May 31, 1924.
55. "Chuban ji xuanchuan wenti an," *Geming wenxian*, vol. 76, pp. 13-14.

dents and Chinese educators who attacked and repressed revolutionary organizations. Colluding with warlords, educational cliques suppressed students and initiated anti-GMD demonstrations to counter the effects of revolutionary propaganda and organization. To ensure the success of propaganda and organizational efforts, party leaders determined to emphasize Sun Yat-sen principles and "push down the education tyrants" *(tuidao xuefa)*.[56]

Despite public assurances that the party would "guarantee the independence of education," First National Congress ideologues scarcely hid their intent to subject education to political and ideological expediencies.[57] Education would be geared to serve party interests. In the words of Lutz, "Since the KMT [GMD] viewed itself as custodian of the national orthodoxy, it was unwilling to permit educators to control education."[58] The charge to Propaganda and Youth Ministry officials was clear: establish new party schools *(dang xuexiao)* and direct all such schools as well as those managed by comrades "to ensure that the direction of education will always be suited to the principles and policy of the party."[59]

Organizational Leverage: Dangtuan *and Popular Forces*

Propaganda and education provided a way for GMD leaders to spread their message into even remote corners of Chinese society. Influencing thought, however, was just the beginning. According to the *First National Congress Declaration*, "All individuals and groups truly opposed to imperialism must enjoy all freedoms and power. Moreover, all who sell out the country and deceive the people *(maiguo wangmin)* by being loyal to imperialism and warlordism, regardless of whether they are part of a group or an individual, should not enjoy these freedoms and authority *(ziyou ji quanli)*."[60] Labels of inclusion and exclusion distinguished the empowered from the disenfranchised—the *guomin* from their enemies. Nevertheless, these labels had power only when they enjoyed ties to real influence. Without any means of bestowing or removing alleged "freedoms and authority," ideological constructs stood alone and frail, particularly since the more passive of the people remained immune to propaganda and/or untouched by party education.

Part of the solution was to expand organizational leverage beyond the party itself. Therefore First National Congress leaders adopted a series of

---

56. "Zhongyang zhixing weiyuanhui," *1-ZXWH*, vol. 4 (June 2, 1925).

57. "Zhongguo Guomindang diyici quanguo daibiao dahui xuanyan," *Geming wenxian*, vol. 69, p. 94.

58. Lutz, *Chinese Politics and Christian Missions*, p. 279.

59. "Zhongguo Guomindang zhongyang zhixing weiyuanhui xuanchuanbu banshi zhangcheng," *1-ZXWH*, vol. 1 (April 24, 1924).

60. "Zhongguo Guomindang diyici quanguo daibiao dahui xuanyan," *Geming wenxian*, vol. 69, p. 90.

Leninist institutions that could add a corporeal arm to the ethereal spirit of ideology. In other words, First National Congress delegates defined methods by which organizations outside the ranks of the revolution could be manipulated for party use.

An invaluable mechanism for extending organization influence was the party's system of infiltration via "party fractions" *(dangtuan)*.[61] As defined in the GMD General Regulations *(zongzhang)*, all party members belonging to other organizations—be they public, private, or secret merchant corps, labor unions, peasant self-help organizations and associations, educational organizations or schools, clubs, companies, provincial assemblies, and so forth—were required to organize *dangtuan*. Through its ministries, the CEC itself oversaw *dangtuan* formation, collected *dangtuan* reports, and planned *dangtuan* activity.[62] In addition to offering intelligence, *dangtuan* provided the CEC a direct, internal connection to their host organization. By voting uniformly and persuading non-party members to support decisions that complemented party objectives, *dangtuan* infiltrators could expand GMD influence and spread Nationalist ideology, thus granting CEC leaders leverage in steering other organizations.[63] *Dangtuan* also helped actualize revolutionary programs. Propaganda campaigns, for example, relied heavily on school or factory *dangtuan* to spread GMD materials within host organizations. *Pingmin* education depended on high school and normal school *dangtuan* sponsorship to arrange facility use.[64] As meticulously described at the First National Congress, coordinating *dangtuan* activities would help spur military, propaganda, and party advances.[65]

Using *dangtuan*, party authorities quickly carved out spheres of influence in non-GMD organizations. *Dangtuan* softened anti-party animosity and corroborated revolutionary invitations for cooperation. Potential matured, however, when *dangtuan* began to commandeer popular movements or federations of organizations—especially those operating at the provincial or national level. Among labor unions, alliances between multiple unions were

---

61. The English term "fraction," common in literature of the period, referred to the practice of capturing control of an organization by forming a subgroup or "fraction" of the whole that voted in unison. The term nicely accounts for at least a portion of the Chinese term *dangtuan*.

62. "Qingnian dangtuan zuzhi ti'an," *1-ZXWH*, vol. 1 (March 12, 1924). The Labor Ministry reported directly to the CEC on *dangtuan* activities related to strikes or labor struggles while the Youth Ministry reported on *dangtuan* action in schools. "Zhongyang zhixing weiyuanhui gebu zhiwu gaiyao," *1-ZXWH*, vol. 1 (February 20, 1924).

63. "Zhongguo Guomindang zongzhang zhiding an," *Geming wenxian*, vol. 76, p. 7; "Diyici quanguo daibiao dahui tongguo Zhongguo Guomindang zongzhang," *Geming wenxian*, vol. 70, p. 54-55. Predictably, the CCP adopted the same policy vis-à-vis the GMD. To maximize effect, party members in *dangtuan* were ordered not to openly debate decisions in the presence of non-party members but discuss plans behind closed doors in order to present a unified stand.

64. "Qingnianbu baogao pingmin xuexiao qingxing," *1-ZXWH*, vol. 2 (June 2, 1924).

65. "Diyici quanguo daibiao dahui tongguo Zhongguo Guomindang zongzhang," *Geming wenxian*, vol. 70, pp. 54-55. See Articles 77 through 84.

commonplace. Immediately after January 1924, however, it was among student union federations that GMD *dangtuan* produced the greatest flurry of activity. Like their Peasant and Labor Ministry counterparts, Youth Ministry officials energetically pushed organizational expansion, creating new student unions *(xuehui)* and infiltrating hundreds of older ones scattered throughout China. As announced by Youth Ministry proclamations, "students must . . . organize . . . in order to enter the proper revolutionary course."[66] Even without GMD encouragement, however, student unions were multiplying. Many had already joined provincial and national alliances, providing unprecedented opportunity for *dangtuan* infiltrators to rise into the upper ranks of alliance leadership. As early as March 1924, the Youth Ministry began targeting the Guangzhou Student Federation:

> With Guangzhou serving as the political center of south China, the student movement of Guangzhou not only has ties to the city or the province, but it has ties to the entire southern portion of China. The organization of the current Guangzhou Student Federation is extremely disordered and cannot call on the student masses to conduct large scale movement. Moreover, our party has no means to govern it. Therefore, our student GMD members must instigate a movement to hasten its reform.[67]

To expand influence, the Youth Ministry outlined the following program: first, reform each student union so *dangtuan* members could vote for each other and have a chance to seize "a bit of influence" *(jifen shili)*; second, organize among party students a committee for unifying Guangzhou's students; and third, send delegates from all respective student unions to demand that the Guangzhou Student Federation reform.[68] Student GMD members were then ordered to form *dangtuan* in their respective schools and join local student alliances. Nationalist district and sub-district branch offices, meanwhile, were instructed to oversee the actions of both while central authorities provided guidance.[69] As similar reforms impacted other student organizations, revolutionary influence expanded through all levels of the student movement.

Dangtuan infiltration vastly extended organizational reach and helped the Guomindang more fully revolutionize *guomin* potential. Nevertheless, since most people were not yet organized enough to host a *dangtuan* or engage in other revolutionary work, Congress leaders also emphasized the creation of new mass organizations among workers, peasants, the youth, and women.

---

66. "Qingnian yundong zhengce jueyian," *1-ZXWH*, vol. 1 (March 12, 1924).
67. "Guangzhoushi xuesheng tongyi yundong jueyian," *1-ZXWH*, vol. 1 (March 12, 1924).
68. "Guangzhoushi xuesheng tongyi yundong jueyian," *1-ZXWH*, vol. 1 (March 12, 1924).
69. Chen, "Zhongyang dangbu qingnian yundong baogao," 1926.

Before 1924, Sun's primary interest in China's masses had been to improve their living conditions with the new laws, institutions and opportunities promised via his People's Livelihood platform.[70] Under Borodin's insistence, however, the party moved to embrace mass-based organizations as a way to engender social and political change. Predictably, this responsibility was also entrusted to the CEC which oversaw mass movements through its respective Labor, Peasant, Youth, and Women's ministries.[71] Branch offices managed their own labor, peasant, youth, and women's bureaus which customized general CEC objectives to fit local conditions. Sometimes other specific duties were added. The Guangzhou Labor Bureau, for example, was ordered to track labor issues and report on labor laws, agitation, communication, and meetings. The Guangzhou Youth Bureau was ordered to spread propaganda in schools, organize the Boy Scouts, and assess attitudes at all Guangzhou schools.[72] At each level, party cadres spread propaganda within their local jurisdiction while shaping mass organizations into sharpened political tools.

CEC leaders outlined the basic responsibilities of the Labor Ministry in February 1924. Highlights included collecting information on worker conditions, coordinating propaganda opportunities, calling nation-wide meetings of worker representatives, "communicating with the leaders of domestic worker groups," and "creating labor leaders able to serve as the backbone of the Nationalist movement."[73]

Despite promise, organizational efforts struggled when wary localist interests refused to participate. In March 1924, Liao Zhongkai tried to centralize GMD control over Guangzhou's labor unions *(gonghui)* by planning a Guangzhou Workers' Delegates Conference. As envisioned, delegates elected by union federations (including the communications, industrial, and handicrafts federations) were supposed to elect a central executive committee to direct labor's participation in the revolution. Liao also hoped to plant ideological corps in unions and set up branch offices among Guangzhou seamen and among workers at the Guangzhou-Hankou Railroad and the

70. On January 1, 1923, Sun's government announced a series of policies aimed at relieving pressures on peasants and workers, including regulations regarding land (rights, ownership, utilization, and taxes); assurances of labor equality and protection; and the promotion of peasant equality and status. Also, the nationalization and central administration of railways, mines, forests and water conservancy, and other large-scale projects affecting the people, and the policy of granting workers engaged in these enterprises a portion of administrative authority, were largely conceived for the benefit of workers and peasants. See "Zhongguo Guomindang xuanyan," *Geming wenxian*, vol. 69, pp. 67-71.
71. "Zhongyang zhixing weiyuanhui gebu zuzhi wenti an," *Geming wenxian*, vol. 79, pp. 1-2. Accordingly, the First National Congress declared, "the national revolutionary movement must rely upon the participation of all of China's peasants and workers." See "Zhongguo Guomindang diyici quanguo daibiao dahui xuanyan," *Geming wenxian*, vol. 69, p. 91.
72. "Zhongguo Guomindang Guangzhou tebieshi zhixing weiyuanhui zhangcheng," *1-ZXWH*, vol. 2 (May 29, 1924).
73. "Zhongyang zhixing weiyuanhui gebu zhiwu gaiyao," *1-ZXWH*, vol. 1 (February 20, 1924).

Guangdong Arsenal.[74] In its ideal form, this comprehensive vision sought to institute everything from a workers' hospital to a China-wide organization embracing virtually all workers in a layered hierarchy extending from the Workers' Delegates Conference, down through labor federations and individual unions. To guard against localist interests and other "reactionary" *(fandong)* opposition, Liao drafted plans for a labor militia.[75]

On May 1, this drive to unite Guangzhou labor under the party banner began with Sun Yat-sen addressing a large Labor Day rally and inviting Guangzhou workers to abandon class interests and join the revolution's fight against foreign privilege. The following week-long conference proved relatively unsuccessful, however, when only a handful of unions participated. The dangers of organizing in warlord China had conditioned labor leaders to be wary of political intrusion. Most unions opted to preserve their political independence by staying with the old federation headed by the Mechanics Union. The Mechanics Union delegate attending the conference criticized the Guomindang, claiming that Chinese employers did not treat workers any better than foreign employers and intimating that the party did not have the best interests of workers at heart. Other divisions also impeded Liao's efforts.[76] Sympathetic unions refused to join a GMD-led federation if it meant uniting with rival unions.[77] Other labor leaders claimed that Labor Ministry radicals sought to seize control of the unions and use them for political rather than reformist purposes.[78] Unwilling to subordinate their own interests to revolution, most union leaders avoided Liao's centralizing overtures.

Narrowing its focus, the party decided to concentrate on workers in key industries and services vital to revolutionary objectives: railways, shipyards, communications (telegraph, telephone, and postal), and the electrical industry.[79] Incrementally, relations improved. Revolutionary party members (especially those with concurrent CCP ties) became well-represented among labor leaders, voting as *dangtuan* blocs to promote fellow comrades until union leadership featured high percentages of revolutionary sympathizers if not actual party members. In June 1924, to formalize central control the CEC approved regulations requiring all unions to comply with Labor Ministry organizational requirements, accept party oversight, and register with the

74. GMD officials provided oversight. Wilbur and How, *Missionaries of Revolution*, p. 106; "Gongren daibiao dahui kaihui jingguo baogao," *1-ZXWH*, vol. 2 (May 12, 1924).

75. "Gongren daibiao dahui kaihui jingguo baogao," *1-ZXWH*, vol. 2 (May 12, 1924).

76. Only unions in the more modernized sector of the economy joined, including, railwaymen, dock workers, printers, and rice-huskers. Chesneaux, *The Chinese Labor Movement*, pp. 246-247.

77. Internal labor issues—resistance to large unions and amalgamation, rivalries between unions, problems with administration, and so forth—defied GMD centralizing efforts. Wilbur and How, *Missionaries of Revolution*, p. 107.

78. Wilbur, *The Nationalist Revolution in China*, p. 15.

79. Wilbur, *The Nationalist Revolution in China*, p. 15.

government.[80] Party by-laws, emerging in August 1924, further subordinated Guangzhou unions by requiring them to submit semi-annual reports that included biographical, financial, job performance, and political activity information on each union member.[81] Party organizers infiltrated existing labor organizations while creating new ones to challenge and draw strength away from those deemed uncooperative. Nationalist influence among workers grew. On May 1, 1925, just one year after its failed campaign to bring labor under its control, the party sponsored the Second National Conference of Chinese Labor. On opening day, roughly 148 delegates representing some 171,300 workers in registered unions attended. Later reports projected that over five hundred delegates, representing eighty-seven unions, would attend some part of the ten-day Guangzhou conference.[82]

Organization among peasants followed a similar trajectory. On February 20, 1924, CEC leaders ordered the Peasant Ministry to research organization, plan a conference, and publish a peasant journal. By March, they added a variety of educational programs headed by GMD county, district, and sub-district offices. Peng Pai, the newly appointed secretary of the GMD Peasant Ministry, oversaw preparations.[83] In June, Sun Yat-sen endorsed a CEC report asserting that "all China's peasants should struggle under one ideology and one organization."[84] With Sun's blessing, party organizers began establishing autonomous peasant associations, each consisting of at least twenty peasants aged sixteen years or older. To guard against usurpation, regulations banned anyone involved in usury, opium or gambling; anyone possessing authority in any religious organization (fathers, ministers, monks, or shamans); anyone owning over one hundred *mu* (one *mu* equals 1/6 of an acre); and anyone connected to imperialism.[85]

As peasant associations spread, they were united via county, provincial, and national federations—all under the control of the GMD Peasant Ministry. By September, forty-five individual associations and five county federations were in operation. Seven months later, organizers claimed ninety-one associations in the five counties nearest Guangzhou (with 10,890 members) and eleven more nearby (with 1,500 members). Sun's home county of Xiangshan proved somewhat more receptive, boasting fifty-eight associations and eight thousand members. In Guangning county, located northwest of Guangzhou, deputies organized 294 associations with 55,000 members by April 1925.

---

80. "Guiding bendang zhi gongren zuzhi zhengce ji ci zhengce duiyu zhengfu zhi guanxi an," *1-ZXWH*, vol. 2 (June 2, 1924).
81. "Gonghui fa cao'an," *1-ZXWH*, vol. 3 (August 7, 1924).
82. Wong, "Farmers and Workers in Canton," p. 301.
83. Galbiati, *P'eng P'ai: and the Hai-Lu-feng Soviet*, p. 173.
84. "Jianyi dayuanshuai pixing nongmin xiehui zhangcheng gongwen," *1-ZXWH*, vol. 2 (June 16, 1924).
85. "Duiyu nongmin yundong zhi xuanyan," *1-ZXWH*, vol. 2 (June 19, 1924).

Additionally, once Haifeng and Lufeng counties had been recaptured from Chen Jiongming, revolutionaries were able to revive Peng Pai's earlier efforts—long dormant—and add some 82,000 members to the total.[86] By May 1925, the GMD press could claim over fifty peasant federations in twenty-two of Guangdong's ninety-six districts, totaling over 200,000 members.[87] That same month, Guangzhou hosted a ten-day Peasant Conference. Flexing their combined political muscle, delegates demanded better economic rights, a stronger federation, support for agricultural science, participation in politics, and solidarity with similar movements around the world.[88]

While GMD links to workers and peasants grew, ties to youth organizations exploded. Active since the May Fourth Movement, students had committed to revolutionizing China's masses even before the First National Congress. In August 1923, student representatives convened the Fifth National Congress of the National Student Union in Guangzhou and declared popular revolutionary work to be "vital" *(qieyao)* if China's masses were to ever be organized enough to destroy imperialism and warlordism.[89] First National Congress decisions thus augmented momentum that had long been building. On March 9, 1924, the Guangzhou Student Federation announced intentions to reorganize and declared, "The people's revolution will never succeed unless the strength of all the nation's masses are first concentrated and then follow formal, clear, and unified goals. Moreover, it will never succeed unless it first arranges students in an organized, systematic, disciplined, and goal-oriented group."[90] Naturally, the force providing the requisite order, discipline, and goals was not the revolution—a non-sentient phenomenon—but the GMD, its self-proclaimed head.

On March 12, 1924, the CEC passed a resolution structuring the youth movement. As designed, GMD district offices *(chubu)* and sub-district offices *(chufenbu)* organized student movement committees of five to ten members which received direction from district offices. Two members selected from each of these committees sat on a student movement committee representative association which also followed district instruction. Two members from each student movement committee joined a higher county representative association, and two members from the county association sat

86. Wilbur and How, *Missionaries of Revolution*, p. 111; Galbiati, *P'eng P'ai and the Hai-Lu-feng Soviet*, pp. 193-202.

87. Wong, "Co-operation, or Non-Intervention, Wanted," p. 362.

88. Heavy Nationalist influence was undeniable. Delegates passed an agenda formed in advance by party leaders while GMD colleges and trade institutions hosted the Conference. Wong, "Farmers and Workers in Canton," p. 301.

89. The Guangzhou Student Federation, like many other organizations, had been founded in 1919 and operated outside the official channels of GMD control yet still enjoyed close ties to the party. "Guangzhou xuesheng lianhehui gaizu xuanyan," April 1924.

90. "Guangzhou xuesheng lianhehui gaizu xuanyan," April 1924.

on a still higher provincial representative association under the provincial party office. Two members from each provincial committee then sat on the highest body, the National Student Movement Committee Representative Association, overseen by the GMD central headquarters. Topping this hierarchical pyramid sat the *dangtuan* officers of the National Student Union who reported directly to the Youth Ministry. At every level, the student union *dangtuan* leaders on these committees enjoyed direct access to party leaders and vice versa, allowing the Youth Ministry to "act among the general student masses."[91] National organizations such as the Shanghai Student Federation, which hosted student unions from all over the country, also enjoyed direct access to CEC financial assistance and leadership. Such access was described as necessary if the party was going to "collect all the youth of China under the banner of the Guomindang" and prevent rivals from usurping power.[92] Coordinating the actions of *dangtuan* in student organizations, clubs, athletic teams, and other student-related groups, the GMD positioned itself to exercise influence far and wide.

When possible, the Youth Ministry took advantage of student movement inertia by regularly offering training, direction, and even funding to student activists. Guangzhou students enjoyed particularly close ties to central GMD officials. In May 1924, Youth Ministry officials invited all Guangzhou students to a series of lectures by top officials, including Wang Jingwei and Dai Jitao, and planned demonstrations celebrating national events.[93] With time, party influence became formal and institutionalized. In September, Ministry officials ordered the Guangzhou Education Bureau and the Guangdong Education Department to survey all schools in the city—both public and private. Requested information included financial resources, faculty names, and information on student organizations. According to Ministry directives, the purpose for the surveys was simple: to better understand "student storms" *(fengchao)* and student conditions.[94] On April 19, 1925, the Youth Ministry reached a milestone in its centralizing efforts when the Guangdong Student Representative Congress determined that all student groups in the province "obeyed GMD directives" and had formed work groups "in all locales." [95]

From the perspective of top Nationalist leaders, mass organizations did not exist for their own sakes but to mobilize *guomin* with revolutionary potential in various movements. At the same time, mass organizations also

91. "Xuesheng yundong jihua jueyian," *1-ZXWH*, vol. 1 (March 12, 1924).

92. "Shanghai zhixingbu qingqiu zengjia yusuan an," *1-ZXWH*, vol. 2 (June 16, 1924).

93. Zou, "Zhongyang qingnianbu buzhang Zou Lu zhi Guangzhou gexiao tonghan," May 1924; "Qingnianbu bugao," August 6, 1924.

94. "Zhongyang qingnianbu zhi Guangdong jiaoyu tingzhang han," September 15 1924; "Zhi Guangzhoushi zhengsuo jiaoyuju diaocha de xia benshi gexuexiao han," September 15, 1924.

95. "Qingnianbu gongzuo baogao," June 25, 1925.

promised to check or even roll back the influence of non-revolutionary organizations. In rural settings, peasant militias protected against gentry forces such as people's corps *(mintuan)* or gangs of hired toughs that occasionally murdered GMD cadres or burned villages to prevent the spread of peasant associations.[96] According to Peasant Ministry regulations, militias had to: (1) conform to military discipline and military organizational methods; (2) exclude anyone not belonging to the peasant association; (3) confiscate any arms within the village not controlled by peasant militia members; and (4) accept absolute government supervision.[97] Militias spread. By June 1924, the Peasant Ministry reported that Foshan had already established a "protection militia" *(baoweituan)* that allied forty-seven different township *(xiang)* militias.[98] Urban areas saw comparable structures wherever unions organized labor militias or armed strike pickets. Labor militias defended worker interests against strike breakers or merchant toughs. Strike committees were granted sweeping powers so they could conduct and enforce strike or boycott regulations. Even students enjoyed martial training and organization, although it never reached the level of maturation found in labor and peasant militias. Against warlord forces, armed mass organizations performed inconsistently. However, when employed against other "enemy" organizations, mobilized mass organizations proved invaluable as a source of coercive force. Even modest degrees of influence and leverage in Chinese society could help pressure reluctant *guomin* or enemies. Anything beyond that had the potential to greatly enhance political opportunities.

Tactical Options: the Dual-Prong

Combining elements of Sun's modernizing vision and Borodin's Leninist system, the First National Congress produced a hybridized revolutionary program. At the head stood a party hierarchy that extended GMD influence to hundreds of smaller party units scattered throughout China. Meanwhile, *dangtuan* and propaganda connections to a vast network of non-party organizations augmented revolutionary might. Collectively, the two networks

---

96. Working with the Communist Youth Corps in the countryside, Peng Pai just escaped *mintuan* violence before heading the GMD Peasant Ministry. Galbiati, *P'eng P'ai and the Hai-Lu-feng Soviet*, pp. 100-172. The first volume of the GMD peasant journal *Zhongguo nongmin* provides detailed accounts of rural tensions in Zhongshan and Haifeng counties. See Luo, "Zhongshan xian shibian zhi jingguo ji xianzai, pp. 39-58, and Peng, "Haifeng nongmin yundong baogao," pp. 59-69.

97. The party promised not to use peasant militia for any purpose beyond defending villages. "Duiyu nongmin yundong zhi xuanyan," *1-ZXWH*, vol. 2 (June 19, 1924).

98. Peasant militias often tried to preserve their autonomy. Peasants in Nanpu, for example, did not join the larger militia of Foshan but maintained an independent force of three hundred men trained by a local elementary school teacher. Liao Zhongkai and representatives from the larger militia attended the opening ceremonies, which were held in May, as a sign of brotherhood and solidarity. "Foshanshu Nanpu nongtuan chengli zhuangkuang," *1-ZXWH*, vol. 2 (June 2, 1924).

gave the revolution the integrity and discipline of a distinctly centralized administrative apparatus while adding a vast decentralized army of popular organizations that offered allied support even while enjoying relative independence and autonomy. Accounting for party control and popular support at the same time, this decentralized centralist blend of revolutionary forces gave the Nationalist Revolution new strength.

First National Congress documents never explained why this arrangement was preferred or how the revolution's various parts would bring about revolutionary objectives. Abrogation of the unequal treaties, for example, was described as the GMD's "most important duty" *(zui zhongyao zhiwu)*. As one policy declaration announced, "the Guomindang considers the abolishment of the unequal treaties and the struggle with imperialism as a necessary precondition to pushing down warlord dictatorships and unifying China through the formation of a democratic government."[99] Nevertheless, despite great effort to flesh out ideological and organizational details of the revolution's ranks, Congress pronouncements failed to outline a plan of action vis-à-vis the unequal treaties or give any indication how they would be destroyed. In fact, all revolutionary goals seemed quite vague. In their treatment of imperialism, for example, Congress pronouncements declined to even identify a concrete target, announcing instead that China's enemy was the generalized system of imperialism and *not* any specific treaty, foreign power, or institution.[100]

Party reluctance to identify how its new revolutionary tools would abrogate the treaties or defeat imperialism stemmed, in part, from the party's recognition of individual choice. Since it fell to China's various interests and individuals to opt for inclusion *or* exclusion, and since not even Sun—sacred vision notwithstanding—could foresee how every group would use that agency, no one could predict how the revolution would play out.

Another, perhaps weightier, reason for Congress silence about its plan of action was the fact that the new revolutionary system contained so many untidy contradictions that its dynamics were too irrational to articulate. Ideological ideals did not match political realities. Thanks to Sun, actors facing the revolution could choose inclusion or exclusion, "people" or "enemy" status. Nevertheless, thanks to Borodin, the Guomindang refused to stand idly by, waiting for people to decide, but determined to actively drive them into ranks of the revolutionized. Sun's spirit of inclusion mandated that anyone hesitating to participate could not simply be destroyed. Borodin's tools of exclusion, however, intimated that they could not be tolerated either. As a result, the Nationalist Revolution represented an odd mix of freedom and coercion, inclusion and exclusion. Those anxious to join the revolu-

---

99. "Bendang muqian zhengce zhi xuanchuan dagang," *1-ZXWH*, vol. 5 (July 23, 1925).
100. "Bendang muqian zhengce zhi xuanchuan dagang," *1-ZXWH*, vol. 5 (July 23, 1925).

tionary movement enjoyed the freedom to do so. Those slower to commit, however, faced various degrees of persuasion to help them make the "right" choice.[101]

First National Congress institutions provided party leaders with a number of options. On one end of the spectrum lay the coercive systems of state control: legal, police, judicial, and military systems tied to the Guangzhou municipal, the Guangdong provincial, and the Guomindang national governments. State-sponsored force—or the threat of it—produced results when nothing else could and backed other persuasive mechanisms. Nevertheless, coercion could not effectively persuade potential *guomin* to join the revolutionized *guomin*. It offered short-term results but long-term hazards; reluctant loyalty at best and cornered defiance at worst. State coercion also had limited value against so-called enemies in Chinese society. The revolution's adversaries did not float about detached and insulated, but maintained tight connections with each other. Even modest erosion of the Chinese base supporting imperialism could not help but attract unwanted attention from the powers and militarists. Thus, state-sanctioned force against even domestic enemies had to be fully justifiable lest it precipitate imperialist or warlord intervention. At the other end of the spectrum, opposite state-sanctioned violence and coercion—sat China's organized, revolutionized, and mobilized *guomin*. Extensive in both number and geographic reach, mass organizations carried propaganda and ideology to the streets via parades, demonstrations, campaigns, and other forms of agitation. Mass movements promised considerable returns by injecting potential *guomin* with ideological sentiment and drawing increasing numbers into the ranks of the revolutionized.

Separately neither GMD state coercion nor mass organizations looked particularly impressive. Collectively the image did not improve much, even after accounting for ideology. The array of enemies obstructing national unification was simply too great. The system crudely outlined at the First National Congress, however, was misleading for its power was not contained within its ideology nor its particular institutions but in the creative ways Nationalist leaders employed both—ways that to be effective best remained unexplained.

The basic *modus operandi* that eventually carried China's revolutionaries to power was worked out between 1920 and 1923, long before the First National Congress. The first ingredient involved labor unionization, which Sun Yat-sen's second Guangzhou regime actively encouraged as a prelude to

---

101. Nationalist ideologues whitewashed this dirty little inconsistency by employing the terms *juewu* or *juexing*—glossed as "awakening"—to identify the transition from inert potential *guomin* to revolutionary *guomin*. The terms imply an inner realization, obfuscating the duress sometimes required to compel "awakening." In short, while the Chinese verbs are predominantly intransitive, revolutionary pressures gave them a distinctive transitive quality as well.

modernization.[102] As unions spread through Guangzhou and into Hong Kong, labor identities and solidarity expanded, creating strong loyalties between workers of both cities. The second element appeared accidentally in April 1920 when some nine thousand striking mechanics abandoned their jobs in various British enterprises and departed for Guangzhou, leaving Hong Kong's modern industrial sector, which was highly dependent on skilled labor, unmanned and idle. Within two weeks, the mechanics had secured a reasonable settlement. Although short-lived, the strike had far-reaching consequences. By offering haven and modest support to Hong Kong strikers, Sun solidified his reputation as a friend of labor and found a way to squeeze Hong Kong and British economic well-being. Similar strikes followed, providing more experience and refined tactics. Sun's greatest triumph, however, came in early 1922 when Hong Kong's ship owners rejected a Seamen's Union request for a pay hike. Encouraged by Sun's government, the seamen struck and deserted Hong Kong by the thousands. As negotiations lagged, the strike assumed greater political significance, quickly became a matter of national prestige, and soon attracted other unions, including those representing engineers, dockers, stevedores, coolie laborers, domestic servants, and so forth. Altogether, some 120,000 workers left Hong Kong.[103]

Through it all, Sun's party played an integral role, providing refuge, hosting the strikers' headquarters, and funding their expenses.[104] Strikers carried identification cards with Sun's picture on one side and organized under the direction of Chen Bingsheng, president of the Seamen's Union and a Guomindang member.[105] When ship owners, union leaders, and the British consulate asked Chen Jiongming and GMD leader Wu Chaogang to arbitrate a resolution, the party gained even greater influence.[106]

Skeptics complained that Sun Yat-sen's involvement was not coincidental but carefully orchestrated to secure nation-building and foreign-relations advantages. Guangzhou enjoyed far too many benefits to suspect otherwise. On the domestic front, the strike spawned resonant class and nationalistic solidarity that spread to cities all over China.[107] As British

102. Fung, *The Diplomacy of Imperial Retreat*, p. 38.
103. Welsh, *A Borrowed Place*, pp. 369-370; Tsin, *Nation, Governance, and Modernity in China*, p. 80.
104. Chesneaux, *The Chinese Labor Movement*, p. 183. The GMD paid out some $100,000 Chinese dollars.
105. Tsin, *Nation, Governance, and Modernity in China*, p. 79; Chen, comp., *BCCM*, vol. J, section 10, p. 8.
106. The initial arbitration meeting at Chen Jiongming's offices included Chen, Frank Lee (Commissioner for Foreign Affairs), five seamen delegates, two Guangzhou labor union representatives, the British Vice-Consul, and Mr. A. E. Wood (Assistant Secretary for Chinese Affairs of Hong Kong) as representative for the Hong Kong government." Chen, comp., *BCCM*, vol. J, section 10, p. 2; Chesneaux, *The Chinese Labor Movement*, p. 182.
107. Chesneaux, *The Chinese Labor Movement*, pp. 184-185.

authorities struggled to maintain their hard-line position, Sun claimed the moral high ground and popularity as a leader able to stand up to imperialism. His rising reputation in turn substantiated party claims to possess national, as opposed to mere regional, appeal. On the international front, the strike offered even more. By assisting in the negotiations, the Nationalist regime enjoyed diplomatic intercourse with British authorities even though London refused to officially recognize the revolutionary government. Denied *de jure* relations, the GMD used strike negotiations to secure *de facto* high-level, official contacts. Best of all, the tables had turned. Instead of Sun asking for favors from Britain, the British now found themselves seeking assistance from the GMD—to head arbitration and prevent strikers from attacking British marines supplying food to Hong Kong.[108]

British officials carefully documented the Nationalists' new-found power. Assessing strike impact, British Consul-general Sir James Jamieson in Guangzhou wrote to the Foreign Office, "Not only Hong Kong, but Kwangtung [Guangdong] and all South China, are face to face with a powerful organization, which has already proved its amazing strength and is prepared at any moment to put it into operation." [109] More begrudgingly, Hong Kong Governor Sir Reginald Stubbs reported that Sun's party had gained prestige and acclaim by assisting the strikes, and that the Seamen's Strike "has shown that [the GMD] can paralyze the trade of [Hong Kong] , and it must be expected that it will again employ similar tactics *whenever it desires to gain some object.*"[110] [Emphasis added.] While Jamieson admired the sheer power labor unrest could unleash, Stubbs worried about who would be wielding that power and what it provided: leverage in the hands of Guomindang officials.

Although British officials strongly suspected that the Guangzhou regime contributed to Hong Kong's labor problem, they struggled to find solid evidence. GMD authorities easily defended themselves, saying that labor unrest had developed quite independent of party involvement. Strikes were erupting all over China and, indeed, all over the globe. In official statements, Sun's foreign policy advisor Chen Youren (Eugene Chen) doggedly announced that the party kept a strict policy of "non-intervention."[111] Indeed, Guangzhou officials publicly maintained as much distance from the strikers as possible—portraying striker financial aid, for example, as "loans." To GMD coyness the British had no retort. Guangzhou clouded the issue by shunting responsibility everywhere and anywhere. Responding to accusations implicating Sun, for example, the *South China Morning Post*—a British paper—reported that a Chinese "gentleman" close to Sun sought to correct

108. Chen, comp., *BCCM*, vol. J, section 10, p. 2.
109. Chen, comp., *BCCM*, vol. J, section 10B, p. 1.
110. Cited in Tsin, *Nation, Governance, and Modernity in China*, p. 81.
111. Chesneaux, *The Chinese Labor Movement*, p. 183.

"misleading information" among the powers by assuring them that there was "no doubt whatever" that Chen Jiongming, not Sun, was to blame for Hong Kong's labor troubles.[112] Some British officials insisted that Nationalist declarations of noninvolvement were insincere, arguing that Sun's pardon of Chen Bingsheng—convicted of murdering his wife—for "good service to the Government" could only refer to his role as a strike leader.[113] Nevertheless, evidence was scanty and circumstantial at best. When Stubbs angrily accused Sun of fomenting the strike to give Guangzhou advantage over Hong Kong, Sun simply denied it.[114] To put remaining doubts to rest, the Guangzhou leader publicly announced that his government "absolutely repudiated" the use of strikes to damage British interests.[115]

With ambiguities abounding, British leaders struggled to formulate a coherent response and argued about whether to pin responsibility on Chen Jiongming, Sun Yat-sen, labor activists, or the strikers themselves. Stubbs and Sir Beilby Alston (British *Charge d'Affaires* in Beijing) viewed the strikes as politically motivated and demanded a strong hand against the GMD. Jamieson, on the other hand, blamed economics, claiming that the strike only became a political problem when the British treated it as one.[116] Accusing his colleagues of poorly handling GMD relations in general and the strike in particular, Jamieson maintained that prolonging negotiations only gave the revolutionary "Bolshevist element" time to "bring the requisite intimidation to bear and to build up the machinery necessary to call out every guild or association in Hong Kong and South China."[117] Sharply divided in opinion, the British failed to reach a consensus. Even if they had, however, they would have struggled to justify strong-handed action to their own constituency, let alone to China's people.

Unable to formulate a better response, Hong Kong authorities vented frustration by repressing the strikers directly. Governor Stubbs issued notice forbidding workers from leaving Hong Kong, leading to conflict on March 3 when a small task force of police and soldiers fired into workers defying the order. The incident, however, did not intimidate and originally planned. Rather, it fanned an outburst of public anger which in turn spawned plans for even more walkouts. Outmaneuvered, Hong Kong's ship owners quickly settled, meeting most of the seamen's demands. In Guangdong, Sun basked in his success.

---

112. Chen, comp., *BCCM*, vol. J, section 10A, p. 1.
113. Tsin, *Nation, Governance, and Modernity in China*, p. 79; Chen, comp., *BCCM*, vol. J, section 10, p. 8; Chesneaux, *The Chinese Labor Movement*, pp. 166, 181.
114. Fung, *The Diplomacy of Imperial Retreat*, p. 38.
115. Sun retorted that his interest in Hong Kong strikers stemmed exclusively from a deep concern for their economic well-being. See Chan, "Labor and Empire," p. 291.
116. Chen, comp., *BCCM*, vol. J, section 10B, p. 3.
117. Chen, comp., *BCCM*, vol. J, section 10B, p. 1.

Even while his regime savored its success, however, Sun's victory was cut short when Chen Jiongming's coup drove him from Guangzhou in June 1922 and left him in humiliating straits as he sought passage to Shanghai. Believing labor disruption would end and foreign interests could again enjoy respect, British papers reported the news of Sun's ouster with relief and celebration. In the long run, however, the strike proved profoundly significant once Sun returned to Guangzhou in January 1923. Although international recognition was still not forthcoming, under the right conditions international notoriety was nearly as good. Acknowledging that Sun's influence over labor could again disrupt Hong Kong, Stubbs and the British Foreign Office reversed their tactics. On February 18, Sun was warmly greeted in Hong Kong as an "honored guest" by Stubbs himself. By all indications, relations between the two men seemed to have improved and, by February 20, praise gushed from both sides. Addressing students of Hong Kong University, Sun applauded the "good government of Hong Kong" and England, before noting, "My fellow students, you and I have studied in this English Colony and in an English University and we learn by English examples. We must carry this English example of good government to every part of China."[118] The *South China Morning Post* suggested that future "financial and other help" from Hong Kong could break "new ground to the great benefit of both."[119] Sun was happy and claimed that his interview with Governor Stubbs predicted good ties between Guangzhou and Hong Kong.[120]

Utilizing mass organization activism, Sun was able to win British attention and even signs of affection. Such cordiality marked a dramatic turnaround. Twice, first in 1922 and then again in early 1923, the Hong Kong governor had requested British government loans to help Chen Jiongming oust Sun, but had to content himself with private donations when the British Foreign Office refused.[121] Before that, Stubbs had even proposed assassinating Sun because he was a "danger to civilization."[122] Explaining Hong Kong's sudden warmth toward Sun, U.S. Naval Intelligence reported that some British and Chinese authorities in the colony "recognize Sun as the one who *can best control the labor situation of South China and prevent serious strikes.*" [Emphasis added.]

At the same time, however, popular forces could only take Sun part way down the road to power. Continuing, the U.S. naval report noted that British support for Sun remained limited and "only moral" because Sun remained in a "very difficult position, [with] little money, no troops of his own, and few

---

118. Chen, comp., *BCCM*, vol. Q, section 2A, pp. 3-4.
119. (Editorial), *South China Morning Post* (February 20, 1923).
120. Chen, comp., *BCCM*, vol. Q, section 2A, p. 3.
121. Stremsky, *The Shaping of British Policy*, p. 13.
122. Stremsky, *The Shaping of British Policy*, p. 12.

capable supporters."[123] Stubbs made a genuine effort to assist Sun. Anxious to avoid further labor troubles and recognizing that Hong Kong's well-being depended on good relations with Guangzhou, he reversed his animosity, writing to the Foreign Office on Sun's behalf that petitions for customs surplus funds be reconsidered.[124] On March 6, 1923, Stubbs again met with Sun, along with Chen Youren and James Jamieson, who hinted that Britain might consider sending advisers to help reform Guangdong's provincial finances. Nevertheless, other British authorities proved less enthusiastic. Two months later, with newspapers declaring a new era of cooperation between Guangzhou and Hong Kong, Sun applied for the promised aid. Stubbs supported the petition, but waffling Foreign Office authorities rejected it on the argument that it violated Britain's pledge to "neutrality" in China's domestic affairs.[125]

Undeterred and still anxious to cash in on extended British munificence, Sun's government forwarded a new petition in September 1923, asserting that the foreign-managed Maritime Customs Service unjustly remitted customs surplus to Beijing, which used them against Guangzhou. Using rational, legal, and moral arguments, the GMD sought all revenues produced by southern ports.[126] Once again, Sun was left hanging when war allowed the British Foreign Office to delay its decision on the hope it would become moot once Sun's regime collapsed. By December, however, the Nationalists had defeated Chen Jiongming's army, forcing the British to respond to Sun's request for control over south China's customs.[127] Unfortunately for party fortunes, the Diplomatic Corps rejected his petition again, arguing that granting Guangzhou favorable preference would only prompt other militarists to take their "fair share" and thereby destroy the customs system. Enraged that Britain still refused any promised assistance, Sun responded with a stronger hand, threatening to seize customs houses in GMD territories.[128] Shortly afterwards, U.S. and British gunboats appeared in Guangzhou waters while authorities threatened to land marines if the party made good on its threat. On December 22, 1923, while visiting Canton Christian College (Lingnan University), Sun blasted Britain's effort to "crush China" with its gunboats and condemned the U.S. government for the "worst blunder" it had

---

123. Chen, comp., *BCCM*, vol. Q, section 2A, p. 3.
124. For his efforts, Stubbs was nearly sacked by the Foreign Office, causing him to place some distance between himself and Sun later. Welsh, *A Borrowed Place*, p. 368.
125. Stremsky, *The Shaping of British Policy*, pp. 14-15.
126. For a full account see Wilbur, *Sun Yat-sen*, pp. 183-190.
127. *FO* 405/244 [F779/3/10], p. 52, Macleay to Curzon, Beijing, December 21, 1923.
128. For the GMD rebuttal, see *USDS* 893.00/5375, Enclosure, C. C. Wu dispatch, Guangzhou, January 14, 1924. Schurman feared that conceding would prompt all other militarists in China to request the same, thus destroying the Customs Service's ability to help pay back foreign loans and debts. "Disintegration in China: Dr. Schurman's Observations," *Peking and Tientsin Times* (January 19, 1924).

ever made. His hostility shocked foreign authorities, leading to a flurry of reports about his "wild" accusations, "unbalanced state of mind," and "extremely dangerous, neurotic state."[129]

This incident—called the customs crisis by contemporary observers—and Sun's defiance did not change foreign opinion, but did produce a modest wave of popular support. New popular organizations dedicated to opposing "foreign invasion," such as the Citizens' Association of Diplomacy for the Guangzhou Government of China, distributed circulars asking foreign soldiers and sailors to join the cause against imperialism and capitalism. Stoking nationalistic fires, Sun continued his attack, calling the foreign gunboat threat one of three "causes of death" facing the Guomindang.[130]

At the same time, however, party leaders recognized that actual conflict outside the realm of rhetorical disapproval had to be avoided. Guangzhou simply did not possess the military strength to challenge a foreign institution like the customs service and worried that any attempt to do so would only bring foreign guns to bear on its own headquarters. Subsequently, as in the past, Sun toned down his anti-imperialism and let the issue wither while turning his attention elsewhere. Within weeks, the crisis had faded and business returned to normal even as Nationalist relations with the powers continued to sour.[131]

By the time Borodin arrived in late 1923 and the First National Congress opened in January 1924, Sun had already discovered the vital link between mass mobilization and foreign relations. He had long sought improved foreign ties, offering gracious terms and rich opportunities if the powers would recognize and aid his regime. He also tried to take advantage of perceived weaknesses. Exploiting East/West rivalries, he called for Japanese support against Anglo-American imperialism. Emphasizing democracy, he appealed to his "friends the American people."[132] Extending guilt, he denounced Britain for "dealing the death blow to democracy in China."[133] Nevertheless, as demonstrated by the Seamen's Strike, no petition forced the

---

129. Sun was invited by the student union. *USDS* 893.00/5348, Enclosure, Hainer, Sun's Remarks at Canton Christian College, Guangzhou. Another report claims that Sun called for an "alliance of the oppressed" nations, i.e., Germany, India, Russia, and Ireland, to oppose the powers. *FO* 405/244 [F568/568/10], p. 63, Enclosure, Sun's remarks at Canton Christian College, Guangzhou, December 22, 1923.

130. Luo, ed., *Guofu nianpu*, p. 690. The other two "causes" were enemies of the party to the east and its own "guest armies" in Guangzhou.

131. U.S. and British leaders carefully watched the southern regime. In January 1924, Sun asked U.S. Minister J. C. Schurman to set up a conference of China's various military and political factions, but he refused. "America's Policy: Dr. Schurman's Interview with Sun Yat-sen," *Peking and Tientsin Times* (January 18, 1924).

132. *FO* 405/244 [F779/3/10], p. 60, Enclosure 6, extract from the *Far Eastern Times* (December 21, 1923).

133. *FO* 405/244 [F799/3/10], p. 53, Macleay to Curzon, Beijing, December 21, 1923.

foreigners' hand as readily as popular anti-imperialism. When compelled to choose between direct dealings with strikers and GMD mediation, foreign authorities—especially the British—generally chose the latter because anything else would only deepen disruption. By encouraging popular agitation against the roots of imperialism and then intervening to mediate a settlement, the Guomindang could extract specific foreign relations advantages.

The stratagem was powerful but only if certain conditions were met. First, popular agitation had to undermine vital imperialist interests, such as Hong Kong's economic stability. Second, the party required sufficiently close ties with agitative forces that it could promise some influence over them; otherwise, foreign leaders would have no cause to request Nationalist aid in negotiating a settlement. Third, party leaders also had to maintain some distance from mass activism lest they be implicated for the destruction it caused. For this reason, it was vital that the strikes be identified as "of the people" and *not* "of the party" because only then could the Nationalist regime avoid culpability. As long as party leaders denied involvement and maintained their own version of "neutrality," there was little that British authorities could do, even if they suspected party duplicity.

Some foreign leaders recognized that Sun had stumbled onto something. In early 1923, Britain's minister to China reported that Sun should be offered friendship if he demonstrated a "genuine desire to improve his relations with the British" by abstaining from *"fomenting labour troubles in British territory."*[134] [Emphasis added.] In fact, it was the hope that they could exchange friendship for abstinence that led Hong Kong authorities to warmly welcome Sun in 1923. Nevertheless, London still withheld advisors and the customs surplus just months later, demonstrating a fatal weakness in Sun's program: any hint that he could not maintain his position and the powers would ignore him. Sun proved he could improve conditions for the laboring class but still struggled to secure practical benefits for his national agenda. Labor agitation got Sun to the negotiating table and warm accommodation of foreign interests kept foreigners smiling, but neither could fully deliver the recognition or support he sought. Something was still lacking.

In sum, the First National Congress carefully described all the requisite components needed to implement this new *modus operandi* but only hinted at how they would fit together. With time, however, patterns began to emerge. Between 1922 and 1923, Sun Yat-sen had employed popular agitation and foreign accommodation sequentially. Gradually, however, GMD leaders discovered how to use them simultaneously—an approach here called

134. *FO* 405/240 [F1107/12/10], p. 124, Macleay to Curzon, Beijing, February 28, 1923. One ambassador tried to reverse the direction of power politics by suggesting that Britain threaten to withhold official recognition of any new government in China that employed labor agitation to rise to power. *FO* 405/245 [F3983/19/10], p. 171, Enclosure, Waterlow note, November 26, 1924.

"dual-prong tactics." Agitation advantaged revolutionary leaders. It could stir up class or nationalistic tensions to pressure party rivals: non-revolutionary localist, provincialist, or even imperialist organizations.[135] Eager to reduce disruptions, those facing agitation had to accept and submit to Nationalist intervention and authority in order to win the Guangzhou regime's help in slowing the agitators. Equally important, the "class struggle," "nationalistic," and "non-party" characteristics of China's popular movements gave them credibility independent of the Guomindang, obscuring party machinations. Non-party revolutionary organizations brought their own agendas and thus legitimized mass-movement agitation as "popular" outgrowths of Chinese nationalism. Playing a mediating role, the southern regime could simply ask beleaguered localist or imperialist targets to better align themselves with the "nation" as the primary means of deflating popular animosity and thereby erode non-revolutionary resistance to party dominance. To encourage movement in the "right" direction, GMD authorities merely had to offer an accommodating hand.

It was these dual-prong tactics—the use of both accommodating and agitative measures against non-revolutionary interests—that bound all components defined at the First National Congress' together into one cohesive and coherent system. Bifurcated nationalism combined state-building with agitative objectives, even though the two were often mutually exclusive. "Decentralized centralism" combined Sun Yat-sen's democratic ideals with Borodin's Leninist system, grafted decentralized agitative branches to the GMD's centralized trunk, and adopted fluid and subjective categories of "enemy" and *guomin* that alternated between invitations of inclusion and threats of exclusion. Dual-prong tactics merely put all the pieces in motion. It gave party leaders the means to manipulate imperialist, provincialist, and localist institutions by playing accommodative state mediation off disruptive popular agitation or, in other words, play the "freedom and authority" advantages of inclusion off the destructive terrors of exclusion, generating tremendous flexibility, leverage, and synergistic power. If bifurcated nationalism represented Sun's and Borodin's envisioned ideal and "decentralized centralism" represented the requisite revolutionary machinery, dual-prong tactics represented the deployment of both.

Surreptitiously stimulating agitation while officially denying any such role, party leaders eventually learned how to erode localist resistance and fold even powerful imperialist systems and institutions into the expanding GMD "nation." Details about how the system would work remained obscure, especially when the party suffered from terrible weakness during the months immediately following the First National Congress. More experience was needed to flesh them out. Unfortunately for GMD leaders, however, even as

---

135. Fitzgerald, "The Nationless State," p. 97.

components of the Congress' revolutionary system were being set in place, the party was forced to confront a combined imperialist, warlord, and localist/provincialist threat. Even before its pieces were assembled, the revolution's bifurcated approach faced its first major test.

3. Pressures and Vulnerabilities
—Evading Localist and Imperialist Collusion, January 1924 - June 1925

Ever since Sun Yat-sen entered Guangdong, the mobster-run, despotic government has been even worse than that of the ancient Qin Dynasty. People are forced to sell their properties and graves. Their traditional dwellings have almost all been destroyed or occupied. Commoners have been dragged into military campaigns. The gentry and well off are compelled to pay enormous ransoms. Severe and exacting miscellaneous levies are collected to the fullest minute amount. Motley soldiers and bandits slay freely at will. Public criticism is heavily punished as criminal slander. Payments even slightly late are treated as . . . criminal rebellion. . . . As a result, the wealthy hide their residences in different locations while the poor tearfully tell the tale of not even having a door. Ravenous leaders extend as far as the eye can see. Thorns and brambles cover the way and yet we can still force the maintenance of order. Those not fully corrupted can rely on the gentlemen with Merchants Corps (shangtuan) for merciful and sincere protection of the people.[1]
—Guangzhou Merchants Corps, August 27, 1924

On the morning of October 10, 1924, a young Guangdongese student named Huang Renjun abandoned his regular routine to review a speech he planned to deliver later that day. Although family elders had given him the traditional name *Benevolent Gentleman* and had sent him to Shanghai to get an education, young Huang's heart was set on revolution. Committed to China's cause, he joined the Shanghai Student Federation, quickly rose through the ranks, and became one of its more outspoken leaders. Huang was excited. Infused with GMD direction and funding, the Federation had conducted several anti-imperialist and anti-warlord demonstrations, but none as grand as those planned for this day—Double Ten Day *(Shuangshijie)*, the Republic of China's founding holiday. Hoping for a good response, the young revolutionary readied his notes.

Although student leaders had been planning this particular event for weeks, disagreements and divisions had taxed Federation effectiveness,

---

1. Wei Yan, pseud., ed., *Guangdong kouxie chao*, juan 2, p. 102.

73

leading to reports that clashes between party members were worse than those with non-party interests.[2] As the events of October 10 unfolded, however, conflict with angered merchant interests soon put revolutionary squabbles into perspective. Denouncing anti-imperialism at the planned rally, student leaders denounced localist merchants as traitorous "compradors" *(maiban)* who benefited from their political and commercial ties to imperialism. Those most maligned took offense, angered that the Federation claimed to be serving China's interests but seemed set instead on advancing a political agenda that favored the Guangzhou regime. As post-rally parades filed through Shanghai streets, merchant corps *(shangtuan)* militiamen retaliated. Slashing through the crowds, corpsmen singled out student leaders, thrashing them severely. Several were left with extensive wounds. At least one—Huang Renjun—was beaten to death.[3]

The same day, another episode of violence erupted in Guangzhou. Marching in support of Sun Yat-sen's government, a column of cadets, peasants, workers, and students wound their way along the riverfront near Xiguan, Guangzhou's wealthiest commercial district. Shouting slogans and waving banners, the paraders tried to pass a cordon of armed merchant corpsmen securing a sensitive weapons transfer—the result of months of contentious negotiations with GMD officials. Provocations between the two sides escalated when merchant corps volunteers began chasing and shooting panicked peasant and labor militiamen. Trying to flee, unarmed paraders jumped into the river and drowned. Some tried to hide in nearby shops while excited corpsmen hunted them in an hour-long shooting barrage. Before it was over, twenty had been killed and scores more had been wounded or captured. Adding insult to injury, merchant volunteers then mutilated the corpses of their victims and forced captives to view the spectacle.[4]

Tensions between revolutionary and non-revolutionary forces permeated all sectors of society, even institutions supposedly under strong revolutionary influence. During the autumn of 1924, for example, tensions at Guangdong First Provincial Middle School in Guangzhou reached the breaking point when student union leaders were criticized by non-union students for pursuing the political goals of the GMD rather than student interests. In October, escalating fighting and violent outbursts between the two factions forced the principal to ban all student organizations. Bewailing their fate to Guomindang superiors and denouncing their rivals as "bad

---

2. Shou, "Shou Hua zhi Zou Lu han," September 2, 1924.
3. "Guangdong xinxueshengshe deng shang zongli deng daidian," October 29, 1924; Zou, "Zou Lu zhi zhongyang qingnianbu han," October 31, 1924. Shocked, but also recognizing that little could be done in far-away Shanghai, the Youth Ministry issued a public notice calling on GMD members to refrain from commenting on the episode until all facts had been gathered. "Zhongyang qingnianbu tonggao," October 25, 1924.
4. *USDS* 893.00/5776, Jenkins to Secretary of State, Guangzhou, October 13, 1924.

elements" *(buliang fenzi)*, the school's revolutionary leaders complained, "Who would have thought that education under the revolutionary government could still harbor such anti-revolutionary students?"[5]

As the shock of October's grisly events wore off, revolutionary students tried to assess blame. In a telegram addressed directly to Sun Yat-sen, the Guangzhou students of the New Student Society lamented:

> New shoots of the people's revolution had only just emerged into view when fascism seized a chance to expand. Spilt blood of the recent Double Ten Day [October 10] massacre in Guangzhou had not yet even fully dried when evil word of the vicious beatings of Double Ten Day celebrations in Shanghai suddenly arrived. Here in Guangzhou, where the revolutionary government has been established, to still find such anti-revolutionary behavior, rips the heart and tears open wounds *(pouxin geshang)*.[6]

Outraged at these and other atrocities against fellow activists, angered students demanded that Nationalist authorities better guard against "reactionaries." Addressing what they perceived to be the source of the problem, students boldly accused Sun himself of betraying the revolution by continually chasing politicking opportunities and cavorting with non-revolutionary interests: "if you want revolution, you must carry out the work with the laboring and peasant masses and must absolutely reject the convenience of plotting with officials, militarists, or compradors . . . who will compromise the end result."[7] No more, the students insisted, should the GMD allow people to be beaten to death for merely criticizing imperialism and no longer could the party allow its ranks to be tainted by guest army, comprador, small shop owner, unemployed politician, intellectual, or gentry interests. Such non-revolutionary interests, the students argued, deserved no place among the "people."

To revolutionary agitators, the students' petition represented only the most fundamental of demands: the exclusion of non-revolutionary interests from which "bad elements" sprang and fuller Guomindang support for the revolutionary masses. Sun, however, was in no position to implement any change. In fact, he was not even in Guangzhou. By all indications he had abandoned the city to evade localist animosity which had swelled to overwhelming levels. Militia and "bad element" attacks, such as those that tormented his supporters and killed young Huang Renjun, represented just the tip of the iceberg. Localist disdain for the southern regime had coalesced into open rebellion which the brutality of October 10 could only foreshadow.

---

5. "Guangdong shengli diyi zhongxuexiao xueshenghui zhongyao qishi," December 19, 1924.
6. "Guangdong xinxueshengshe deng shang zongli deng daidian," October 29, 1924.
7. "Guangdong xinxueshengshe deng shang zongli deng daidian," October 29, 1924.

Although often eclipsed by the GMD's great enemies—warlord armies and imperialist backers—riled localist and provincialist interests represented a powerful threat in their own right. Entrenched in the heart of Guangzhou, they attracted outside support and extended the reach of warlord and imperialist rivals deep into the Nationalist base. Unfortunately for the party, efforts to retool Chinese society as prescribed by First National Congress directives had only intensified anti-revolutionary resistance.

Provincialist/Localist Ire in Guangdong, 1923-1924

Anti-revolutionary hostility had been mounting steadily since early 1923 and continued long after the events of October 1924. Despite Borodin's call for better party relations with the local populace, animosity prevailed. Most historical accounts blame the party's "guest armies" *(kejun)*—the colorful array of mercenaries guarding the Nationalist base against Zhili clique armies in Guangxi, Hunan, Jiangxi and Fujian and minor threats to the south and east. In all, Sun's piecemeal force included nearly forty thousand troops of varied quality and origin. Xu Chongzhi's Guangdong Army consisted of an assortment of brigades and divisions. Wu Tiecheng commanded a provincial peace preservation force while Li Fulin maintained a private army on Henan island just south of Guangzhou. Four autonomous corps of Yunnan soldiers, an army from Guangxi, Tan Yankai's Hunanese troops, and somewhat less significant units from Jiangxi, Hubei and Henan comprised the remainder of Sun's so-called military.[8] Although ostensibly employed by the Guomindang, the guest armies deeply undermined its control. Few harbored any ideals about national unification; those with ideological views, such as the Yunnanese, generally preferred provincial federalist ideals over Sun's centralist views.[9] Most simply sought cash and promotions.

After defeating Chen Jiongming in late 1922, these "guests" carved Guangzhou into four spheres, each jealously guarded and exploited as a private territory.[10] Seizing the armory, mints, railways, taxing stations, transit tax *(lijin)* offices, and so forth—anything that could produce money or guns—the guest armies left little for Sun's regime to tap. Thus, although annual revenues jumped from $3 million in 1922 to $9 million the following year, some $6.2 million went straight to the war chest to pay for "military expenditures." Denied access to Guangzhou's most lucrative institutions and required to make heavy payment to its mercenary forces, the southern regime always lacked funds.[11]

---

8. Wilbur, *Sun Yat-sen*, pp. 167-168.
9. Sutton, *Provincial Militarism and the Chinese Republic*, p. 279.
10. The four "empires," as Sutton calls them, include the North River at Shaoguan, Guangzhou's commercial district of Xiguan, Guangzhou's commercial district of Nanguan, and Foshan. Sutton, *Provincial Militarism and the Chinese Republic*, pp. 280-281.
11. Wilbur, *Sun Yat-sen*, p. 168. Also see Sutton, *Provincial Militarism and the Chinese*

Still, Sun was willing to pay; without mercenary support he could not hold Guangdong, a fact grimly substantiated by the fate of his predecessor. In 1922, Chen Jiongming had forfeited control over Guangzhou in large part because he could not pay his troops. Despite efforts to secure foreign and domestic loans, Chen's government could not stop Guangdong Provincial Bank notes from sinking to about 15 percent of face value.[12] At the same time, efforts to improve local administration by curbing troop lawlessness (i.e., looting or pressing funds) and eliminating gambling—a common source of troop payments—reduced fiscal options. When asked by his subordinate General Ye Ju to reopen the gambling houses to calm disquieted troops, Chen reportedly declared that he would rather give up office than reinstitute the vice. Putting principle before power, he left himself vulnerable to betrayal at the hand of his own officers and Sun's mercenaries took advantage, seizing Guangzhou in early 1923.[13] Almost immediately the tables had turned. Finding itself in equally compromising circumstances, the GMD made every effort to keep its restless armies happy.

Mercenary contentedness, however, came at the expense of the Guangdongese who could scarcely hide their scorn for the party's "guests." As one editorial pleaded of Sun, "[Banish] this human refuse as soon as possible so as to protect life and liberty and prevent Guangdong from being a market for gambling, opium and other immoral traffic."[14] Lax GMD control led to mercenary abuses but also tainted regime practices in the process. Failing to secure donations, loans, or foreign support, party leaders found creative ways to wrest revenue from a base that had already relinquished its best resources to guest army control.[15] One unpopular measure involved the confiscation and sale of public property. Land endowments had long been set aside for disaster relief, charitable work, schools, hospitals, and so forth.[16] Through 1923 and 1924, public properties worth millions of dollars were seized and sold to meet Guomindang military expenses.

In late 1924, for example, Sun's regime announced the nationalization of charitable institutions and hospitals in Guangzhou still holding valuable

---

Republic, pp. 281-282. Unless otherwise indicated, all currency refers to Hong Kong dollars.

12. Chen, comp., *BCCM*, vol. P, section 5B, p. 1.

13. Chen, comp., *BCCM*, vol. P, section 3A, p. 7; section 3A1, p. 5; section 5B, p. 1.

14. "Kuomintang Should Appeal to People for Support," *The Canton Times* (January 25, 1923). Later reports proved that localist fears were not unfounded as "guest armies" quickly proceeded to expel occupants and turn "every available building into a gambling house." "Two Farcical Events," *Hong Kong Telegraph* (January 27, 1923).

15. Yunnanese mercenaries controlling Guangzhou's river defense, for example, sold government transports and launches for their own profit, raising criticism that public interests had been compromised. *CWR* 31 (February 25, 1925); Wong, "The Passing of the Kuomintang in South China," p. 74.

16. Wilbur, *Sun Yat-sen*, p. 157; *USDS* 893.00/5152, Tenney to Schurman, Guangzhou, July 28, 1923; Chen, comp., *BCCM*, vol. Q, section 2B, pp. 5-7; "Canton Land Sale," *Hong Kong Telegraph* (April 10, 1923); "Canton Land Sale," *Hong Kong Telegraph* (April 11, 1923).

property. Affected directors argued that property endowments could not be readily liquidated for war funds and thus should not be taken, but to no avail.[17] In one ten-day frenzy, over twenty institutions and hospitals were raided and confiscated, generating considerable public outcry.[18] In Foshan, party leaders recruited peasant corpsmen to capture and hold four gentry officers until they surrendered famine funds which they controlled as public trustees.[19] Structures built on public lands were also targeted. Along streams or canals, for example, property owners routinely built on or otherwise encroached into public space. Rather than restoring the land to the public, however, Guomindang officials confiscated the illegal buildings and resold them for profit, thus converting public lands into private properties.[20]

Justifying party actions, Sun Ke, the mayor of Guangzhou and son of Sun Yat-sen, claimed that "so-called public lands" were often leased to private individuals. Therefore confiscating them for the purpose of raising municipal funds represented no significant change except to private administrators with vested control.[21] Even Sun Ke, however, could not excuse the GMD practice of seizing *private* property which became common as lucrative public property opportunities were exhausted. Private sector resources with military or political value were particularly susceptible. Military officers commandeered transport vessels or supplies, as on March 5, 1925, when the Nationalist Army seized twelve junks transporting half a million catties of rice.[22] When foreign and northern naval forces blockaded Russian arms imports, the GMD "borrowed" needed supplies or weapons from private merchant vessels plying the rivers of Guangdong.[23] Newspapers fell to a variety of impositions and often lost advertising space to party authorities or had to surrender their operations entirely.[24] Even private landholdings were confiscated, as the U.S. consul in Guangzhou reported in early 1924:

> The seizure of real estate under the pretext that the titles of the individual holders are defective continues, and it is estimated more than Hong

---

17. *CWR* 34 (October 17, 1925): 174.

18. *CWR* 34 (November 7, 1925): vi.

19. Such funds were typically reserved for dike repair, famine relief, and so forth. *CWR* 34 (October 31, 1925): 218; *CWR* 34 (November 7, 1925): vi.

20. *CWR* 34 (November 7, 1925): 242.

21. "Sun Yat-sen's Son in Shanghai," *North China Daily News* (September 29, 1924). Sun Ke defended party seizures of temple properties, stating that "street temples had nothing that could be called art" but only "musty clay idols" which may have been damaged or sold. Temples worthy of being called "national treasures" were protected.

22. *CWR* 32 (April 4, 1925): 145. A Chinese unit of measure, one catty is about 1.1 pounds.

23. *CWR* 34 (November 21, 1925): 288.

24. The *Canton Gazette* came under Guomindang control after it refused to publish an anti-foreign manifesto in September 1924. *USDS* 893.00/5729, Jenkins to Bell, Guangzhou, September 17, 1924. The Guangzhou daily *Kuo Wen Sin Wen* was confiscated by Huangpu cadets. Other papers lost space when they were forced to publish CEC declarations and propaganda. *CWR* 32 (May 30, 1925): 372.

Kong $15,000,000 worth of property has been taken from private owners in this way. The Government immediately disposes of these confiscated lands at extremely low prices because buyers are doubtful as to their rights should another government succeed that of Dr. Sun in Canton [Guangzhou].[25]

The nationalization of Guangdong's railway system proved particularly provocative. Parts of the system were confiscated as early as January 1923. By 1925, the party had taken most remaining lines from private stock holders or guest army control. Lines open to passenger and freight service subsidized the operating costs of those dedicated to troop transport and passed the expense to customers.[26] To maximize profits GMD administrators cut management and maintenance, driving some lines to near collapse and prompting complaints from railway managers and workers, the general public, and stock owners still hoping to recover control. When Generalissimo Hu Hanmin ordered the Guangzhou-Hankou Railroad, for example, to cut salaries and dismiss 178 persons to save $10,000 in monthly expenses, his intent was *not* to make the railroad more efficient but to generate more revenue.[27] The Nationalists extracted some $6,000 a day while beds rotted, rails warped, and engines fell into disrepair. By late 1925, cumulative neglect had curtailed operations, produced several serious accidents, and generated managerial complaints that the only two still-functioning locomotives limped along under barely "tolerable" conditions. Similar deterioration and problems with the Guangzhou-Sanshui Railroad aroused complaints that the line would have to suspend operations unless authorities dropped the daily impost of $3,000.[28]

Localist critics also reproved other regime monopolies, including those overseeing fuel, alcohol and tobacco, salt, opium, and cereal products. The harshest scorn, however, was heaped on government management of shipping, the Guangzhou Water Works, the Guangdong Electricity Supply Company, and the Guangdong Cement Works. In each case, the general managerial approach was always the same: to maximize revenues, the Industrial Affairs Bureau manipulated supplies, services, and prices.[29] Consumers and producers alike were displeased. Popular animosity directed at

---

25. Chen, comp., *BCCM*, vol. Q, section 2B, pp. 10-11; "Canton Grievances: A Public Complaint," *Hong Kong Telegraph* (November 3, 1923); "Canton House Seizures," *Hong Kong Telegraph* (October 17, 1923).

26. The Guangzhou-Hankou Railroad was nationalized January 16, 1923. In late 1925, the party took over all Guangdong railroads to ensure ready troop transport and defray operating costs among them. Song Ziwen became the managing-director. *CWR* 34 (October 31, 1925): 216.

27. *CWR* 32 (March 21, 1925): 86.

28. *CWR* 34 (November 14, 1925): 262.

29. *CWR* 35 (January 16, 1926): 194. GMD authorities in Wuzhou controlled even firewood. *CWR* 35 (December 26, 1925): 106.

the oil monopoly approached volatile levels. In mid-1925, GMD authorities imposed a double duty levy on kerosene imports. Rather than pay anything beyond the five percent defined by treaty, U.S. and British oil firms—including the Standard Oil Company and the Asiatic Petroleum Oil Company—boycotted shipments to Guangzhou. Russian imports from Vladivostok tried to meet demand but fell far short.[30] When efforts to stabilize supplies stalled and prices soared, straining the stretched resources of the poor, popular outrage exploded.[31] By early 1926, oil in Nationalist territories cost $12.50 to $17.60 a case compared to the $5.00 per case encountered everywhere else in China.[32] Shortages caused oil-dependent factories to suspend operations and cut electrical output at power plants, in turn leading to further shutdowns among factories dependent on electricity.[33] When party leaders farmed the monopoly out to the highest bidder, again to maximize income, popular hostility only rose further.[34]

The most rancorous Guomindang practices, however, involved the liberal distribution of assorted taxes, levies, and fines. Those aimed at the wealthier segments of society generally aroused little popular response.[35] Others, however, were widely rebuked as crude extortion. Taxes on specific commodities, such as silk, cement, meat, jewelry, cosmetics, jade, timber, land, and even water, among other items, angered producers, sellers, and customers alike. Imposts on monopoly goods, including charcoal, kerosene, and alcohol, were particularly heavy.[36] Taxes on specified activities hit restaurants, hotels, and Guangzhou's entertainment sector.[37] The GMD charged a 20 or 30 percent surcharge on admissions to places of amusement. Officers running the munitions factory collected fees on mahjong sets and gaming tables in Guangzhou's public restaurants and clubs while other authorities focused on brothels and unregistered girls.[38] Occupation-specific taxes targeted sampan and launch operators, food hawkers, rickshaw drivers, pawnshop owners, native bank managers, providers of motor car services,

---

30. *CWR* 32 (May 23, 1925): 343; *USDS* 893.00/6105, Jenkins to State Department, Guangzhou, February 19, 1925; *USDS* 893.00/6189, Jenkins to State Department, Guangzhou, April 3, 1925.

31. *CWR* 34 (November 21, 1925): 288.

32. *CWR* 36 (March 27, 1926): 99.

33. *CWR* 35 (January 9, 1926): 168. Coal shortages also compelled local industries and railways to suspend operations. *CWR* 36 (March 27, 1926): 98. When the GMD assumed control of Guangxi, Wuzhou plants faced similar problems. See *CWR* 35 (December 26, 1925): 106.

34. The Nanhua Syndicate gained control of the oil monopoly in eastern Guangdong by promising to pay taxes on a minimum of 75,000 cases a month. *CWR* 35 (December 26, 1925): 107; *CWR* 36 (March 6, 1926): 13.

35. In 1925, for example, only mild protests challenged new land taxes and a GMD "capital" tax of one percent on all possessing over $500. *CWR* 34 (September 26, 1925): 92; *CWR* 34 (October 31, 1925): 216.

36. *CWR* 34 (November 7, 1925): 242; *CWR* 35 (January 16, 1926): 194.

37. Control over lucrative enterprises often led to skirmishes between rival commanders.

38. *CWR* 32 (March 28, 1925): 114; *CWR* 36 (April 3, 1926): 127.

and embroiderers of silk shawls and "dainty articles," among many others. Double-taxing was commonplace. Collectors representing different military groups or GMD government offices often taxed a single enterprise, refused to recognize the existence of each other, and/or failed to acknowledge payments already made under a former arrangement.[39]

Even escalating dissatisfaction with new levies, however, could not compare to the popular outrage generated by the southern regime's odious collection methods. Coercion was common. In early 1925, for example, when the Finance Ministry sought an emergency loan of $600,000 from Guangzhou's reluctant trade guilds, Nationalist affiliates in the General Chamber of Commerce pressed the funds out of them.[40] Government authorities sold tax farming contracts to those promising the greatest returns, leading to abuses.[41] In October 1925, party agents threatened to close all mutual fire insurance companies that refused to pay an impost of $10,000.[42] That same month, party leaders announced that customers withdrawing money from Shamian banks had to "contribute" four percent of the withdrawn amounts to government expenses or face "interference."[43] Even those with no apparent resources were not safe. Reports hotly denounced GMD press gangs for conscripting coolie labor in Sanshui and defying traditional proscriptions against seizing numerous men from the same family.[44]

When not itemizing Guomindang offenses, critics of the southern regime savaged its deleterious influence on the economy in general. A February 1925 report, for example, complained that since 1920 the price of common foodstuffs and commodities, such as rice, firewood, native sugar, and bean oil, had risen from 200 to 400 percent.[45] High taxes prompted merchants to close their shops or direct goods to markets outside Guangzhou. Imposts on imported cement drove up construction costs and produced severe shortages when importers stopped shipments to protest government surcharges.[46] Nationalist seizures of rolling stock elevated freight and passenger railway costs, raising prices on transported goods.[47] The party's habit of commandeering vessels and commodity shipments along water routes, such as Hu-

---

39. "Canton War Taxes," *Peking and Tientsin Times* (January 15, 1924).
40. *CWR* 32 (March 7, 1925): 21; *CWR* 32 (April 18, 1925): 204. The party extended influence over the General Chamber of Commerce early and often used it to influence decisions of Guangzhou's other three chambers of commerce.
41. *CWR* 32 (April 11, 1925): 175; *CWR* 36 (April 3, 1926): 126.
42. *CWR* 34 (October 17, 1925): 174.
43. "Contributions" started at one percent of the total withdrawn amount but later increased to four percent. *CWR* 34 (October 31, 1925): 218; *CWR* 34 (November 21, 1925): 287.
44. *CWR* 34 (November 21, 1925): 287.
45. *CWR* 32 (March 7, 1925): 21.
46. The Masons Guild in Guangzhou, the Building Contractors Association, and British and Japanese consular representatives all complained. *CWR* 32 (March 14, 1925): 51.
47. "Canton War Taxes," *Peking and Tientsin Times* (January 15, 1924).

men (Bocca Tigris)—the primary artery through which imported rice flowed—destabilized markets and exacerbated inflation.[48] Unsympathetic reports roundly denounced "short-sighted" government policies that destroyed native industries. In early 1926, for example, when sugar producers refused to pay new surtaxes, party authorities placed an embargo on native sugar, threatening to destroy the $4 million per year industry and replace it with foreign imports.[49] Others criticized party involvement in or failure to control currency manipulation and depreciation. By mid-1925, guest army officers in Guangzhou ran twenty-nine illicit mints that churned out some $400,000 in subsidiary coins daily—all without approval from southern regime authorities.[50] Dumped on the market, low-grade copper coins quickly depreciated coinage from 100 to 180 coins per dollar, injuring those dealing in small denominations such as newsboys and rickshaw drivers.[51] Private mints and depreciation in Guangxi, meanwhile, were blamed for a 200 percent increase in prices and spawned allegations of market chaos.[52] At the same time, souring economic conditions forced the Guangzhou treasury to devalue its notes to 30 percent of face value.[53]

Alongside criticisms of Nationalist economic policy were scathing allegations that the party had also destroyed Guangdong's progressive political climate. Sun had not only restored the hated guest armies (pejoratively called "foreign" invaders for their non-Guangdong origins), he also killed modernizing reforms started by Chen Jiongming. In the place of Chen's "rest and savings," the Guomindang had substituted a warlike mien that spoke incessantly of military action northward.[54] Many viewed Sun's variety of nationalism as both impractical and destructive—a hopeless charge that promised only to consume Guangdong's precious resources on the battlefields of central China. As one *Huazi ribao* editorial noted in July 1924,

> Prior to returning to Canton [Guangzhou], [Sun and his followers] attacked [Chen Jiongming's] government each day for being corrupt, evil,

---

48. *CWR* 32 (May 9, 1925): 291.

49. Foreign imports jumped 600 percent. *CWR* 36 (April 10, 1926): 152.

50. Some of these mints employed over fifty workmen each. *CWR* 32 (April 18, 1925): 204.

51. *CWR* 32 (May 16, 1925): 319. To minimize strain on money markets, the importation of copper coins was banned and visitors to Guangzhou were allowed to bring no more than one hundred. *CWR* 32 (May 30, 1925): 372.

52. *CWR* 32 (May 23, 1925): 343; *CWR* 36 (April 24, 1926): 210. Having faced it before, Guangxi citizens were particularly sensitive to currency manipulation. Warlord general Lu Rongting, a former bandit chief, built a fortune before his overthrow in 1922 by forcing the people to circulate paper money while he collected specie for himself. *CWR* 34 (October 31, 1925): 216.

53. *CWR* 36 (May 22, 1926): 328.

54. *USDS* 893.00/5355, Jenkins to Schurman, Guangzhou, January 17, 1924. Most maddening to critics was the fact that, in 1920, it was Sun and Chen who liberated Guangdong from the so-called "foreign" troops in the first place.

and barbaric. They advocated the Three Principles of the People and a Five-Authority Constitution. They promised that they would save the country and serve the people. We, being simple-minded common people, believed them and supported them with money and labor. . . . Alas, however, as soon as they gained control of the government they did exactly the opposite of what they had preached! Sun's government has brought to Guangdong nothing but destruction. Its arbitrary use of power is unmatched by the absolute monarchies of the past.[55]

By the time this editorial was published in July 1924, the regime had already dissolved Guangdong's elected provincial assembly and most of the other democratizing institutions cultivated under Chen's regime. Less than two years later, Guangxi's provincial and district assemblies were dismantled as well, spawning protests that the Nationalists had destroyed the most successful democratizing efforts in all of China.[56] Newspapers in Guangzhou kept modestly quiet, but not because they had no complaints. The media, relatively free under Chen Jiongming, faced heavy censorship under Sun's subsequent regime, which limited access or simply told reporters what to print.[57] Even party papers were subjected to heavy censorship under the Chief of Staff of the GMD Army.[58] In early 1926, rumors spread that the Guomindang would implement a 30 percent tax on advertising, not to produce revenue, but to drive all independent, non-party, and non-subsidized papers out of business.[59] Meanwhile, police screened all postal deliveries and arrested addressees receiving "seditious material."[60] In September 1925, government authorities began inspecting and censoring all telegraph transmissions.[61] In October, the minister of home affairs received permission to search bookstores and destroy literature deemed "detrimental" to the southern regime and its revolution.[62]

---

55. Editorials in Hong Kong and Shanghai were particularly condemnatory. Chen, "A Tale of Two Cities," pp. 13-14. (For smoother reading, Chen's translation has been slightly modified.) See the original text in "Wo ye tantan Sun zhengfu," *Huazi ribao* (July 14, 1924).
56. *CWR* 36 (April 3, 1926): 127.
57. In October 1921, a visitor described the unusual freedom accorded the Guangzhou press: "Of the 33 daily newspapers published in Canton [Guangzhou], some are critical of the Canton Government, some are even sympathetic to the Beijing Government, but none have been censored by the authorities." Huang, *Yisui zhi Guangzhoushi*, p. 52. In late 1925, reporters were banned from the headquarters of the Guangzhou Strike Committee. *CWR* 34 (November 28, 1925): 318. When fighting broke out near the eastern front between GMD factions, reporters were told that all was merely a campaign to clean up pirate infestations and that reports must avoid any mention of possible civil war. *CWR* 36 (April 24, 1926): 208.
58. Press censorship was enforced by police until April 1926 when the Guomindang Military Council took charge. *CWR* 36 (April 24, 1926): 208; *CWR* 34 (October 17, 1925): 175.
59. *CWR* 36 (March 6, 1926): 13.
60. *CWR* 36 (March 13, 1926): 46; *CWR* 36 (April 24, 1926): 210; *CWR* 36 (March 6, 1926): 14.
61. *CWR* 36 (March 13, 1926): 46.
62. *CWR* 34 (October 31, 1925): 218.

Scandals also marred the regime's image. Critics blasting poor GMD management of the Guangzhou-Hankou Railroad gained more steam when four former party directors were found to have embezzled some $500,000.[63] Butchers claimed that the Department of Public Health relied on unscrupulous meat inspectors who wrongfully levied heavy fines.[64] Customs brokers protested after two Nationalist agents raided fifteen customs offices in Jiangmen and fined each for construed "improprieties."[65] In April 1925, a special auditor announced that the Land Deeds Inspection Bureau had failed to submit $120,000 charged to sixty thousand landlords to have their deeds photographed, and had in its possession $250,000 emergency treasury notes beyond what it had actually been issued.[66] Among detractors already condemning party graft, news that corruption had been cleaned up did not redeem the government but merely provided more evidence that its officials used their posts to enrich themselves. As one critic exclaimed,

> Petty officials in the districts have become tyrants of the worst type and bandits and pirates organizing themselves also as Kuomintangites [Guomindangites] under a Red standard, are now acting as if they have license to loot and kill. In Canton [Guangzhou], however, where politicians are intriguing against one another for the spoils of office things have not been so bad, and corruption within the judiciary, the railroad administrations, water works, and other government departments is being exposed one after another due to efforts of those who are idle but will find openings upon dismissal of dishonest incumbents.[67]

Those angered at conditions in revolutionary Guangzhou also decried the general immorality of Guomindang policy. State-sanctioned gambling, for example, had been stamped out by stringent policies set by Chen Jiongming himself. In August 1925, however, despite popular concern that the party was abandoning principle for lucre, party officials legalized and licensed all forms of free gambling in Guangzhou. In November 1925, Song Ziwen reintroduced the lottery. Within weeks, gambling began to pour $4,000 to $5,000 each day into the party's war chest, prompting some to note that gaming in Guangzhou had become some ten times bigger than it was in Macao where state gambling had always been encouraged.[68] Lowering ethical inhibitions even further, the party embraced the opium trade. A

63. *CWR* 35 (December 26, 1925): 106.
64. *CWR* 32 (April 4, 1925): 146.
65. Managers were accused of submitting false custom returns and heavily fined. *CWR* 32 (April 4, 1925): 145.
66. *CWR* 32 (May 2, 1925): 263.
67. *CWR* 35 (December 5, 1925): 20.
68. *CWR* 34 (September 5, 1925): 23; *CWR* 34 (November 21, 1925): 288; *CWR* 35 (December 12, 1925): 53; *CWR* 35 (December 26, 1925): 106.

government monopoly charged licensing fees on product and smoking lamps while allowing free distribution of stamped (state authorized) opium in clubs and gambling houses. Song Ziwen oversaw sales and distribution via a special office attached to the Finance Ministry, which issued some 4,500 licenses and convicted 1,500 people for smoking without one. Shantou authorities went further, levying a ten-cent "daily fee" on each of the city's nine hundred licensed opium lamps. Guomindang expansion only spread the opium monopoly and its wares, drawing heavy criticism that the Guangzhou "Bolshevists" did not subscribe to their own standards.[69] In March 1924, for example, via his official dispatch the American Consul complained:

> Opium dens and gambling places continue to flourish in Canton [Guangzhou]. The so-called Opium Suppressing Bureau, recently established by the government, is actually designed to secure revenue and as far as can be seen, is encouraging the use of drug rather than attempting to curtail it or suppress it. The gambling houses enjoy the protection of the troops, who evidently derive considerable revenue from that source.[70]

Critics also noted that the Nationalists had eroded rule of law, human rights, and personal liberties. Military authorities detained anyone considered a threat, leading to thousands of arrests, including some five hundred individuals held without charge.[71] Even while slashing courts to save costs, the party expanded prison space, particularly at the Huangpu Military Academy where political prisoners were incarcerated, interrogated, and executed. The judiciary system suffered as fees in the regular court system skyrocketed due to competition from military tribunals, strike committee "prize courts," and other self-appointed courts that took business from the regular system.[72] Clandestine attacks on individuals reluctant to embrace regime policies routinely cast doubt on the Guangzhou regime's commitment to its own laws. In May 1925, for example, two well-known Hong Kong merchants were abducted. Although party officials blamed bandits dressed in GMD uniforms, critics suggested that local Guomindang leaders had actually planned the kidnappings because the two had helped block kerosene and flour imports to protest tax hikes.[73]

---

69. *CWR* 34 (October 17, 1925): 175; *CWR* 34 (November 21, 1925): 287; *CWR* 35 (December 5, 1925): 21; *CWR* 35 (December 26, 1925): 106.
70. Chen, comp., *BCCM*, vol. Q, section 2B, p. 10.
71. Reports unsympathetic to the practice decried the fact that sixty such prisoners had been imprisoned by individuals that were no longer even associated with the GMD. *CWR* 35 (December 5, 1925): 21
72. *CWR* 36 (April 3, 1926): 127.
73. According to reports, the two merchants plotted with The Standard Oil Company, the Asiatic Petroleum Oil Company, the Texas Oil Company and various Chinese merchants to boycott oil shipments as a way to protest GMD tax hikes. *CWR* 32 (May 9, 1925): 291.

Reports also excoriated the party for spiking martialization and violence in Guangdong. Labor, peasant, and student groups all hosted militia. Nationalist military academies churned out cadets steeped in martial culture while party officials publicly honored party assassins.[74] The exaggerated role of army officers, propaganda celebrating military conquests, and violent rivalries between the guest army officers fed a general sense of impending destruction. State violence was devastating. In 1926, for example, reports blamed the party for a campaign in Jiujiang that destroyed the town, massacred many, and rendered over 61,000 homeless.[75] In April 1926, reports claimed that fighting in a southern Guangdong district, which allegedly killed 40 percent of the population, wasted 60 to 70 percent of the land, and destroyed two-thirds of the homes, stemmed from battles between "GMD factions" associated with Guangzhou and Chen Jiongming, respectively, as if both legitimately represented the party.[76]

Critics also denounced the regime for failing to eliminate the thousands of bandits and pirates plaguing Guangdong's rail and waterways.[77] Heavily armed gangs operated in broad daylight. In early 1926, press releases noted that nineteen major gangs based in West River districts would soon hold a conference to elect new leaders, fix booty cuts, and determine the daily pay of regulars when not on maneuvers.[78] Although the meeting was openly reported in the press, the southern regime failed to intervene. Localist interests anxious to slow bandit predations and gain government assistance first had to pay "protection fees." Any community unwilling to hire regime troops took its chances with the bandits who, often enough, were the same troops demanding fees in the first place.[79] As if the line between brigands and government troops was not blurry enough, organized criminals regularly dressed as GMD troops. In March 1926, Guomindang branch leaders in Guangdong's North River districts publicly announced that bandits attacking town markets and destroying up to sixty houses at a time were not GMD Hunanese mercenaries but robbers disguised as party troops. Unconvinced, local townspeople begged the party to help, offering assurances that "no contribution will be denied" if it would convince the renegade Hunanese to obey the law.[80]

---

74. *CWR* 35 (January 9, 1926): 170.

75. *CWR* 35 (January 9, 1926): 168.

76. A shared history and continued negotiations between Sun and Chen undoubtedly cemented the view that Chen still enjoyed some link to the Nationalists. *CWR* 36 (April 17, 1926): 179. Rejecting party claims about fighting bandits in eastern Guangdong, reports blamed destruction there on rivalries within the GMD army. *CWR* 36 (April 24, 1926): 208. Near Jiangmen, meanwhile, the foreign press blamed GMD troops, initially sent to calm a feud, for destroying hundreds of homes and huts. See *CWR* 36 (May 15, 1926): 298.

77. *CWR* 36 (April 17, 1926): 178.

78. *CWR* 36 (March 6, 1926): 13.

79. *CWR* 35 (January 16, 1926): 192.

80. *CWR* 36 (March 27, 1926): 98.

To many localist and provincialist observers, these and other problems only confirmed that the entire revolutionary movement was but a murky union of aggrandizement that promised little except to strangle Guangdong's prosperity. Decline would continue as long as the Nationalists tolerated "Bolshevistic" inclinations and continued to sacrifice local and provincial well-being to chase idealized visions of national unification.[81] Those most outspoken were banished—a fate incurred by Hin Wong of Shanghai's *China Weekly Review*. In March 1925, however, Wong fired a parting shot by condemning GMD profiteering before summarizing conditions from the perspective of Guangzhou's localist interests:

> For the last two years the people of Kwangtung [Guangdong] have seen nothing but officials intriguing against each other for offices of profit and militarists fighting one another for territories of defense, which means that military commanders stationed within the territory may commandeer local revenue, impose new taxes, and exact protection fees from shipping, gambling, opium, and other traffics illegal or otherwise. Under the pretext of land classification and deeds examination, thousands of sites and buildings belonging to the people have been confiscated and sold in order that the proceeds might be divided among the unscrupulous politicians and militarists. By subjecting everything to inspections and registration and requiring heavy fees on every act, at least $120 million have been extorted from the Cantonese in the last two years by the terrorists in power. Taking advantage of the once necessary act of commandeering ships for military transportation, the mercenary bandit-troops in Kwangtung have forcibly taken so many launches and small steamers and junks and tow-boats that many large companies have been forced to register their vessels in foreign consulates in Shameen [Shamian] with the hope of avoiding the authorized piracy so frequently practiced in Canton [Guangzhou] waters the last two years.
>
> By charging those opposing them as being traitors to the government and kidnapping persons under the excuse of impressing them for military transportation service in the battle fronts, both the politicians and the militarists have been able to extort large sums of money from the wealthy residents and rich merchants. In the last two years in Kwangtung every tax rate has been doubled and sometimes quadrupled, besides the addition of hundreds of new imposts. Those Kuomintang [Guomindang] members who have failed to enrich themselves either through political persecution of helpless individuals or by military extortion on the public have resorted to enlistment in the Bolshevist rank in order to fatten

---

81. Merchants feared a "Bolshevist" regime in Guangzhou. *USDS* 893.00/5650, Enclosure 1, Jenkins to Bell, Guangzhou, September 2, 1924. The revolution's "communistic" elements proved a ready scapegoat for any policy distasteful to foreign, provincialist, or localist interests.

themselves by the liberal subsidies from outside sources. Today the Kuomintang insignia of blue sky and white sun has been mounted on the left corner of the red flag, under which the Kuomintang may now flourish.[82]

The significance of Wong's reproof lies not in its veracity but in its illumination of a major source of localist and provincialist frustration: the caustic side-effects of decentralized centralism. In the context of foreign relations, decentralized centralism proved hugely advantageous as evidenced when Sun played labor off British might during the Seamen's Strike of 1922. By obscuring ties to strike agitation and adopting an accommodating mediatory role, Nationalist leaders garnered political influence and a seat at Britain's negotiating table. In the context of GMD domestic relations, however, dynamics were inverted because localist and provincialist interests held the party accountable for everything the revolution's decentralized portions did. Sun's regime paid the guest armies and depended on their military power. Thus popular resentment bred by their abuses fell squarely on party shoulders and made regime leaders, at best, guilty of not providing better government.

In short, the revolution's system of decentralized centralism produced positive results for the GMD regime, but only if the revolution's centralized portion could manage its sundry decentralized parts, allies, and ancillary organizations. Despite Sun's quest for unity and centralized control, he often enjoyed neither. (Even supposedly steadfast institutions, such as the Huangpu Military Academy, could demonstrate considerable license.[83]) Without full control, Sun's regime had to spend considerable effort just to avoid falling prey to its own allies.[84] In this context, decentralization was a liability. When funds were needed, as they always were, any of the revolution's various parts could simply announce new tax laws and send out collectors. Guest army officers levied their own imposts, as could *anyone*

---

82. Wong, "The Passing of the Kuomintang in South China," p. 72. Surprisingly, although banished from Guangzhou, Hin Wong continued to enjoy loose party ties and spoke favorably of Sun Yat-sen when later asked to speak at a memorial service honoring him in Hong Kong.

83. Jiang, *Sue zai Zhongguo*, p. 23. Li points out that Chiang threatened to resign as commandant of the Huangpu Military Academy in order to compel greater access to influential leaders such as Sun and Liao Zhongkai, setting a precedent for military noncompliance with civilian procedure. Li, *Student Nationalism in China*, pp. 16-17.

84. Despite its best efforts, the party lost salt revenues, railway receipts, and hotel taxes to the "guest armies." *CWR* 32 (March 7, 1925): 21; *CWR* 32 (March 14, 1925): 42; *CWR* 32 (May 16, 1925): 319. In March 1925, rumors announced that acting Generalissimo and Civil Governor Hu Hanmin would leave Guangzhou and be replaced by Yunnan general Yang Ximin, and that the CEC considered moving party headquarters and the military academy to Shantou to avoid the reach of mercenary forces. *CWR* 32 (March 28, 1925): 114; *CWR* 32 (May 9, 1925): 291. Militarist clashes and jostling spawned fighting, looting, and destruction that sometimes left whole towns burned to the ground. "Canton War Taxes," *Peking and Tientsin Times* (January 15, 1924).

tenuously claiming party authorization and showing enough muscle to enforce payment. Even allegedly legitimate government collectors depended on troops and threats of arrest to shore up their authority. As long as the party was weak, the ambitious could justify almost any action by simply claiming allegiance to the revolution, party, and/or government. In the end, GMD power was compromised.

British/Merchant Collusion, A Dual-Prong Response

Unwilling to remain idly by while conditions under GMD misrule continued to decline, a great many localist and provincialist groups responded. Shop proprietors, roadside food hawkers, rickshaw drivers, and others found ways to resist, often by paralyzing commercial markets or disrupting the economy. Strikes and boycotts abounded. Commenting on localist disruptions, the American Consul in Guangzhou recorded,

> The Sun government continues to arrest and force coolies into military services. This has been the cause of much discontent on the part of the common people. Extraordinary tax levies have also been the causes of *complaint and frequent strikes.* Among these levies may be mentioned special taxes on fish dealers, rickshaw coolies, theaters, hotels and restaurants. The tax on the fish dealers was followed by a strike. . . . The restaurant tax has resulted in the *closing of all eating houses* in Canton [Guangzhou]. . . . As the result of a claim on the part of the local authorities that the Custom House Brokers' Guild had defrauded the government of certain revenues, the police are demanding a fine of $100,000 Hong Kong currency from the Guild. This the Guild is *refusing to pay and a strike of stevedores and others connected with the Association is now on.*[85] [Emphasis added.]

It is interesting to note that unhappy localist and provincialist interests used the same economic leverage to defy revolutionary Guangzhou that Sun had used to challenge imperialist Hong Kong. With the regime systematically organizing the masses and localist defiance rising at the same time, individuals began to gravitate to one or the other, prompting reports that Sun had indeed become "the most hated and best loved" of China's political leaders.[86] Tensions between the two sides, however, had few outlets. The regime refused to offer protestors any recourse or voice in the political process, leaving little maneuvering room within the GMD legal framework.[87] Formal

---

85. Chen, comp., *BCCM*, vol. Q, section 2B, pp. 9-10.
86. "Sun Yat-sen's Son in Shanghai," *North China Daily News* (September 29, 1924).
87. Guangdong's difficulties with militarism were not unique but reflected what everyone else in China routinely experienced. What differed was how Guangdongese responded by organizing armed resistance. Localist interests elsewhere copied Guangzhou developments. Merchants in Chongqing, for example, established their own merchant militias and began applying to the

complaints could be submitted to party headquarters, but they were widely recognized as having minimal effect even when laws existed and arrangements had been made.[88] As a result, many interests opted to challenge the government directly. Through October 1924, most betting observers put their money on the Guomindang's localist and provincialist rivals. They enjoyed initiative, momentum, considerable popular support, allies, and infrastructural advantages that foretold a brief and inglorious end to Sun's southern regime.

Central to this anti-Nationalist movement was Guangdong's wide array of self-defense groups, militias, and corps. In 1912, Beijing's Republican government chartered such groups to deter bandits and renegade troops. Enjoying status as legal, auxiliary branches of local governments everywhere, private armies helped local military and police forces maintain law and order. When central authority collapsed with Yuan Shikai's regime, local militias proliferated in the resulting political vacuum. In Guangdong alone, some 150,000 volunteers participated in various units scattered among the province's leading 138 towns and cities.[89] To neutralize GMD advantage and strengthen their own military muscle, Guangzhou merchants unified these autonomous groups. On May 27, 1924, the Merchants Association convened a Merchants Militia Congress aimed at consolidating Guangdong's militias into a single federation. Hugely successful, the congress attracted roughly three hundred delegates representing some ninety-eight different people's corps *(mintuan)* and merchant militias *(shangtuan)* into an umbrella organization called the Merchants Volunteer Corps. Forces in Guangzhou alone boasted four thousand armed regular troops, another four thousand in reserve, and some $3.5 million invested in weapons and barracks—not including the uniforms and arms provided by each volunteer.[90] Gates, causeways, ramparts, and iron palisades around Xiguan, meanwhile, separated Guangzhou's wealthiest commercial district from the rest of the city, making it an ideal base for the Merchants Association and its Corps.[91]

Although Guomindang leaders could not deny that mediocre administration and recurrent problems had soured their ties with Guangzhou's merchants, there remained the nagging worry that merchant defiance owed its initiative to foreign interests seeking to undermine the southern regime.

---

government for permission to buy arms. *CWR* 35 (January 16, 1926): 191.

88. Media reports scoffed at petitions by Guangzhou merchants seeking the return of twelve junks and half a million catties of rice taken by the Guomindang Army on March 5, 1925. *CWR* 32 (April 4, 1925): 145. According to the cynical observers, recompense was highly unlikely.

89. *CWR* 35 (February 6, 1926): 291. Li estimates Guangdong's collective militia strength in mid-1924 to have ranged from thirty to forty thousand men under various units. Li, *Student Nationalism in China*, p. 24.

90. Xu, "Yijiuersi nian Sun Zhongshan de beifa yu Guangzhou shangtuan shibian," p. 2. Also see *CWR* 35 (February 6, 1926): 291.

91. Luo, ed., *Guofu nianpu*, p. 1241.

Cordial relations between Sun and Britain depended on GMD strength. With merchants sounding a challenge through various strikes and militia organization efforts, the party suspected that Britain—finding Sun a greater threat to labor stability than a solution—had seized an opportunity to turn the tables by helping the merchants. Key ties binding Merchants Corps interests to British commercial enterprises in Hong Kong deepened Nationalist concerns.[92] Heading the Merchants Association, for example, was Chen Lianbo (a. k. a. Chen Bolin), a powerful comprador of the British-owned Huifeng Bank (Hong Kong and Shanghai Banking Corporation).[93] Chen conveniently made his headquarters in the foreign concessions of Shamian where he enjoyed ready access to foreign financial circles and refuge from GMD police. Rumors maintained that Chen was encouraged by certain foreigners who sought to institute a new merchant-led government in Guangzhou. One of these individuals, A. G. Stephen, the Chief Manager of the Hong Kong and Shanghai Bank, even allegedly went as far as to underwrite international weapons orders for the Merchants Corps. Other rumors asserted that Stephen enjoyed the tacit support of the Hong Kong governor—a notion that Governor Stubbs strongly denied.[94]

Motive was not hard to understand. A merchant coup in Guangzhou promised British interests revenge and relief from further labor strikes or customs disruptions. Nevertheless, official British statements staunchly declared "neutrality" in China's domestic affairs and denied any shady dealings with Guangzhou merchants. Unable to determine what support—if any—the Merchants Corps was actually receiving, the southern regime anticipated the worst: collusion between merchants, Chen Jiongming, and certain Hong Kong interests aimed at destroying Guomindang power. Dealing with the threat, real or imagined, proved difficult. Beyond raising public sympathies through anti-foreign statements, the party had few options. On May 7, Sun accused the foreigners of disregarding all "government, laws, and rights."[95] Nevertheless, GMD anti-foreignism seemed tepid. In the face of Merchants Corps' strength and popularity, the party simply lacked the confidence and capacity to challenge its foreign opponents with something stronger.

Opportunity presented itself on June 19, however, when an Annamese revolutionary tried to assassinate French Indochina's governor-general by bombing the Victoria Hotel in Shamian. Although entirely unconnected to Guangzhou's recent political developments, the bombing aroused foreign

92. Isaacs, *The Tragedy of the Chinese Revolution*, p. 68.
93. Chen was employed by the Guangzhou branch of the Huifeng Bank. Xu, "Yijiuersi nian Sun Zhongshan de beifa yu Guangzhou shangtuan shibian," p. 2.
94. Welsh, *A Borrowed Place*, pp. 368-369.
95. Sun directed his comments at the Diplomatic Corps in Beijing. *USDS* 893.00/5466, Enclosure, Sun's speech at Pui Ching Baptist Academy, May 7, 1924.

fears about anarchists from Korea, India, and other countries. Japan's Eiji Amau, the senior consul of Guangzhou's foreign representatives, criticized the government, claiming that "plotters" were using Guangzhou as a base and insisting that the Nationalists more thoroughly suppress anarchist agents.[96] Capitalizing on this development, the party responded with dual-prong tactics. On one hand, top officials stimulated popular anti-imperialism by retorting with indignation to Amau's critiques and publishing angry editorials.[97] On the other hand, Governor Liao Zhongkai warmly assuaged foreign fears, claiming that Guangdong's government and people had always maintained attitudes "friendly to foreign representatives and [had] never supported such plots." Promising to protect foreign interests with largesse so sweet that it bordered on sarcasm, Liao then asked Amau for details about the terrorists, allegedly so "proper measures" could be taken, before fishing for a *quid-pro-quo* arrangement. Turning Amau's remonstration around, Liao accused the foreigners of harboring "terrorists" of their own:

> It is a well known fact that some people who are hostile to this Government [have] not only indulged in circulating groundless rumours but are plotting overthrowal [sic] of this Government by establishing some organization at some place within jurisdiction of the Government represented by you, and by using that place as the base of political and military operation. I hope that the authorities concerned shall take more strict measures in that respect and help in improving the cordial relations between us.[98]

If Liao hoped to gain anything by comparing merchant leaders in Shamian to anarchist plotters housed in Guangzhou, he must have been disappointed. The foreign community was in no mood to cut deals. Waves of bandit, pirate, mob, and militarist attacks against foreigners throughout China had already made the powers hypersensitive.[99] Anti-foreignism was sweeping the country. Unwilling to entrust Shamian's safety to GMD promises, British and French ratepayers voted on June 30 to safeguard the concession themselves by implementing new traffic regulations. Most affirmed mundane laws, such as prohibitions against walking on the grass, but others required Chinese entering Shamian after 9:00 P.M. to show a pass with picture identification. Instead of stabilizing conditions, however, the plan

---

96. Amau lodged his complaint with the governor's office. *USDS* 893.00/5528, Schurman to Washington, Beijing, July 25, 1924; *USDS* 893.00/5523, Enclosure, Amau to Liao Zhongkai, June 26, 1924; *FO* 405/247 [F117/117/10], pp. 7-9, Macleay to Chamberlain, Beijing, November 22, 1924.

97. *FO* 405/247 [F117/117/10], pp. 7-9, Macleay to Chamberlain, Beijing, November 22, 1924.

98. *USDS* 893.00/5523, Enclosure, Liao Zhongkai to Amau, Guangzhou.

99. The year 1923 marked a banner year for bandit and pirate attacks against foreigners. "Ninety-two Outrages against Foreigners in China," *North China Daily Mail* (January 15, 1924).

played directly into the hands of anti-foreign agitators. Chinese were offended that foreigners were not required to show identification even though the alleged anarchists were all non-Chinese. Harnessing anti-foreign displeasure, labor agitators quickly organized a general boycott against Shamian. On July 15, labor pickets representing twenty-six different unions began "encouraging" Shamian's Chinese workers to strike by blocking bridge access to anyone without strike committee authorization.[100] Students and even major compradors also contributed, generating broad-base enthusiasm for the Anti-Shamian Boycott that, unlike earlier strikes, was purely anti-imperialist and entirely political. In the middle of it all was the Nationalist Labor Ministry which oversaw the strike committee.[101]

The Anti-Shamian Boycott offered GMD leaders many of the same benefits provided by the earlier Seamen's Strike of 1922. It stimulated popular support and provided propaganda material. It granted Guangzhou modest strategic advantage by inserting a cordon of popular forces between the British and insurgent Merchants Volunteer leaders in Guangzhou while avoiding provocative military or police actions. Pickets harassed anyone wanting to enter Shamian, compromising communications between the merchant corpsmen in Guangzhou and their leader Chen Lianbo in Shamian and disrupting any flow of weapons or funds by paralyzing Shamian banks, businesses, and docks dependent on Chinese clerks or laborers. Most significantly, however, it gave the party another chance to employ its dual-prong revolutionary approach and thereby translate mass activity into political leverage. Anti-foreign Guomindang statements directed at the *guomin* maintained popular interest in the strike while official overtures readied for foreign consumption maintained strict "neutrality," allowing party leaders to mediate and again play the two sides off each other.

Given Guangzhou's tinderbox conditions, however, the line between success and failure was a fine one. Much depended on the overt qualities of agitation and how it was perceived. Agitators had to be visible. As Michael Tsin notes, "[they] had to *appear* to be organized and active participants for the cause."[102] [Emphasis added.] Mass mobilization was intended to *appear*—to be seen—and thereby showcase popular energy and unity. Activity was thus choreographed to produce as large a show as possible, often within sight of the foreign concessions or some other high profile setting where it could not be missed. At the same time, however, direct regime involvement—the fiscal support, planning, and direction necessary to animate

100. Wilbur and How, *Missionaries of Revolution*, p. 107.
101. *USDS* 893.00/5650, Enclosure 2, Jenkins to Bell, Guangzhou, September 6, 1924.
102. While Tsin's "cause" refers to the construction of an imagined community and swelling sense of modernization, his observation applies equally well to the "cause" of securing Guomindang foreign policy advantages. Tsin, *Nation, Governance, and Modernity*, p. 145.

popular activism—had to remain *invisible*.[103] Popular anti-foreign agitation had to *appear* spontaneous to be perceived as legitimate. Any sign of GMD involvement would be interpreted as disingenuous "Bolshevist" meddling and possibly provoke an imperialist backlash.

To avoid direct confrontation, the party spared no effort to accommodate and assuage foreign concerns. The pattern had precedence. Six months earlier in January 1924, for example, one day after Sun enflamed anti-imperialist sentiment with a blistering speech at Canton Christian College, his advisor on foreign affairs Chen Youren visited the school to recant the statements. As one foreign witness explained, "[Chen] made strenuous efforts to smooth away his chief's erratic statements and made it appear that he had not been talking seriously in all he had said."[104] By the time of the Anti-Shamian Boycott, the GMD had greater reason to avoid culpability. It is for this reason that C. Martin Wilbur exclaimed, "Sun's government *pretended not to be directly involved*, which was only technically the case."[105] [Emphasis added.]

In general, party theatrics worked. Determining where popular spontaneity ended and GMD inducement began was nearly impossible. Anti-imperialist agitation predated Sun's latest regime, could be found throughout China, and included many organizations operating independent of the party Labor Ministry. Although Douglas Jenkins, the U.S. Consul General in Guangzhou, eagerly sought proof that the Guangzhou regime backed anti-foreign agitation, the best evidence he could muster was the speculative observation that agitative groups routinely posted circulars on party buildings—an act requiring government approval.[106] Even explicitly anti-foreign speeches and statements were explained away by party headquarters as the private feelings of individuals. Unable to pin responsibility on the southern regime, the imperialists found themselves arrayed against the *guomin* of China—a position hosting few options. In 1922, during the Seamen's Strike, Hong Kong leaders had tried to restrain the spread of the strike using forceful means, but they only provoked more agitation. By July 1924, with the Anti-Shamian Boycott in full swing, foreign authorities had learned to recognize when they were outmaneuvered. Acknowledging the strikers' upper hand, U.S. minister Jacob Gould Schurman had to advise that, "As the Chinese are in a position where eventually they will *in all probability be able to force compliance with their demands*, the sooner the opposing parties

---

103. Tsin distinguishes between "emancipatory" and "disciplinary" forms of government involvement. Tsin, *Nation, Governance, and Modernity*, p. 145.

104. Sun had even threatened war. *USDS* 893.00/5348, Enclosure, Brownall, Sun at Canton Christian College, Guangzhou, December 21, 1923.

105. Wilbur, *Sun Yat-sen*, p. 227.

106. *USDS* 893.00/5348, Enclosure, Jenkins to Schurman, Guangzhou, December 28, 1923. Also see Sharman, *Sun Yat-sen*, p. 256.

settle their differences the better."[107] [Emphasis added.] In short, the only viable recourse was to seek GMD arbitration. For its part, the party could earn a measure of *de facto* recognition, a psychological victory, and proof that it could exercise responsible administration. To encourage the British to take a step in the right direction, the party's Guangzhou Municipal Government reaffirmed its "neutrality" before offering to host negotiations and mediate a settlement satisfactory to all.[108]

Although it seemed to hold all the strings, the Guomindang soon discovered that it was not the only force able to employ popular mobilization. In late July, rupturing relations with the merchants gave the party a taste of its own medicine. The turning point came when Guangzhou municipal authorities imposed new road levies, ostensibly to unify road authority and improve surfaces. Refusing to pay, the Merchants Association threatened to close Guangzhou's markets and called for a general uprising against anticipated government suppression. Regime officials were intimidated and retracted their plans, temporarily diffusing the standoff but emboldening the merchants in the process.[109] In the meantime, Chen Lianbo secured Sun Yat-sen's permission, at a cost of $50,000 Mexican silver dollars, to import almost ten thousand rifles, pistols, and revolvers plus three million rounds of ammunition.[110] Militias routinely bought arms and applied for import permits from local authorities. This particular shipment, however, worried GMD leaders. Its enormous size extended well beyond even the capacity of the Merchants Corps. More troubling still was the observation that some items—such as spare aircraft parts—seemed destined for Chen Jiongming's forces. Suspecting that the armaments might be employed against the regime by Chen, the Merchants Corps, and/or even the guest armies, party officials decided to seize the shipment.[111] In mid-August, when the cargo ship *Hav* arrived from Belgium, two Nationalist warships escorted it to the Huangpu Military Academy where cadets hastily unloaded the cargo.[112] Angered, Merchants Association leaders stirred up their own popular movement, parading over one thousand protesters to party headquarters and threatening immediate strikes unless the weapons were surrendered. Trying to maintain the peace, GMD leaders sought assurances that the weapons would not be used against the government.

---

107. *USDS* 893.00/5528, Schurman to Washington, Beijing, July 25, 1924.
108. Wilbur and How, *Missionaries of Revolution*, p. 108.
109. Luo, ed., *Guofu nianpu*, pp. 1214-1215.
110. Altogether the shipment was valued at 1.6 million Chinese *yuan* (Chinese currency). *CWR* 35 (February 6, 1926): 291; Li, *Student Nationalism in China*, p. 25.
111. For a breakdown of the *Hav*'s manifest, see Tsin, *Nation, Governance, and Modernity*, pp. 217-218, notes 103-104. In addition to the small arms and ammunition, the shipment included some large machine guns, mountain guns, and parts for two airplanes.
112. Luo, ed., *Guofu nianpu*, p. 1216.

As tensions over the arms seizure escalated, attention shifted away from the Anti-Shamian Boycott. Chen Lianbo relocated to Hong Kong where the boycott could not reach and where he found even greater reception than in Shamian. Rumors claimed that certain British interests there had even promised that if he would overthrow the GMD he would become "China's Washington." A British consular official—likely Bertrand Giles—substantiated the hearsay when he warned Sun that illegal collaboration between Chen and a small circle of British interests had indeed arisen.[113] Under the threat of a larger and looming Merchants Corps crisis, any advantage offered by the Anti-Shamian Boycott seemed trivial indeed. At best, it threatened to weaken British commitments to "neutrality" and motivate fence-sitters to side with conspirators supporting Chen. As a result, when asked about it by foreign authorities, Sun engineered a hasty compromise that abruptly ended the boycott at noon on August 19.[114]

Zealous agitator leaders were disappointed. When several Chinese servants trying to return to their jobs in Shamian found their positions terminated, boycott leaders accused the foreigners of reneging on the settlement agreement and called for further strike action. Nevertheless, without regime support nothing came of it.[115] Party attention had turned to focus exclusively on the merchant threat. The same day that Sun ended the boycott against Shamian, GMD officials denounced the merchants, accusing Chen of conspiring to use the Association's military might to topple the government. Merchants retaliated by demanding that the regime return all weapons unconditionally, grant permission for a United Self-Defense General Headquarters, and cancel a warrant for Chen's arrest.[116] When the party rejected these demands, Chen Lianbo rallied guild support and declared a market strike on August 25. The move was a shrewd one. Not only did it cut GMD revenues, it also pinched the pockets of guest army commanders who then pressured Sun to resolve the issue. Gradually, mediation by two Yunnanese generals produced a compromise: the merchants agreed to end the market strike on August 30 and pay $500,000 while the party promised to withdraw government troops from merchant areas and return the confiscated arms. Merchant leaders also agreed to submit the Merchants Volunteer Corps to civil governor oversight and swear allegiance to the southern regime in exchange for amnesty for all Corps leaders.[117]

113. Luo, ed., *Guofu nianpu*, pp. 1214-1215; Wilbur, *Sun Yat-sen*, p. 250.

114. *FO* 405/247 [F117/117/10], pp. 7-9, Macleay to Chamberlain, Beijing, November 22, 1924.

115. *USDS* 893.00/5650, Enclosure 2, Jenkins to Bell, Guangzhou, September 6, 1924.

116. The official denunciation was entitled "An Explanation of the Unreliability and Sedition of the Merchants Association" (*Xiaoyu shangtuan wufu he panni*). Luo, ed., *Guofu nianpu*, pp. 1220-1221.

117. *USDS* 893.00/5650, Enclosure 1, Jenkins to Bell, Guangzhou, September 2, 1924; *FO* 405/247 [F117/117/10], pp. 7-9, Macleay to Chamberlain, Beijing, November 22, 1924.

Despite its promise, the truce quickly collapsed when a corpsman was shot for spying.[118] As prospects for peace declined, signs arose that the merchant threat was broadening. Rumors asserted that Yunnanese guest army officers would side with the Merchants Corps while reports claimed that Chen Jiongming had already been paid $500,000 and was promised another million dollars (or millions of dollars) if he would also intervene against the Nationalists.[119] (To raise the needed funds, Corps officers telegraphed overseas Chinese organizations for contributions.)[120] Meanwhile, Britain, France, and Japan weighed in by warning the Guangdong governor that any GMD gunboat fire against merchant defenses would provoke a foreign retaliation to protect foreign lives and property.[121] Challenged by the Merchants Corps, the Yunnanese, Chen Jiongming, and a collection of foreign nations all at the same time, the revolutionary government could do little except mobilize popular forces. Party officials formed a federation of revolutionary militias called the Citizens Volunteer Corps that combined loyal labor, peasant, merchant, and local militias under central GMD control.[122] Meanwhile, inflammatory government statements aroused popular energies. On September 1, Sun blasted British "meddling" and announced,

The relations, spirit, and various loans of strong imperialist nations have invariably helped the anti-revolutionaries. We would like to view imperialist actions as not plotting to destroy the GMD regime but find it impossible because an open rebellious movement faces our government today and its leader is a representative of British imperialism's most powerful organization. Even while we seek to take forceful measures to oppose this rebellious movement the so-called British Labour Party government threatens to knock over our government. What does this

118. *USDS* 893.00/5650, Enclosure 1, Jenkins to Bell, Guangzhou, September 2, 1924.
119. *USDS* 893.00/5538, Bell to Secretary of State, Beijing, September 18, 1924; *USDS* 893.00/5743, Jenkins to State Department, Guangzhou, September 30, 1924. Suspicions rose when reports broke that General Yang Ximin, commander of the three Yunnan armies in Guangzhou and a "firm" supporter of Sun Yat-sen, had been replaced by General Fan Shisheng who was known to be friendly with the merchants. Luo, ed., *Guofu nianpu*, p. 1241. Sun, meanwhile, also tried to recruit Chen Jiongming's support. *USDS* 893.00/5729, Dispatch, Jenkins, Guangzhou, September 17, 1924; "Sun Yat-sen's Son in Shanghai," *North China Daily News* (September 29, 1924).
120. *USDS* 893.00/5651, China Society of America to State Department, New York, October 14, 1924. The China Society of America was contacted by an organization calling itself the Hong Kong Chinese General Chamber of Commerce Volunteers for donations.
121. *USDS* 893.00/5650, Enclosure 1, Jenkins to Bell, Guangzhou, September 2, 1924. Jenkins reported that Britain's senior naval officer in south China claimed he had orders to sink any Chinese gunboat firing on the merchants in Guangzhou. *USDS* 893.00/5650, Enclosure 3, Jenkins to Bell, Guangzhou, September 6, 1924. Sun, of course, protested. "Dr. Sun Denounces British Premier's Policy in China," *Canton Gazette* (September 24, 1924).
122. *USDS* 893.00/5650, Enclosure 2, Jenkins to Bell, Guangzhou, September 6, 1924; *FO* 405/247 [F117/117/10], pp. 7-9, Macleay to Chamberlain, Beijing, November 22, 1924.

mean? This GMD regime that imperialism hopes to destroy is still the only government in the country striving to protect the revolutionary spirit, and the only one attacking the center of the anti-revolutionaries, the real target British guns ought to fire at. . . . Today begins a new era, we will anxiously overthrow imperialism's interference with China and sweep aside the greatest obstacle to completing our revolutionary work.[123]

On September 7, the Nationalists organized great parades featuring soldiers representing the Huangpu Military Academy, the Peasant Army, the newly formed Labor Corps, and some loyal Yunnanese units, in addition to students and common citizens. Peasants and workers carried banners attacking imperialism, militarism, and the Consular Body while calling for a boycott of British and U.S. goods. The following day Sun added his personal disappointment with the powers by issuing a manifesto decrying British and U.S. imperialism, denouncing unsupportive supporters (such as certain Yunnanese mercenaries), and denying any "Bolshevist" ambitions.[124]

Despite the blustery front, however, Sun seemed to have been deeply intimidated by the threat facing his regime and little comforted by Guangzhou's popular demonstrations. In early September 1924, therefore, when shifts in the northern political landscape opened for Sun an opportunity to again snatch at national power, he jumped at it. Reverting to old habits, he called for a campaign against rival warlords and requested that friendly militarists help him form a federation regime in Beijing. On September 13, eager to begin the charge and certain that Guangzhou would soon be lost, Sun left for Shaoguan, located 140 miles north of Guangzhou.[125] In a manifesto published on the eve of his departure, he admitted that things had not gone well in Guangzhou. Blaming the guest armies and unscrupulous officials, he promised to lead all troops out of south China's greatest city and cancel all unusual taxes while adding that the people should elect a new mayor of Guangzhou as a step toward self-government.[126] (Sun Ke had already re-

---

123. "Wei Guangzhou shangtuan shijian duiwai xuanyan," *Geming wenxian*, vol. 69, pp. 108-109. Subsequent pronouncements denounced the British for alleged "atrocities" against the GMD. "Fandui diguozhuyi ganshe wuguo neizheng zhi xuanyan," *Geming wenxian*, vol. 69, pp. 109-111.

124. *USDS* 893.00/5650, Enclosure 4, Jenkins to Bell, Guangzhou, September 9, 1924; "Boxer Protocol Is Charter of Organized Imperialism in China," *Canton Gazette* (September 8, 1924). Staunch denials of Bolshevism were published in the *Canton Gazette* on September 12, 1924.

125. *USDS* 893.00/5650, Enclosure 2, Jenkins to Bell, Guangzhou, September 6, 1924; "Kuomintang's Declaration Regarding the Objects of The War," *Canton Gazette* (September 22, 1924).

126. "President Sun's Manifesto to the People of Kwangtung," *Canton Gazette* (September 13, 1924). Jenkins believed that Sun had given up on Guangzhou. *USDS* 893.00/5729, Jenkins to Bell, Guangzhou, September 17, 1924; *USDS* 893.00/5650, Enclosure 5, Jenkins to Bell, Guangzhou, September 17, 1924.

signed as mayor and had departed along with other party officials, leaving Hu Hanmin as acting Generalissimo and Chiang Kai-shek heading the Huangpu Academy.)[127] Sun Yat-sen then ordered GMD troops holding the eastern front against Chen Jiongming's armies to join him in Shaoguan and even offered to "pardon" Chen if he would support the new campaign against the north. Chen did not respond, but party forces heeded by leaving eastern Guangdong for Guangzhou.[128] On September 22, party headquarters tried to augment its might by ordering all worker and peasant militias *(gongtuan* and *nongtuan)* to join Sun in Shaoguan and make ready to unify China.[129]

By late September, foreign observers gleefully reported that the expedition had stalled. Neither the Yunnanese mercenaries nor Chen Jiongming had signed up. Meanwhile, Guangzhou merchants refused to forward revenues. Once again, Sun's base had turned against him. In the words of the American Consul General,

> It seems safe to say that Dr. Sun has lost much support during the past two months and his controversy with the merchants has come very near forcing him out of office entirely. Were it not for the presence of the Yunnanese, whose allegiance is doubtful, it is believed that Sun would have had to flee. As things now stand his sole support rests with certain radical elements in the labor unions, although in the last analysis the situation depends . . . upon the Yunnanese troops.[130]

Unable to press northward and equally unable to return to Guangzhou, Sun found himself stranded in Shaoguan. Out of options, he pinned all hope on northern militarist allies whom he believed would somehow form a coalition and rush to aid his northern expedition.[131] Writing to Chiang Kai-shek, Sun noted: "Since coming to Shaoguan I have come to feel we should quit Canton [Guangzhou]. . . . With the situation today looking as dangerous as it does, I hope you will promptly abandon the lonely island of Whampoa [Huangpu], bring all the arms and cadets, and quickly come to Shaoguan so that we might

---

127. *USDS* 893.00/5538, Bell to Secretary of State, Beijing, September 18, 1924; *USDS* 893.00/5650, Enclosure 2, Jenkins to Bell, Guangzhou, September 6, 1924. According to foreign observers, Sun Ke's resignation was intended to calm merchants who blamed him for unpopular methods of revenue collection. The appointment of his replacement—General Li Fulin, who had refused to align himself with the party—was seen as a gesture of conciliation on the part of the Guomindang. *USDS* 893.00/5729, Jenkins to Bell, Guangzhou, September 17, 1924; *USDS* 893.00/5743, Jenkins to State Department, Guangzhou, September 30, 1924.

128. *USDS* 893.00/5650, Enclosure 6, Jenkins to Bell, Guangzhou, September 18, 1924.

129. "Kuomintang's Declaration Regarding the Objects of The War," *Canton Gazette* (September 22, 1924).

130. *USDS* 893.00/5730, Jenkins to Bell, Guangzhou, September 23, 1924.

131. Sun's northern ally Duan Qirui sent a representative (Xu Shiying) to encourage Sun to hasten preparations and absolve differences with Chen Jiongming so a coordinated attack on Wu Peifu's forces could be launched. *USDS* 893.00/5743, Jenkins to State Department, Guangzhou, September 30, 1924.

make the northern expedition our sole focus."[132] Chiang, however, resisted Sun's urgings, writing back that he would stay and fight to the last man.[133] Mustering local labor and peasant militias, GMD leaders still in Guangzhou braced for the worst.[134]

Revolutionary Victory and Assimilation

Most observers assumed that the Nationalist regime could not survive, leaving conjecture to revolve around speculation about who would deliver the fatal blow. In many ways, the patterns unfolding in Guangzhou looked strikingly familiar. Raising the specter of imperialism and encouraging popular organizations to set up the Anti-Shamian Boycott should have given Guangzhou authorities leverage as mediators. It did not work, however. With merchant interests laying claim to a powerful segment of the *guomin* and threatening the regime with popular mobilization and economic disruptions of their own, dynamics had reversed, this time in favor of the Merchants Association. Organized, ambitious, and strong enough to defend themselves, the merchants held Guangdong markets hostage while they negotiated with the Nationalist regime to get what they wanted. As a result, party leaders found themselves outflanked and challenged by the same tactics they had used during the Seamen's Strike of 1922. Merchant market strikes strangled Guangzhou's economic well-being just as labor strikes had stifled Hong Kong's productivity in 1922. Market strikes offered political leverage by forcing the party to negotiate the fate of confiscated arms just as labor strikes had forced Hong Kong authorities to deal with a regime they refused to recognize. Both groups also enjoyed external support in spats with their respective regimes; the Guangzhou merchants of 1924 took courage from Chen Jiongming and British interests while the Hong Kong workers of 1922 had been encouraged by GMD Guangzhou. Lastly, British authorities denied any ties to Guangzhou merchants just as Sun's regime had secreted overt encouragement for Hong Kong strikers earlier.

On closer inspection this schematic fractures, rendering it pointless, except for the fact that *it* is not as important as the observation that the primary actors of both the 1922 and 1924 episodes were largely the same. Some of them, such as Chen Jiongming's Guangdong Army, had switched sides while others, such as Hong Kong workers, sat on the sidelines in 1924, but

---

132. Luo, ed., *Guofu nianpu*, p. 697. Efforts to attract troops and funds seemed doomed. The "guest armies" refused to leave Guangzhou and sent little more than token contingents while merchants refused to transfer funds. *USDS* 893.00/5743, Jenkins to State Department, Guangzhou, September 30, 1924.
133. Wilbur concludes that Chiang acted as described here, refuting an uncorroborated Soviet report that he hid in his bedroom. Wilbur and How, *Missionaries of Revolution*, p. 118.
134. Peasant and labor militiamen immediately wanted to know how much they would get paid. *USDS* 893.00/5650, Enclosure 2, Jenkins to Bell, Guangzhou, September 6, 1924.

most had played the game or at least seen it played before from the front row. Given Sun's success with the strike of 1922, Guomindang leaders could not have missed the danger of their predicament in 1924. Nor could merchants have overlooked their advantage. After all, only thirty months separated the two episodes. There was, however, one major difference between the strikers of 1922 and the merchants of 1924. Unlike the Seamen's Union walkout, Merchants Association defiance did not first seek economic benefit. Enjoying a position of ascendancy, Guangzhou merchants pursued political power. Economic benefit, a byproduct of rescinded GMD taxes and imposts, was secondary.

To accommodate merchant demands and mitigate hostility, Sun had promised tax reprieves on the eve of his departure for Shaoguan. On October 10, after party leaders failed to follow through, signaling either party weakness vis-à-vis the guest armies or insincerity or both, the merchants again closed the markets. That same day, Chiang agreed to return four thousand rifles.[135] Under these tense conditions, while the transfer was underway, paraders ostensibly celebrating Double Ten Day filed past the heavily guarded Merchants Corps fortifications.[136] Paragraphs opening this chapter describe the ensuing scuffle which killed over twenty paraders, swung public sympathy toward the southern regime, and justified a stronger show of Nationalist force.[137] The incident, however, merely signaled the beginning of hostilities. Readying for a final confrontation, merchant leaders repositioned their troops and announced that since the party had returned only half of their weapons, they would open only half of the closed stores. Meanwhile, Merchants Association leaders ordered people's corps *(mintuan)* allies in the North River districts to head off Sun's forces should they try to return to Guangzhou.[138]

On October 13, five thousand troops loyal to Sun reached Guangzhou from the East River front.[139] Wasting no time Chiang deployed all available Nationalist troops and cadets around Xiguan and attacked at 4:00 A.M. the following morning. Bombarding the defenses, government forces broke

135. The initial agreement involved five thousand rifles plus ten to twenty thousand rounds of ammunition. In return the party would get 200,000 *yuan* from the Merchants Association, one month's building rents, and immediate end to the market strike. See Luo, ed., *Guofu nianpu*, p. 1241.

136. See Luo, ed., *Guofu nianpu*, p. 1241.

137. *USDS* 893.00/5776, Jenkins to Secretary of State, Guangzhou, October 13, 1924. Li claims that the incident turned popular support back in favor of the GMD. Li, *Student Nationalism in China*, p. 26. Also see Wu, *Wu Tiecheng huiyilu*, pp. 77-86. Although thought to sympathize with the merchants, General Li Fulin denounced them after the skirmish on October 10 and declared allegiance to Sun's regime. *USDS* 893.00/5777, Jenkins to Secretary of State, Guangzhou, October 18, 1924.

138. Luo, ed., *Guofu nianpu*, p. 1242.

139. *USDS* 893.00/5620, Bell to Secretary of State, Beijing, October 16, 1924.

merchant lines and occupied Xiguan after half a day of fierce fighting. For three days, fires raged throughout Guangzhou's wealthiest district, destroying property valued at some $30 million. What the fires left fell to looters until a government prohibition and the threat of capital punishment slowed them significantly.[140] Rumors that merchant leaders planned retaliatory uprisings kept Sun in Shaoguan.[141] Reports of death and destruction prompted U.S. authorities to order the *U.S.S. Pampanga* and *U.S.S. Sacramento* to Guangzhou but neither made any move to stop the violence.[142] British ships also stood quiet. In the end, Chiang's military strike was quick, effective, and over before many realized it had begun.

The Merchants Association movement was crushed, thanks to the timely arrival of troops from the eastern front, Chiang's willingness to destroy Xiguan, and dumb luck that the powers did not intervene as they had promised. Failed tactics and negotiations led to coercive measures generally reserved for the worst "enemies." According to its own doctrines, the GMD regime could not tolerate a direct challenge to its authority. The First National Congress stated clearly the fate of all who "betray the nation and ensnare its people" *(maiguo wangmin)* by remaining loyal to imperialism and warlordism. Be they an individual or a group, they had to be excluded from the ranks of the *guomin* and stripped of all "freedoms and rights" *(ziyou ji quanli).*[143] Similar declarations issued as the merchants crisis escalated warned that there would be "no middle ground" between the *guomin* and their enemies.[144]

Despite its own threats, however, actual Nationalist policy proved accommodating to the point of appearing almost soft. It seemed that there actually was a middle ground between the *guomin* and their enemies and it was considerable. On August 29, party leaders issued a proclamation that divided Guangzhou's merchants into five categories. Of these, only the very smallest—top Merchants Association leaders involved in imperialist-aided plots to overthrow the government—were to be "excluded in every case" *(zaisuo bichu).* All "rebels" in the other four categories were granted considerable license; their offense could be "overlooked" *(guzhi)* or "indulged" *(guxi)* because they had been manipulated by leaders of the first category.[145]

---

140. *USDS* 893.00/5623, Bell to Secretary of State, Beijing, October 17, 1924. Later reports claimed that 1,100 buildings were burned and six hundred establishments looted, particularly native banks. *USDS* 893.00/5790, Enclosure, Jenkins to Bell, Guangzhou, October 23, 1924.
141. *USDS* 893.00/5650, Bell to Secretary of State, Beijing, September 20, 1924.
142. *USDS* 893.00/5620, Bell to Secretary of State, Beijing, October 16, 1924.
143. "Zhongguo Guomindang diyici quanguo daibiao dahui xuanyan," *Geming wenxian*, vol. 69, p. 90.
144. Tsin, *Nation, Governance, and Modernity in China*, p. 111.
145. "Zhongguo Guomindang dui Guangzhou bashi shijian xuanyan," *Geming wenxian*, vol. 10, p. 50.

This early offer of amnesty, however, represented more than an attempt to split the ranks of the merchants and isolate their leaders. While fires in Xiguan still raged, the party freely and widely extended forgiveness and offered inclusion. When the assistant head of the Merchants Corps visited Chiang Kai-shek and pled for a reprieve on October 14, for example, he received it, bringing the violence to a quick conclusion.[146] The only stipulation sought in return was that the merchants lift their market strike.

Bypassing the temptation to demonize and destroy the merchants as an "enemy within," the party embraced the majority of corpsmen and Merchants Corps leaders. It had good reason to exhibit a gracious face. Harshness was difficult to justify when even Sun Yat-sen had acknowledged that government failings had produced the popular dissatisfaction that provoked the merchant uprising.[147] Sun Ke, meanwhile, explained popular hostility another way:

> We tried to establish a modern municipality, but *most of the people* could not understand what we were about. We came in touch with vested interests and we had to overcome all sorts of difficulties. One of our most serious problems was to finance the municipal government. We found that Canton [Guangzhou], like other cities, was *a merger of many villages. These little units were running their own shows, without regard for the general interests of the city.*[148] [Emphasis added.]

Motivated primarily by narrow non-revolutionary interests, most Chinese sat in the category of potential *guomin* only, ensuring that party leaders could not afford to write them off even if they did challenge the party because doing so would leave no one with whom to create the "nation."

In short, even severe measures of exclusion, such as military suppression, did not ultimately aim to destroy but to subdue and ready individuals for inclusion among the revolutionized *guomin*. Per Sun's vision of the "nation"—an integrated home for all Chinese—the machinery of exclusion sought national inclusion whenever possible. For this reason, GMD leaders rejected the petitions of Huang Renjun's cohorts introduced at the beginning of this chapter. Strident and uncompromising, they had insisted that the party crush all "bad elements" and drive from the revolution all guest army, comprador, small shop owner, unemployed politician, intellectual, and gentry

---

146. Luo, ed., *Guofu nianpu*, pp. 1243-1244; *USDS* 893.00/5777, Jenkins to Secretary of State, Guangzhou, October 18, 1924.

147. "President Sun's Manifesto to the People of Kwangtung," *Canton Gazette* (September 13, 1924).

148. "Sun Yat-sen's Son in Shanghai" *North China Daily News* (September 29, 1924). Despite Sun Ke's critiques, the GMD itself was not immune to fragmentation. At the First National Congress, Dai Jitao specifically identified the destruction of *provincialist and localist loyalties among GMD cadres* as the first of three major responsibilities facing local party branch offices. "Zhongguo Guomindang zongzhang zhiding an," *Geming wenxian*, vol. 76, p. 8.

interests.[149] Spurning the black-and-white demands generally pursued by agitators eager to destroy the revolution's enemies, Guomindang authorities forgave the vast majority of merchants and folded them into the "nation."

At the same time, however, at least one feature of this inclusion was different. Because violence had been required to bring about merchant submission, the Merchants Association never again enjoyed the type of autonomy characterizing organizations that voluntarily submitted to regime oversight and revolutionary transformation. As Merchants Corps leaders discovered firsthand, those who rejected freely-offered invitations to join the revolutionary *guomin* faced the rude hand of party intrusion. Per Borodin's vision, involuntary inclusion required some guarantees to preserve party power. As a result, the form of inclusion extended to the Merchants Association involved more disciplinary oversight and less participatory independence. Changes subordinated commercial organizations and enhanced regime influence within the merchant community. As Tsin describes,

> The subjugation of the merchant class to the new disciplinary regime began with a reconstruction of its organizational structure. The Nine Charitable Halls, a symbol and bastion of the merchant establishment of Canton since the turn of the century, were formally put under the control of the municipal authority in October 1925. . . . The roles of the General Chamber of Commerce and the Municipal Chamber . . . were also greatly reduced. . . . In their place a new government-sponsored Merchant Association was founded in early 1925 to represent and mobilize the merchant class.[150]

Defeated interests, in short, found themselves assimilated into the "nation" on the party's own terms—controlled and contained to better serve the interests of the state.

---

149. "Guangdong xinxueshengshe deng shang zongli deng daidian," October 29, 1924.
150. Tsin, *Nation, Governance, and Modernity in China*, p. 112.

4. "Safe" Anti-Imperialism
—Harnessing the Anti-Christian Movement, January 1924 - June 1925

It is undeniable that Christian education, in so far as it is subsidised and staffed by the West, is under suspicion to-day in China. There are various causes which have led to this state of things: the policy of "peaceful penetration" on the part of Japan in connection with the development of schools, etc., in Manchuria; the fact that before the World War the German Government was proposing to subsidise German mission schools in China for the direct purpose of spreading German "Kultur" and benefiting German trade; the action of the Associated British Chambers of Commerce in contributing a large sum of money towards British schools and hospitals, and the widespread apprehension as to possible use that will be made of the released Boxer indemnity funds. These and similar events have all helped to produce an attitude of suspicion on the part of leading Chinese as to the true motives underlying such an investment of men and money in educational enterprises in China. This suspicion has manifest itself in a double line of attack upon mission schools, partly political and partly anti-religious.[1]
—Dr. Harold Balme, President of Shandong Christian University, April 6, 1925

On April 7, 1925, a German national on his way to work painstakingly picked his way through a dense crowd of mourners in Chongqing. All over China, communities were conducting memorial services to honor the passing of Dr. Sun Yat-sen—posthumously identified by the Beijing regime as modern China's greatest national hero. In Chongqing, organizers planned for six straight days of events. Available seating at the Chamber of Commerce building, however, filled quickly, spilling large numbers into streets already congested with student processions.

Trying to reach his office, M. Meyer found the throng unforgiving. Many Chinese resented his foreignness. Unable to contain his contempt, a youngster in a Boy Scout uniform spat and cursed at Meyer as he passed. The German countered, cuffing the boy over head with his open palm. Instantly,

---

1. *FO* 405/247 [P 544/544/145], p. 212, Anti-Christian Movement memorandum, March 5, 1925.

nearby Scouts blew whistles of alarm, shouting, "Kill the foreigner who attacked a Chinese." Alarmed, Meyer fled into a nearby office building where surprised British staff hid him in a back room. Moments later a posse of angry students and Boy Scouts surrounded the building, burst through the door, and hunted basement to roof for the "criminal." Determined to see "justice" served, the angered patriots seized two Englishmen and dragged them roughly back to the Chamber of Commerce building to face a hastily erected drum-head court. Upon confirming with the alleged victim that neither of the two had been involved, the Scouts promptly escorted them safely out of harm's way. Meyer, meanwhile, stayed put for hours, secretly escaping only after the angry youth had withdrawn and the German vice-consul had arrived.

The next day the matter was dropped when apologies were exchanged between student representatives and the German consul. British consul Allen Archer, however, was not satisfied. Anti-foreign incidents had risen all over China. Blaming local authorities for failing to maintain the peace, Archer paid a visit to General Liu Xiang, a noted militarist and the civil governor of Sichuan. As Archer relayed and complained about Meyer's unhappy en- counter, however, General Liu suddenly burst into laughter and recounted his own experience that day. Riding in a sedan chair the general too had found the streets impassable. As he approached a dense gathering of mourners, young Chinese surrounded him, compelled him to descend, and ordered him to walk humbly by if he wanted to pass. Foreigners, Liu retorted, were not the only ones harassed.

In the right context, a pubescent Boy Scout enjoyed more power than a foreign adult or even a Chinese general-governor with his own military. Social hierarchy had been inverted. Even Archer acknowledged that Meyer's physical exchange with the boy had been "unwise." Youth power did not solely stem from their collective strength, however, but from the cumulative weight of Republican history. As Michael Palairet, the British *Charge d'Affaires* in Beijing, explained:

> The republican calendar unfortunately contains a growing number of anniversaries which provide the students with pretexts for mass meetings and demonstrations. Moreover, under much of the prevailing turbulence and unrest are complex currents of feeling, connected with the growing spirit of nationalism, which are liable to come unexpectedly into play. The student agitations, together with the kindred movements against Christianity, the foreign treaties, &c., must thus be regarded as a serious and uncertain factor, which is likely to have a bearing on many questions affecting foreign interests and activities.[2]

---

2. *FO* 405/248 [F2794/144/10], pp. 23, Palairet to Chamberlain, Beijing, May 22, 1925.

Significantly, student vigor contrasted sharply with plummeting Nationalist vitality in Guangzhou. Chiang's crackdowns through the end of October 1924 greatly reduced the Merchants Corps threat but did not, by any stretch, clear the party of its base-area problems.[3] Merchant suppression had come at a high price: flagging GMD authority and mushrooming anti-regime activity. The mayor's office, the most important of Guangzhou's municipal government, had "practically ceased to function." The Secretary of Finance post remained unfilled because no one—including the usually energetic and ambitious Liao Zhongkai—would take the unpopular job.[4] The War Department remained unstaffed and virtually invisible, as did the Foreign Affairs Ministry. The Provincial Treasury Department hosted a chief but fumbled along because he could never be found in his office. Hu Hanmin continued as Guangzhou's most powerful civil leader, but he shouldered most of the blame for anti-merchant destruction and thus walked on eggshells. Describing political conditions in Guangzhou, one foreign observer reported that Guomindang leaders were so "deplorably weak" that they could not even enforce their orders.[5] Rumors about the party's immediate future once again differed only over the question of who would strike the fatal blow. Regrouping in Hong Kong, escaped Merchants Corps leaders courted anti-GMD militarists and prepared to reconstitute the militias. Other localist opponents—various rural interests, some student and worker organizations—cemented ties with provincialist forces, prompting talk of an upcoming war. Confident that conflict would doom the regime, hundreds of Guangzhou citizens whisked their valuables off to the safety of foreign banks in Shamian. Thousands more moved to Hong Kong.[6]

Northern developments further darkened revolutionary prospects. On October 23, warlord Feng Yuxiang turned against his commander Wu Peifu, forcing talk of a new regime in Beijing. Eager to share in the new order, south China's militarists took action. Since 1920, General Tang Jiyao of Yunnan and other provincialists had promoted the Federal Self-Government Movement by restoring provincial assemblies and forming provincial constitutions in Yunnan, Hunan, Guangdong, and Sichuan.[7] Hoping to strengthen his voice in the upcoming Beijing talks, Tang accelerated his efforts to ally these

---

3. Mop-up exercises against merchant organizations followed in other Guangdong cities. *USDS* 893.00/5875, American Foreign Service Report, Guangzhou, November 28, 1924.

4. *USDS* 893.00/5730, Jenkins to Bell, Guangzhou, September 23, 1924; *USDS* 893.00/5743, Jenkins to State Department, Guangzhou, September 30, 1924.

5. Many basic administrative functions did not exist in any recognizable form. *USDS* 893.00/5875, American Foreign Service Report, Guangzhou, November 28, 1924.

6. *CWR* 34 (November 21, 1925): 287; *USDS* 893.00/5777, Jenkins to Secretary of State, Guangzhou, October 18, 1924; *USDS* 893.00/5798, Enclosure, Jenkins to Bell, Guangzhou, October 23, 1924.

7. Duara, *Rescuing History from the Nation*, p. 179. Hunan promulgated the first provincial constitution on January 1, 1922. Chesneaux, "The Federalist Movement in China," p. 108.

provinces, along with Guizhou and Guangxi, under his command. From Guangzhou, Tang's plans looked menacing. They reflected Chen Jiongming's provincialist views better than Sun's centralist vision and threatened to isolate the party by uniting its most proximate militarist rivals. More frightening, however, were Tang's claims that Yunnanese mercenaries in Guangzhou remained loyal to him and would soon help him "restore order" in Guangdong. Perhaps the only news remotely comforting to Nationalist officials was that so little stock was placed in their chances that Tang may have overestimated his influence.[8] Through November, rumors of a Yunnanese invasion combined with speculation that Chen Jiongming and the merchants would join forces to dislodge the GMD. By December, conjecture crystallized into frightening reality when Chen publicly announced his intentions:

> Our Cantonese Army has always looked upon the restoration of peace and integrity of Kwangtung [Guangdong] as its primary duty. . . . If we fail to act at once, how can we fulfill the expectation of the people? Since the massacre of the people and the destruction of property at the Western City [Xiguan] of Canton [Guangzhou], delegation after delegation of Canton and Hong Kong merchants have approached us at Hoifung [Haifeng] and Swatow [Shantou] with requests to move our troops to save the people from further suffering. Under this urgent pressure, we cannot refrain from hastening our mission of relief. The false report that I, Chiung-ming [Jiongming], [am] not in favor of advancing towards Canton has been a fabrication of the enemy only. The Cantonese people are ready to welcome our return, and we cannot shirk our duty. Let us all be united with one heart and one spirit in the cooperation for the salvation of Kwangtung. All officers and men of our Army are hereby ordered to return immediately to their several posts and be prepared for the attack. Detailed orders will be issued soon after further conference of chief commanders. Be prepared to advance for the relief of Kwangtung without further delay.[9]

Ideologically, GMD nationalism offered no particular advantage. Both Tang and Chen promoted their respective causes with ideological claims and

---

8. Yunnan general Fan Shisheng hated Tang, who had executed Fan's father. Other Yunnan generals, meanwhile, hesitated to join Tang if it meant losing their prime positions in Guangzhou. *USDS* 893.00/5959, Foreign Service Report, Guangzhou, December 16, 1924; *USDS* 893.00/6145, Jenkins to State Department, Guangzhou, March 17, 1925. Tang did express a willingness to cooperate with Sun if doing so would serve his own federation, yet foreign consular authorities assumed that any such union would be temporary at best since Tang did not expect the Guomindang regime to survive much longer. *USDS* 893.00/5847, Myers to Secretary of State, Yunnanfu, October 29, 1924.

9. *South China Weekly Review* (December 6, 1924); *USDS* 893.00/5959, Foreign Service Report, Guangzhou, December 16, 1924.

petitions geared to stimulate and motivate popular loyalty and support. Chen specifically appealed to provincialist identities of the Guangdongese, asking them to rise up for the "salvation of Guangdong." Tang's military force, named the Army United to Establish the Nation *(Jianguo lianjun)*, appealed to nationalistic sympathies of a federalist stripe. Militarily, meanwhile, the Nationalists faced threats from the east, west, and even from inside their own base, yet, because Sun had ordered General Tan Yankai to drive north and link up with allies in the lower Yangzi, the party's most loyal troops were no longer in Guangzhou. Indeed, by early December, Tan's troops had bogged down in Jiangxi and thus were completely unable to assist in Guangzhou's defense.[10]

Discouraged, Sun turned his attention northward to more national politicking and a chance to wrest away some measure of political influence. Leaving Shaoguan and arriving in Guangzhou on October 30, he immediately announced his plan to travel north and participate in the Beijing talks. To bolster Sun's claim to represent south China, GMD leaders issued propaganda glorifying his platform and aiming, in the sardonic voice of one foreign critic, to "create the impression that the mass of the people were intensely interested."[11] On November 13, before leaving Guangzhou forever, Sun sought reconciliation with the city's citizens by issuing a declaration that called for an inclusive People's Congress in Beijing. As Sun envisioned, the congress would represent all Chinese interests and mark the first step toward ending warlordism and revoking the unequal treaties.

With his status as a regional authority eclipsed by Tang Jiyao and popular acclaim diluted by the burning of Xiguan, Sun required another form of legitimacy to bolster his Beijing trip. As a result, he turned to the only options left. On one hand, he renewed his anti-imperialist rhetoric, hoping to generate a wave of popular sentiment and ride it into power. Arriving in Shanghai in mid-November, he issued what one foreigner called, "the most defiant message that has ever been uttered by any Chinese entitled to be heard on any public occasion. . . . It is likely to ignite whatever smoldering embers there may be of anti-foreign feeling."[12] Within the week, Sun again savaged the imperialists and swore to do everything in his power to end their "evils."[13] On the other hand, he again began to energetically court the powers. Convinced that Soviet ties would not help him much in Beijing, Sun left for Japan

---

10. *USDS* 893.00/5959, Foreign Service Report, Guangzhou, December 16, 1924; *USDS* 893.00/5962, Price to Secretary of State, Fuzhou, December 22, 1924.
11. *USDS* 893.00/5845, Jenkins to Secretary of State, Guangzhou, November 15, 1924.
12. *USDS* 893.00/5852, Cunningham to Secretary of State, Shanghai, November 18, 1924.
13. *USDS* 893.00/5854, Cunningham to Secretary of State, Shanghai, November 25, 1924; Calls in Shanghai's foreign papers for Sun's banishment from the foreign concessions only further fueled anti-foreign sentiment and bolstered his visibility. "Dr. Sun's Attack on Foreigners," *Shanghai Times* (November 18, 1924).

on November 22 and made a pitch for Japanese aid. Blaming the West for China's problems, he petitioned Japanese support in his bid to overthrow the unequal treaties and hinted at an "Asia for the Asiatics" alliance. Although they received him politely, however, the Japanese kept their distance. (Unfortunately for Sun, the move also offended patriotic Chinese and left his party struggling to justify his strategy.)[14]

Reaching north China in December, Sun was greeted enthusiastically by Guomindang supporters but denounced by the foreign press.[15] Before his proposals for a People's Congress could get off the ground, however, he was diagnosed with cancer, sickened, and died some three months later on March 12, 1925.

Sun Yat-sen's passing wrecked any prospect the party may have hoped for in Beijing just as Guangzhou braced for attacks from Chen in the east and Tang in the west. At the same time, Sun's strident anti-foreignism had aggravated the British, threatening to add their fire to the mix. To quiet things down, GMD leaders in Guangzhou did not dare to either stimulate labor agitation—as witnessed during the Hong Kong strikes—or challenge imperialism's economic, political, or military systems—as occurred during the Guangzhou Customs Crisis. Responding with docility instead, top party leaders officially retracted threats to seize the customs office and promised to resolve the issue by negotiation with the foreign Diplomatic Corps—the imperialists' primary decision-making authority vis-à-vis treaty rights.[16] Taking meekness as a sign of resignation, critics described the party's "closing chapter" with confident certainty.[17]

---

14. "China Depends Upon Japan For Aid in Abolishing All Treaties Conferring Extraterritoriality," *Japan Times and Mail* (November 25, 1924). Signaling cordial feelings toward Japan, several GMD officials attended an official reception at the Japanese consulate celebrating the emperor's birthday. *USDS* 893.00/5844, Jenkins to Secretary of State, Guangzhou, November 12, 1924. Japanese officials delivered lectures on "Asia for the Asiatics" in Guangzhou that were well received. *USDS* 893.00/5959, Foreign Service Report, Guangzhou, December 16, 1924. Sun's hopes for Japanese support, however, never materialized. *USDS* 893.00/5791, Bancroft to Secretary of State, Tokyo, November 25, 1924.

15. Foreign press editorials denounced Sun for various issues and his "Bolshevist" leanings. "Chinese Merchants and Politics," *Peking and Tientsin Times* (November 15, 1924); "Canton Bolshevism," *Peking and Tientsin Times* (November 20, 1924); "An Unwelcome Guest," *Peking and Tientsin Times* (December 4, 1924); "Merchants and the Conference," *Peking and Tientsin Times* (December 6, 1924); "Great Asia," *Peking and Tientsin Times* (December 6, 1924); "The 'Great Asia' Stunt," *Peking and Tientsin Times* (December 8, 1924); "Sun Yat-sen's Little Programme," *Peking and Tientsin Times* (December 8, 1924); "Sun Yat-sen Ill," *Peking and Tientsin Times* (December 8, 1924); "Sun and the Treaties," *Peking and Tientsin Times* (December 10, 1924); "Sun Beats Us," *Peking and Tientsin Times* (December 10, 1924).

16. Ironically, Nationalist conciliation came just as foreign stridency had declined. Only the British insisted on defending the customs office, yet, even then, only if the other powers helped. *USDS* 893.00/5813, Enclosure, Jenkins to Mayer, Guangzhou, October 31, 1924.

17. Critics openly predicted the party's "inevitable" extinction. Wong, "The Passing of the Kuomintang in South China," p. 72.

Borrowed Momentum: Anti-Christianity, 1920-1922

The party did enjoy one point of optimism amidst the portents of doom: an anti-imperialist student movement expanding among a constituency far broader than just zealous Boy Scouts. One problem, however, reduced effectiveness. Activism that confronted imperialism in the abstract, theoretical sense struggled to sustain itself. Only when it attacked concrete targets did anti-imperialist agitation mature and expand. Identifying suitable candidates, however, proved difficult. Although Guangzhou students operating under Guomindang patronage could freely agitate against specific imperialist institutions, those functioning outside the base area found anti-imperialism extremely dangerous. In April 1924, for example, revolutionaries and Chinese educators planned a China-wide campaign to oppose some 450 Japanese schools and one hundred libraries founded to consolidate Japanese control in Manchuria through language, culture, and pro-Japan curricula. Party organs such as *Republican Daily (Minguo ribao)* and *Political Weekly (Zhengzhi zhoubao)* enhanced public awareness while Nationalist and educator agitators planned boycotts and protests demanding that the schools be closed. Before the campaign could gather steam, however, Japanese threats of reprisal against local Chinese officials and the media dissolved the movement.[18] Other events proved equally discouraging. In Fujian, for example, students protested questionable Japanese business practices and attacked local merchants selling Japanese products from Formosa. Shortly thereafter, student unions and an organization calling itself the Society for the Preservation of Human Bones demonstrated against foreign land use. All ended, however, when Japanese pressure forced local militarist and civil authorities to crack down on "destabilizing influences."[19] In sum, when arrayed against specific institutions, student anti-imperialism provoked suppression, stunting growth, limiting recruitment, and killing momentum.

What was needed was a concrete target for anti-imperialist activism that would not generate such harsh reactions. Fortunately for party leaders, Christian institutions fit the bill perfectly. Precedent had already proven the effectiveness of anti-Christianity. In 1920, May Fourth activists had launched the Anti-Christian and Educational Rights Movements. Interest deepened in February 1922 when Christian leaders announced that Beijing would host the Eleventh World Student Christian Federation Conference and the China Continuation Committee published a comprehensive outline of Protestant

---

18. Lutz, *Chinese Politics and Christian Missions*, pp. 116-118.
19. *USDS* 893.00/5788, Price to Secretary of State, Fuzhou, October 18, 1924; *USDS* 893.00/5962, Price to Secretary of State, Fuzhou, December 22, 1924. Agitation construed as pro-GMD was met with sharp repression. Wu Peifu's ally Zhou Yinren showed little restraint when his forces were attacked by popular revolutionary forces anticipating the arrival of Tan Yankai's Guangdong Army.

work in China for an upcoming National Christian Conference to be held in Shanghai in May. As if on cue, anti-Christian activity exploded. On March 9, 1922, Shanghai students formed the Anti-Christian Student Alliance which was joined two days later by the Grand Anti-Religion Federation formed by Beijing University students. Active mirror and branch organizations followed, springing up in Tianjin, Baodingfu, Taiyuan, Wuhu, Wuhan, Shaoxing, Changsha, Nanjing, Xiamen, and Guangzhou.[20]

As the 1922 Anti-Christian Movement expanded, so too did acrimonious exchanges between Christians and anti-Christians. Most interactions were limited to intellectual argument. Battles took place in newspapers and over the rostrum. Some Shanghai groups condemned Christianity's exploitation of China's proletariat, but most opposition was founded on humanist critiques that superstitious religion had been superseded by rational science and thus served no useful purpose in modern China. *Chinese Educational Review (Jiaoyu zazhi)*, for example, published lengthy editorials supporting the view that science trumped religion and applauding anti-Christian student activity.[21] Christian apologists responded by emphasizing the religion's "modernizing" components. Differences over the political role of Christian education, however, most divided the two sides. Christians claimed that mission schools represented a religious and therefore neutral agenda, but critics retorted that education could not be fully divorced from politics, that missionary education constituted "cultural imperialism," and that Britain and America posed a greater threat in this regard than Japan. Defending China's "educational interests," Anti-Christian and Educational Rights Movement leaders demanded that the unequal treaties granting educational liberties to Christian missionaries be revoked, that mission schools be subordinated to Chinese educational administrative authority, and that religious education be curbed.[22]

After an impressive showing, the Anti-Christian Movement of 1920-1922 faded, largely because it failed to capture broader attention and because China's most active student revolutionaries had dispersed for summer vacation.[23] Nevertheless, while the movement only lightly affected Chinese society, it heavily impacted the Chinese Christian community. Jonathan Tien-en Chao identifies three criticisms that aroused particular concern among Chinese Christians: (1) Christianity's allegedly unscientific nature, (2) its close ties to foreign institutions, and (3) its identification with imperialist aggression in China. Significantly, two of the three major attacks

---

20. Chao, "The Chinese Indigenous Church Movement," pp. 136-139.
21. Beijing anti-Christians favored rationalist critiques while Shanghai and Guangzhou organizations leaned toward Leninist arguments. Lutz, *Chinese Politics and Christian Missions*, pp. 58-63; Chao, "The Chinese Indigenous Church Movement," pp. 140-141.
22. Lutz, *Chinese Politics and Christian Missions*, pp. 104-106.
23. Lutz, *Chinese Politics and Christian Missions*, pp. 66-67.

on Christianity involved its ties to foreign might, prompting many Chinese Christians to seek greater control over the Chinese church, closer affinity with the Chinese nation, and discontinued dependence on gunboat diplomacy. By indigenizing *(bendihua)* Christian institutions—defined as augmenting the role of Chinese leaders and minimizing influence from abroad—and distancing them from imperialism, reform-minded Chinese and foreign Christian leaders alike hoped to build credibility within Chinese society. How to best do this, however, divided Chinese Christians and foreign missionaries, producing exploitable cracks between them.[24]

By late 1924, these developments combined synergistically to make Christian institutions the perfect target for flagging revolutionary anti-imperialism. As long as some Christian leaders repudiated reliance on foreign military might and supported indigenization as a way to shed the stigma of "imperialism," the Christian enterprise could not respond with unanimity, leaving it vulnerable to revolutionary action. Christian institutions were also scattered over wide regions of China. Even small communities hosted potential targets, making Christianity virtually indefensible, even *if* the powers had been willing to protect Christian treaty rights. Students gave anti-Christianity an additional layer of protection. Their reputation for selfless action—in contrast to the allegedly self-serving motives of labor agitators enmeshed in "Bolshevik" subterfuge—meant that shooting students earned instant opprobrium. Laughing at his own encounter, Chongqing's General Liu Xiang intimated that even militarists gave students some license—a courtesy rarely granted labor activists. Missionary leaders were even more loath to exceed reprimands or expulsion, allowing students some immunity from suppression. As a result, student-led anti-Christianity did not—with few exceptions—trigger the type of heavy intervention encountered by other anti-imperialist actions, making foreign Christian institutions an effective and "safe" other against which revolutionary anti-imperialism could define itself.

Other advantages only sweetened the attraction. The broad distribution of Christian institutions gave anti-Christian forces further reach than even labor agitation which remained centered in large urban centers. Through their extensive ties to Chinese students, teachers, nurses, patients, clients, and patrons, foreign missionaries sought to extend social influence. At the same time, however, since all these groups were susceptible to revolutionary propaganda, Christian institutions could do little to defend themselves from infiltration. Perhaps the greatest advantage of anti-Christianity, however, arose from its soft impact on Chinese society. Few Chinese harbored any vested interest in the Christian enterprise while those who did harbored little interest in a *status quo* dominated by foreign missionaries. Labor agitation

---

24. Chao, "The Chinese Indigenous Church Movement," pp. 148-163.

against imperialist economic institutions generated violent reactions from Chinese interests dependent on the system. In contrast, while anti-Christianity could stimulate modest complaints from mission school alumni or student bodies, it rarely produced reactions elsewhere. Anti-Christian demands for educational reform struck a resonant chord among even devout Chinese Christians who stood to gain responsibility, status, and control as missionary roles diminished. Thus, instead of dividing Chinese into economic interest groups, as labor activism often did, student-led anti-Christianity cemented national unity. It aligned a spectrum of political views ranging from radical revolutionaries to moderate Christians and showcased a national crisis: a controversy of national significance capable of generating broad waves of popular support across class lines.[25] Even organizations and interests fully opposed to the Guomindang on political or economic grounds sympathized with anti-imperialism defined in cultural and educational terms, allowing the movement to operate openly far outside Nationalist territory.

Popular Anti-Christian Agitation

From Guangzhou's shaky perspective, any advances that could deflect attention away from base-area calamities were welcome indeed. The party had long supported anti-Christianity. Since its foundation in 1923 as a joint venture between the GMD and CCP, Shanghai University had headed a distinctly anti-Christian charge. In March 1924, the Youth Ministry added, "We want students to understand the intention behind schools run by foreigners in China and ensure they oppose these schools . . . so they can better oppose imperialism."[26] Interest in the movement notwithstanding, contributions from central authorities lagged behind student initiative. Indeed, the National Student Union—energized with GMD money and support—had to urge the party Youth Ministry to be more proactive in pushing educational rights as a pillar of national consciousness.[27]

It was students at Guangzhou's Holy Trinity College's middle school, however, that provided the spark that ultimately revived the Anti-Christian Movement. The students had petitioned school officials for their own government but without success. When they then refused to apologize for alleged "impertinence," Trinity's principal closed the school, cleared out the campus, and expelled the students. Many absconded for Chinese schools, swearing they would suffer death before submitting to one more day of "slave education" *(nuli jiaoyu)*. As news spread via revolutionary organs such as *Republican Daily, China Youth (Zhongguo qingnian),* and *Awakening Lion Weekly*

---

25. Lutz, *Chinese Politics and Christian Missions*, p. 102.
26. "Qingnian yundong zhengce jueyian," *1-ZXWH*, vol. 1 (March 12, 1924).
27. Lutz, *Chinese Politics and Christian Missions*, p. 106.

(Xingshi zhoubao), similar "student storms" *(fengchao)* erupted in other middle schools throughout central and southern China. In May 1924, former Trinity students published a "Declaration of Withdrawal," explaining two major tactics that quickly reshaped the Anti-Christian and Educational Rights Movements. The first sought government action to restore China's educational rights and subjugate foreign schools to Chinese control. The second asked the people of China to rise up in opposition to foreign cultural encroachment.

Simultaneous appeals to government authorities and fellow countrymen, however, did not reflect equal expectations. As the Trinity declaration implied, one side was not holding up its end. Efforts by the people were praised as having a "great effect" *(da de gongxiao)*, but government involvement in the quest to recover educational rights was criticized as "unreliable" *(kaobuzhu de)*, "slack and unresponsive" *(huan bu jiji de)*, and producing "few results" *(shouxiao bu shenda)*. Disappointed by official inaction, the students closely aligned with the approach that offered the best return: mass propaganda and popular agitation. Laying China's future at the feet of patriotic Chinese—China's best hope—the Trinity authors concluded with an emotionally charged appeal printed in enormous, bolded characters:

> Dear compatriots! Imperialism's cultural invasion is not a casual affair but will affect the survival or destruction of the Chinese race! All students who have suffered under slave education, all Chinese faculty who teach for the imperialists, if you can still think, must have realized that foreigners have cheated and poisoned China's young people by taking advantage of our psychological weakness. You should ally yourselves with all those who are suffering to fight against the cruel invasion. *We cannot depend solely on the government to retrieve the right of education. Only when we have the strength of the masses will we have an impact. When the loud cries of all the masses rise up, then will we succeed and the whole Chinese nation will survive!* [28] [Emphasis added.]

As student storms spread, organizational activity surged. In June, the Guangzhou Student Union demanded that, (1) all foreign schools submit to government registration, (2) Chinese direct all academic programs, (3) compulsory religious instruction be banned, and (4) students be granted the right to organize, publish, and assemble. In mid-July, former Trinity students at Guangzhou Normal College moved to unify disparate student groups by contacting branches of the National Student Union, Guangzhou's New Student Society, Fuzhou's Young Student Society, Hangzhou's Young United Progress Association, and various parochial student groups.[29] By July,

---

28. "Guangzhou 'Shengsanyi' xuesheng tuixue xuanyan!," May 20, 1924.
29. Lutz, *Chinese Politics and Christian Missions*, pp. 126-127.

over fifty student unions had aligned with peasant, labor, and women's associations to produce Beijing's Great Anti-Imperialism League which demanded an end of foreign privilege and the recovery of China's lost rights.[30] Revolutionary organs such as Shanghai's *Republican Daily*, the local GMD Youth Bureau's *Revolutionary Youth (Geming qingnian)*, and the CCP's *The Guide Weekly (Xiangdao zhoubao)* helped by popularizing the anti-imperialist message.[31] On August 2, 1924, party CEC leaders Liao Zhongkai and Wu Zhihui founded the Anti-Christian Federation before establishing *The Non-Christian (Fei Jidujiao)* which featured a flood of editorials and articles by Shanghai University professors.[32] Federation officials, often Guomindang Youth and Propaganda Ministry cadres, mentored and directed responsive students although non-party groups were also very active. By late August 1924, anti-Christianity dominated the center stage of the anti-imperialist movement and flared hottest in cities with a strong Nationalist presence: Changsha, Guangzhou, and Shanghai.[33]

The timing was perfect. Just when military concerns forced Guangzhou to temper anti-imperialist propaganda and labor activism, anti-Christian agitation emerged to take its place. This did not mean, however, that the party had to settle for second-rate anti-imperialism. Anti-Christianity may have been "safe" but that did not make it any less potent; indeed, nothing could beat it at expanding agitative infrastructure. For example, in August 1924, Hubei's revolutionary leaders measured progress almost exclusively in terms of the number of new recruits and branch organizations, but they soon discovered, to their great surprise, that nothing produced better results than anti-Christian agitation. In fact, eulogizing Sun Yat-sen's memory was the only theme that could remotely compete with anti-Christianity. In the words of one Wuchang organizer, all other propaganda themes "had nothing to show for themselves."[34]

On the back of anti-Christian activity, Hubei revolutionary organizations spread. In late March 1925, local Wuchang leaders directed sixty agitators through eleven branch organizations and special branches in Hankou, Qiaokou, Hanyang, Huangpo, and Huanggang. By May, the numbers had jumped to 120 active members in thirteen branches and eight special

---

30. "Fan diguozhuyi yu feichu bupingdeng tiaoyue zhi yundong," *Dongfang zazhi* 22:6 (August 1924): 127-141.

31. Chao, "The Chinese Indigenous Church Movement," p. 176.

32. Wasserstrom, *Student Protests in Twentieth-Century China*, p. 48; Chao, "The Chinese Indigenous Church Movement," pp. 176-177. The Shanghai Girls' School for the Masses trained the party's female cadres. Lutz, *Chinese Politics and Christian Missions*, pp. 103-104.

33. Lutz, *Chinese Politics and Christian Missions*, p. 104.

34. *HGLW*, vol. 2, pp. 18-19. Even memorial services for Sun, however, employed an anti-Christian approach since so many mission school students attended. *HGLW*, vol. 2, pp. 28-31. Organizers readied expert speakers and prepared over forty leaflets specifically designed for such memorial services. *HGLW*, vol. 2, pp. 56-57.

branches.[35] In Wuhan, organizers reported that agents had penetrated virtually every student union, study society, and book-reading club tied to the Wuhan Student Union Federation. To ready its many new recruits, the Wuhan New Youth Regional Committee sent trainers to weekly branch meetings to report on ideology, propaganda, agitative methods, and so forth.[36] Propaganda specialists taught how to use anti-Christian slogans, link propaganda to Christian festivals, and utilize propaganda organs such as the *Wuhan Review (Wuhan pinglun)*.[37] Organizational progress came rapidly, but primarily among students rather than workers or peasants. Not only did Wuchang student organizations outnumber worker organizations by a spread of thirteen to four, students comprised over two-thirds of all revolutionaries and more actively participated in agitative events.[38] Warlord suppression stifled labor recruitment while long work schedules left little time for prescribed training and meetings. Student branches, on the other hand, enjoyed both time and motivation—judging from the high praise revolutionary leaders heaped upon them for their strict adherence to party procedure.[39] In May, while workers struggled to hold even basic meetings, Hubei's student groups established a branch of the Anti-Christian Federation and formed the Hubei New Youth Groups Alliance.[40]

By the spring of 1925, Hubei's anti-Christian forces were ready for larger campaigns. In early April, students distributed anti-foreign propaganda at the All-Hubei Athletic Meet, attracting extensive press coverage when their spokesman was forcibly removed from the grounds. In early May, New Youth leaders followed with Propaganda Week, a series of activities aimed at highlighting the revolution and its anti-Christian platform. On May 1, agitators distributed leaflets and convened the New Youth Alliance Conference to Oppose Christianity. On May 4, over one thousand participants attended anti-Christian speeches and conducted a parade through Wuchang. Demonstrations and speeches at various schools rounded out the week. As activities concluded, organizational work in Wuchang soared, prompting New Youth leaders to beg central headquarters for more agents and financing.[41]

Students, especially those from Wuchang, comprised the bulk of participants and occupied most leadership positions in both the Hubei

---

35. Progress in Hankou, meanwhile, raised talk about its promotion to a regional group *(difang tuan)*—the same status enjoyed by Wuchang. *HGLW*, vol. 2, pp. 18-19, 28-31, 48-49, 53.

36. *HGLW*, vol. 2, pp. 15-16. Interestingly enough, cell organizers complained that native place associations were worthless. *HGLW*, vol. 2, pp. 2-3.

37. Reports excitedly noted that Wuhan Middle School produced a weekly anti-imperialist journal while eye-catching reports on anti-Christmas activities could even be found in the foreign press. *HGLW*, vol. 2, pp. 3-4.

38. *HGLW*, vol. 2, pp. 1-2, 22-23, 29.

39. *HGLW*, vol. 2, p. 56.

40. *HGLW*, vol. 2, pp. 1-2, 28-31, 56-57.

41. *HGLW*, vol. 2, pp. 62-64.

Anti-Christian Federation and the New Youth Alliance.[42] This heavy dependence on students, however, meant anti-Christian anti-imperialism was susceptible to collapse during the summer and winter recesses. Energies also waned when approaching graduation soured student enthusiasm with fears that expulsion could endanger educational investments. Through late 1924 and early 1925, Hubei's revolutionary leaders complained bitterly about moribund momentum. As one reported, "Fine, I won't raise any more complaints. What is the situation? Since winter break till now some three months have passed, the situation has completely ground to a halt, and is yet to get off the ground even now." [43] Despite momentary setbacks, however, anti-Christianity continued to enjoy privileged status within the revolutionary program; indeed, New Youth Alliance leaders identified it as "the highest priority of all important work."[44] Gradually, organization strengthened. By late 1925, field reports asserted that virtually every student in Wuhan participated in the Wuhan Student Union Federation and that the New Youth Alliance had grown from twelve participating youth groups in May 1925 to forty in October.[45] With time, anti-Christian agitation outgrew the simple task of recruitment. As one Hubei New Youth organizer predicted,

> My school educates Christian school students about the importance of opposing Christianity and the methods of doing so. As a result, Christian schools have been heavily influenced. Wen Hua Middle School students are in the middle of opposing prayer and establishing secret student organizations. All student dormitories have placards with leaflets opposing cultural encroachment. Most likely, in the near future, Christian schools will experience an explosion.[46]

Through 1924 and 1925, anti-Christian progress in Hubei was paralleled in other provinces. As organization saturated key revolutionary centers such as Guangzhou, Shanghai and Changsha, activists exported propaganda, know-how, and agents to surrounding communities as far away as Chongqing. These cities then became core regional nodes of anti-imperialist and anti-Christian influence within a wide network combining student unions, provincial educational associations, GMD and CCP branch organizations, New Youth, local anti-Christian associations, educational rights restoration leagues, and so forth. Shanghai's Anti-Christian Federation headed this vast system and, through its branches, coordinated activities in schools through-

---

42. Each comprised twelve participating organizations. *HGLW*, vol. 2, pp. 62-64.
43. *HGLW*, vol. 2, pp. 4-5, 8, 28-31; *USDS* 893.00/6118, Enclosure 2, Meinhardt to Schurman, Changsha, February 2, 1925.
44. *HGLW*, vol. 2, p. 66.
45. "Hubei shengdangbu yinianban jingguo gaikuan," *1-ZXWH*, vol. 5 (November 6, 1925); *HGLW*, vol. 2, pp. 63-64.
46. *HGLW*, vol. 2, p. 66.

out Anhui, Zhejiang, Henan, Hunan, Hubei, and Guangdong.[47] As Federation leaders planned anti-Christian events, the National Student Union, the Young China Party, and other independent anti-Christian groups pooled their strength. Spontaneous agitation often erupted in individual schools or communities but seldom without stimulating coordinated anti-Christian activity and propaganda throughout the entire web.

Within this broad system, GMD leaders enjoyed unrivaled influence. Through his ties with Shanghai University and the Anti-Christian Federation, GMD labor minister Liao Zhongkai oversaw anti-Christian events in central China.[48] As president of Guangdong University, GMD youth minister Zou Lu enjoyed comparable authority in south China.[49] Exporting anti-Christian agents and propaganda from these two agitative centers, the party extended its outward reach far beyond Guangzhou.

To enhance revolutionary clout, the Anti-Christian Movement hosted a full compliment of institutions that imitated Christian philanthropic, educational, and recreational functions. Schools with a distinctly anti-Christian flavor, such as Shanghai's popular Guanghua University, formed by former St. John's University students, arose to absorb defections from mission schools.[50] Anti-Christian organizers in Guangzhou, Hangzhou, Jinan, and Changsha engineered "anti-Christmas" celebrations and exchanged "anti-Christmas" cards with one another. Anti-Christian religious reformers in Guangzhou even cooperated with local bookstores to revive Buddhism as an alternative to Christianity.[51]

Propaganda, meanwhile, juxtaposed the nation and Christianity and demanded that Christians "caught in the snare of deceit" choose between the two. As one leaflet argued, "Quickly with your whole strength ally yourselves with your fellow countrymen in an indissoluble union to destroy Christianity and its missions, which are institutions for promoting superstitions and encroaching upon the sovereignty of China!"[52] Everywhere anti-Christian demonstrations, parades, and strikes challenged the patriotism of mission school students and decried the role of foreign education.[53] Infiltrators, meanwhile, enrolled in Christian and government schools, converting dormitories into agitative headquarters for organizing secret student unions,

47. Yip, *Religion, Nationalism, and Chinese Students*, p. 41; *FO* 405/247 [F1260/194/10], pp. 206-207, Enclosure 4, Archer to Macleay, Chongqing, February 6, 1925.
48. Yip, *Religion, Nationalism, and Chinese Students*, p. 40.
49. *USDS* 893.00/5994, Jenkins to Department of State, Guangzhou, January 7, 1925.
50. *CWR* 34 (September 12, 1925): 44; Yip, *Religion, Nationalism, and Chinese Students*, p. 55.
51. Yip, *Religion, Nationalism, and Chinese Students*, p. 41; *CWR* 32 (March 14, 1925): 51.
52. *FO* 405/247 [F1260/194/10], p. 205, Enclosure 2, Hangzhou leaflet, December 21, 1924.
53. Student unions or New Youth generally headed the activities, but rallies could often include some worker or peasant groups to exhibit multi-class support. In Guangzhou, demonstrations denouncing the YMCA showcased defecting Christian students.. Yip, *Religion, Nationalism, and Chinese Students*, pp. 41-42.

planning agitative activities, spreading propaganda, and steering school policy. Most who abandoned mission schools offered nationalistic zeal to signal they had shaken off imperialist brainwashing and were quickly embraced by anti-Christian organizations in return. On occasion, however, anti-Christian leaders advised young recruits to stay in mission schools or even accept Christian baptism—despite propaganda demands to the contrary—in order to maintain an inside vantage point.[54]

While assaulting mission schools, anti-Christian agitators took special precautions to guard against government suppression. In early 1925, for example, after a series of successful anti-Christmas demonstrations in Chongqing, foreign missionaries asked Chinese authorities to restore order. Sichuan civil officials and even the governor responded by lecturing and warning student leaders.[55] Taking the advice seriously, the Chongqing branch of the Anti-Christian Federation publicly renounced any action that might spark a government reaction, including: (1) reckless slander, (2) attacks on specific individuals, (3) destructive or violent action, and (4) anti-foreignism. Federation leaders meticulously added that they opposed only Christianity and no other foreign enterprise, decried communism, rejected anarchism, and repudiated "foolish, uncivilized, anti-foreign behavior"—a reference to the Boxer Uprising of 1900.[56] Championing China's well-being while assailing only Christianity's deleterious impact on the youth, anti-Christian agitators found few opponents.

Anti-Christian activism in late 1924 impacted China's Christian community with a force far beyond anything generated during the movement of 1922. In mid-December, after authorities at Changsha's Yale-in-China rejected student calls to register with the government and expelled a student leader for holding an unauthorized meeting, 80 percent of the students withdrew, prompting speculation that the school would have to close. Strikes at St. James School in Changsha, Albright High School in Liling, and John D. Wells School in Xiangtan soon followed. Beijing's YMCA School of Finance, Yanjing University, and a Fuzhou college maintained by the Women's Foreign Missionary Society faced similar interference.[57] Revolutionized mission school students energized a new burst of student storms through early 1925. Hoping to mitigate disruption, even Chinese Christian teachers and students loyal to their schools called on foreign missionaries to

54. Critics of the Guomindang pejoratively referred to infiltrators as "Bolshevist disciples." Wong, "Co-operation, or Non-Intervention, Wanted," p. 362; *HGLW*, vol. 2, p. 66; Chao, "The Chinese Indigenous Church Movement," p. 183.

55. *FO* 405/247 [F1260/194/10], p. 204, Palairet to Chamberlain, Beijing, February 25, 1925.

56. *FO* 405/247 [F1260/194/10], p. 208, Enclosure 5, extract from *Hsin Shu Pao*, Chongqing, January 31, 1925.

57. *FO* 405/247 [F1260/194/10], p. 203, Palairet to Chamberlain, Beijing, February 25, 1925; Also see Yip, *Religion, Nationalism, and Chinese Students*, pp. 39-40.

renounce imperialist privilege and the unequal treaties. Others formed exclusively Chinese organizations and schools to distance themselves from
imperialism. Foreign authorities asked missionaries to report all
anti-Christian sentiment and agitation in major cities. While some regions
reported no significant change, F. L. Hawks Pott of St. John's University in
Shanghai—the center of the anti-Christian energy—noted that the wave was
much worse than originally thought and reflected the political agenda of the
Guomindang.[58]

Chinese Christians freely offered advice. Wang Zhengting (C. T. Wang),
a Beijing foreign relations official and noted Christian leader, wrote the
British editor of the *North China Daily Herald*, saying, "The important
thing . . . for the missionary to-day is not to combine more closely with
foreign business, but to do all that he can by works, attitudes, actions and
spirit to make clear that the religion of Christ has *nothing in common with the
politics and activities of foreign Governments and business interests as they
are motived [sic] and constituted to-day.*"[59] [Emphasis added.] Wu Zhenchun, a Christian member of Beijing's Education Ministry, wrote in the
Chinese weekly *Truth (Zhenli)* that the church should not shield itself behind
the unequal treaties but seek government registration.[60] Even foreign educators began to call for a new missionary role. Dr. Harold Balme, president of
Shandong Christian University, concluded a detailed analysis of the rising
crisis surrounding Christian education by declaring that mission schools
should conform to government regulations, grant Chinese more administrative positions, employ only honorable and culturally sensitive missionaries,
and drop missionary support for treaty rights.[61]

Beyond conceding, missionaries could do little to defend themselves.
Since the late Qing they had argued that their work sought only to impact
culture and thus operated outside the scope of official government interest.
Now the same argument—that popular anti-Christian activity sought merely
cultural change which did not affect foreign governments—could be used
against them. At the same time, while obliged to protect missionary lives and
property, few western consuls felt justified opposing the right of students to
protest against Christian institutions. Any imperialist attempt to intervene
could only confirm what anti-Christian agitators had argued all along—that
missionaries relied on imperialist might and therefore *did* harbor a political
agenda. By early 1925, therefore, popular anti-Christian agitation was already fragmenting the Christian enterprise. Cracks separated radicalized

---

58. *USDS* 893.00/5951, Schurman to Secretary of State, Beijing, January 16, 1925.
59. *FO* 405/247 [F1260/194/10], p. 211, Enclosure 8, extract from *North China Daily Herald*,
January 10, 1925.
60. *FO* 405/247 [P 544/544/145], p. 219, Harold Balme letter, January 21, 1925.
61. *FO* 405/247 [P 544/544/145], p. 215, Anti-Christian Movement memorandum, March 5,
1925.

students from those loyal to Christianity and split both of these groups from the missionaries running Christian institutions. Further fissures divided Chinese Christian leaders and foreign missionaries and alienated each of these vested interests from imperialist political and commercial leaders. All that was needed was a way to exploit the divisions.

Official Anti-Christian Regulation

From Guangzhou's perspective, the Anti-Christian Movement worked wonderfully. It divided Christian loyalties, attracted popular support, expanded revolutionary organization, and did so while being virtually unassailable. Best of all, Nationalist leaders enjoyed uncontested influence at its highest decision-making levels—a fact that did not go unnoticed by Christian leaders. YMCA educational secretary Liu Zhan'en, identified four differences that distinguished the Movement after 1924 from earlier anti-Christian activity of 1920-1922: (1) Christian institutions, not its doctrines, were now targeted; (2) loosely associated societies relying on editorials had given way to a nation-wide system coordinating student agitation and propaganda; (3) mission school students attacked Christian institutions instead of defending them; and (4) through ties to the National Student Union and other organizations supported by the GMD, anti-Christian forces advanced a specific political agenda.[62] In short, anti-Christian forces were far more organized and politicized than before. Comprehensive as it was, however, the YMCA report could have added another item: government pressure on Christian institutions had begun to gain steam.

Since the late Qing, the Chinese state had sought control over Christian schools but under very different circumstances. In 1905, missionary educators had eagerly sought government registration as a way to validate mission school diplomas but found their petitions rejected by Qing officials unwilling to legitimize foreign education.[63] With the advent of warlordism and decline of central authority, however, Christian schools offering modern scientific curricula enjoyed booming popularity and growth, giving them their own legitimacy and eroding all inclinations to seek regime sanction. With time, missionaries began to view registration as an impediment to educational autonomy and integrity.[64] By 1919, however, nationalistic considerations had changed government views regarding education. To reverse social and political disintegration, China's most respected educators moved to unify education along the lines of its greatest secular institutions: Beijing University, Nankai University (Tianjin), and Dongnan University (Nanjing).[65] By

---

62. Ford, *The History of Educational Work in the Methodist Episcopal Church in China*, p. 162.
63. Lutz, *Chinese Politics and Christian Missions*, p. 120.
64. *FO 405/247* [P 544/544/145], p. 216, Harold Balme letter, January 21, 1925.
65. *FO 405/247* [P 544/544/145], p. 217, Harold Balme letter, January 21, 1925.

restoring order in the educational world, many reformers believed, schools would become a stabilizing influence, define the nation, and socialize Chinese students to be loyal subjects. With education playing a central role in this process of nation-defining, any institutions controlled by Russians, Japanese, or Christian missionaries represented a threat. Advocating China's right to shape its own development, educators demanded that China's government regulate foreign schools.[66]

Disagreements, however, divided Chinese educators about the best way to proceed. Inspired by liberal commitments to cultural reform, Hu Shi and Jiang Menglin asserted that good education must remain independent of politics. To promote their views, these and other moderate cultural reformists founded journals—including *New Education (Xin jiaoyu), Chinese Educational Review (Jiaoyu zazhi)* and *China's Educational World (Zhonghua jiaoyu jie)*—and set up educational associations—including the Society for the Promotion of New Education, the National Federation of Provincial Educational Associations, and the National Society for the Advancement of Education. Acknowledging the contributions of mission schools and the value of educational autonomy, liberal reformists helped squelch a drive by Beijing's Education Ministry to nationalize mission schools in mid-1924.[67] Nevertheless, even the liberals rejected the missionaries' Christianizing agenda, favoring instead a secular program promoting pragmatic curricula and social improvement. Thus, in July 1922, Hu Shi called for a ban on religious education in elementary schools on the grounds that it limited student individuality and potential.[68]

Other reformers repudiated notions that education could be independent at all. Viewing culture and education as extensions of political power, critics such as Cai Yuanpei claimed that the government should control all national education and forbid all religious instruction.[69] Nationalistic organizations were even more antagonistic toward mission schools. Young China Party *(Zhongguo qingnian dang)* propaganda, for example, urged the destruction of all "domestic traitors" and "foreign authoritarian forces"—Chinese Christians and foreign missionaries, respectively. Founded in Paris in 1923 by Zeng Qi and Li Huang, the Young China Party was a secret organization that used the name Chinese Nationalistic Youth Corps *(Zhongguo guojia zhuyi qingnian tuan)* as a front. Many Young China leaders were former anarchists who strongly opposed religion in general and stridently advocated secular

---

66. Foreigners noticed. As one report indicated, "The strongest unifying force in the land has been that of education." *FO* 405/247 [P 544/544/145], p. 214, Anti-Christian Movement memorandum, March 5, 1925. Lutz notes that China's literati instinctively focused on education as a means of creating the "nation." Lutz, *Chinese Politics and Christian Missions*, pp. 107-109.
67. Lutz, *Chinese Politics and Christian Missions*, p. 116.
68. Yip, *Religion, Nationalism, and Chinese Students*, p. 34.
69. Cai Yuanpei, "Beijing feizongjiao dahui yanjiang zhi yi."

education as fundamental to China's unification and independence. To them, mission schools not only represented a denationalizing force, they also diluted what education they imparted with religious indoctrination.[70] By the fall of 1924, the Young China Party had set up branches of the Anti-Christian Federation, the Educational Rights Movement, and its own Awakening Lion Society in schools ranging from universities to middle schools throughout China. Meanwhile, other activists, such as Chen Qitian, savaged mission education in Young China Party journals such as *Awakening Lion Weekly (Xingshi zhoubao)*.[71]

With student agitators, educator reformers, and nationalistic groups all clamoring for government control over mission schools, Beijing's Education Ministry could scarcely resist. According to Shandong Christian University's president Harold Balme, educational societies in particular carried irresistible weight with the Ministry and could get their recommendations acted upon "in almost every instance."[72] Under pressure, the education minister promulgated new regulations in the autumn of 1922. Although the changes ostensibly sought to democratize curricula in accordance with the views of John Dewey and Paul Monroe of Columbia University, most educators read in the reforms a strong push for greater secularization and centralization within a national system.[73] In July 1924, for example, leaders of the National Society for the Advancement of Education argued strongly that parochial schools should be nationalized, closed down, or at least strictly regulated. Moderates toned down demands but still sanctioned a resolution calling for government registration of foreign schools and constraints on schools engaged in "aggressive" designs.[74]

The Educational Rights Movement—so named for its drive to restore Chinese control over national education—reached a watershed on October 15, 1924 when the National Federation of Provincial Educational Associations convened its annual conference at Kaifeng. The Federation, a consortium of provincial educational systems, maintained no political standing and could not enforce its decisions. Nevertheless, its declarations routinely impacted

---

70. Protesting GMD and CCP ties to the Soviets, the Young China Party avoided close association with either party and focused on cultural/educational issues rather than political/economic ones. *FO* 405/248 [F3250/194/10], p. 43, Enclosure, extract from *Peking Leader*, May 22, 1925; Yip, *Religion, Nationalism, and Chinese Students*, p. 34.
71. Lutz, *Chinese Politics and Christian Missions*, pp. 113-114. Chen also used his position as editor of *China Educational World (Zhonghua jiaoyu jie)* to attack foreign education in China.
72. *FO* 405/247 [P 544/544/145], p. 216, Harold Balme letter, January 21, 1925.
73. Lutz, *Chinese Politics and Christian Missions*, p. 110. Specific objectives were championed by organizations such as the Chinese Vocational Educational Association and the Mass Education Society.
74. The conference was held in Nanjing. "Zhonghua jiaoyu daijin she chudeng jiaoyuzu yijue an," in *Guonei jinshinian lai zhi zongjiao sichao*, comp. Zhang, pp. 271-272. Attention focused primarily on middle and primary schools. *FO* 405/247 [P 544/544/145], p. 217, Harold Balme letter, January 21, 1925.

government educational policy and represented ideals to which many Chinese educators subscribed. Describing mission school education as "religious propaganda" *(zongjiao zhi xuanchuan)* and "political aggression" *(zhengzhi shang zhi qinlue)* masquerading as charity, delegates in Kaifeng issued two statements. The first summarily demanded that foreign schools: (1) accept government registration or face punishment; (2) comply with national and provincial laws regarding school establishment, teacher qualifications, government supervision, student tuition, and protocol; and (3) restrict religious preaching. The second clarified point three, calling for: (1) a ban on religious teaching, proselytizing, scripture reading, prayer, and any other religious activity, (2) strict government supervision to limit such activities, and (3) total equality of all students and teachers—Christian or otherwise.[75] In the spring of 1925, the Beijing regime confirmed the Kaifeng statements by ordering mission schools to register with the Education Ministry, adding government pressure to the agitative variety mission schools already faced.

Compared to the Beijing government, which actively pushed mission school regulation, Guangzhou's revolutionary regime had little to show for itself. The contrast was striking. GMD/CCP leaders enjoyed unrivaled influence within the Anti-Christian Movement, both through low-level agents and prominent organizations such as The Anti-Christian Federation which hosted an executive committee comprised fully of Nationalist members.[76] GMD aid sustained the National Student Union while CCP leaders headed New Youth, both of which were extremely active within the Anti-Christian Movement. Leaders of both parties, meanwhile, headed the Great Anti-Imperialism League based in Beijing. In Guangzhou, the Youth Ministry investigated Christian student groups, organized rallies, held a five-day conference for youth group leaders, and established *dangtuan* in all institutions and groups, including Christian schools. (Since most revolutionary students had already withdrawn from it, Holy Trinity College posed a problem, prompting the Ministry to matriculate new students in order to formulate a Trinity *dangtuan*; Lingnan University, meanwhile, hosted seven party-controlled work groups to carry out GMD mandates.)[77]

Given its interest in anti-Christian agitation, it is peculiar to note the party's reluctance to challenge Christian institutions with any official regulatory efforts. While Beijing's Education Ministry pressured mission schools

---

75. "Quanguo shengjiaoyuhui lianhe huiyi jue an," in *Guonei jinshinian lai zhi zongjiao sichao*, comp. Zhang, pp. 339-342. For the entire declaration see "Quanguo jiaoyuhui lianhehui dishijie nianhui gailue," *Jiaoyu zazhi* 16:12 (December 1924): 1-9.

76. Chao lists the executive committee: Tang Gongxian (CCP member); Xu Hengyao; Li Chunfan (editor of the GMD's *Minguo ribao*); Zhang Qiuren (CCP member); and Gao Erbo (secretary of the Guomindang's Propaganda Bureau in Shanghai). Chao, "The Chinese Indigenous Church Movement," p. 177.

77. "Qingnianbu gongzuo baogao," June 25, 1925. A *dangtuan* was also established within the Guangzhou Student Federation.

and sought registration, the southern regime remained silent. Thriving agitation in the GMD base represented the model for student mobilization everywhere. Nevertheless, *official* governmental efforts to bring Christian institutions under control were noticeably absent, leaving *de facto* initiative and leadership to the Beijing regime—even when educational rights demonstrations arose in Guangzhou. Anti-Christian calls for registration could only infer Beijing's regulations because Guangzhou had not produced any.

Actually, the GMD regime was far more interested in denying ties to the Anti-Christian Movement than in legislating control over mission schools. Even when directing anti-Christian agitation, revolutionary officials preferred to remain behind the scenes, and manage operations through popular, ancillary groups rather than through Guomindang branch offices.[78] In communications with foreign authorities, the Guangzhou regime strongly denied involvement in anti-Christian activity. On February 11, 1925, for example, Sun Ke ardently rejected allegations that the party viewed Christianity as the vanguard of imperialism, harbored an anti-Christian agenda, or even contributed to the Anti-Christian Movement. While conceding that some revolutionaries backed anti-Christian activity as individuals, Sun maintained that others supported the religion's enterprises, especially party leaders of the Christian faith such as himself, Sun Yat-sen, Song Qingling, Xu Qian (justice minister), Wei Que (Sidney Kok Wei, member of the education committee), Song Ziwen (T. V. Soong, finance minister), and Kong Xiangxi (H. H. Kung).[79] Such rebuttals were not unpersuasive. One Christian leader blamed agitation on the CCP, student unions, and nationalistic groups, arguing that the Nationalists maintained no anti-Christian agenda because Sun Ke had so stated.[80] Even critics convinced that the party did aim to seize mission schools could produce no evidence beyond circumstantial support for anti-Christian organizations offered by some officials.[81]

GMD Leverage, Revolutionary Advantage

Despite the Guomindang regime's revolutionary image and close ties to agitative forces, Christian institutions in Guomindang territory enjoyed relative freedom from government interference. Party officials surveyed conditions in Guangdong's mission schools but otherwise left them alone, making Beijing oddly more "revolutionary" in its pursuit of educational rights than Guangzhou.[82] Yip Ka-che implies that factional divisions be-

78. Yip, *Religion, Nationalism, and Chinese Students*, p. 40.
79. "Guanyu Guomindang yu Jidujiao di taolun," *Shengming* (January 1926): 1-2. See Yip, *Religion, Nationalism, and Chinese Students*, p. 65.
80. Lee, "The Anti-Christian Movement in Canton," pp. 220-226.
81. Guangzhou's New Student Society, for example, received some support. Yip, *Religion, Nationalism, and Chinese Students*, pp. 39-40.
82. "Qingnianbu gongzuo baogao," June 25, 1925; *USDS* 893.00/6105, Jenkins to Secretary of

ANTI-IMPERIALISM*

tween pro-Christian and anti-Christian officials produced these inconsistencies. His evidence, however, is unconvincing.[83] Another possible explanation claims that threatening crises distracted party attention to the point that officials could not implement reconstructive reforms or formulate a broader educational vision. In October 1924, for example, while northern educators were meeting in Kaifeng, Nationalist leaders were still engaged in the bloodily suppression of the Merchants Association. Even this argument, however, collapses when the fate of Guangdong's *Chinese* educational institutions is considered.

Party interest in Chinese schools appeared quite early. In February 1921, Sun Yat-sen's second Guangzhou regime issued provisional municipal regulations that outlined the primary responsibilities of the Education Bureau: (1) run all municipal schools and reformatories; (2) supervise private schools within the municipality; (3) suppress theaters and public entertainment establishments; and (4) oversee charitable institutions and their activities.[84] Later reforms sought to raise private school performance to match GMD standards and enroll young Chinese in school—threatening parents and employers who might find other uses for them. In April 1923, Guangzhou's hundreds of traditional academies *(sishu)* and non-accredited private Chinese schools were closely scrutinized. Those complying with regulations found themselves welcomed into the southern government's educational system; non-compliant schools were ordered disbanded and their students distributed among Education Bureau schools.[85] To help private schools and *sishu* improve and ready themselves for inclusion within the party system, special "circulating professors" *(xunhui jiaoshou)* were rotated from school to school.[86]

In 1924, party interest expanded when the Youth Ministry surveyed all Guangzhou schools as a precursor to instituting centralizing reforms.[87] Backed by popular agitation, government intrusion encountered little resistance. By mid-1924, through his posts on the CEC, the Financial Management Committee, and Guangdong University's administration, youth minister Zou Lu commanded "absolute control" over Guangdong's educational world.[88] In early August, all municipal school staffers were ordered to

State, Guangzhou, February 19, 1925.
83. Yip asserts that Sun's two funerals, one Christian and one secular, reveal factional tension within the party. Yip, *Religion, Nationalism, and Chinese Students*, pp. 65-66.
84. Huang, *Yisui zhi Guangzhou*, p. 9.
85. "Guangzhoushi diyiqi chouban yiwu jiaoyu jihua shu," in Huang, *Yisui zhi Guangzhou*, p. 71; "Guangzhoushi shixing yiwu jiaoyu zhanxing guicheng," in Huang, *Yisui zhi Guangzhou*, p. 69.
86. The circulating professors added specialty courses (i.e., music and physical education), watched hygiene, and raised performance, among other things. "Jiaoyuju xunhui jiaoshou zhanxing zhangcheng" in Huang, *Yisui zhi Guangzhou*, pp. 75-77.
87. "Guangzhou gexiao yilan biao," 1924.
88. *Huazi ribao* (March 25, 1924): 3.

join the Guomindang.[89] In September, the party's provincial government ordered all teaching and administrative staff in provincial schools to join the party.[90] By January 1925, the Youth Ministry had set up the GMD School Principals Association to promote Nationalist educational policy.[91] On January 26, Youth Ministry officials met with GMD educators to identify how education could further party objectives.[92] In February, party authorities commanded *all* staff, principals, and teachers in *all* Chinese educational institutions to join the party *en masse*. Anticipated resistance from independent thinkers was squelched with the warning: "Any message conveyed from University of Guangdong students or faculty that the college is the highest seat of learning and that freedom of thought is imperative *will be disregarded*."[93] [Emphasis added.] That same month, the Youth Ministry introduced plans for instituting universal education.[94] By March, a CEC committee began inspecting textbooks to weed out "anti-revolutionary," "capitalistic," and "imperialist" curricula.[95] On March 13, Zou ordered *dangtuan* to report on their particular school's political conditions, student organizations, relative support of GMD objectives, and so forth.[96] In April, the CEC announced plans to change the name of Guangdong University to Sun Yat-sen University as the first step toward instituting "true reform."[97]

GMD demands for compliance were backed by considerable weight. In Taishan, a Chinese middle school principal was dismissed for showing insufficient sympathy to the memory of Sun Yat-sen. (He was accused of raising the five-color flag of the early Republic instead of the GMD flag, failing to attend a memorial service for Sun, and twice "feasting" during the month of mourning Sun's death.)[98] Similarly, a new middle school, a girl's normal school, and a Chinese medical school were all threatened with closure unless they better followed party directives and regulations. Private Chinese

---

89. (Discussion item #4), *1-ZXWH*, vol. 3 (July 31, 1924). All Education Bureau staff had one month to join, while municipal school principals and teachers had until the end of summer vacation.

90. Yuan, "The 'Partification' of Education," p. 36.

91. Zou ordered further surveys of all public and private school principals and organized a committee to investigate textbooks. "Zhongyang qingnianbu zhi jiaoyu tingju han," January 21, 1925; "Shisinian yiyuefen gongzuo baogao," January 31, 1925. The Guomindang employed the Principals Association for numerous tasks, including universal education, entertaining and comforting the troops, and so forth. See "Shisi eryuefen gongzuo baogao," February or March, 1925. The Guangzhou Education Bureau claimed that all public school principals belonged to the Principals Association, but private school principals did not. "Guangzhou shi jiaoyuju zhi zhongyang qingnianbu han," February 7, 1925.

92. "Shisinian yiyuefen gongzuo baogao," January 31, 1925.

93. "Guomindang shixing dangjiaoyu zhengce," *Jiaoyu zazhi* 17: 2 (February 1925): 16.

94. "Qingnianbu pingmin jiaoyu yundong buzou," February, 1925.

95. *CWR* 32 (March 28, 1925): 114.

96. "Zhongyang qingnianbu zhi gedi xuexiao han," March 13, 1925.

97. "Zhongyang zhixing weiyuanhui zhi Xu Chongqing han," April 16, 1925.

98. *CWR* 32 (May 2, 1925): 263.

schools were particularly vulnerable. By March 1925, after some efforts to raise educational standards in Guangzhou's numerous *sishu*, the party praised 160, closed nine for low teacher competency, and threatened 361 with closure unless improvements were made.[99]

The Nationalist regime clearly possessed an educational vision and the resources to implement it, at least over Chinese schools. Party silence vis-à-vis Christian mission schools, therefore, must have had another explanation. The most obvious, of course, is that any policy concerning mission schools first had to account for foreign ties, alleged treaty rights, and imperialist intervention. Surrounded by other military threats, the last thing Guangzhou officials needed was an incident that might attract foreign gunboats. While this argument accounts for soft GMD attitudes toward Christian institutions, it—like the others—begins with the assumption that there was only one way to deal with mission schools. Indeed, any attempt to explain Nationalist hesitancy presumes weakness, suggesting that the party lacked sufficient power to formulate a stronger policy. However accurate they may be, however, such arguments do not acknowledge revolutionary strengths. In short, *official* party refusal to regulate Christian schools does not necessarily mean GMD disinterest, panic, or factional paralysis, nor does it prove that measures to influence Christian education were not being taken. It *does* indicate that revolutionaries did not follow the same path used by Beijing.

Steps *were* being taken to bring mission schools under party control. They simply took a different direction. Through 1924 and early 1925, the party's primary focus was to expand agitative influence throughout the Christian enterprise. In the fall of 1924, the Youth Ministry began surveying conditions at Guangzhou's Christian schools. A report on Lingnan University dated October 10, 1924, for example, claimed that students felt alienated from and resented school authorities but respected revolutionary objectives. Party sympathizers enjoyed status within the student body but were often criticized over matters of GMD policy. Faculty members were split between those supportive of students and those siding with the imperialists. Some Lingnan students engaged in low-level revolutionary action, such as fund-raising, boycotting Sunday services, or attending demonstrations, but many—the children of local businessmen—had been strongly affected by "American-style capitalism" and required considerable reforming. At the same time, aggressive efforts to revolutionize these "Americanized" students would likely prompt powerful reactionary forces to intervene. In spite of its dismal assessments, the report did give some cause for celebration. Ling-

---

99. *CWR* 34 (November 7, 1925): 242; *CWR* 32 (March 21, 1925): 86. Reports also claimed that *sishu* remained popular despite the closings and that the number had actually risen to 532. After investigations, a government oversight committee declared that 27 were well-conducted, 133 performed at acceptable rates, and 372 would be closed unless significant improvements were made. *CWR* 32 (March 14, 1925): 51.

nan's Agricultural Department was administered by Chinese rather than foreigners, and at least one Lingnan official had already proposed removing Christian curricula and turning school administration over to Chinese control.[100]

Unlike Beijing, which routinely broadcast top-down policies it could not enforce, Guangzhou adopted a bottom-up approach. While Beijing sought foreign complicity by fiat from without, Guangzhou used agitation to inspire or pressure mission school administrators to reform from within. While Beijing openly defied foreign privilege, Guangzhou officials spun illusions of detached disinterest. Although encouraged and supported by party leaders, anti-Christianity existed quite independent of them. As a result, while the Guomindang regime was accountable for anti-Christian destruction in Guangdong, it could not necessarily be held liable for any disruption arising under the banner of anti-Christian organizations elsewhere. Party officials, such as Guangdong's Commissioner of Foreign Affairs Fu Bingchang and Chief of Police General Wu Tiecheng, routinely promised to end disorder and offered assurances that no "responsible" government officials approved of anti-Christian agitation. Blame, they declared, lay with a minority headed by Liao Zhongkai or Huangpu cadets. Guangdong Governor Hu Hanmin, GMD foreign affairs minister Wu Chaogang, and Sun Ke went even further, entertaining foreign consuls at a dinner party to assuage concerns about anti-Christian activism and to pledge regime intervention against its excesses.[101] To foreigners, at least, anti-Christianity was presented as a popular, not an official, phenomenon. Foreigners seeking evidence of GMD involvement struggled to find any, satisfying U.S. Consul General Douglas Jenkins enough that he could declare with confidence, "The consular body has taken no official action in respect to [anti-Christian] agitation because it is generally felt that the matter can best be handled by the Chinese themselves."[102]

Stimulating anti-Christian agitation while also denying any hand in it meant that party leaders could influence change from a safe yet commanding position on the sidelines. Nevertheless, even dual-prong tactics illuminate but one small portion of the larger political picture. It has already been implied that from the perspective of Guangzhou, anti-Christianity delivered ideological and cultural value far beyond the narrow task of bringing mission schools to heel. The question of why Christian schools remained untouched by state regulation, in short, may be the wrong one because, in some ways, the party gained more by *not* extending state oversight. Anti-Christianity

100. "Guangzhou Lingnan daxue diaocha biao," October 7 and 10, 1924.

101. *USDS* 893.00/5993, Jenkins to Secretary of State, Guangzhou, January 6, 1925; *USDS* 893.00/5994, Jenkins to Secretary of State, Guangzhou, January 7, 1925; *USDS* 893.00/6026, Jenkins to Secretary of State, Guangzhou, January 16, 1925.

102. *USDS* 893.00/5994, Jenkins to Department of State, Guangzhou, January 7, 1925.

inspired agitative energy, attracted popular support, and detached foreign systems from their Chinese base, giving the party something to show for its anti-imperialist platform. Championing cultural unity gave the revolution a safe focus, allowing party officials to deflect attention away from Guangzhou's severe political and economic problems as well as sidestep conflict with localist Chinese interests tied to the political and economic interests of the imperialist-dominated *status quo*. The Anti-Christian Movement's far-flung network provided top party leaders a mechanism for projecting influence beyond Guangdong and expanding leverage among other nationalistic organizations. Anti-Christianity also served as a "nexus of common cultural interest" through which the revolution could popularize its version of the Chinese "nation" while elevating the threat of a dangerous (but vulnerable) "other" and defining GMD nationalism in contrast to it.[103] In short, anti-Christianity enjoyed a higher revolutionary calling than merely co-opting mission institutions.

Ideological and cultural influence, however, was only the beginning. With a China-wide system in place, the Anti-Christian Movement also provided potent political leverage against Guangzhou's domestic rivals. According to contemporary observers, one reason that party leaders intentionally excused themselves from a prominent official role in student agitation was so they could entangle non-revolutionary regimes in awkward situations. In early 1925, for example, Chongqing's British consul expressed suspicions that Guangzhou stimulated anti-Christian and student agitation to embarrass Sichuan's provincial government as an act of revenge for Sichuan's expulsion of GMD officials a year earlier.[104] Circumstantial evidence substantiated such mistrust. Agitators and radicalized students angered at slow government efforts to pursue educational rights often attacked political figures. In the spring of 1925, for example, students from the Russian College stormed the Beijing Foreign Office, demanding that the director of their school be sacked. At roughly the same time, students at Beijing's Girls' Normal University voted the principal out of office, seized control of the campus, cordoned off the grounds to "former" administrators, and took over all school operations.[105]

Government efforts to contain student disturbances often enough only stimulated more. Anticipating student disruptions in conjunction with Na-

---

103. Lutz, *Chinese Politics and Christian Missions*, p. 102; Duara, *Rescuing History From the Nation*, p. 103.
104. *FO* 405/247 [F1260/194/10], p. 207, Enclosure 4, Archer to Macleay, Chongqing, February 6, 1925.
105. (The Foreign Office oversaw the Russian College because it was supported by proceeds from the Chinese Eastern Railway for the purpose of teaching Russian and training railway workers.) Heavily implied in Dailey's account is the assumption that if *all* authorities met student disruption with stiff resistance, agitation would disappear. Dailey, "Bolshevik Students Put Check on American Donations," p. 357.

tional Humiliation Day on May 7, for example, Beijing authorities held a police review in Central Park (where the students had planned to meet), banned parades, and proclaimed a school holiday. Angered at the regime's lack of support, students wrecked the house of education minister Zhang Shizhao and beat up policemen sent to protect it. Authorities arrested seventeen student leaders but only incited further demonstrations the next day when throngs of students, including many from Christian schools, denounced the government, the education minister, and the police for buckling to foreign demands. Students then stormed the residence of Marshall Duan Qirui, China's provisional chief executive, demanding the dismissal of the minister Zhang and redress for the injuries they had sustained during their clashes with police earlier. Restrictions did nothing to slow student zeal, but their failure deeply impacted entangled officials. After the student attacks, Zhang begged Duan to accept his resignation before fleeing with his family to the safety of Tianjin.[106]

Student agitation was powerful. As one report indicated, National Humiliation Day had turned into the Beijing regime's "Humiliation Day," especially after the arrested student leaders were released with government apologies and without being charged.[107] The anecdote opening this chapter demonstrated how a handful of Boy Scouts could debase and/or threaten even foreign and militarist authorities. Encouraged by their successes, student activists only became more emboldened. High-profile cases, however, eventually convinced some local leaders to stand firm. Hunan's governor responded to student agitations in Changsha by canceling anti-Christmas activities scheduled for the end of 1924. Consular reports claimed that the governor of Shaanxi was also "sick of students" and had decided to crack down on them.[108] In January 1926, Hubei militarists went even further. Warned by a British petroleum industry employee that newly arrived youth agitators from Wuchang would enflame student disruptions in Xiangyang, military authorities ordered the local magistrate to arrest the two agents on January 10. One was captured, but the other escaped and incited three hundred students to gather at the magistrate's yamen to demand the release of his detained cohort. When the magistrate refused, students attacked, cursing and beating him about the head. Bodyguards fired their guns into the air, attracting the notice of troops and the local general stationed nearby. Believing that the general had come to help them, the students cheered, but they soon

---

106. Zhang was also concurrently the Minister of Justice. *FO* 405/248 [F2794/144/10], pp. 22-23, Palairet to Chamberlain, Beijing, May 22, 1925; Dailey, "Bolshevik Students Put Check on American Donations," p. 356; *USDS* 893.00/6320, Mayer to Secretary of State, Beijing, May 19, 1925.
107. "The Government's Humiliation Day," *Peking and Tientsin Times* (May 13, 1925).
108. Dailey, "Bolshevik Students Put Check on American Donations," p. 356; *FO* 405/247 [F1260/194/10], pp. 203-204, Palairet to Chamberlain, Beijing, February 25, 1925.

found that he had other plans. Twenty-seven demonstrators were summarily arrested, scattering the others. Local authorities closed all schools, severely reprimanded their principals for not maintaining order, sentenced one Wuchang agitator to three years in prison, and ordered the arrest of any student creating disruptions. According to reports, most Xiangyang students left the city, while those that remained dared not appear in public.[109]

As more and more Christian school students became radicalized and sought to prove their revolutionary vigor through agitation, their bright reputations as docile, obedient citizens tarnished, prompting fierce government backlashes. Beijing Methodist Academy students, for example, who had participated heavily in the attacks against minister Zhang, were subsequently set upon by police who swarmed Academy grounds, beating up any suspicious-looking student they encountered. In short, the time when a regional military commander could laugh about rowdy Boy Scouts did not last.

Once again, however, this development also advantaged the Nationalists. Swelling anti-Christian and anti-imperialist agitation forced local authorities to defend themselves as well as imperialist interests from social disruption and implicating international incidents. Each time local officials suppressed agitation, however, they weakened their own legitimacy among the revolutionized masses and alienated activist students, peasants, and workers, deeply tearing the social fabric of Chinese society outside the revolutionary base. Given the variety of political options produced by anti-Christianity inside Guangdong and out, the situation of Guangzhou's revolutionary government appears far less weak than political reports seemed to indicate.

---

109. *FO* 405/251 [F1521/307/10], pp. 12-13, Enclosure 2, student disruption and boycott report, Fancheng, January 14, 1926.

5. Control and Expansion
—Severing the Popular Roots of Imperialism, June 1925 - June 1926

The workers have in their hands the most effective weapon for the destruction of imperialism. This weapon, as you can understand, is the strike which you have instituted. That the strike is an effective weapon is a recognized fact throughout the country. Its effectiveness increases as its sphere expands. Our present movement should not be confined to a fixed locality, like Canton [Guangzhou], for instance. . . . British residents who are willing to obey Chinese laws and jurisdiction shall have our adequate protection for their lives and properties. Those who refuse to put themselves under the control of the Chinese laws shall be driven out of the country.[1]
   —Zhou Enlai, Chief Political Officer of the GMD army, November 13, 1925

On November 7, 1925, a young and energetic Zhou Enlai stood proudly triumphant before expectant crowds in the eastern Guangdong city of Shantou. As the Guomindang military's chief political officer, it was his job to rally popular support. Generals Chiang Kai-shek and He Yingqin sat nearby awaiting their turn, but, for the moment at least, Zhou owned the rostrum as he recounted why the whole province celebrated the party's latest achievements.

There was much to review. Just eight months earlier, eastern Guangdong had been part of Chen Jiongming's sprawling base and was mobilizing to destroy the revolution. Through February, as Sun Yat-sen's health worsened and party rule foundered, neighboring warlords took advantage. Launching a pincer campaign against Guangzhou, Chen's forces marched from the east while Yunnan militarist Tang Jiyao drove from the west. In March, however, the campaign met a shocking defeat when Nationalist troops dispersed Chen's armies and Tang's dispirited forces abandoned their plans.

Shortly thereafter, the guest armies—supposed "allies" of the Nationalists—initiated an anti-revolutionary crusade of their own. Yunnan commanders asked Britain to help them help topple the southern regime and its

---

1. *FO* 405/250 [F110/1/10], p. 19, Zhou Enlai speech of November 12, Shantou, November 13, 1925.

"Bolshevik" extremists—identified as Liao Zhongkai, Zou Lu, and Chiang Kai-shek. The British refused, but party leaders took notice.[2] In June, therefore, once Tan Yankai's army returned from Jiangxi, it was immediately ordered to help Chiang's Huangpu cadets drive Yang Ximin's Yunnan and Liu Zhenhuan's Guangxi mercenaries out of Guangdong. Once again revolutionary forces prevailed. By June 12, the party enjoyed exclusive military control over its base.

Two days later, Nationalist leaders met to reframe Guangdong's political order. On July 1, the Guomindang founded a national government and began forming all requisite and concomitant legal, political, military, and financial organs. The Guangdong provincial and Guangzhou municipal governments were also reorganized. By the end of the month, the southern regime possessed a national administration rivaling that of Beijing.[3] Under the direction of Wang Jingwei, head of the GMD left-wing, Guangzhou authorities redoubled their commitment to mass activism and anti-imperialism.

Extraordinary advances notwithstanding, Zhou's rendition of recent revolutionary triumphs was still building to climax, for he had not accounted for progress against the imperialists. In mid-1925, despite exciting developments vis-à-vis regional rivals, party leaders could not calm the lingering fear that the northern warlords and/or Hong Kong authorities might attack Guangzhou, completing the task that nearby merchant, guest army, and warlord lackeys had left unfinished. On June 26, Chiang Kai-shek warned,

> The [GMD] Government should complete within three to six months military preparations for an armed struggle against the British. British influence in the Far East has indeed reached a climax! I believe that, besides employing peaceful means of struggle (such as a boycott of British goods), our Party should start military preparations to be completed within half a year for a long period of struggle against the British (which may last for three to five years).[4]

As it turned out, Chiang's "peaceful means of struggle" proved far more explosive and effective than he realized. Spark was provided by the May Thirtieth and the Shaji Incidents. On May 30, British troops fired into a crowd of Shanghai demonstrators, killing thirteen and wounding dozens more. Incensed, Guangzhou's anti-imperialist mass organizations responded.

---

2. *FO* 405/248 [F2789/2/10], pp. 17-18, Enclosure, Jamieson to Palairet, Guangzhou, May 8, 1925.
3. Provincial and municipal reorganizations occurred July 3 and July 4, respectively. The CEC appointed a National Government Military Council on July 5 and the National Government's Finance Ministry on July 24. Wilbur and How, *Missionaries of Revolution*, pp. 153-155. Top appointments included: General Xu Chongzhi as minister of war, Hu Hanmin as minister of foreign affairs, Liao Zhongkai as minister of finance, and Xu Qian as minister of justice. *FO* 405/248 [F3819/194/10], p. 155, Enclosure 2, Chinese press notes, July 4, 1925.
4. "Chiang Kai-shek's Letter to Bliukher," in *Missionaries of Revolution*, p. 503.

On June 23, as a parade of 100,000 protesters made their way along Shaji Street, however, British and French troops watching from Shamian suddenly opened fire with pistols and machine guns. In all, sixty-one Chinese were killed and at least another 150 were wounded. Popular fury resulting from the two massacres elevated anti-foreign energies to record heights, precipitating a China-wide boycott against all things British. Merchants cleared their shelves of British goods. Employees deserted British employers. Ports refused service to British ships. In Wuhan, local chambers of commerce helped organize massive land and river parades that attracted, as one foreigner described, "practically all mercantile and civilian organizations in Hankou, Wuchang and Hanyang."[5] Similar demonstrations erupted in Changsha and Zhengzhou where worker, peasant, and merchant volunteer corps set up strike committees to institute and enforce the boycott.[6] Soon boycott organizations and agitation could be found throughout the country.

In north and central China, Anti-British Boycott vigor faded after two months or so, once merchants found it too costly to maintain, but in the Guomindang's Guangdong base it showed unusual stamina.[7] Leading the charge was the Guangzhou Strike Committee (GSC). Carrying out its boycott mandate, labor leaders controlled warehouses for confiscated goods, operated their own courts to manage strike offenders, and directed strike pickets to enforce Committee rulings. The GSC maintained a treasury, lodging-houses, a commissariat, armed police, and even jails.[8] Its greatest strength, however, stemmed from the thousands of Hong Kong workers who flooded Guangzhou to support the boycott. By mid-September, some 51,851 strikers had registered with the GSC in Guangzhou alone.[9] By January 1926, over three thousand of these had been organized into picket lines, equipped with uniforms, guns, and a dozen patrol boats, all dedicated to severing ties with Hong Kong and Macao at Guangdong's nineteen major ports.[10] Pickets searched persons and property, seized "contraband," repulsed ships touching at Hong Kong, and cut travel to and from "imperialist" territories. In many

---

5. *CWR* 34 (September 19, 1925): 64. The Hankou Chamber of Commerce even dispatched delegates to upper Yangzi districts to help spread the Anti-British Boycott. *CWR* 34 (September 12, 1925): 44; *CWR* 34 (September 5, 1925): 24.

6. *CWR* 34 (September 19, 1925): 65. Chongqing merchant volunteers scoured the city for British and Japanese goods. *CWR* 34 (October 17, 1925): 177.

7. Pinched by the boycott, the Hankou Chamber of Commerce sought relief for needy merchants from Marshall Xiao Yaonan but without success. *CWR* 34 (October 10, 1925): 144. By late October, Boycott enforcement had fallen to Guomindang agents, irritating the Hankou Chamber of Commerce which refused to support a movement headed by a party that had caused its members so much trouble. *CWR* 34 (October 31, 1925): 214.

8. Chan, *China, Britain, and Hong Kong*, pp. 181-182; Gannett, "Why Canton is Radical Center of Asia," p. 30.

9. *CWR* 34 (September 19, 1925): 66.

10. Chan, *China, Britain, and Hong Kong*, p. 183; *CWR* 35 (January 30, 1926): 262; *CWR* 35 (December 12, 1925): 53.

ways, the GSC resembled a government in its own right, operating independent of the Nationalist regime but sharing its role as a champion of Chinese sovereignty.

Economically, the boycott deflated British trade in south China. Shipping sank from over 2.2 million tons during the last five months of 1924 to just 260 thousand tons during corresponding months in 1925. What did manage to get shipped barely supplied Shamian which had become a ghost town of sandbags, barbed wire, and armed guards. The British consul, as one reporter put it, sat "alone in his office with nothing whatever to do . . . except to meditate on June 23."[11] British elsewhere in Guangdong supplied and unloaded their own food since no Chinese would sell to them. Meanwhile, stripped of some 200 thousand skilled Chinese workers, Hong Kong's industrial productivity sank. Real estate values followed. Even the colony's ensuing tranquility was shattered when strikers stole into the New Territories to shoot at Hong Kong police and throw bombs at non-striking workers.[12]

Cresting anti-imperialism did not limit itself to boycott objectives but spilled over into other areas. On July 9, for example, soldiers burst into the English Presbyterian Mission compound located in the small community of Wujingfu near Shantou. After stripping, robbing, and beating what missionaries they found, troops looted the mission safe and ordered the foreigners to clear out within three days. Terrified, they left before that very evening. Reporting the incident to his superiors, one British official based in Beijing sternly warned, "Unless the central and provincial authorities take immediate steps to check the activities of the irresponsible agitators who are now inflaming the minds of both soldiers and common people against foreigners, the incident at Wujingfu will be followed by similar and perhaps even more serious outrages against the persons and property of foreign residents in other parts of China."[13]

Guangzhou authorities, however, were busy *stimulating* anti-imperialist agitation, not checking it. In November 1925, the party's Second Eastern Expedition captured Shantou and scattered the armies of Chen Jiongming. To counter the influence of localist interests—the base on which Chen had depended—Guangzhou rushed in one hundred propagandists and a battalion of strike pickets to institute the Anti-British Boycott in eastern Guangdong.[14] By November 7, Guomindang officers had stabilized military control to the

11. Gannett, "Why Canton is Radical Center of Asia," p. 30.

12. Gannett, "Why Canton is Radical Center of Asia," p. 30. British police arrested Guangzhou workers trying to visit Hong Kong for nothing more than possessing labor union cards. *CWR* 35 (December 26, 1925): 106; *CWR* 35 (February 27, 1926): 368; *CWR* 36 (March 27, 1926): 100; *CWR* 36 (April 3, 1926): 128; *CWR* 36 (May 1, 1926): 236.

13. *FO* 405/248 [F4126/194/10], pp. 264-265, Enclosure, Palairet to Soeu-ling, Beijing, July 15, 1925.

14. *CWR* 35 (February 13, 1926): 316; *USDS* 893.00/6080, Schurman to Secretary of State, Beijing, March 11, 1925.

point that they could begin addressing large rallies, such as the one featuring Zhou Enlai, Chiang Kai-shek, and He Yingqin.

Completing his account of major revolutionary advances over the last eight months, Zhou stopped reporting and began exhorting. He called the boycott strikers the "most effective weapon for the destruction of imperialism" and warned that the revolution could only free China's people and produce lasting peace if the people would support it.[15] Calling them the "pawns of imperialistic Hong Kong" and "servile dependents" of Britain, Zhou described how Chen's armies had "suppressed the people's patriotic movement, imperiled the constitution of our Revolutionary Government, and robbed the inhabitants of [Guangdong] of their wealth." Concluding his address, Zhou then identified what was needed specifically: "The many and varied disasters, sufferings and other perils that the Province of Kuangtung [Guangdong] has undergone during the past years were entirely the work of Ch'en Ch'iung-ming [Chen Jiongming] and his followers and *the result of treacherous conspiracies on the part of Imperialists*. For this reason we should overthrow Ch'en Ch'iung-ming's militarism, *just as we are overthrowing Imperialism*."[16] [Emphasis added.] Allegiance to Chen, in short, equaled association with imperialism.

Fiery anti-imperialistic speeches, as presented on November 7, translated directly into revolutionary benefit. With Guomindang leaders pledging imperialism's overthrow, aroused Shantou workers and merchants alike threw their weight behind the Anti-British Boycott, closing Guangdong's last open link to Hong Kong. New mass organizations spread quickly though the region, assisted in mop-up campaigns against Chen's followers, and helped check Shantou's localist interests. The consequences of defying GMD rule were heavy. On November 16, Chiang Kai-shek intimated what they were in an address to the Shantou Chamber of Commerce. After assuring merchants that the party harbored no plans to "communize" their property, he turned to discuss the fate of foreign property:

> You may rest assured, gentlemen, that in present-day China Communism is impossible. On the other hand, in Britain, Japan, America and France Communism must be introduced because in these countries there are real capitalists—oil kings, steel kings, automobile kings, etc., who besides devouring the small capitalists, cause the lower classes to go without their daily bread. Do you not think that Communism is necessary under such circumstances? I sincerely believe it is so. *I therefore*

15. *FO* 405/250 [F110/1/10], p. 19, Zhou Enlai speech of November 12, Shantou, November 13, 1925.

16. *FO* 405/250 [F408/1/10], p. 156-157, Enclosure 2, mass meeting speeches, Shantou, November 7, 1925. After Zhou, He Yingqin followed with his own anti-imperialist statements before Chiang Kai-shek reassured the crowd that overthrowing imperialism would be a "simple matter."

maintain that we should communize foreign, not Chinese, property.[17] [Emphasis added.]

The implications were clear. If Chen Jiongming's followers could be painted with the "imperialist" brush, so too could others who opposed the Nationalist regime. Labels designating what was "imperialist," after all, had less to do with nationality than political alignment. Withholding support for the revolution was all it took to be linked with imperialism and risk all one possessed.

Ironically, veiled threats aimed to keep localist interests in check were accompanied by strict warnings directed at revolutionary anti-imperialist organizations. Five days after the rally of November 7, Zhou Enlai again stood before a large gathering of Shantou labor unions. Filled with anti-imperialist content, his address climaxed with a vow that all foreigners refusing to submit to Guomindang rule would be expelled from China. At that point, however, Zhou suddenly qualified his remarks. Activism was necessary and powerful, he argued, but it had to adopt limits. In his words, "We strikers are not against the British residents as individuals; we are against Hong Kong imperialism. Beyond this, however, *all our acts should be highly civilized, because we are only at the stage of giving warnings and not at that of declaring war.*"[18] [Emphasis added.]

If Zhou had any specific incident in mind—like Wujingfu, for example—he gave no indication. What was clear was that although revolutionary authorities proudly trumpeted the power of popular anti-imperialism, they did not want to provoke a war. This left them walking a perilously thin line between arousing agitation with anti-imperialist propaganda on one hand and dampening agitative escalation with reminders of "civilized" action on the other. In sum, GMD anti-imperialism sought something short of its own rhetorical demands, something less than driving the imperialists into the sea. Statements encouraging attacks against "imperialist lackeys" such as Chen Jiongming showed little restraint, but calls for direct action against foreigners urged distinct restrictions.

Several valid explanations can account for Zhou's interest in limited anti-imperialism: fear of foreign reprisals, eagerness to impress the powers about GMD intentions, desire to maintain the moral high ground, and so forth. All legitimately contributed to CEC concerns about active mass organizations. The primary observation to be emphasized here, however, is that the party did not intend to use popular forces to attack imperialism as much as to undermine its local roots—the allies upon which imperialism depended.

---

17. *FO* 405/250 [F622/1/10], p. 292, Enclosure 2, Chiang Kai-shek speech, Shantou, November 16, 1925.
18. *FO* 405/250 [F110/1/10], pp. 18-19, Zhou Enlai speech of November 12, Shantou, November 13, 1925.

The Anti-British Boycott: GMD Political Control

As the uprising of October 1924 had already shown, localist interests such as the Merchants Corps were fully capable of challenging Nationalist power. Destroying the Corps' infrastructure and assimilating its institutions, however, had failed to reduce localist hostility. Through late 1924, seditious energies continued to fester. Some interests employed passive resistance or non-compliance. People hid in their homes, secreted valuables, or left Guangdong to avoid taxation, confiscations, or conscription. Proprietors took items off their shelves to avoid government imposts. Sellers hid old books to evade censors. Tow-boat, freight junk, steamer, and armament owners concealed property. Restaurants closed their doors, factories suspended operations, and merchants left town to avoid fines or taxes.[19]

Others used more active means to protest. One group demanded that authorities stop collecting stamp duties on contracts predating the Guomindang's rise to power. Junk owners complained of high protection fees. Radio enthusiasts denounced restrictions on wireless sets. Refugees sought redress for destroyed homes. The Chinese Shipping Merchants Guild took matters into its own hands, voluntarily offering its ships to GMD "service" but then rotating participation between ship owners so the burden would not fall on a few unfortunate individuals.[20] A steady stream of petitions sought relief from regime impositions, but it was widely acknowledged that pleas to the government had little or no effect.[21]

Angered that dealings through official channels proved so unproductive, some localists took proactive steps to a higher level, precipitating waves of demonstrative strikes and boycotts. Refusing to pay a new luxury tax, jewelry shops suspended business. Pawn shops threatened the same if pressed "loans" and license fees were not revoked. Guangzhou telegraph employees took to the streets to defy unpopular regime-appointed managers while students from the Girls' Industrial School boycotted their party-appointed principal.[22] Rickshaw coolies struck when ordered to join the party and were followed by workers at the Guangzhou-Hankou Railroad eager to protest political intrusion and nepotistic GMD management. In September 1925, a strike at the Guangzhou-Sanshui Railroad sought to nullify the appointment of their latest chief—Wang Jingwei's brother-in-law. Even Guangzhou's six thousand embroiderers of silk shawls and "dainty articles" launched protest

---

19. *CWR* 32 (April 18, 1925): 204; "Canton War Taxes," *Peking and Tientsin Times* (January 15, 1924); *CWR* 34 (October 31, 1925): 218; *CWR* 34 (November 14, 1925): 264.
20. *CWR* 34 (September 5, 1925): 23; *CWR* 34 (September 19, 1925): 66; *CWR* 34 (October 31, 1925): 216; *CWR* 34 (November 21, 1925): 288; *CWR* 35 (January 2, 1926): 140; *CWR* 35 (January 9, 1926): 168; *CWR* 35 (January 30, 1926): 262; *CWR* 35 (February 13, 1926): 316.
21. *CWR* 32 (April 4, 1925): 145; *CWR* 36 (March 27, 1926): 98.
22. *CWR* 32 (April 18, 1925): 204; *CWR* 34 (September 5, 1925): 23; *CWR* 34 (November 14, 1925): 262, 264.

walk-outs when the party ordered them to join a Guomindang union and march in political parades.[23] (They had no interest in politics and organized a strike to prove it!)

Localist unrest raised government alarm. It was popular, widespread, and often violently opposed to GMD policy. On May 1, 1925, government land surveyors were attacked by villagers fearful that the party aimed to confiscate public property and local cemeteries. Food hawkers in Xiaolan raided the local Nationalist Health Bureau and drove its chief out of town when he tried to license peddling and impose "quality" inspections. Near Taishan, after the local magistrate took over charitable institutions, two hundred blind inmates stormed and occupied his office for two days before troops drove them off. Even top officials were not immune. Ten thousand jade carvers and luxury industry workers threatened to wreck the home of Acting Generalissimo Hu Hanmin unless he repealed the hated luxury tax.[24]

Organizations spread. On February 20, 1925, the Merchants Association appointed a committee to form a new defense corps *(mintuan)* and ordered all firms with six employees or more to sponsor at least one volunteer or pay support.[25] Citing government failure to provide security, towns along shipping and railway routes set up corps to fend off bandits and maintain order.[26] Through 1925, the number of defensive militias climbed dramatically. Corps leaders in Dongguan and Luogang united multiple villages under mutual defense agreements.[27] To the regime's dismay, such organizations could quickly turn against GMD agents, officials, or even troops. Shunde volunteer corpsmen, for example, arrested and expelled female Labor Ministry agents for "inciting unrest." Similarly, villagers west of Guangzhou captured and "mistreated" the chair of the Guangzhou Women's Emancipation Association and her associates for spreading propaganda among the area's women.[28]

Popular animosity was more than an inconvenience, particularly when it intersected localist organizations and enemies outside Guangdong. The Merchants Association routinely solicited aid from overseas Chinese to oppose GMD rule while Hong Kong merchants promised to fund anyone willing to destroy "Bolshevism."[29] Strikes at the Guangzhou Water Works

---

23. *CWR* 34 (November 7, 1925): 242; *CWR* 34 (October 31, 1925): 218; *CWR* 32 (May 2, 1925): 263; *CWR* 34 (September 19, 1925): 66; *CWR* 34 (November 14, 1925): 264.

24. *CWR* 32 (May 16, 1925): 318-319; *CWR* 34 (November 14, 1925): 264; *CWR* 34 (November 7, 1925): vi; *CWR* 32 (May 9, 1925): 291.

25. *CWR* 32 (March 7, 1925): 21.

26. *CWR* 34 (October 17, 1925): 174. Village volunteers were hired and armed by railway management to guard rail lines. *CWR* 34 (November 14, 1925): 262.

27. *CWR* 34 (October 31, 1925): 216.

28. *CWR* 32 (March 21, 1925): 85-86; *CWR* 32 (March 14, 1925): 42; *CWR* 35 (January 16, 1926): 192.

29. *USDS* 893.00/5651, China Society of America to State Department, New York, October 14, 1924.

were rumored to be the work of residual Yunnanese interests hoping to weaken party control.[30] Reports explaining why Hong Kong merchants withheld flour imports and Shantou businessmen closed their shops also implied that outsiders were trying to undermine the Guomindang regime.[31]

Clear evidence of collusion rose in the spring of 1925 when Chinese kerosene dealers protested party taxes by arranging with the Standard Oil Company, the Asiatic Petroleum Oil Company, and the Texas Oil Company (among others) to block oil shipments to Guangdong. Nationalist officials set up a monopoly to regulate supplies but, as prices rose from $5.00 to $17.60 a case, popular animosity soared. In fact, conditions became so acute that monopoly officials dared not even announce price hikes. In Wuzhou and Nanning, bands of angry citizens drove the Oil Sales Bureau director out of town, forcing authorities to reduce prices to $5.50 a case. In outlying districts, crowds attacked monopoly agents, requiring troops to restore order. Workers, peasants, and other citizens denounced the monopoly for "enriching" party leaders while impoverishing everyone else, eventually inducing the government to abolish it outright.[32]

With the scapegoat guest armies gone and the regime shouldering all hostility, party officials backed down with surprising regularity. Protests by Guangzhou women compelled the government to scratch cosmetics from the luxury tax list; others got water stricken before officials dropped the tax outright.[33] Xinhui pawn shops forced the party to withdraw a $300 per shop impost by threatening a strike.[34] Guangzhou's butchers managed the same by warning that they would close the hog market.[35] Even as late as April 1926, merchant intimations of a rice boycott killed GMD plans to seize rice stored in foreign warehouses.[36] Unlike petitions, popular challenges to Nationalist authority got results, spawning further unrest each time the regime yielded.

Struggling to manage localist unrest, CEC leaders welcomed the Anti-British Boycott as a breath of fresh air. Strategically, it complimented Guangdong's defenses and helped cut localist ties to external enemies. The party already tightly controlled southern approaches to Guangzhou and other base area cities. Mine fields blocked water access near Humen (Bocca Tigris), forcing ships to rely on special Nationalist pilots to navigate the passage. Xiwan channel, the only water access to Jiangmen, was partially blocked with old

---

30. *CWR* 34 (September 5, 1925): 23; *CWR* 34 (October 31, 1925): 215.
31. *CWR* 32 (May 9, 1925): 291; *CWR* 36 (April 17, 1926): 175.
32. *CWR* 32 (March 28, 1925): 114; *CWR* 32 (May 9, 1925): 291; *CWR* 35 (January 16, 1926): 194; *CWR* 36 (March 27, 1926): 99; *CWR* 36 (April 17, 1926): 174.
33. *CWR* 32 (May 2, 1925): 263; *CWR* 32 (May 9, 1925): 291; *CWR* 32 (May 23, 1925): 343.
34. *CWR* 34 (November 7, 1925): vi. In Wuzhou, however, threats backfired when the GMD opened its own pawn shops and established a monopoly. *CWR* 35 (December 26, 1925): 106.
35. *CWR* 32 (April 4, 1925): 146; *CWR* 32 (May 2, 1925): 263.
36. *CWR* 36 (April 24, 1926): 210.

hulks while troops regulated traffic. [37] Strike pickets amplified this semi-isolationist defensive scheme by regulating movement along Guangdong's waterways. The function was an important one—so much so that scarce GMD troops were even occasionally sent to back up sagging picket lines trying to hold the line against remnant militarist forces. [38] Strike pickets also acted as a buffer, ensuring that Guomindang troops and police did not directly encounter foreign troops—conditions that might generate conflict. Reports from Jiangmen, for example, credited pickets with keeping the peace by separating U.S. and British gunboats from three Nationalist naval vessels docked nearby. [39] In additional, because pickets eager to enforce boycott regulations boarded incoming ships before foreign customs officials did, the revolutionaries could bypass foreign inspectors trying to maintain weapons bans. [40]

Politically, the boycott offered even more advantages. It provided a new crisis—one grander than even anti-Christianity—with which to mobilize and organize mass organizations. Better yet, it presented a uniquely potent opportunity to implement dual-prong tactics. Activating the agitative prong, CEC leaders lent full support to the Anti-British Boycott, going as far as to plan a conference in October to determine how revolutionary mass organizations could contribute and how they should participate. [41] The CEC ordered the Propaganda Ministry to arrange special classes on *British Imperialism* and various revolutionary topics to be taught by Borodin, Tan Pingshan, Wang Jingwei, Gan Naiguang, Chen Gongbo, and other top leaders. [42] Ministry officials, in turn, issued circular telegrams asking all Chinese to defy imperialism through strikes, donations, and boycotts. [43] Provocative statements from top Nationalist figures—including Zhou Enlai, Chiang Kai-shek, and Borodin—encouraged popular support for the boycott and lionized the strikers. As Sun Ke declared,

> The people of Kwangtung [Guangdong] . . . will finally make Hong Kong yield. The imperialists now do not dare insult the Nationalist Government nor the people of Kwangtung. If we are able to extend our national revolutionary movement throughout the whole country and to

---

37. *CWR* 34 (October 31, 1925): 216; *CWR* 34 (November 21, 1925): 288.

38. A battalion of Huangpu cadets reinforced picket ranks in Qianshan while the party provided three gunboats to help pickets close a route used by many to "illegally" return to Hong Kong via Macao. *CWR* 34 (September 19, 1925): 68; *CWR* 34 (October 17, 1925): 175; *CWR* 35 (December 12, 1925): 53.

39. *CWR* 34 (November 21, 1925): 288; *CWR* 34 (September 19, 1925): 68.

40. *FO* 405/250 [F1392/1/10], p. 543, Enclosure 1, Jamieson to Macleay, Guangzhou, February 22, 1926.

41. "Tongyi Guangdong gejie daibiaohui dagang," *1-ZXWH*, vol. 5 (October 8, 1925).

42. (Discussion item #4) and "Guomindang zhengzhi xuanchuan weiyuanhui tebie xuanchuanban kemu biao," *1-ZXWH*, vol. 5 (October 8, 1925).

43. *FO* 405/250 [F618/71/10], p. 275, weekly summary, Foreign Office, February 12, 1926.

remove the Nationalist Government to Peking [Beijing], *we shall be able to use the name of China to declare war against England, and I am sure that the victory will be ours.*[44] [Emphasis added.]

Dual-prong's accommodative prong, meanwhile, was actuated as well. In its official communications with foreign representatives, the southern regime vigorously denied any hand in the boycott, claiming that British offenses had spawned it and that the Guangzhou Strike Committee directed it. In August 1925, when the British Consul General at Shamian asked about new regulations that prohibited vessels touching at Hong Kong from approaching Guangzhou, Guomindang leaders deflected the question, noting that the rules had been issued by the GSC, not the party.[45] When dealing with foreign representatives and similar inquiries, top revolutionary officials projected an image of neutrality and even suppressed anti-imperialist agitation as a sign of good faith. After activists tore down the French flag flying over a foreign hospital in January 1926, for example, Nationalist regime apologized and sent uniformed NRA troops to run it back up with full salute.[46]

Denials notwithstanding, revolutionary leaders *did* enjoy influence and routinely tightened or loosened the boycott cordon as opportunity presented itself. [47] Press reports carefully tracked fluctuations. British pugnacity spawned anti-imperialist rhetoric from CEC authorities and tighter picket lines as a result, while a conciliatory mien from the foreigners minimized GMD statements, quieted agitation, opened access to Shamian's banks, loosened travel restrictions to Hong Kong, earned special passes through picket lines, and so forth.[48]

Although subtle, that influence gave the party considerable power. It tempted non-British foreigners to abandon ties with Britain to preserve their own economic opportunity, thus dividing imperialist solidarity. It allowed, as dual-prong tactics generally did, the southern regime to intervene in a mediating capacity, forcing British diplomats to Guangzhou's negotiating table. That, in turn, could be parlayed into other advantages. As the Hong Kong governor described with clear irritation, "For several months past there have been direct dealings with the Canton [Guangzhou] Government of to-day, both by the Hong Kong Government and by His Majesty's consul-general at Canton, and *to that extent* [the Nationalist regime] *has already been recog-*

---

44. *FO* 405/250 [F756/1/10], p. 350, Enclosure, extract from *Canton Gazette*, January 13, 1926.
45. *CWR* 34 (September 5, 1925): 23; *CWR* 34 (September 12, 1925): 48.
46. *CWR* 35 (February 6, 1926): 291.
47. When the party decided to court wealthy merchants from Hong Kong and invite them to Guangzhou, it successfully ordered the Strike Committee to abstain from all interference. *CWR* 35 (December 26, 1925): 107.
48. *CWR* 34 (September 19, 1925): 68; *CWR* 34 (October 31, 1925): 218; *CWR* 34 (November 21, 1925): 288; *CWR* 35 (January 16, 1926): 194; *CWR* 35 (January 23, 1926): 222; *CWR* 32 (March 6, 1926): 6-8; *CWR* 36 (March 13, 1926): 46.

nized."[49] [Emphasis added.]

Dual-prong tactics were not risk-free. The autonomy enjoyed by mass organizations meant that they could easily set their own course whenever tensions rose—as they routinely did. In September 1925, for example, Hong Kong police boarded the *S.S. Yick*—a former Hong Kong merchant vessel confiscated earlier by pickets—before detaining the 150 GMD troops on board, seizing their weapons, and restoring the ship to its former owners. In May 1926, Portuguese authorities captured a picket launch, taking captives as well as arms and property worth $50,000.[50]

While these and other incidents generally passed with apologies from both sides, any friction they produced played directly into the hands of those seeking escalation, such as local and foreign interventionists eager to settle the boycott by force. The British inspectorate-general of the Maritime Customs Service routinely argued for naval and troop action. Foreign residents of Shamian and Hong Kong, still riled about the Seamen's Strike and the Anti-Shamian Boycott, repeatedly asked why the Hong Kong garrison's three thousand troops were not being "better" used. Talk about a possible economic blockade or naval bombardment received ready reception among foreign mercenary soldiers impatient for a battle. Some demanded an alliance with anti-Guomindang militarists to relieve Guangzhou's "oppressed and terrorized" citizens. Others insisted that Britain militarily defend its treaty rights and Hong Kong prosperity or face even grander crises in the future.[51]

The British Foreign Office refused to take action, but others did not. In October, Hong Kong's Governor-in-Council declared an arms embargo against Guangzhou. In support, the Beijing regime sent gunboats and cruisers south to track Vladivostok shipments and aid "anti-red" forces. What remained of Chen Jiongming's troops aligned with Wu Peifu while overseas Chinese pledged to help underwrite a new campaign against Guangzhou.[52] Once again, the southern regime faced a conspiracy aimed at its destruction.

Guomindang prospects improved, however, when the Nationalists' Second Eastern Expedition destroyed Chen's base and took over eastern Guangdong. The northerners withdrew their naval forces while French, U.S., and Japanese firms abandoned Shamian for offices in Guangzhou, enabling

---

49. *FO* 405/250 [F1357/1/10], p. 539, Enclosure, Clementi to Amery, Hong Kong, February 10, 1926.

50. The detained NRA soldiers, enroute to Shantou, were later sent to Guangzhou by train. *CWR* 32 (May 30, 1925): 372; *CWR* 34 (October 10, 1925): 148; *CWR* 36 (May 22, 1926): 326.

51. *FO* 405/247 [F2694/2/10], p. 309, Algen memorandum, Chinese Maritime Customs, June 29, 1925; *CWR* 32 (May 9, 1925): 290; *CWR* 34 (September 5, 1925): 23; *CWR* 34 (September 26, 1925): 90; Wong, "British Ask Intervention Against Bolsheviks," p. 35.

52. *CWR* 34 (September 26, 1925): 90; *CWR* 34 (October 31, 1925): 216, 218; *CWR* 35 (January 16, 1926): 192. Wu allegedly gave Chen $200,000 to gather his forces in Hunan where Zhao Hengti, Hunan's commander *(duban)*, would grant him a station. *CWR* 36 (March 6, 1926): 12.

them to gobble up British market shares.[53] Hong Kong interventionists remained active, but by November 1925, the latest anti-GMD campaign had faded—prompting celebratory speeches, including the November 7 rally in Shantou featuring Zhou Enlai, Chiang Kai-shek, and He Yingqin.

Once again the southern regime had dodged a bullet. November's events did change one thing, however. They taught British officials something about revolutionary tactics. After receiving word of Zhou Enlai's statements in Shantou, consul Jamieson reported, "In view of this very candid exposition of the policy of the Nationalist Government proclaimed to the world . . . by one of their own responsible agents, *disingenuous communications to myself and the press, in which they, as a Government, dissociate themselves from the strike movement and from the shipping boycott of Hong Kong, would seem futile.*" [54] [Emphasis added.] Foreign convictions about Guomindang dual-prong duplicity solidified in February 1926 when British officials intercepted a secret telegram. According to Sir Cecil B. Clementi, Hong Kong's new governor since November 1925, it was now, "impossible for [the Nationalist] Government to dissociate itself from the activities of the strike committee, for which it has been accustomed to deny responsibility."[55] CEC involvement could no longer be doubted. Again in Clementi's words,

> The Canton [Guangzhou] Government, although called upon to do so, and having adequate military force at its disposal, has not prevented illegalities nor punished the guilty parties. On the contrary, it publicly recognizes the Strike Committee . . . and has given the help of its gunboats in picketing operations. *Full responsibility for the illegalities committed by the Canton Strike Committee falls, therefore, upon the Canton Government.*[56] [Emphasis added.]

---

53. *CWR* 34 (November 21, 1925): 288; *CWR* 34 (November 28, 1925): 318, 319; *CWR* 34 (September 26, 1925): 94. Afterwards, only Hainan island retained minor anti-revolutionary militarist resistance. *CWR* 35 (January 16, 1926): 192. As imperialist solidarity fragmented, France offered sanctuary to Soviet propagandists to curry favor with Moscow. *FO* 405/250 [F1275/307/10], p. 509, Enclosure, Barton to Macleay, Shanghai, January 16, 1926.
54. Zhou declared that the GMD: (1) sought the overthrow of imperialism—particularly the Hong Kong government, (2) would support, encourage, and direct labor attacks on imperialism, (3) would drive out British citizens refusing to subordinate themselves to Chinese law, and (4) viewed Britain as the primary target of anti-imperialism. *FO* 405/250 [F120/1/10], p. 26, Enclosure, Jamieson to Commissioner for Foreign Affairs, Guangzhou, December 5, 1925. Jamieson twisted the party's refusal to acknowledge its influence over the GSC into embarrassing conundrums. When asked by the GMD Fireworks Bureau for Hong Kong saltpeter, potash, and other items, Jamieson sarcastically quipped that the Strike Committee would never concede to such a shipment. If the party could secure GSC permits for saltpeter, he claimed, then surely it would never have let the strikers block food shipments to Shamian. *FO* 405/250 [F120/1/10], p. 27, Enclosure, Jamieson to Macleay, Guangzhou, December 7, 1925.
55. *FO* 405/251 [F1766/1/10], pp. 74-75, Enclosure 1, Clementi to Avery, Hong Kong, February 26, 1926.
56. *FO* 405/250 [F1357/1/10], p. 541, Enclosure, Clementi to Amery, Hong Kong, February 10,

Clarity about who was to blame notwithstanding, there was little Britain could do. The presence of boycott pickets sharply cut its options. On January 25, 1926, Clementi, Jamieson, and others proposed a multi-nation blockade against Guangzhou and diplomatic pressure on Moscow to withdraw its "Bolshevik" advisors from Guangdong. Sir Austen Chamberlain, Britain's minister to China, however, vetoed the plan in the hope that the party would either moderate policy or disappear entirely once Wu Peifu made good on his promise to destroy the southern regime. The British Foreign Office, meanwhile, produced its own list of possible responses: (1) force, (2) blockade, (3) aid to anti-communist leaders, (4) pressure on Moscow, and (5) conciliation. Like Chamberlain, Foreign Office officials concluded that only the latter two options were viable. Memory of the May Thirtieth and Shaji Incidents tainted more forceful measures, especially since the failure of nearby militarists meant that British action would have to contend directly with Chinese nationalism and likely enflame anti-foreign agitation everywhere. Only the Nationalists could calm picket agitators and mediate an end to the boycott. Thus, as one British report noted, "the only alternative is patience."[57]

Whether forced or voluntary, British patience presented the party with a window of opportunity and encouraged the southern regime to improve its foreign relations. In November, Guangzhou authorities instituted judicial reforms aimed to impress foreign interests.[58] A truer test of GMD priorities arose on December 5, 1925, when the party ordered local officials to take control of the Shantou Salt Inspectorate. Although Shantou's Inspectorate was still under foreign administration, the move surprised no one since the Guomindang had just captured Shantou and Guangzhou's own Salt Inspectorate had been under Chinese control since 1918. Crisis arose, however, when zealous Shantou leaders also then seized control of the Native Customs Office on January 19. Directed by the foreign-run Maritime Customs Service, the Native Customs underwrote China's international debts. Its loss, therefore, precipitated a flurry of consular protests, although no one expected them to have any impact.[59] Nevertheless, to the surprise of many foreigners, GMD central headquarters quickly returned the Native Customs to foreign control and sacked the head of the Shantou commissioner of foreign affairs for interfering with the administration of the customs and for failing to consult with Guangzhou. The Guomindang's response angered agitative leaders, as well as Chiang Kai-shek, who accused the CEC of "truckling" to imperialist

---

1926.
57. *FO* 405/250 [F441/71/10], p. 152, weekly summary, February 1, 1926; *FO* 405/250 [F618/71/10], p. 275, weekly summary, Foreign Office, February 12, 1926; *FO* 405/250 [F1357/1/10], pp. 538-543, Colonial Office to Foreign Office, London, March 29, 1926.
58. A special commission, for example, was ordered to reform the court and prison systems to ready them for foreign inspection. *CWR* 34 (November 21, 1925): 288.
59. *CWR* 35 (December 19, 1925): 82; *CWR* 35 (February 6, 1926): 291.

threats.[60] Nevertheless, the gesture deeply impressed British officials. By year's end, party relations with Hong Kong and Britain, while not cordial, had entered a warming spell.

Using dual-prong tactics, Guomindang leaders utilized the Anti-British Boycott to extort British "patience" and force an improvement in foreign relations. At the same time, the boycott helped extend influence over localist interests and consolidate control on the domestic front. The dynamics, however, differed. While GMD anti-imperialism employed limited and largely accommodative applications, revolutionary dealings with localist interests looked far more unlimited and assimilative.

The Guomindang's Second National Congress, held in January 1926, called for strong action against any and all domestic threats, claiming that even anti-imperialist action should first target the tools of the imperialists: warlords, corrupt officials, compradors, and rural bullies *(junfa, guanliao, maiban, tuhao)*. Official Congress declarations promised to purge society of all "counter-revolutionaries" *(fan geming)* and sweep out all traitors. [61] Technically, however, those so maligned represented only the very worst domestic "enemies." Between them and the revolutionized "people" *(guomin)* lay a vast stretch of hostile localist interests that required something short of destruction—something closer to pacification.

In some ways, the Anti-British Boycott worsened anti-GMD energies. To many groups, it was insufferable on several levels. Localist leaders in some districts tried to minimize the impact of the strike pickets by declaring that they preferred to manage the boycott at the local level, without GSC involvement. Others sought exemptions for the Chinese New Year, entreated the regime to expel striker squatters from apartments, or begged a respite from picket "abuses." Plagued by disruptions, residents of Shiqi district in Xiangshan petitioned to have the GSC withdraw its pickets outright. [62] Through the latter half of 1925, individuals routinely tested picket lines in an attempt to reach Hong Kong or restore old trading links. Smuggling and the seizure of contraband occurred daily, often generating intense disputes about whether or not a particular shipment constituted "smuggling." In October, the Merchants Volunteer Corps of Gongyi forcibly disarmed and expelled pick-

---

60. The Commissioner was also the Superintendent of Customs. *CWR* 35 (February 20, 1926): 344; *FO* 405/251 [F1567/71/10], p. 17, weekly summary, Foreign Office, April 12, 1926; *FO* 405/251 [F1563/1/10], pp. 18-19, Enclosure, Jamieson to Macleay, Guangzhou, March 8, 1926.
61. "Zhongguo Guomindang dierci quanguo daibiao dahui xuanyan," *Geming wenxian*, vol. 69, pp. 161-162, 167.
62. *CWR* 34 (November 21, 1925): 288; *CWR* 34 (September 5, 1925): 23; *CWR* 34 (September 19, 1925): 66; *CWR* 35 (January 2, 1926): 140; *CWR* 35 (January 30, 1926): 262; *CWR* 36 (May 15, 1926): 298. Shipping companies insisted that party representatives accompany searches for "contraband" so ship owners and captains would not be blamed for items smuggled by crew members. *CWR* 35 (February 13, 1926): 316; *CWR* 36 (March 27, 1926): 96.

ets for seizing native goods that had been certified for safe passage by the government. In Taiping, fighting allegedly resulted in more than fifty casualties and led to the disappearance of all pickets, prompting local party cadres to beg CEC authorities for troops to help regain control. Battles elsewhere, meanwhile, reportedly killed over two hundred peasant corpsmen and numerous cattle and pigs.[63] Boycott pickets and *mintuan* militiamen in Qianshan (near Macao) clashed for months before local villagers shot a picket, later arrested all his cohorts, and handed them over to anti-GMD forces.[64]

Nevertheless, although it aggravated localist interests, the boycott also effectively reduced their influence. Without ready access to Shamian or Hong Kong, localist organizations struggled to secure weapons and funds. Anyone in Guangdong seeking contact with the British risked arrest and imprisonment. Any attempt to trade with them jeopardized one's goods. Pickets were more than well-equipped to handle any challenge to GSC directives. In one incident, pickets near Macao arrested over sixty passengers and crew for violations. In another episode, pickets in Guangzhou netted two hundred crates of silk enroute to Hong Kong worth $2 million. Merchants hoping to avoid such interferences had to apply for GSC permits, allowing Strike Committee leaders to watch even legitimate trade.[65]

The strikers also offered modest military defense against *mintuan*. When Guomindang forces took Beihai, for example, leaders called on strike pickets to safely conduct the new Commissioner for Foreign Affairs to his station.[66] Once party forces conquered eastern Guangdong, it was pickets that took over policing responsibilities, freeing troops for other tasks. As already discussed, mass organizations could engage military rivals; Haifeng peasant corps took Chen Jiongming's hometown before NRA troops arrived while labor and peasant corps supported party victories in Shantou. Nevertheless, their greatest contribution came in checking localist backlash. As Chiang Kai-shek exclaimed in January 1926, mobilized masses played a valued role in providing local defense so regular troops could engage militarist enemies.[67]

---

63. *CWR* 34 (October 31, 1925): 216; (Discussion items #20 and #21), *1-ZXWH*, vol. 5 (November 6, 1925); *FO* 405/250 [F758/1/10], p. 352, Enclosure 1, Jamieson to Macleay, Guangzhou, January 18, 1926.

64. *CWR* 34 (September 19, 1925): 68; *CWR* 34 (November 7, 1925): vi.

65. Travelers could only get to Hong Kong via Xiamen or Haiphong (Vietnam). Wong, "Co-operation, or Non-Intervention, Wanted," p. 366; *CWR* 34 (September 19, 1925): 68; *CWR* 35 (December 5, 1925): 21; *CWR* 36 (April 3, 1926): 127; *CWR* 35 (December 5, 1925): 21. After pickets arrested a petty pork hawker and ate his wares, no one dared even go near the gates to Shamian. *CWR* 34 (September 5, 1925): 23.

66. *CWR* 35 (December 19, 1925): 84; *CWR* 35 (January 2, 1926): 140.

67. *CWR* 32 (April 11, 1925): 175-176. Hin Wong noted the value of peasant and labor corps in replacing deserting mercenary troops. Wong, "Farmers and Workers in Canton," p. 301; Wong, "The Passing of the Kuomintang in South China," p. 76. "Proposed Reforms in Kwangtung Red Army," *CWR* 35 (January 2, 1926): 138. Chiang allegedly claimed that peasant corps, because of

More important was the breathing room that boycott pickets offered party leaders. With the British kept at arm's length, nothing restricted government action against localist power. In November 1925, party officials ordered all volunteer corps and militias to disarm. The real push, however, began in early 1926 when peasant associations petitioned the CEC to disband all merchant and village volunteers because they were controlled by "interests unfriendly toward the GMD." Urged by "popular" demand, the party complied. In January 1926, the Second National Congress instructed the Nationalist Government to subdue all volunteer organizations.[68]

Although couched in sharp terms, regime measures did not seek to suppress militias but to fold them into the party hierarchy. In February, therefore, Guomindang leaders dissolved all militia administrations and subordinated their resources (as well as those of GMD labor corps and peasant militias) to a new organ—the Bureau of People and Peasant Volunteer Corps. As directed by the party's Military Council, the Bureau could appoint or remove volunteer officers and/or disband militias. In late March, the party added a short-term military school to train militia officers in basic drilling, military science, and party doctrine. By April, the Bureau was training new leaders, overseeing actions, and promoting (enforcing) the party's regulations governing volunteer corps.[69] Some militia chiefs rejected regime overtures and refused to conform to mandatory inspections. In fact, so many ignored regime directives, especially in Guangdong's outer districts, that Nationalist officials specifically ordered all rural volunteer corps to submit a list of strength and arms before July 1, 1926. Still, some militias refused out of fear that they would lose what weaponry they still had.[70]

Despite some hesitancy, most localist groups found themselves overwhelmed and began to drop their resistance. In January 1926, Guangzhou authorities announced that anyone opposing regime financial measures (i.e., taxation) or interfering with revenue officials discharging their duties would be liable to criminal proceedings, and that protests, strikes, boycotts, and business suspensions would no longer be tolerated. Police or troops dispersed demonstrators and disarmed militiamen. Marine Volunteers—armed guards protecting water traffic between Guangzhou and Foshan—were among the first targeted. In West River districts, troops forcibly disarmed other militias and scattered a force of seven thousand anti-GMD fighters.[71]

---

their number, were more helpful in defeating Chen Jiongming than his own Huangpu cadets. Galbiati, *P'eng P'ai and the Hai-lu-feng Soviet*, p. 194.

68. *CWR* 34 (November 28, 1925): 318; *CWR* 35 (January 16, 1926): 192; *CWR* 35 (February 6, 1926): 291.

69. *CWR* 36 (March 6, 1926): 13; *CWR* 36 (April 17, 1926): 179; *CWR* 36 (May 1, 1926): 232; "Guanyu mintuan wenti jueyian," *ZWDL-XJ*, pp. 40-41.

70. *CWR* 36 (April 17, 1926): 179; *CWR* 36 (April 24, 1926): 210.

71. *CWR* 34 (November 28, 1925): 318; *CWR* 35 (January 30, 1926): 261; *CWR* 36 (March 27, 1926): 98; *CWR* 36 (April 24, 1926): 208.

Occasionally, revolutionary mass organizations augmented state coercion and helped put down localist forces. The most significant contribution of the masses, however, was less direct. Noncompliant merchant enterprises faced strikes from revolutionized labor unions, often one after another in rapid succession. The GMD Central Bank called anyone unwilling to accept its banknotes at full value "counter-revolutionaries." Employees striking at the Guangzhou Water Works for higher wages were denounced by government officers as "aiding the enemy." Fearful of adverse labels that could justify mass agitation—in addition to state criticism, attacks, or jailings—localist interests found themselves unable to seek foreign aid or cooperate with each other, thus diluting their strength.[72]

Heavy-handed state-driven and agitative steps had the greatest effect when softer measures—such as economic, social, and political reforms—undermined the *raison d'être* for localist defiance. To rectify unpopular and widely recognized abuses, the Guomindang trained government tax collectors and prohibited anyone else from commandeering property or exacting taxes. A Department of Finance board rose to investigate tax delinquency, end smuggling, and protect shipping against piracy. Finance reforms in late 1925 expanded revenues six times over the same period in 1924. Political censors visited county magistrates to ensure that party direction and ideals were followed. In Guangdong's cities, improved regulations and policing clamped down on vagrancy, begging, prostitution, and indecency, spawning laudatory reports that crime had fallen significantly.[73] Laws were instituted to manage student organizations and *dangtuan* to prevent agitator abuses.[74]

In February 1926, Chiang Kai-shek promised to sweep away all disaffected militarists and politicians so Guangzhou could again be a city "fit to live in." Free to act like a civil government instead of a besieged warlord power, the Nationalist Government began ambitious developmental projects and announced a period of civic development that promised piracy and banditry suppression, a provincial census, land surveys, a provincial police system, and a highway network.[75] As law and order rose and corruption declined, localist hostility toward Guomindang rule lost the fueling frustrations that kept it at peak levels.

To this, the party added proactive steps to improve relations with localist interests. Authorities promised to prevent troops from disrupting silk and rice

72. *CWR* 36 (April 10, 1926): 152; *CWR* 36 (April 3, 1926): 126; *CWR* 34 (September 5, 1925): 23; Wong, "Co-operation, or Non-Intervention, Wanted," p. 362.
73. *CWR* 34 (September 12, 1925): 48; *CWR* 35 (January 2, 1926): 140; *CWR* 35 (January 23, 1926): 220; *CWR* 36 (March 6, 1926): 13, 14; *CWR* 36 (April 24, 1926): 208.
74. "Dangtuan ganshi weiyuan zhixing weiyuan huiyi shixiang," August 5, 1926.
75. *CWR* 35 (February 13, 1926): 315; *CWR* 35 (February 20, 1926): 344; *CWR* 36 (March 6, 1926): 14; *CWR* 36 (April 24, 1926): 208.

shipments. In January 1926, as a conciliatory gesture to localists, the party declared itself friendly to labor but not opposed to capitalists. Shortly thereafter, the regime began returning confiscated ships to their original owners, forced corrupt railway directors to return embezzled funds, and restored the Guangzhou-Hankou Railroad to stockholder control.[76] To set aside rumors castigating the southern regime and demonstrate that state control over charitable institutions had actually improved conditions, the Guangzhou Municipal Council invited leading citizens to inspect hospitals run by the Department of Public Health. During the inspections, Wu Chaogang—chair of the Guangzhou Charity Board—promised that government seizures had only intended to streamline administration, sweep away "irregularities," and reform management.[77]

Gradually more and more localist interests came to see party rule as improved and permanent. Those most offended by the Nationalists had already left. Factory and shop owners still in Guangdong needed government mediation if and when labor strikes broke out and thus sought connections with the regime.[78] Taxes and imposts continued, but they spawned less anti-regime hostility. By March 1926, even rising land taxes failed to provoke any significant outbursts. Fewer still arose when regime officials began collecting some $5 million via treasury bonds, new levies on home owners, imposts on landlord rents, a monopoly on medicinal wines, higher amusement taxes, and so forth, to finance the Northern Expedition.[79] With time, militias insufficiently committed to party principles were disbanded, as were labor unions and peasant associations not registered with the Nationalist Government.[80] Party officials even replaced the old Merchants Association with a new Nationalist-controlled organization by the same name. Despite these and other unpopular moves, the party still secured merchant promises to help stabilize currency.[81] By mid-1926, all signs indicated that most localist defiance in Guangdong had been silenced.[82]

76. *CWR* 34 (October 31, 1925): 216; *CWR* 35 (January 23, 1926): 222. Some one hundred vessels taken over a three-year period were returned. *CWR* 35 (February 20, 1926): 344; *CWR* 36 (March 27, 1926): 96; *CWR* 35 (February 6, 1926): 291. Deteriorating equipment, among other problems, dropped stock values from $5.00 to 35 cents a share. *CWR* 36 (March 13, 1926): 44, 46; *CWR* 36 (May 1, 1926): 234.

77. *CWR* 35 (January 2, 1926): 142; *CWR* 35 (February 13, 1926): 315.

78. *CWR* 35 (February 13, 1926): 316; *CWR* 36 (May 15, 1926): 300.

79. *CWR* 35 (February 13, 1926): 316; *CWR* 36 (March 13, 1926): 42; *CWR* 36 (March 27, 1926): 99; *CWR* 36 (April 17, 1926): 175; *CWR* 36 (April 24, 1926): 208.

80. *CWR* 34 (November 28, 1925): 318; *CWR* 35 (January 23, 1926): 220.

81. *CWR* 35 (January 2, 1926): 142; *CWR* 35 (January 23, 1926): 220.

82. *Guanyu zhengshou lijuan yanxijuan fangzujuan ji zhulujuan gexiang faling*, *GHGZ*, April 1926. Regulations adopted in October 1926 denounced *mintuan*, but then extended some degree of tolerance as long as militia chiefs submitted to Nationalist training and accepted financial, legal, and membership limitations. "Guanyu mintuan wenti jueyian," *ZWDL-XJ*, pp. 40-41.

The Anti-Christian Movement: "Partyized" National Culture

Following the May Thirtieth Incident of 1925, popular and regime actions collaborated with fine-tuned efficiency to contain foreign imperialists, defeat rival warlords, and subdue localist interests. Success changed Guangdong's political landscape. Consolidating power—both military and political—freed the Guomindang from the most immediate pressures threatening its authority. This security, in turn, meant the southern regime could move beyond issues of crude survival and begin implementing Sun Yat-sen's vision of national reconstruction.

Within this larger drive to build the "nation" envisioned by Sun, the party heightened its interest in the educational institutions that defined national culture. Unfortunately for educators, party oversight had not been kind to Chinese schools. Financial conditions were bleak. Although Guangdong's 1920 constitution guaranteed 20 percent of the provincial budget for education, Nationalist leaders had not complied.[83] As of May 1925, Guangzhou teachers had not been paid for eight months, threatening to close schools and inducing the education commissioner to resign in frustration. In November, educators begged Wu Chaogang, chair of the Guangzhou Municipal Council, not to slash in half salaries that had already been reduced by 30 percent.[84]

Political threats had only exacerbated financial problems. As one Youth Ministry report complained, "Since party members in Guangdong must focus on eliminating foes and attend only to military and political affairs, they cannot give full support to education."[85] In the past, officials had generally circumvented anemic financial conditions by seeking the aid of private sponsors. Privatization was very effective at expanding educational reach without increasing government financial commitments. However, it created other quandaries. During the early 1920s, for example, fiscal shortages had spurred Chen Jiongming's Guangzhou regime to encourage private schools. Localist organizations raised funds for "people's schools" *(guomin xuexiao)* while county officials solicited private monies to support high schools. Meanwhile, officials encouraged the expansion of mission schools to ease Guangdong's educational burden.[86] While helpful in the short run, privatization fractured local education by introducing divisions and vested interests. In 1921, the U.S. Consul in Guangzhou explained,

> The Department of Public Education is faced with a difficult problem. The Cantonese standard of education is probably higher than elsewhere in China, but governmental responsibility and activity . . . has been

83. *Huazi ribao* (January 16-21, 1921).
84. *CWR* 36 (May 16, 1925): 319; *CWR* 34 (November 28, 1925): 318; *CWR* 36 (April 17, 1926): 180.
85. Chen, "Zhongyang dangbu qingnian yundong baogao," 1926.
86. Chen, *Chen Jiongming and the Federalist Movement, p.* 129.

meager. There are thousands of private schools in the city, made necessary by reason of the inadequacy of the public school system. To institute an efficient public school system would be to interfere to a
considerable extent with an established private industry.[87]

By the fall of 1925, efforts to institute an efficient system combined with
Nationalist measures designed to seize control of all education and convert it
into an organ of revolution—generating more than just the predicted "interference." Since most rank-and-file teachers and administrators had already
been inducted into the party, Guomindang officials turned their attention to
other resources, challenging whatever entrenched vested interests they encountered.

In December 1925, the GMD regime nationalized all private educational
endowments set aside to promote clan or locale education. Some, like those
in Dongguan, were worth millions of dollars, prompting fierce resistance
from localist gentry managers—but to no avail.[88] Faculty at National
Guangdong University put up a bigger fight. In October, when party authorities announced reforms aimed at politicizing higher education, GMD
president Zou Lu denounced the changes as "Bolshevik," students and
alumni protested, and over fifty faculty members resigned.[89] Undeterred,
party officials sacked Zou and appointed Gu Mengyu, a communist from
Beijing's Chinese Government University, in his stead. Angered at this
"intrusion," most remaining non-GMD faculty then submitted their resignations. Committed to following through, the party continued to implement
changes, officially renaming the school Sun Yat-sen University before converting it into south China's keystone revolutionary training institution.
Comintern agents took over financing and administration while students
were organized into cadet corps and trained in ideology, propaganda, organization, military science, and tactics.[90]

The spat with Guangdong University had an impact. As word spread that
party leaders intended to close the University because it had failed to fully
register with the government, a mad scramble ensued as students elsewhere
denounced lax Chinese school principals who feverishly sought to rectify
oversights, comply with regulations, and avoid government interference.[91]

---

87. Chen, *Chen Jiongming and the Federalist Movement,* p. 141.
88. *CWR* 35 (December 12, 1925): 53.
89. *CWR* 35 (February 27, 1926): 367; *CWR* 34 (November 7, 1925): vi. In February 1924, Sun
Yat-sen hard ordered GMD educator Zou Lu to turn what had been the Guangdong Higher
Normal College, the Law School, and the Agricultural College of Guangzhou into a single
institution: National Guangdong University. Lee, *Modern Canton*, p. 110.
90. Zou Lu proposed the name change in September 1925. (Discussion item #6), *1-ZXWH*, vol. 5
(September 15, 1925); *CWR* 34 (November 7, 1925): vi. Zou's expulsion was complicated by
factional conflicts. *CWR* 35 (December 5, 1925): 21; *CWR* 35 (January 9, 1926): 168; *CWR* 35
(February 27, 1926): 367; *CWR* 36 (May 15, 1926): 300; *CWR* 36 (May 22, 1926): 327.
91. *Guangdong dazhong xuexiao qiu li'an, GHGZ,* September, 1925-October, 1926.

Even the parents of students could not resist the party's plans for education. In early 1926, for example, officials noticed that children were being pulled from Guomindang schools and enrolled in old-styled private academies *(sishu)*. Many parents were angry that their sons and daughters were being forced to participate in compulsory political activities that wasted study time (20 days in the latter half of 1925 alone), exploited naïve youngsters for political gain, and exposed them to potentially dangerous conditions.[92] In response, the party prohibited unlicensed educators from taking students and tightened teacher qualifications. Inspectors closed several *sishu* and threatened the administrators of many more unless they strictly adhered to party standards.[93]

By late 1925, the ideals behind this drive for educational control came to be called "partyization" *(danghua)* and involved injecting institutions and curricula with revolutionary political standards in order to prepare students for revolutionary participation.[94] In February 1926, after resuming his post following a six month hiatus in Shanghai, Education Commissioner Xu Chongqing accelerated *danghua* efforts by ordering all Guangzhou higher education to include military training.[95] In March, the Commission required the study of Sun Yat-sen doctrine and his Three Principles in all public schools. After being prompted by the Propaganda Ministry, the provincial Education Department announced that education would focus on making revolution and training teachers who excelled at preparing revolutionary students.[96]

By April, a new Three Principles text was approved and Guangxi public schools were ordered to implement courses. The party also initiated preliminary measures toward eliminating "biased" and out-dated texts prepared by individual schools. In May, *danghua* became the primary topic of the Sixth Guangdong Educational Conference. Meanwhile, the Youth Ministry

---

92. *FO* 405/250 [F1246/1/10], p. 523, Enclosure, Jamieson to Macleay, Guangzhou, February 15, 1926; *CWR* 35 (February 27, 1926): 367.

93. *CWR* 35 (February 27, 1926): 367.

94. The fluid Chinese term *danghua* is often awkwardly rendered in English as "partify" or nominalized as "partification." To preserve the party's centrality in the *danghua* process and preserve the term's grammatical flexibility, I translate *danghua* as "partyize" or "partyization."

95. *CWR* 34 (October 10, 1925): 150; *CWR* 34 (November 7, 1925): 242, vi; *CWR* 35 (December 19, 1925): 82; *CWR* 35 (February 13, 1926): 316; *CWR* 35 (February 27, 1926): 367.

96. (Discussion item #12), *1-ZXWH*, vol. 5 (November 27, 1925). Also see *CWR* 36 (March 13, 1926): 46; *CWR* 36 (March 27, 1926): 100. Chen Gongbo identified the Youth Ministry's "Ten Plans" vis-à-vis the youth movement: (1) watch party activities in school, (2) unify the youth movement, (3) recover educational rights, (4) edit textbooks to match party principles, (5) implement *danghua* in schools, (6) establish ties with all nationalist, youth, and revolutionary parties, (7) expand mass education, (8) promote ties between the student, peasant, and workers movements, (9) steer students toward social involvement rather than intellectualism, and (10) encourage all students to join the Nationalist Revolution. Chen, "Zhongyang dangbu qingnian yundong baogao," 1926.

actively gathered information about schools in Guangzhou to assess and expand revolutionary capacity [97] By mid-1926, with Nationalist leaders carefully adjusting policy and instituting curricular reform, most Chinese education in Guomindang territory had come to ardently serve the revolutionary agenda.

While Chinese educators found themselves grappling with heavy top-down intrusion by the state, mission school administrators, as usual, did not. Instead, they faced pressure of another sort that sought partyization of different variety. In this case, the power exercised to redefine mission education welled up from the bottom portions of Chinese society—largely in the form of anti-Christian student-led agitation. Here, the party did not seek outright control of mission schools, but to revolutionize them by compelling them to "voluntarily" embrace the GMD platform. Once again, the Nationalists turned to dual-prong tactics.

After the May Thirtieth and Shaji Incidents, anti-foreign agitation exploded. The National Student Union's Seventh National Congress of July 7, 1925 led the way by calling for new student unions and the revival of old ones dormant since 1922. Delegations from Shanghai and Guangzhou visited major cities, in their own words, "(1) to promote an anti-imperialism alliance, (2) to organize a general alliance of labor, agriculture, commerce, and education, (3) to hasten the spread of student unions, and (4) to explain the views of the National Student Union regarding acts of imperialist aggression."[98] Unions were organized, demonstrations were held, and armed student and labor corps proliferated. Within a year, anti-foreign organizations could be found in sixteen of China's twenty-two provinces and were connected through some 320 municipal and county student union alliances, most of which maintained some allegiance to Guangzhou. The Anti-Christian Federation expanded, reaching even small towns, while the National Student Union's Bureau of Workers and Peasants employed drama troupes, lectures, and protests to spread anti-Christianity among the masses.[99]

---

97. (Report #11), *2-ZXWH*, vol. 2 (April 27, 1926); Zhong, et. al., "Jiaoyu xingzheng weiyuanhui weiyuan Zhong Rongguang deng fu zhongyang zhixing weiyuanhui han," April 23, 1926; "Qingnianbu sanyuefen gongzuo jingguo baogao," April 1,1926; *CWR* 36 (March 27, 1926): 100; *CWR* 36 (May 29, 1926): 352; "Xuesheng dangyuan diaocha biao," 1926; *Jiaokeshu bianshen weiyuanhui zhangcheng*, *GHGZ*, April-October 1926.

98. The Congress was held in Shanghai. "Quanguo xuesheng zonghui yijue an," in *Guonei jinshinian lai zhi zongjiao sichao*, comp. Zhang, pp. 395-400; *CWR* 34 (September 26, 1925): 94; *CWR* 34 (October 17, 1925): 176.

99. *FO* 405/250 [F1275/307/10], pp. 509-510, Enclosure, Barton to Macleay, Shanghai, January 16, 1926. Anti-foreign agitation erupted in cities as widely scattered as Jinan, Qingdao, Changsha, Fuzhou, Xiamen, Beijing, Wuhan, and Guangzhou. Yang, *Minguo shiwunian Zhongguo xuesheng yundong gaikuang*, pp. 66-69; Chao, "The Chinese Indigenous Church Movement," p. 183; *CWR* 34 (September 26, 1925): 94. Also see Yip, *Religion, Nationalism, and Chinese Students*, pp. 51-52.

Caught in China's latest anti-Christian maelstrom, mission schools found their operations disrupted like never before. Four days after the May Thirtieth Incident, when school administrators refused to fly the flag at half mast to honor the slain, five hundred students and nineteen teachers struck at St. John's University in Shanghai. Over six hundred students withdrew from Tianjin's Anglo-Chinese College while other protests broke out in Beijing, Fuzhou, Kaifeng, Changsha, Wuchang, Hankou and Hanyang. In Shantou, agitators forced virtually all British-run schools to close or drop their British principals. As fall semester approached, the Nanchang Student Union and the Wuhan Student Union Federation, representing thirty public schools, urged mission school students not to return for classes. Guangzhou's Lingnan University and Changsha's Yale-in-China began the school year on schedule, but other schools were not so fortunate. Wuchang's Wesley College lost all students *en bloc* while so many withdrew from Hankou's Griffith John College that it had to close. Nanning mission schools shut down after five thousand students and workers launched anti-imperialist demonstrations.[100] Wuchang Catholic College students boycotted classes to protest curriculum revisions. St. Joseph's School students called on administrators to register with the government and abolish religious teachings and services. Lingnan University students and teachers forced out the foreign vice-president. Disruption was widespread. According to the Nationalist Commissioner of Civil Affairs, all large missionary institutions faced at least some form of disruption.[101]

The new face of anti-Christian agitation deeply impacted missionary attitudes. Before the May Thirtieth Incident, most missionaries defended educational autonomy and refused government registration.[102] In April 1925, for example, the China Christian Education Association—a union of primary and secondary schools and eighteen Protestant colleges and universities—met in Shanghai to formulate policy vis-à-vis the Beijing government's demands for registration. As the meeting concluded, Association delegates issued a formal declaration:

It is in accordance with the spirit of democracy and with the practice in all democratic nations of the modern world that permission should be granted to individuals or to social groups, who so desire, to establish and maintain private educational institutions, in addition to the public system of education maintained by the state. . . . It is generally agreed that progress in education is dependent upon the existence of diverse types of

100. Yip, *Religion, Nationalism, and Chinese Students*, pp. 55-56; *The China Press* (January 6, 1926); *CWR* 34 (September 12, 1925): 44; *CWR* 34 (September 19, 1925): 64; *CWR* 34 (September 26, 1925): 94-95; "Qingnianbu siyuefen gongzuo jingguo baogao," May 20, 1926.
101. *CWR* 34 (September 5, 1925): 23; *CWR* 34 (October 3, 1925): 126; *CWR* 36 (May 22, 1926): 328; Yip, *Religion, Nationalism, and Chinese Students*, pp. 54-55.
102. *FO* 405/250 [F407/7/10], p. 153, Macleay to Chamberlain, Beijing, December 7, 1925.

schools and the largest possible freedom of variation. To deny the right of variation, and to insist that all schools follow the same uniform procedure would be contrary to the educational interests of the state.[103]

Delegates favored government registration in principle—out of respect for accreditation standards—but rejected its attempt to strip religion from their schools. Equally concerned, Catholics used another approach. On March 6, 1925, Rev. Fr. William F. O'Shea, the Hong Kong procurator of the American Maryknoll Catholic Mission in China, proclaimed,

> Throughout China the necessary money for supporting state schools has for years been so hard to get that these schools have frequently, and for long periods, suspended operations altogether, while the mission schools, being independent of taxation, have been able to keep going steadily. . . . As to the charge that foreigners, particularly American, finding themselves excluded from other means of influencing the Chinese, have chosen school building and the teaching of the Gospel, to conduct their propaganda, nothing can be more untrue. American missionaries in China whether Protestant or Catholic, are devoted to China's needs rather than to America's. They are in no sense government agents.[104]

Whether they used a democratic or economic rationale, missionaries identified the value of mission education with its autonomy and dismissed Chinese accusations that independence favored an ulterior agenda.

Missionaries spoke of "China's needs" as if they were self-evident, asserted that mission schools aided China's development, and, therefore, claimed not just the right but the duty to defend institutional independence. Government oversight threatened their entire value system, prompting some missionaries to claim that institutional closure was better than compromise through registration.[105] A few particularly committed zealots suggested a Christian counterstrike, arguing: "Christian forces of conscientious native pastors and foreign missionaries must be augmented and better equipped to fight Bolshevism and hesitation to openly recruit and mobilize will mean the fear that this religion may not be equal to the occasion. The YMCA organizations throughout the country must rise to save the young men of China from false doctrines."[106]

---

103. "The Reply to the Anti-Christian Agitation," *CWR* 32 (April 18, 1925): 184-185.
104. "The Reply to the Anti-Christian Agitation," *CWR* 32 (April 18, 1925): 184. Catholics also often refused to renounce the unequal treaties. *FO* 405/250 [F407/7/10], p. 153, Macleay to Chamberlain, Beijing, December 7, 1925.
105. "Chinese Christian Education," *Chinese Recorder* (57): 340-344. Missionaries debated the issue back and forth. One argument calling for qualified acceptance of treaty revision claimed that German missionaries enjoyed good treatment despite having no treaty protection. Heeren, "Missionaries and Governments," pp. 112-113.
106. Wong, "Co-operation, or Non-Intervention, Wanted," p. 364.

Missionaries of this mindset, however, based their resolve almost exclusively on rational or ideological argument. As soon as the May Thirtieth Incident and its anti-foreignism burst onto the scene, lofty assertions about what China needed and the debatable value of educational independence became moot. Institutions and organizations, not ideas, were under attack. Under these conditions, foreigners could muster little defense. In Shanghai, a coalition of representatives from twelve different nations formulated plans to launch a broad-based educational movement among workers and students to offset agitation, but nothing came of it.[107]

Christians were simply too divided to cobble together any meaningful response, let alone arrange a way to defend their position. Agitators targeted fissures and opened wide gaps between foreign missionaries and Chinese Christian leaders who had long endured missionary condescension and glass-ceiling restrictions. Disruptive anti-Christian agitation alone might have cemented Christian solidarity but, by 1925, it was not alone. Agitation advocating Christianity's exclusion was balanced with generous offers of inclusion from revolutionary leaders trying to get Christians to side with the "nation." Agitators did not attack the religion *per se* but its ties to imperialism, thus granting Chinese Christians an opportunity to redefine themselves. By abandoning the foreign Christianizing agenda, cutting dependence on the unequal treaties, and emphasizing their "rational" contributions, Chinese Christians could enter the "people" and retain their religion at the same time.

Only one route could convey Christianity away from alienation, agitation, and national exclusion, and it was clearly marked. To counteract agitative propaganda, Chinese Christians declared support for Sun Yat-sen's movement, criticized foreign tinkering in Chinese affairs, condemned the May Thirtieth "massacre," repudiated the unequal treaties, called for greater social relevance, and promised closer alignment with the Chinese people.[108] Complaining that missionary-led churches could not muster the support enjoyed by anti-Christian forces, many Chinese Christian leaders recalled the views of Cheng Jingyi who had argued since 1922 that only indigenization could bring about a Christianized China.[109]

Other Chinese Christians took active steps to distance the church from imperialism. On November 18, Chinese persuaded the National Christian Council of China, which was founded in 1922 to coordinate the activities of Protestant missions, to recommend terminating all treaty protection for Christians.[110] Quoting promises from Guomindang leader Liao Zhongkai

107. *FO* 405/250 [F1275/307/10], p. 510, Enclosure, Barton to Macleay, Shanghai, January 16, 1926.
108. Chao, "The Chinese Indigenous Church Movement," pp. 200-201.
109. Cheng was the secretary of the National Christian Council of China. Cheng, "The Development of an Indigenous Church in China," p. 370.
110. Chao, "The Chinese Indigenous Church Movement," p. 200. The National Christian

who said, "We must attack Christianity until it gets rid of its imperialistic elements, then we will welcome it as we have welcomed other religions in China," Guangzhou's outspoken YMCA head Li Yinglin (Y. L. Lee) argued that Chinese Christian leaders, "must do [their] best to help to get rid of the unequal treaties, for they are against Christian principles."[111]

Some went further still, trying to detach Christianity from foreign ties altogether. Baptists in Kaifeng renounced their association with the China Inland Mission and established their own churches.[112] Wenzhou Christians proclaimed, "Now that non-Christians are accusing us Christians of being the running dogs of foreigners, the good name of our faith is being maligned; so let us separate ourselves from the foreigners and flee from the power of the imperialists. We have been talking about independence for so long. Now is the time to rise up for independence."[113] On October 15, Chinese Baptists of Guangdong and Guangxi sent to all GMD organs and media outlets a declaration soundly denouncing the unequal treaties as well as all missionaries who still defended them.[114] Missionaries were still divided over the issue of indigenization, but Chinese Christian leaders widely embraced it as the best way to reduce anti-Christian agitation.[115]

Severing foreign ties may have removed the stigma of imperialism from Christians, but it alone did not necessarily justify inclusion within the "nation."[116] To prove that China's Christians were worthy to stand among the "people," they required, in the words of Jonathan Chao, "affirmation of identification" with China's national interests.[117] After the May Thirtieth Incident, demonstrations of this solidarity became common. The Christian National Salvation Alliance of Guangdong contacted the Nationalist Labor Ministry to condemn the Shanghai shootings and call for protest marches. Three days after the Shaji Incident, Guangdong and Guangxi Baptists issued similar pronouncements, decrying Britain's hand in the slaughter and calling for the annulment of the unequal treaties.[118] In November, the China Chris-

---

Council of China replaced the earlier China Continuation Committee which was founded in 1913 for the same purpose. Cui, *The Cultural Contribution of British Protestant Missionaries*, p. 21.

111. *FO* 405/250 [F119/1/10], pp. 24-25, Enclosure, Y. L. Lee report on Anti-Christian Movement, Guangzhou, November 9, 1925.

112. "Kaifeng neidihui quanti jiaoyou yin Hu'an yu Yingren wanquan juejiao xinzucheng 'Kaifeng Zhonghua Jidujiaohui' zhi xuanyan," *Shengming yuekan* V-9 (July 1925): 41-42.

113. "Wenzhou shengdaohui zili xuanyan," *Shengming yuekan* V-9 (July 1925): 42-43.

114. "Jidujiao liangguang jinxinhui daibiao dahui xuanyan," 1925.

115. Chao, "The Chinese Indigenous Church Movement," p. 207.

116. Anti-Christian forces based their opposition on a number of arguments. See *FO* 405/250 [F119/1/10], p. 24, Enclosure, Y. L. Lee report on Anti-Christian Movement, Guangzhou, November 9, 1925.

117. Chao, "The Chinese Indigenous Church Movement," p. 221.

118. "Guangdong Zhonghua jidutu jiuguo dalianhehui shang zhongyang gongrenbu daidian," June 26, 1925; "Liangguang jinxinhui banshisuo zhi zhongyang gongrenbu daidian," June 6,

tian Education Association accepted government registration, hired Chinese principals to replace foreigners, and made Bible-related courses elective.[119] Chinese Christians organized patriotic associations, such as the Supporters of the Shanghai Incident, which established branches in Beijing, Shanghai, Suzhou, Hangzhou, Changsha, Fuzhou, Ningbo, Harbin and elsewhere, and pressured the National Christian Council of China to demand a fair settlement for May Thirtieth Incident victims. Beijing Christians sided with the Shanghai Student Union in seeking treaty revisions.[120] The Shanghai Christian Student Union raised money for anti-British strikers while Nanjing and Shanghai Christians organized for the abolition of the unequal treaties. YMCA facilities routinely served revolutionary purposes.

In September, Henan's General Labor Union held its inaugural ceremonies in Zhengzhou's YMCA. The Chongqing YMCA, meanwhile, hosted demonstrations decrying foreign imperialism while the Young Men's Guild of the United Church of Canada Mission hosted comparable events.[121] To bolster its revolutionary image, the Lingnan University Student Union published an account of Lingnan's legacy that emphasized ties to Sun Yat-sen's old Revolutionary Alliance (Tongmenghui), campus visits by Sun himself, and the Lingnan student and teacher martyred during the Shaji Incident. Lest anyone confuse the students' intent, the declaration concluded by claiming, "Those who vilify Lingnan are not familiar with the history of the school and those going as far as to accuse Lingnan of anti-party and pro-imperialist views must have some vicious purpose. We hereby declare that we would like to express our sympathy to the Guomindang and the Nationalist Government."[122]

As Chinese Christian roots detached themselves from Christianity's foreign component, some foreigners retaliated. F. L. Hawks Pott, president of St. John's University in Shanghai, for example, became increasingly inflexible. Boone College issued a statement, warning, "While having deep sympathy with the Chinese students in their high nationalist ideals, the school feels that steady progress must be made in their school work for the advancement of Chinese education and citizenship. In the event of student strikes, the school will declare holiday at any time as it sees fit. Under such circumstances, students will be requested to leave the school with no re-

1925.

119. Wu, "Jiaohui xuexiao li'an yihou," p. 2.

120. "Beijing Zhongguo Jidutu Hu'an houyuanhui xuanyan," *Shengming yuekan* V-9 (July 1925): 35.

121. Yip, *Religion, Nationalism, and Chinese Students*, p. 47; *CWR* 34 (October 3, 1925): 124. The Zhengzhou YMCA shared a close relationship with labor organizations and helped organize them. Tso, *The Labor Movement in China*, p. 79; *CWR* 34 (September 5, 1925): 24.

122. "Lingnan daxue tongxuehui duiyu muxiao yiye tongxue fasheng jiufen shi xuanyan," April 1926.

funding of tuition."[123] When news of disruption diverted European and North American contributions to other causes, some China missionaries accepted salary reductions in order to continue.

In spite of these and other modest examples of hardening and belt-tightening, however, missionary resistance began to buckle. Immediately after the May Thirtieth Incident, several missionary associations renounced privileged protection under the unequal treaties, as did associations based in the U.S. and London. By January 1926, eighteen mission societies, including the larger ones, had repudiated treaty rights and demanded treaty revisions. The National Christian Council discouraged missionaries from relying on foreign consuls for aid and renounced special treaty protections.[124] Mission schools in Wuhan moved to register with the Beijing government while Christian students pressured the local Education Commissioner to enforce registration regulations.[125] By mid-1926, those still advocating *status quo* mission school independence and continued defiance of government regulations had lost considerable ground.

Revolutionary Choice: State-Building or Agitation?

Between June 1925 and June 1926, the southern regime chalked up some impressive triumphs. British and localist hostility had been checked by the Anti-British Boycott and state coercion, respectively. Chinese schools were becoming increasingly partyized while both Chinese Christians and foreign missionaries were detaching themselves from imperialism. Momentum notwithstanding, the party proceeded very cautiously in its official dealings with Christian institutions.

As expected, the GMD maintained support for the Anti-Christian Movement. Second National Congress declarations adopted in January 1926 reviled mission schools and church charities as imperialism's "throat, tongue, claws, and teeth" *(houshe yu zhuaya)*. Praising agitation, the Congress promised close party direction over all *guomin* struggling to carry out the Nationalist Revolution and swore, "even if the imperialists and their tools oppress us, we will not be shaken. . . . The time of their overthrow and destruction cannot be distant. In the end, final victory will be ours."[126] Reporting on the youth movement, Chen Gongbo proposed increasing the number of agitators, "so students can combat foreign school education and thus further the fight against imperialism. The youth are revolutionary even if some are not yet organized. We shall lead those who are already organized

---

123. *CWR* 34 (September 5, 1925): 25.
124. Dailey, "Bolshevik Students Put Check on American Donations," p. 356; *FO* 405/250 [F407/7/10], pp. 153-154, Macleay to Chamberlain, Beijing, December 7, 1925.
125. *CWR* 34 (September 26, 1925): 95.
126. "Zhongguo Guomindang dierci quanguo daibiao dahui xuanyan," *Geming wenxian*, vol. 69, pp. 154, 167.

and on the right track. We shall organize those who are not . . . and provide training."[127]

True to his word, Chen assumed control of the Anti-Christian Federation and broadened its reach.[128] Guangzhou Youth Ministry officials routinely attended demonstrations, issued propaganda, hosted conferences, and so forth. Lower-level party officers encouraged the anti-Christian agenda. Thus the Fujian Revolutionary Youth League could report to the Youth Ministry, "[our] objective is to awaken the Fujian people and encourage them to participate in the Nationalist Revolution for liberation. Future work will begin by promoting party principles as well as all other political policies so that the people of Fujian can obtain a better understanding of both the Nationalist Revolution and our enemies."[129] Even student unions in small villages decried imperialism and condemned foreign schools.[130]

As usual, the party benefited.[131] Seeking respite from disruptive agitation, missionaries sought help from Guomindang authorities rather than the unequal treaties, providing party officials *de facto* recognition and heightened status while devaluing that of the treaties. Mediation also gave party leaders a chance to urge missionaries to accept registration and renounce the unequal treaties in order to reduce the "imperialist" stigma that motivated anti-Christian agitation in the first place. As foreign affairs minister Wu Chaogang explained to a gathering of foreign guests, Chinese harbored no ill feelings toward foreigners, only the unequal treaties which injured China's well-being. "If such sentiments as these are anti-foreign, I much confess that I am anti-foreign myself and proud of it," Wu proclaimed.[132] The antidote to agitation was simple: tear up the unequal treaties. Chinese Christians were given the same option—comply and the regime will help you.[133] In both cases, the Nationalists enticed voluntary submission with powerful incentives.

Distinct advantages notwithstanding, GMD-sponsored anti-Christian agitation also produced complications. Success raised agitator expectations

---

127. "Guangzhou tebieshi zhixing weiyuanhui qingnianbut eryuefen gongzuo jinguo baogao," March-April, 1926; Chen, "Zhongyang dangbu qingnian yundong baogao," 1926.
128. *CWR* 35 (January 9, 1926): 168.
129. "Jiangsusheng qingnianbu siyuefen baogao," May 1926; "Fujian geming tongzhi qingniantuan zhi zhongyang qingnianbu han," May 13, 1926; "Fujian geming tongzhi qingniantuan zhi zhongyang qingnianbu han," May 1926.
130. "Maping qingniantuan xuanyan," April 16, 1926.
131. In small ways, anti-Christian forces augmented Guangzhou's defenses by scrutinizing the actions of foreigners. CEC investigators responded quickly, for example, after *dangtuan* reports from Lingnan University warned that school officials had expelled youth movement agitators, resisted Education Commission orders, and smuggled over one hundred handguns into the campus from Shamian. (Report #10), *2-ZXWH*, vol. 2 (April 23, 1926); "Zhongyang zhixing weiyuanhui zhi qingnianbu han," December 29, 1925.
132. *USDS* 893.00/6026, Jenkins to Secretary of State, Guangzhou, January 16, 1925.
133. *CWR* 36 (April 17, 1926): 174.

and demands. The First Congress of Peasant Associations, for example, pressured Guomindang headquarters for more secular schools to offset mission school influence. Success also elevated anti-Christian violence and destructiveness. Wesley College agitators assaulted other students trying to attend classes. In Guangzhou, agitators in GMD uniforms kidnapped fifty-six students from their dormitories at Presbyterian Guangzhou Union Middle School. Other attacks broke out at Holy Trinity College and Gongyi (Kung Yee) Nursing School.[134] Some institutions collapsed from the pressure. A blockade against Lingnan threatened to starve out students and teachers.[135] Cutting water and electricity at the U.S. missionary-run Guangzhou Hospital, labor pickets forced it to close. Crowds in Guilin and Longzhou destroyed mission property.[136]

Labor interests greatly intensified agitation's destructive potential. Recruited into the Anti-Christian Movement, labor organizers found a ready welcome among employees at Christian institutions, adding an additional layer of labor disruption to the anti-Christian variety already facing Christian institutions. A Youth Ministry report, for example, explained that, "In places other than Guangdong, it is the students who are guiding the peasants and workers movements, but in Guangdong . . . it seems the peasants and workers are guiding the students."[137] Labor agitation commonly generated cycles of active and reactive violence between police and strikers, a phenomenon made especially fiery when union rivalries were added to the mix.[138]

The magnitude of anti-Christian disorder *within* GMD territory presented party leaders with a difficult choice: (1) pursue agitative objectives by overpowering Christian institutions but risk provoking the war Chiang Kai-shek and Zhou Enlai had warned about, or (2) improve foreign relations and pursue concessions from the powers by limiting agitation but risk undermining support among the masses. The choice placed the Guomindang in ironic straits for it was the same dilemma confronting northern authorities. Despite rhetoric denouncing "reactionary" Beijing, however, the party responded just like its northern rivals by siding with state-building over agitation.

---

134. Yip, *Religion, Nationalism, and Chinese Students*, p. 52; *CWR* 34 (October 10, 1925): 144; *CWR* 34 (October 3, 1925): 126; *CWR* 36 (May 22, 1926): 328; *CWR* 36 (May 15, 1926): 300.

135. Hostilities arose when Lingnan expelled three students for "misconduct." *CWR* 36 (May 15, 1926): 300.

136. Roosevelt, "Russia and Great Britain in China," p. 236. The suppression of agitation also proved violent. Catholic organizations in rural districts with strong ties to peasants occasionally repelled agitators. Yip, *Religion, Nationalism, and Chinese Students*, pp. 53-55.

137. Chen, "Zhongyang dangbu qingnian yundong baogao," 1926.

138. Agitators fostered bloody clashes between police and striking workers. *CWR* 34 (September 19, 1925): 64; *CWR* 34 (September 26, 1925): 92, 94; *CWR* 34 (October 3, 1925): 124; *CWR* 34 (October 10, 1925): 146; *CWR* 35 (January 2, 1926): 143.

In April 1926, Lingnan University administrators expelled three students for encouraging strikes among university workers. Four Lingnan professors sided with the agitators but most of the student body stood by school authorities, dividing the campus. Supporters of the three agitators denounced Lingnan's "foreign slaves" *(yangnu)* and "counter-revolutionaries" before demanding: "We urgently request closure of the school and the proper arrangement of staff who are party members. The school should be prohibited from reopening and the land should be confiscated so that imperialist conspiracies will be completely destroyed." [139] In contrast, unsympathetic Lingnan University student leaders asked the party to banish the agitators. Similarly, the Lingnan Student Representatives Group appealed directly to the "people," condemning the agitators and four supportive faculty members a public letter while asking: "Have we shaken the foundation of Lingnan University by expelling bad students? We hope the four professors can tell us the answer for the sake of the future of education and for the sake of *private education's future development as protected by the government*." [140] [Emphasis added.] Both sides fully expected regime support, but it was the agitators who were shocked when Guomindang authorities decided against them and refused to close the school.

Under certain conditions, agitators found themselves left in the cold, a pattern that repeated itself beyond the Lingnan case and generated considerable irritation among student leaders. [141] Complaining to Guomindang authorities about a school which expelled seventeen students for shouting revolutionary slogans, one student petition lamented, "We cannot understand why this kind of reactionary event could take place *under the leadership of the revolutionary party*." [142] Striking Trinity students lodged similar complaints in May 1926. When school authorities expelled student leaders, cut dormitory food, and banned all meetings, strikers sought aid from party headquarters but were treated only to indifferent silence before being told to contact the Youth Ministry. Reporting to Ministry officials, the students complained, "The strike has lasted for more than a month while the school has rejected our requests. Guangzhou Education Bureau negotiations have failed several times. On May 7, school authorities announced school closure and forced us to leave the school but refused to return our paid tuition. We hereby ask for help from the Youth Ministry to tell Guangdong University to

---

139. "Lianyi haiwai jiaotongbu tebie dangbu shang zhongyang zhixing weiyuanhui cheng," April 25, 1926.

140. "Guangzhou lingnan daxue quanti xuesheng wei qingchu buliang fenzi xuanyan," April 6, 1926; "Jinzhiwen Wei Tang Liang Liu siwei xuesheng de xuanyan," April 13, 1926.

141. See *Guanyu Yue Gui liangdi xuexiao xuesheng bake shijian yijiao jiaoyu xingzheng weiyuanhui banli zhi wenshu, GHGZ*, April 1926.

142. The incident took place at Chenghai County Number Two High School. "Wei 'Xianli ergao xuesheng bei yapo' xuanyan," April 27, 1926.

enroll all of us and waive tuition so that dozens of students will not be homeless."[143]

If anyone received special assistance from Nationalist authorities, it was Guangdong's Christian leaders and missionaries. In late 1925, party leaders helped negotiate the release of students kidnapped from Presbyterian Guangzhou Union Middle School.[144] Mediation by government educational officials helped end a blockade against Lingnan University. Ordering that electricity and water be restored, the GMD Labor Commissioner broke the cordon around Guangzhou Hospital in March 1926. Continuing his arbitration between the two sides, the commissioner then pushed the workers to soften their demands and tried to convince the Americans not to close the hospital since the workers' revised demands were not unreasonable and had not been conceived with malicious intent. In January 1926, party headquarters ordered district magistrates to protect the freedom of religion as guaranteed by the constitution and to meet anti-Christian violence with action. In March, foreign papers reported that GMD authorities were even talking about forcing Guangdong University, a fountainhead of anti-imperialist agitation, to stop using its facilities for anti-Christian rallies. The reason presented in these reports was that the university was public property and therefore belonged to all citizens—including Christians.[145]

Surprised foreigners saw other signs of regime rapproachment with Christians. The rabidly anti-foreign Guangzhou Strike Committee granted special exit papers to the YMCA secretary while denying the same to almost everyone else. Strike leaders even let overseas Chinese visit Guangzhou directly from Hong Kong so they could attend activities hosted by the Guangzhou YMCA and Christian schools. In May 1926, under party pressure, the GSC forbad its pickets from entering the premises of foreign institutions or properties, particularly mission schools.[146] When the *Guangzhou People's Daily (Guangzhou renmin ribao)* dropped an anti-Christian supplement, a few enthusiastic observers used the occasion to exclaim that the move confirmed that very little anti-foreignism could be found among the party's education authorities.[147]

---

143. Ye, et. al., "Shengsanyi quanti bake xuesheng daibiao Ye Yaoqiu deng cheng zhongyang qingnianbu han," May 18, 1926.

144. The party blamed the crime on ordinary bandits—even though the kidnappers used GMD military launches, wore GMD uniforms, and denounced the school's non-revolutionary students, teachers, and alumni. *CWR* 34 (October 31, 1925): 218; *CWR* 35 (December 12, 1925): 53; *CWR* 35 (December 19, 1925): 84.

145. *CWR* 32 (March 14, 1925): 51; *CWR* 35 (January 16, 1926): 192; *CWR* 36 (March 27, 1926): 98; *CWR* 36 (May 22, 1926): 328.

146. *CWR* 34 (September 19, 1925): 66; *CWR* 35 (January 23, 1926): 220; *CWR* 36 (May 22, 1926): 328.

147. *CWR* 36 (March 13, 1926): 46; *USDS* 893.00/5423, Jenkins to Schurman, Guangzhou, April 2, 1924.

Oddly enough, no one worked harder to accommodate missionaries and offer them a warm hand than Mikhail Borodin. In December 1925, he told two YMCA secretaries that Christianity held much in common with communist principles, and that he did not oppose the religion unless it served as an anti-nationalistic force. That same month, when the Anti-Christian Federation announced a special "Anti-Christian Week," Borodin summarily quashed it, counseling revolutionaries to avoid action that might provoke the powers. Instead he advised cooperation, calling for a "united front" with Christians supporting national emancipation and the revolution.[148]

Fear partially explains the party's soft treatment of Christians after mid-1925. Borodin himself warned against provocative anti-foreign incidents that might justify an imperialist response. Evidence also indicates, however, that he and other party leaders were motivated by higher objectives. Borodin's quickness to silence anti-Christian activity and aid beleaguered institutions caught the attention of both Chinese Christian and missionary leaders. Many routinely approached the Soviet advisor in hopes of mitigating agitation. On December 31, 1925, Borodin met with Dr. James M. Henry of Lingnan University and explained his motives, expressing concern that anti-Christian activity would create a negative impression of the Nationalist regime in the eyes of other nations and that such activity could not be tolerated if the party leaders hoped to produce a positive image abroad.[149]

Agitation had long been used to pressure foreign interests, as the Seamen's Strike, Anti-Shamian Boycott, and the Anti-British Boycott attested. What Borodin described to Henry, however, was the opposite—government *restraints* on anti-Christian agitation as a way to improve foreign relations. British authorities already knew that only the Nationalists could control agitation, and Borodin knew they knew.

In simple terms, party encouragement of anti-Christian agitation was carefully balanced with efforts to accommodate foreign interests. From a state-building perspective, however, support for anti-Christian forces sought more than just mission school registration. In key ways the Anti-Christian Movement functioned as a pawn in the higher stakes game of foreign policy and international relations. Nevertheless, its role was not as minor as the term "pawn" implies. In the realm of power politics—dominated by grappling British and Strike Committee interests—there existed few opportunities for the party to offer conciliation as dual-prong tactics required. Something had to counterbalance the weighty Anti-British Boycott, win foreign sympathies, and neutralize British interventionist impulses. Returning Shantou's native customs to foreign control helped, but it was too isolated a case. Accom-

---

148. *Minguo ribao* (December 6, 1925); Chao, "The Chinese Indigenous Church Movement," p. 183; Yip, *Religion, Nationalism, and Chinese Students*, p. 63.
149. *FO* 405/250 [F756/1/10], pp. 353-354, Enclosure 2, Henry's interview with Borodin, Guangzhou, December 31, 1926.

modating Christians, therefore, became doubly important. Borodin offered aid to Chinese believers and missionaries alike while even revolutionary leaders directly engaged in fanning agitation, such as Zhou Enlai, called for "civilized" anti-imperialism. Any offer of assistance to missionaries provided evidence that the government could and would deliver stability and fairness if foreigners simply acknowledged regime authority. It also won missionary allies against the unequal treaties.

In this light, accommodation of foreign interests did not reflect a policy reversal, factional shift, or weak-kneed cowardice. Conditions had changed. In 1922 and in 1924, the party had tried to hide behind dual-prong tactics to avoid foreign accusations and intervention. After June 1925, however, it used the same strategy to entice improved foreign relations from a position of strength.

As further evidence of Guomindang strength and interest in improving foreign relations, the southern regime finally began to promulgate an official policy vis-à-vis mission schools but then made few efforts to enforce it. In July 1925, just after consolidating military control in Guangzhou and initiating the Anti-British Boycott, the party modestly proclaimed that mission schools must register with the Nationalist Government. Announcing the regulations through the Guangdong Education Department rather than the Guomindang's Education Ministry, central authorities cautiously framed the change as a provincial educational concern rather than a national foreign policy one. Significantly, the party also demanded only the most basic of changes: schools could not use scripture as texts nor require attendance at religious services.[150]

Compared to Beijing's directives, Guangzhou's looked feeble. On November 11, 1925, Beijing's Education Ministry repeated demands that missionary schools register with the government, hire Chinese principals, and stop mandatory religious instruction.[151] Five days later, the Ministry announced six rules for mission school accreditation, warning that any school failing to comply would face closure.[152] Guangzhou, on the other hand, made no mention of enforcement or punishment for the noncompliant. Not sur-

---

150. "Yuejiaoting qudi jiaohui xuexiao zhi banfa," *Jiaoyu zazhi* 17: 7 (July 1925): 8.

151. Chao, "The Chinese Indigenous Church Movement," p. 216.

152. The rules required that all foreign-run schools: (1) apply for government accreditation; (2) add the word "private" *(sili)* to the school name; (3) appoint a Chinese principal or vice-principal; (4) ensure that at least half of the board of directors was Chinese; (5) avoid proselytizing as a primary objective; and (6) utilize Ministry-approved curricula and eliminate compulsory religious courses. "Beijing jiaoyubu bugao dishiliu hao," in *Guonei jinshinian lai zhi zongjiao sichao*, comp. Zhang, pp. 370-371. Attempts to register private Chinese schools went nowhere. Beijing's financial problems ensured that compliance brought few incentives while noncompliance produced no real inconvenience. "Jiaobu duiyu sili daxue zhi qudi," *Jiaoyu zazhi* 17: 11 (November 1925): 5; "Sili xuexiao zhuce tiaoli zhi gongbu," *Jiaoyu zazhi* 17: 12 (December 1925): 9; *CWR* 35 (February 27, 1926): 373.

prisingly, therefore, the GMD regulations generated little attention among Christian educators. Confident that the Nationalist Government would soon collapse anyway, most of Guangzhou's missionaries voted to reject the Nationalists' directives a few months later, claiming that the Bible would still be taught and that disapproving parents could enroll their children elsewhere.[153]

Despite their tepid, timid, and tardy appearance, Guangzhou's regulations were actually stronger than Beijing's. Hard or soft regulatory language in no way reflected actual influence. Blustery threats meant little as long as the Beijing regime lacked the power to enforce its directives, and everyone, including officials in Beijing, knew it. In a letter seeking advice on how to best curb proselytizing in mission schools, Beijing's education minister asked the foreign affairs minister, "Can we even do this?"[154] The Beijing government was even weaker when agitation entered the picture. Northern authorities found mission schools troubling but viewed anti-Christian disruption as a vexation requiring a swift and sound solution. In Wuchang, local authorities threatened to close all schools and incarcerated student activists while demanding that schools guarantee student behavior. In April 1926, Hubei's warlord government banned "radical" student speeches.[155] National and regional educational leaders concurred, distancing their own calls for reform from agitative propaganda by calling it "Bolshevik," "red," or "radical." At the October 1925 conference of the National Education Association of China, delegates from virtually every province voted to condemn revolutionary agitators from Shanghai and Guangzhou and denounce the manipulation of students for "political purposes."[156] Even agitators found agitation uncomfortable. In Wuchang, student organizers publicly repudiated claims that their rallies sought to commemorate "red" successes in south China.[157] As implied, regime suppression could slow agitative disruption, but it also aligned local authorities with imperialism, undermining their credibility and legitimacy.[158]

Profiled next to Beijing, Guangzhou looked strong. Through its influence over agitation, the revolutionary regime could easily pressure Christian schools. Nevertheless, with larger geostrategic issues at stake, Guomindang leaders stopped short, limiting official involvement to soft-peddled regulations seeking "uniform accreditation standards" and generous accommoda-

---

153. *CWR* 34 (September 5, 1925): 23.
154. "Waibu duiyu xianzhi jiaohui xuexiao chuanjiao zhi yijian," *Jiaoyu zazhi* 18: 4 (April 1926): 7.
155. *CWR* 35 (January 2, 1926): 143; *CWR* 36 (May 1, 1926): 236.
156. *CWR* 34 (September 26, 1925): 94; *CWR* 34 (October 17, 1925): 177; *CWR* 34 (November 7, 1925): 237.
157. *CWR* 34 (November 21, 1925): 288.
158. "Qingnianbu siyuefen gongzuo jingguo baogao," May 20, 1926.

tive efforts on behalf of the missionaries. This is significant. While Beijing and Guangzhou both checked anti-Christian agitation, their motives were quite different. Beijing's flailing aimed to curb revolutionary influence. The Nationalists, on the other hand, deftly quieted agitation to help produce a "positive image abroad" while holding its full fury over the head of foreign interests. While anti-agitative crackdowns painted the Beijing regime as "reactionary," agitative-dampening commentary in the south portrayed the Guangzhou regime as "civilized." Beijing used violence while Guangzhou employed party directives and negotiation. Foundering, Beijing had lost control; holding all the strings, Guangzhou seemed to fully enjoy it.

Under these circumstances, missionaries themselves became a tool of anti-imperialism by reporting on and confirming Nationalist sincerity. With time, they shifted from imperialism's "throat, tongue, claws, and teeth" to party propaganda organs in their own right, pressuring London and Washington to leave the southern regime alone and work toward a better relationship. Offered payment in kind—full inclusion within the new Guomindang "nation"—missionaries responded. In a sense, the party needed mission schools to be independent more than the missionaries did. Placed under full government control like Chinese educational institutions, Christian schools and their educators would have lost credibility and persuasive power abroad. Thriving, autonomous, and intact, however, they could more effectively influence their foreign constituencies. From the revolutionary state-building perspective, Christian institutions stood side by side with anti-Christian forces; both represented mechanisms for eroding the roots of imperialism and cultivating better foreign ties.

6. State-Building Dominance
—Negotiating Domestic and Foreign Stability, July - November 1926

The Anti-British Strike has attracted world attention. We persisted for 15 months [and] helped the imperialists realize that we would not be insulted. The past 15 months, however, also proved very dangerous because we could not back the strikes with military force. We were not strong enough to resist the enemy even if not engaged in the Northern Expedition. The only thing we could do was deal with them through diplomatic approaches. . . . We were doomed to fail if we did not change because diplomacy is highly dependent on military force. Without this "last resort," we could not continue the strike. It would have been discouraging for the workers and disgraceful for the country if our strike failed to achieve good results. We wanted to reach an agreement with the British through negotiation and end the strike from the very beginning but the British would not agree to our conditions and seemed to lack sincerity. To the contrary, they did everything to sabotage it which is why negotiations did not show any progress. The strike's future was not optimistic and depended solely on the strength of the pickets. . . . Military intervention was inevitable . . . if things had continued like this. Therefore, after discussing with fellow workers, we realized that the old way no longer worked and required a change. We will, therefore, now use propaganda instead of pickets.[1]

  —Tan Yankai, GMD military commander and CEC member, October 15, 1926

On the morning of May 21, 1926, a group of pickets enforcing the Anti-British Boycott gathered near the British consulate in Shantou. Equipped with posters and glue, the band readied itself for the day's first task. The scene had repeated itself for months, ever since Guomindang troops liberated the eastern Guangdong city in November 1925. By strike committee order, the mission of the pickets was not to attack or destroy but to isolate and irritate—duties at which they excelled. Under their watchful eyes, no Chinese vendors would sell to British customers and no workers would lift a finger to offer service, forcing British bluejackets to shoulder the burden of offloading needed supplies from Japanese ships. Encouraged by picket

---

1. Tan, "Tan Yankai tongzhi zhongyang zhengzhi baogao," *ZWDL-YS* (October 15, 1926).

pressures, Chinese staff and domestic servants deserted British factories, institutions, and homes, increasing the demand for white Russian, Indian, and Eurasian help.[2] The British consulate was particularly quiet. Since no Chinese would enter the compound, Consul Cecil Kirke had to venture into town if he had business.

On the morning of May 21, Kirke left for an early meeting with the GMD Commissioner of Foreign Affairs. With the consul away, the strikers spread out along the consulate compound's outer wall and began affixing their posters. Each showcased a prominent hammer and sickle insignia above vermillion text denouncing British imperialism and capitalism. In no time, the drab wall featured a festive hue. This was not the first time the consulate had been so adorned. The outer walls were popular with mass organizations eager to revile British imperialism. For months, Kirke had sought police protection from such insult and "vandalisms" but without success, despite Nationalist promises to protect foreign lives and property. Upon his return and discovery of the picket's latest installment, therefore, the frustrated consul proceeded, as usual, to tear the posters down one by one. This time, however, the angry pickets reacted, quickly surrounding him and demanding that he explain himself. Ignoring their protests, Kirke detached another sheet when a picket leader screamed into his face and attacked. Instantly, chaos erupted as six or seven other pickets joined in the fist-flying frenzy. Kirke resisted briefly before retreating hastily into the compound—dodging a stick hurled after him as he fled.

Catching his breath, the consul found his adrenaline and rage peaking. Although pickets had meted out the beating, he reserved his hottest reproach for the Shantou police, several of whom had passively watched the entire incident without so much as blowing a whistle. Stripped of all confidence that GMD officials could or would maintain the peace, Kirke ordered in British bluejackets from the nearby *H.M.S. Hollyhock*, scattering the pickets in a panic as soon as the troops arrived.

Kirke's move ended the standoff with the boycott pickets but immediately opened another one with local Guomindang officials when he announced that the troops would remain until Chinese authorities apologized, banned further mass belligerence, punished the perpetrators, and cleared all pickets from the consulate vicinity. Shantou's Commissioner of Foreign Affairs could not have been pleased with the picket attacks or Kirke's demands. Striker assaults had provoked British troops to land on Chinese soil which, in turn, only incited more anti-British agitation and striker attacks. From the Commissioner's perspective, avoiding escalation required dexter-

---

2. *FO* 405/252a [F3424/1/10], p. 167, Enclosure 1, Kirke to Macleay, Shantou, June 29, 1926. Northern Chinese caught working for the British consulate risked arrest, trial, and expulsion. *FO* 405/250 [F999/1/0], pp. 433-434, Macleay to Chamberlain, Beijing, January 11, 1926.

ous handling, especially since the combined mass of Shantou's agitative forces and British military might far outweighed his own authority. In a surprisingly weak move, he first appealed to China's treaty rights, asking Kirke to withdraw the troops since their presence broke international law and treaty arrangements. Furious that party officials had failed to prevent strikers from trampling British treaty rights, Kirke refused to budge and a week later rejected Foreign Affairs office apologies. As a result, the Commissioner found himself in an unenviable position. Although he ordered deeper police vigilance and asked strike leaders to punish the picket assailants, the British had demanded something that he could not provide—a guarantee. Visiting the consulate in person, the Commissioner "begged" Kirke to accept his apology and withdraw the bluejackets, explaining that no Shantou official possessed the power to punish renegade pickets or curb their activities and that Britain's troop presence only enflamed them more. Aware that holding out longer would only jeopardize the well-being of British subjects and the Commissioner's fragile authority alike, and convinced that he had gained the upper hand, Kirke happily reported:

> I was satisfied that the Commissioner for Foreign Affairs himself had done all he could and I was anxious to reach a settlement, if possible, before the 30th May, the anniversary of the Shanghai [May Thirtieth] incident, as I was aware that popular demonstrations were arranged for that date, and, while I personally was in no danger, I thought that the presence ashore of an armed guard of British sailors might provide an excuse for the agitators to stir up hostility against British subjects in the city and so create a situation which would be very difficult to deal with. . . . *I believe that the [GMD] officials now realize that if they continue to close their eyes to the unchecked hooliganism that goes on in the city, they may at any time find themselves in a situation that will not enhance their dignity.*[3] [Emphasis added.]

Explaining why circumstances had developed as they did, Kirke observed: "The fact is, of course, that the police fear the pickets much more than they fear the Commissioner for Foreign Affairs or their own officers."[4]

In Shantou, at least, the pecking order was clear: at the top sat the strike pickets, followed by the slightly weaker government police, and finally the GMD Commissioner of Foreign Affairs. Party officials were not immune from agitative excesses. Even Shantou's mayor was arrested, detained, and rebuked by pickets for a full twenty-four hours for a "deplorable lack of patriotism."[5] In short, while very effective at splitting localist interests from

---

3. *FO* 405/252a [F2953/1/10], pp. 58-59, Enclosure, Kirke to Macleay, Shantou, June 10, 1926. Also see *FO* 405/251 [F2192/71/10], p. 195, weekly summary, May 26, 1926.

4. *FO* 405/252a [F3424/1/10], p. 168, Enclosure 1, Kirke to Macleay, Shantou, June 29, 1926.

5. *FO* 405/252a [F3424/1/10], p. 168, Enclosure 1, Kirke to Macleay, Shantou, June 29, 1926.

British supporters and alienating Chinese Christians from foreign mission-aries, the corrosive effects of dual-prong tactics could also splash back on the revolutionary state-builders supposedly them. Even when top CEC officials ordered it, in short, popular agitation could refuse to stay limited.

Sun Yat-sen had warned that unrestrained Soviet-styled mass move-ments would pursue their own agendas. Decentralized and undisciplined, they were untrustworthy. Borodin's assurances persuaded party members to set aside misgivings and embrace popular mobilization, but they did not erase the problems that Sun had foreseen. Party leaders tried to minimize agitative excesses. To prevent localist interests from infiltrating and steering mass organizations, the party prohibited workers and peasants from entering merchant corps and prevented merchants and landlords from joining labor unions or peasant associations.[6] These and other regulations, however, overlooked the possibility that workers, students, and peasants could *them-selves* defy central authority. Even worse, from the perspective of the GMD, Nationalist statutes had no impact on the vast number of organizations with only loose ties to the party.

Decentralized agitative autonomy may have freed CEC officials from culpability and expanded their reach, but it also gravely undermined central control once agitative forces began to discover their full-blown potential. In March 1926, for example, anti-imperialist Christians connected to the Guangxi Chinese Christian Promotion Association attacked Wuzhou's Stout Memorial Hospital. When U.S. Baptist missionaries offered joint Chi-nese/missionary control but then failed to produce a definite timetable, anti-Christian agitators besieged the hospital while Association leaders publicly renounced all ties of friendship with the missionaries. On March 31, the Americans closed the hospital and departed through a long cordon of pressing and jeering crowds.[7] Rather than praising the agitators' "success," however, central GMD officials sided with the missionaries and rejected Guangxi provincial government petitions for permission to seize the com-pound. The Guangxi governor protested, arguing that if Guangzhou officials could confiscate Gongyi (Kung Yee) Medical College and Hospital then he should be allowed to seize the Stout Hospital. CEC officials countered, claiming that Gongyi facilities were Chinese while Stout Memorial Hospital was property of the American Baptist mission and, therefore, had to be handled differently.[8] Despite the clear position of central headquarters, however, Guangxi authorities occupied the American hospital anyway. Anti-Christian activists celebrated, but CEC officials were greatly irritated.

---

6. Wilbur and How, *Missionaries of Revolution*, p. 107.
7. *CWR* 36 (April 17, 1926): 180; Daily, "How the 'Reds' Drove American Missionaries From Wuchow," pp. 156-158.
8. *CWR* 36 (May 29, 1926): 352; *Guangdong daxue jieshou gongyi xuexiao jingguo qingxing*, *GHGZ*, July 1925-August 1926.

The Anti-British Boycott produced even deeper cracks in the revolutionary camp. Many high Guomindang officials tired of it for economic reasons. Acute shortages of consumer goods, such as refined sugar, flour, and leather, pinched consumers and industry alike. The boycott devastated rural economies along Guangdong's coastal regions, prompting peasant attacks against picket lines.[9] Tax revenues dipped, non-British trade slowed, and failing fuel oil, coal, and raw material stocks threatened munitions production.[10] Worse still were the problems generated by unruly strikers. Self-appointed pickets, operating without Guangzhou Strike Committee consent, sought nothing more than their own profit.[11] Others defied GMD authority. Although the Finance Ministry stamped 2,950 cases of badly needed Hong Kong kerosene for safe passage into Guangzhou, for example, picket leaders confiscated the consignment anyway. Guangzhou's Commissioner of Municipal Reconstruction repeatedly promised to protect postal functions, but he could not stop picket seizures even when party officials tried to intervene on the spot. In March 1926, rising incidents of "illegal" striker interference prompted Guangzhou's foreign-run Customs Administration to threaten to close the port to *all* trade, forcing the Nationalist regime to employ police to keep the strikers in line. Even deepened law enforcement authority, however, did not guarantee success. For example, when police in Foshan tried to convey a shipment of dyes through picket lines, they were overpowered and lost the contested parcels anyway.[12]

Popular agitation produced other unhealthy consequences. Party efforts to secure the defection of General Tang Shengzhi in southern Hunan, for example, collapsed when revolutionary agitators attacked his authority.[13] Zhang Zuolin consistently offered to align with the Guangzhou regime if it would sever ties with Russia and stem mass-based disruption in the north. In short, agitation—so effective against GMD enemies—became a liability when those same enemies wanted to become friends.

Central control also struggled with the natural results of mass movement independence and autonomy. Labor, peasant, and student organizations often

---

9. Deng, *Zhongguo zhi gong yundong jianshi*, pp. 192-193.

10. *FO* 405/250 [F1246/1/10], p. 523, Jamieson to Macleay, Guangzhou, February 15, 1926.

11. Some pickets took bribes for favors. *CWR* 34 (September 26, 1925): 94. In June 1926, the Committee controlled some $5 million dollars while expending only eleven cents a day per striker, leaving it exceptionally well-funded for an extra-government organization and tempting others to participate as well. Su Zhaozheng, chair of the GSC and head of the Seamen's Union, reported that most funds came from contributions and the sale of confiscated "contraband." Chan, *China, Britain, and Hong Kong*, pp. 183-184; Gannett, "Why Canton is Radical Center of Asia," p. 31.

12. *CWR* 34 (November 28, 1925): 318; *CWR* 35 (January 9, 1926): 168; *CWR* 36 (March 13, 1926): 44, 49; *CWR* 36 (March 27, 1926): 98; *CWR* 36 (April 3, 1926): 126; *FO* 405/250 [F1246/1/10], p. 523, Jamieson to Macleay, Guangzhou, February 15, 1926.

13. Jordan, *The Northern Expedition*, p. 72.

pursued partisan objectives in ways that made them more closely resemble localist interests than the obedient Leninist cogs originally envisioned at the First National Congress. Popular organizations had hearts and minds of their own. Labor strikes and unionization automatically pursued economic benefit. Many unions defined their membership by dialect, geography, family, or personal ties, thus introducing inter-union divisions that ran counter to the unifying vision presented by the Guomindang's purveyors of nationalism. In Guangzhou, for example, two coolie labor unions—one comprised of locals and one of workers from Shantou—fought vicious battles for control over jobs.[14] Rival unions locked in inter-labor struggles for turf and domination greatly complicated grander revolutionary plans. Meanwhile, equally motivated by conflicts of personality or petty advantage, student unions could be just as challenging.

Grand revolutionary vision and momentum toward nationalistic objectives, in short, had to accommodate the narrow pursuits of low-level revolutionary interests. When their particular objectives coincided, high and low revolutionary forces could challenge even imperialist institutions such as mission schools. When those interests clashed, however, revolutionary energies lost their synergy, stalling momentum and generating unintended consequences.[15] During times of GMD weakness, raging agitation gave party leaders mediating opportunities. As the party became stronger, however, state-building required more than just mediation opportunities; it also needed compliance. As long as CEC leaders could control the revolution's agitative forces, the two revolutionary branches shared a fruitful symbiosis. Nevertheless, state-building dominance could not always be assured. At that point, the divisive nature of dual-prong tactics proved as capable of alienating revolutionary agitators from revolutionary state-builders as it was at splitting non-revolutionary interests.

Agitative versus State-Building Objectives

Hoping to stabilize socioeconomic and central political control, the CEC made several attempts to bring the Anti-British Boycott to an end. Through late 1925 and early 1926, however, each time party leaders tried to open negotiations the Guangzhou Strike Committee refused to cooperate. Frustrated, Chiang Kai-shek moved unilaterally to curb GSC authority.[16] On March 20, forces under his command raided the Strike Committee headquarters, disarmed the more "troublesome" pickets, and ordered several

---

14. Chan, "Labor and Empire," pp. 215-217, 239-240.
15. Tsin, *Nation, Governance, and Modernity in China*, p. 144.
16. *CWR* 34 (September 26, 1925): 92; *CWR* 34 (November 21, 1925): 288; *CWR* 34 (November 28, 1925): 318; *CWR* 35 (December 5, 1925): 21; *CWR* 35 (December 12, 1925): 53; *CWR* 35 (February 6, 1926): 291; *CWR* 36 (March 6, 1926): 13.

strike leaders to step down.[17] With Chiang's coup, GMD political policy swung from the left to the right, emphasizing central control over mass-activism and anti-imperialism.

Sensing a change in the political winds, some strikers returned to Hong Kong while others reluctantly signed up for work on reconstruction projects.[18] A few strike leaders defied the regime, forming a "picket fleet" from confiscated launches and announcing that mercenaries in the Third and Fourth Army Corps would rebel if the party continued its "double-cross." Police and military forces prevailed, however, allowing Chiang to disband non-GSC pickets, plant agents to watch union meetings, and oversee picket inspection proceedigns. Soon thereafter, picket disruptions declined.[19]

Official GMD and CCP histories accurately describe Chiang's coup as a reaction to communist intrigue. Nevertheless, curbing communism was not the sole objective. Authorities rounded up *all* unemployed men for deportation or employment on state projects in order to bring agitation further under state control and proceed toward ending the boycott. In late April, a subdued GSC announced that it would follow party direction and prepare to end the strike.[20] A month later, on May 31, the CEC published eight resolutions aimed at augmenting social stability. To the delight of Guangzhou's localist interests, five of these resolutions promised to abolish the hated oil monopoly, suppress brigandage, establish an arbitration board for mediating labor/capital disputes, earmark revenues for education and development, and end government corruption. The remaining three specifically targeted agitation. Resolution two ordered the Foreign Affairs Ministry to conclude the boycott. Resolution five added, "Henceforth, no civilian organization of the people may use force . . . and all violators of this order will be treated as rebels." Resolution seven warned, "The military and police are ordered to suppress all sedition and attempts to create disorder."[21] Excepting bandits, a few village militias, and an occasional spy, no one sat as clearly in the cross-hairs as Guangzhou's own mass organizations.[22] By all indications, regime interest in popular agitation had faded.

---

17. *FO* 405/250 [F1355/71/10], p. 524, weekly summary, March 26, 1926; *CWR* 36 (April 3, 1926): 126. Although most scholars point to Chiang's running feud with Soviet advisors and rising CCP influence as the source of the crackdown, it is interesting to note that contemporary foreign observers saw it as a move against "anti-Red" troops by the most strident of the "ultra-Reds"—Chiang Kai-shek. *CWR* 36 (March 27, 1926): 99.

18. *CWR* 35 (January 16, 1926): 192; *CWR* 35 (February 27, 1926): 368; *CWR* 36 (March 6, 1926): 13; *CWR* 36 (April 3, 1926): 126.

19. *CWR* 36 (March 6, 1926): 12; *CWR* 36 (April 3, 1926): 126; *CWR* 36 (May 1, 1926): 236; *CWR* 36 (May 29, 1926): 352. Reports dated March 29, for example, noted that in contrast to the usual volume of disruption, only two riots and one attack against police had occurred that day. *CWR* 36 (April 17, 1926): 178.

20. *CWR* 36 (April 3, 1926): 126; *CWR* 36 (May 29, 1926): 352.

21. *CWR* 37 (June 12, 1926): 44.

22. *CWR* 37 (June 5, 1926): 12; *CWR* 37 (June 12, 1926): 44.

In July, however, all changed when opportunities in Hunan, pressures from Wu Peifu, and mounting hostility from the east encouraged Nationalist commanders to launch the Northern Expedition. Aimed to destroy warlordism and unify the country, the campaign surpassed all expectations. Early setbacks in Hunan only temporarily delayed National Revolutionary Army (NRA) forces which seized Changsha on July 17, Yuezhou on August 22, and Hankou and Hanyang on September 6. By early October, after a successful month-long siege at Wuchang, the party had captured Hunan and Hubei. A second offensive in September encountered fierce resistance from Sun Chuanfang in Jiangxi before taking Nanchang and Jiujiang in November. A third route followed the coastline eastward to Fuzhou in November and then to Zhejiang in January 1927.

Northern Expedition successes greatly complicated the relationship between state-building and agitation. Requiring the full mobilization of every available resource, CEC officials again began encouraging the spread of mass organization forces, especially in areas outside Guangdong. In Shanghai, for example, Nationalist labor bureau chiefs collected information on labor structures, working conditions, worker status, cost of living, strikes, publications, rival parties, women workers, unions, and so forth, to assess revolutionary potential. Propaganda incited labor support by drawing attention to the party's pro-worker platform, working conditions, unions, imperialism, armaments, Sun Yat-sen ideology, and so forth. Provincial and municipal party offices were ordered to unite labor unions under GMD control and organize worker conferences. Shanghai leaders set up secret "fighting" *(zhandou)* corps called Worker National Salvation Teams. Central Headquarters trained and controlled units *(zu)* consisting of ten members each, groups *(tuan)* comprising ten units, and teams *(dui)* each containing ten groups. In GMD-controlled regions, these teams operated in the open. In enemy territory, however, they operated underground, copying a system used by Germany's early Nazi Party. According to party directives, "Secret training will be made under the guise of athletic associations and military studies associations. Field training will be done under the guise of field trips so our enemies will not know what we are actually doing."[23] Priority targets included imperialist concessions, foreign-owned mines and railways, and large treaty ports, including, Shanghai, Hankou, Chongqing, Tianjin, Hong Kong, Guangzhou, Dalian, Nantong, Changsha, Harbin, Qingdao, and Yichang.

Guomindang youth bureaus made great strides of their own. Using fronts to avoid unwanted attention, student unions formed alliances with other schools, published journals, distributed leaflets, and celebrated Northern Expedition successes. School administrators reacted to perceived revolu-

---

23. "Gongren yundong jihua cao'an," Shanghai (1926).

tionary infiltration by expelling leaders who, often enough, were also local party officers.[24] Those thus ejected moved to Shanghai where they joined the All-China Repressed and Expelled Students Union, a collection of some two hundred former student leaders committed to fueling agitation with full party support. Other youth leaders, especially within the Boy Scouts, routinely sought military training and weaponry for use against revolutionary enemies. Weapons shortages ensured that students got very few. Instead, youth groups were encouraged to support propaganda, fund-raising, and the "comfort and entertainment of troops" via Northern Expedition Committees.[25] Quickly, popular forces spread.

Mass organizations complemented the Northern Expedition in two distinct ways. First, they supported NRA military strikes by weakening warlord authority with agitative disruption. In June 1926, a record forty strikes broke out in Shanghai before crackdowns in July and August reduced the number to thirty-one and fifteen, respectively. Pro-GMD sentiment flourished in virtually every city of Fujian, Jiangxi, Zhejiang, Jiangsu, and Anhui.[26] In September 1926, when Sun Chuanfang's troops left Fuzhou to defend Nanchang, rising revolutionary incidents prompted local authorities to declare martial law. Nanchang commanders, meanwhile, complained that sympathetic police had opened the city gates to Nationalist troops.[27] Weekly reports observed that spies, propagandists, labor unions, and popular sentiment aided southern troops at every turn. Suspecting intrigue, Nanjing authorities quashed anti-British activities planned for Double Ten Day. Xuzhou leaders declared martial law when reports alleged that educators were smuggling arms to students.[28]

By October, a pattern was clearly discernible. As Nationalist troops approached, boycotts, strikes, and defections compromised warlord infrastructure. Railway workers gave GMD forces access to rolling stock or slowed warlord retreats by hiding equipment. Hanyang Arsenal workers struck for a full month before the arrival of GMD troops. Wuhan agitators used Red Cross insignias to disguise sabotaging efforts. Occasionally, mass

---

24. The director of Fujian's Tong'an county youth bureau, for example, was a student at Jimei Normal School struggling under the threat of his own expulsion. "Fujian Tong'anxian dangbu qingnianbu zhuren shang zhongyang qingnianbu han," June 9, 1926.
25. "Zhongyang qingnianbu yizhou gongzuo baogao," August 7, 1926; "Guangdong quansheng xuesheng lianhehui changwu weiyuanhui shang zhongyang qingnianbu han," August 22, 1926; "Sichuan linshi sheng zhixing weiyuanhui shang zhongyang zhixing weiyuanhui cheng," June 17, 1926; "Guangzhou xuelianhui zhixingyuanhui dierci changhui jilu," July 11, 1926.
26. *FO* 405/252 [F535/144/10], pp. 52-53, Enclosure 3, Barton to Macleay, Shanghai, October 9, 1926. A Nationalist agent in Hubei, for example, was shot by *mintuan* forces eager to stop him from organizing peasant associations. (Discussion item #11), *1-ZXWH*, vol. 5 (October 8, 1925).
27. *CWR* 38 (October 2, 1926): 140.
28. *CWR* 38 (October 23, 1926): 226; *CWR* 38 (October 16, 1926): 197; *CWR* 38 (November 20, 1926): 310, vi.

organizations even seized strategic locales, as in the case of Hangzhou which fell to labor union forces, or harassed militarists, as in Fujian where peasant militias checked remnant Chen Jiongming armies.[29]

Second—and far more significant—mass organizations helped secure newly conquered territory. As one student declaration asserted, "If we want Northern Expedition armies to be successful . . . we must [construct] a suitable movement with sufficiently tight organization *to act as their rear shield*" *(houdun).*[30] [Emphasis added.] Donald A. Jordan argues convincingly that agitative forces played a minor role against warlord armies and do not deserve the praise gushed by Chinese historians. Nevertheless, their impact on other allies of imperialism cannot be so easily discounted.[31] Consolidating power required a vast army of officials, staffers, and security personnel to take over in the wake of advancing Nationalist forces. Within this secondary wave of revolutionary influence—what some foreign observers called the "political unit" of the GMD—mass organizations played a paramount role.[32] The "rear shield" checked localist and foreign interests alike. According to CEC member Gan Naiguang, for example: "the majority of old *mintuan*, group protection bureaus *(tuanfangju)* and defense corps *(baoweiju)* are but illegal militias for bullies and evil gentry. These types of military forces are often utilized by imperialists, warlords, and reactionaries to break people's movements and shake the GMD and Nationalist Government's foundations, endangering the future of the party and the government."[33] By Guomindang fiat, any community already protected by a peasant militia could not also host a people's corps *(mintuan)*. Peasant associations ensured it.

The rapid expansion of agitative forces offered security against localist reactions, but generated worries as well. As early as September 1926, CEC and provincial authorities—including left-wing and right-wing leaders such as Borodin, Xu Qian, Tan Yankai, Sun Ke, Gan Naiguang, Gu Mengyu, Zhang Renjie, and Li Jishen—met to assess progress and establish new revolutionary objectives for the Northern Expedition. Deliberation focused on two primary state-building concerns: political control and foreign relations. Political control offered the economic and social stability needed for national development, while healthy foreign relations could affirm revolutionary victories, dissolve the unequal treaties, and deny loans and weapons to rivals. Both required legal reforms, improved communications, recon-

---

29. Jordan, *The Northern Expedition*, p. 199; *Xiangdao zhoubao* (November 4, 1926): 1843; *CWR* 37 (July 24, 1926): 198; *CWR* 38 (September 4, 1926): 18; Schwartz, "The Siege of Wuhan: From Day to Day," p. 74; *CWR* 39 (December 25, 1926): 108.

30. "Heyuan xuesheng lianhehui gaizu chengli xuanyan," October 16, 1926.

31. Jordan, *The Northern Expedition*, p. 201.

32. *FO* 405/252 [F1329/144/10], p. 209, Enclosure, Hunan political report, December 31, 1926.

33. "Gan Naiguang deng tichu guanyu mintuan wenti jueyi cao'an," *ZWDL-YS* (October 28, 1926).

struction, educational reforms, and efforts to register foreign schools. Both sought cooperative relations with merchants, schools, non-party unions, village militias, and other localist and foreign interests. Both also pursued stable control through all Nationalist territory.[34]

Unfortunately for the Guangzhou leadership, demand far outstripped resources; there simply were not enough trained cadres. Organization Ministry officials strove valiantly but had to report in October that they could not keep up with the torrent of new party organs.[35] Desperate to fill posts, harried local officials bent the rules, prompting CEC orders that, "Without special permission, government organs cannot use non-GMD members to fill positions."[36] Other CEC directives warned against opportunism and automatically denied party membership to all "bandits, local bullies, evil gentry, false officials, compradors, and indifferent selfish politicians."[37] Despite their best efforts, Jiangxi leaders still complained that under-trained cadres did not understand organization or propaganda, that "evil gentry and local bullies" had infiltrated all county bureaus, and that many posts remained vacant because there was no one to fill them.[38]

As the Northern Expedition proceeded, CEC officials faced an interesting conundrum. In Guangdong, solidifying control meant restricting agitation. Elsewhere, behind advancing Northern Expeditionary forces, however, gaining control required expanding agitation.[39] With state-building institutions still underdeveloped and party infrastructure struggling to consolidate power in newly conquered territories, agitative organizations emerged as the primary means for watch dogging localist and foreign interests. At the same time, attenuated party oversight—the result of too much territory and too few cadres—meant no one was there to scrutinize agitation.[40] Unchecked by state-building authorities, it could rise to threatening proportions. Balancing the benefits and dangers of agitation was an old problem that had generally prompted CEC calls for greater discipline.[41] In January 1926, delegates at the Second National Congress threatened "various

---

34. (Draft agendas for meetings #1, #3, #4 and #5), *ZWDL-QC* (September 14, 17, 20, and 22, 1926).

35. (Report #8), *2-ZXWH*, vol. 5 (October 30, 1926).

36. The only exceptions were personnel in technical or professional posts. (Discussion item #11), *2-ZXWH*, vol. 5 (November 13, 1926).

37. "Zai zhanlingdinei zuzhi linshi dangbu zhouxu ji tiaoli," *2-ZXWH*, vol. 3 (July 17, 1926).

38. "Quansheng dangwu zong baogao jueyian," *J3QD* (n.d., early 1927).

39. Agitation continued in Guangdong but under the watch of central authorities. Thus, in late August, the Youth Ministry ordered all Guangzhou students to parade and protest against imperialism. "Zhongyang qingnianbu zhi Guangzhou gexuexiao tongqi," August 29, 1926.

40. (Report #8), *2-ZXWH*, vol. 5 (October 30, 1926).

41. In May 1925, the CEC had warned that "power must be concentrated in the party to keep the majority of comrades within bounds. All party members must follow only party principle and not their individual will." "Xunling cao'an," *1-ZWQH* (May 22, 1925).

counter-revolutionary, false-revolutionary, and non-revolutionary elements" *(fan geming jia geming bu geming zhongzhong fenzi)* while insisting that workers and peasants be armed, trained, and unified, to combat imperialism.[42] The two calls contradicted each other. Armed, trained, and unified, anti-imperialist agitators had even more power to engage in "counter-revolutionary, false-revolutionary, and non-revolutionary" activity should discipline fail to control them.

Anti-Imperialist Fury versus Foreign Provocation

Agitation's affinity for indiscriminate disruption was the Achilles heel of revolutionary bifurcated nationalism, particularly during the Northern Expedition. Before June 1926, CEC leaders acknowledged that the powers would never sign new treaties with the southern regime until China was unified under a single national government; foreign relations would improve once the NRA successfully conquered its domestic rivals.[43] After June 1926, however, as the Northern Expedition spread Guomindang military might thinly over south China, CEC leaders realized that healthy foreign relations were a prerequisite to national unification, not just a desired result of it.[44] Troop departures left Guangzhou lightly defended at the same time that Anti-British Boycott tensions strained ties with Hong Kong, prompting GMD fears that Britain might take advantage. To provide Guangzhou some modicum of security, therefore, Chiang Kai-shek, CEC leaders, Moscow officials, and the CCP Central Committee all voted to end the boycott and try to improve relations with Hong Kong.[45]

Signs of détente had already begun to appear. In April, a new British consul-general, J. F. Brenan, arrived in Guangzhou with orders to pursue conciliation with the Nationalist regime. Assessing conditions, he confidently reported that most GMD leaders—excepting Chen Gongbo—sought a settlement.[46] In May, British reports applauded party efforts to stifle anti-foreign agitation on the anniversary of the May Thirtieth Incident. Subsequent reports praised the Guangzhou regime for its honesty, tax collection, fiscal policy, municipal administration, reconstruction, and even

---

42. "Zhaoji dierci quanguo daibiao dahui xuanyan," *1-ZXWH*, vol. 5 (December 11, 1925).

43. (Draft agenda for meeting #5), *ZWDL-QC* (September 22, 1926).

44. Zhang Zuolin told a British official that Guomindang successes had spread the party thin and that it would "collapse" like the Taiping Rebellion of the nineteenth century. *FO* 405/252 [F1934/2/10], p. 237, Lampson to Chamberlain, Beijing, January 3, 1927.

45. (Draft agenda for meeting #1), *ZWDL-QC* (September 17, 1926); "Zhongyang zhixing weiyuanhui tichu yi'an," *ZWDL-YS* (October 15, 1926); Wilbur and How, *Missionaries of Revolution*, p. 331.

46. *FO* 405/251 [F2175/1/10], p. 197, Enclosure 1, Brenan to Macleay, Guangzhou, April 19, 1926; *FO* 405/252a [F2783/1/10], p. 13, Enclosure, Brenan to Macleay, Guangzhou, May 31, 1926.

street cleaning.[47] The CEC, meanwhile, appointed Chen Youren as the GMD's foreign affairs minister on June 4 and ordered him to offer talks. A British memorandum, produced in July, explained Guangzhou's rationale:

> The motive which chiefly influences the Cantonese is their acute need of money, mainly for military expenditure. This they doubtless hope to obtain from the proposed Hong Kong loan. . . . The Russians, including Borodin, and even Karakhan himself, are believed to be in favour of ending the boycott, because they fear a revulsion of feeling against them, such as has developed in North China, if the struggle is prolonged indefinitely. In view of the threat of a war with the North and with Yunnan, General Chiang Kai-shek would probably welcome the additional security to his base which would result from a settlement.[48]

By August, Hong Kong's Governor Clementi was even arguing for an end to the arms embargo, *de jure* recognition of the GMD regime, and British advisers in Guangzhou.[49]

While relations between Hong Kong and Guangzhou authorities showed signs of softening, ties between other interests remained intensely combative. Back in December 1925, Hong Kong merchants had offered to pay handsomely to end the boycott, but they were rebuffed by labor minister Wu Chaogang before they could even submit a proposal. Instead of embracing settlement offers, the Guangzhou Strike Committee opted to deepen its picket lines. Frustrated, the merchants accused strike leaders of perpetuating the boycott to maintain their "get-rich-quick opportunities."[50] Conversely, when the party tried to open talks the following March, it found opinions in Hong Kong had changed. Merchants had already paid off debts, directed trade northward, hired new workers, and adopted a new attitude: strong opposition

---

47. *FO* 405/252a [F2783/178/10], p. 14, Enclosure, Brenan to Macleay, May 31, 1926; *FO* 405/252a [F2790/1/10], p. 19, Anti-British Boycott negotiations memorandum, Guangzhou, July 13, 1926.

48. *FO* 405/252a [F2790/1/10], p. 20, Anti-British Boycott negotiations memorandum, Guangzhou, July 13, 1926; For details on Chen's appointment see *FO* 405/252a [F3049/1/10], p. 83, Brenan to Macleay, Guangzhou, June 17, 1926.

49. *FO* 405/252a [F3228/1/10], p. 99, Amery to Hong Kong governor, August 4 1926; *FO* 405/252a [F3179/10/10], pp. 128-130, Colonial Office to Foreign Office, August 7, 1926. Brenan, Macleay, and others countered, arguing that Guangzhou had not formally sought recognition and that offering it would only alienate British allies elsewhere in China. *FO* 405/252a [F3179/10/10], p. 137, Enclosure 4, acting consul-general to Chamberlain, Guangzhou, August 19, 1926; *FO* 405/252a [F3728/1/10], p. 139, Enclosure 2, Macleay to Chamberlain, Beijing, August 11, 1926; *FO* 405/252a, p. 158, Chamberlain to Brenan, August 16, 1926; *FO* 405/252a [F3458/71/10], p. 161, weekly summary, August 20, 1926.

50. *FO* 405/252a [F2790/1/10], pp. 19-20, Anti-British Boycott negotiations memorandum, Guangzhou, July 13, 1926; *FO* 405/251 [F1741/71/10], p. 40, weekly summary, Foreign Office, April 23, 1926; *CWR* 35 (December 12, 1925): 53; *CWR* 34 (November 21, 1925): 288; *CWR* 34 (November 28, 1925): 318; *CWR* 36 (March 13, 1926): 42; *CWR* 35 (February 27, 1926): 368.

to striker compensation in any form.[51] This time it was the GSC that lashed out, denouncing "treacherous merchant bandits" *(youjian shangfei)* and pledging "total victory" *(zuihou shengli)*.[52] In short, by the time preliminary talks opened in June 1926 the issue of compensation sorely divided both sides; GSC leaders and the GMD Labor Ministry demanded it while indignant Hong Kong merchants and Brenan refused, calling it "blackmail."[53]

On July 15, 1926, settlement talks opened. Optimistic, the British dismantled sandbag fortifications around Shamian.[54] GSC leaders, however, remained suspicious, especially after being excluded from the talks and learning that Guomindang negotiators showed less concern about labor interests than party need. Trying to allay striker concerns, Nationalist authorities held a mass meeting, promised to secure compensation, and offered GSC representatives a chance to air their concerns in front of party negotiators, although most saw these measures as but courtesies aimed to pacify labor "clamoring."[55] Labor leaders, however, would not be quieted. Guangzhou's moderate Central Labor Union, some 100,000 workers dominated by the Mechanics Union, favored a quick settlement so its members could reclaim their good-paying jobs. (Leaders supported the GMD but shunned communism and radical views of working class emancipation.) In contrast, the Workers' Delegates Conference, founded by Liao Zhongkai in 1924 and claiming approximately 170,000 workers, wanted to extend the strike since most of its members had already lost their jobs to scabs or bankruptcies, and they had nothing to go back to afterwards.[56] To reward the sacrifice of its members, Workers' Delegates and GSC leaders demanded striker compensation as fundamental to any settlement.

---

51. Hong Kong offered development loans but refused to consider any striker payments. *FO* 405/252a [F2790/1/10], pp. 19-20, Anti-British Boycott negotiations memorandum, Guangzhou, July 13, 1926; *FO* 405/251 [F1741/71/10], p. 40, weekly summary, Foreign Office, April 23, 1926; *FO* 405/251 [F1567/71/10], p. 17, weekly summary, Foreign Office, April 12, 1926.

52. (Discussion item #3), *2-ZXWH*, vol. 4 (August 17, 1926).

53. *FO* 405/252a [F2783/1/10], p. 13, Enclosure, Brenan to Macleay, Guangzhou, May 31, 1926; *FO* 405/251 [F2175/1/10], p. 197, Enclosure 1, Brenan to Macleay, Guangzhou, April 19, 1926; *FO* 405/250 [F1246/1/10], p. 523, Enclosure, Jamieson to Macleay, Guangzhou, February 15, 1926; *CWR* 37 (June 5, 1926): 12.

54. *CWR* 37 (July 31, 1926): 222.

55. Early reports claimed that the party sought: (1) Hong Kong's recognition that Guangdong was independent of the Beijing regime, (2) permission to open a branch of the GMD Central Bank and to sell war bonds in Hong Kong, (3) passage of arms and ammunition through Hong Kong, and (4) the right to customs surplus from Guangdong, Guangxi, and Hunan. None related to labor interests. Nevertheless, party leaders also hinted that Strike Committee demands would "not be denied a hearing." *CWR* 37 (July 31, 1926): 220, 222; *CWR* 37 (August 7, 1926): 248.

56. Mechanics Union workers constituted what Chesneaux calls a "labor aristocracy." Traditional craftsmen comprising the Workers' Delegates Conference, on the other hand, often found themselves marginalized. Almost half of Guangzhou's thirteen thousand un-mechanized oil mill union members, for example, were unemployed. Chesneaux, *The Chinese Labor Movement*, pp. 303-305.

Eager to swing momentum in their favor, unions representing both labor factions began agitations that quickly escalated into street battles.[57] On July 18, Workers' Delegates pickets kidnapped the tea-house waiters' union chief—a Central Labor Union leader—before the Mechanics retaliated with vigilante mayhem. Regime authorities ordered both sides to stop while police called perpetrators "counter-revolutionaries" and "traitors." Still, fighting continued. In late July and early August, street fighting killed ten workers and injured fifty more. Clashes in Shantou drew in some three to four thousand workers, killing and wounding nearly fifty individuals. [58] The Guomindang Military Council had already prohibited pickets from arresting persons, but authorities lost control through July as police warnings went unheeded. Troops joined police patrols along major thoroughfares and secret service men watched union leaders. Even after his forces embarked for Hunan, Chiang Kai-shek remained behind in an attempt to prevent violence from jeopardizing the negotiations. By late July, however, he could no longer wait. Sending his staff ahead, Chiang again ordered Guangzhou's chief of police to suppress the rioting and then declared martial law on July 29, specifically restricting all "public assembly, formation of associations, strikes, suspension of trade, newspapers, magazines, pictures, and other printed matter."[59]

Despite Chiang's best efforts, however, settlement talks foundered. The British refused to submit their garrisons and gunboats to GMD regulations, compensate May Thirtieth or Shaji Incident victims, or offer striker relief funds.[60] Hong Kong did propose a developmental loan of $10 million, earmarked exclusively for non-military use, but Guangzhou officials were not interested. Unable to wrest striker funds from Hong Kong, Nationalist negotiators withdrew, ending the talks on July 23.[61] Smelling victory, the GSC

57. Chesneaux, *The Chinese Labor Movement*, pp. 306, 310. Chesneaux blames conflict on the rising influence of "right-wing elements" such as Sun Ke, who foreigners denounced as a "radical" that granted labor unions excessive authority.
58. *CWR* 37 (July 24, 1926): 198; *CWR* 37 (July 31, 1926): 222-223; *CWR* 37 (August 7, 1926): 246; *CWR* 37 (August 21, 1926): 303; *CWR* 38 (September 4, 1926): 19; *FO* 405/252 [F535/144/10], pp. 47-48, Enclosure 2, Brenan to Macleay, Guangzhou, September 30, 1926.
59. *CWR* 37 (June 12, 1926): 46; *CWR* 37 (July 24, 1926): 198; *CWR* 37 (July 31, 1926): 222; *CWR* 37 (August 7, 1926): 246, 248; *CWR* 37 (August 14, 1926): 276-277.
60. *FO* 405/252a [F3689/1/10], p. 191, Enclosure 1, Brenan to Macleay, Guangzhou, July 26, 1926. As long as Guangzhou sought striker compensation and Shaji Incident damages, Hong Kong demanded boycott compensation and remuneration for damage to Shamian residents. *FO* 405/252a [F2790/1/10], pp. 28-31, Macleay to Chamberlain.
61. *FO* 405/252a [F4326/1/10], p. 271, events of Guangzhou Boycott, October 13, 1926; *FO* 405/252a [F3024/71/10], p. 67, weekly summary, July 23, 1926; *FO* 405/252a [F3138/1/10], p. 98, Chen to Chamberlain, London, August 3, 1926; *FO* 405/252a [3297/1/10], p. 159, Chamberlain to Chen, August 18, 1926; *FO* 405/252a [F3473/1/10], pp. 173-181, Enclosure 1, Brenan to Macleay, Guangzhou, July 20, 1926; *FO* 405/252a [F3689/1/10], pp. 191-194, Enclosure 1, Brenan to Macleay, Guangzhou, July 26, 1926; *FO* 405/252a [F4326/1/10], pp. 270-276, events of Guangzhou Boycott, October 13, 1926. The British believed that the Nationalist negotiating

quickly recruited, trained, and armed two thousand more pickets while pressing party officials to take a harder stance against imperialism. On August 5, Guangzhou Strike Committee leaders issued a nation-wide proclamation pledging to "make whatever sacrifice national interests may demand."[62] Writing to Chen Shuren—the GMD's new labor minister—GSC leaders argued for continuing the fight, declaring, "Whatever choice of action the movement takes here and now will greatly determine our future destination. Naturally [we] dare not fail to publicly call for advancing to the bitter end."[63] Anti-foreignism rose. Picket boats attacked British ships and Chinese trying to skirt picket lines. Brenan criticized the Nationalists for making no effort to stop "organized brigandage."[64] With relations cooling, government statements began to heat up, enflaming agitative forces. In late August, the GSC invited over five hundred delegates representing 116 mass organizations to a series of events called "Strikers Week," allegedly designed to decide on the boycott's future. Highlights included speeches in which government officials urged a huge rally of some thirty thousand demonstrators to "keep fighting."[65]

Facing a new surge of anti-foreignism, the British reconsidered their options and sent intelligence officers to investigate military opportunities. With NRA troops engaging warlord rivals, force had again become a viable alternative to British "patience." In the West River, British naval forces successfully scared off picket boats shooting at passengers as they climbed gangways onto Hong Kong steamers. Encouraged, Brenan proposed staging an incident as a pretext for further intervention.[66] Theatrics were unnecessary, however, for the requisite incident came on its own. On August 28, picket boats surrounded and fired on a foreign motor launch shuttling Chinese passengers to a Hong Kong ship. Retreating to the customs wharf, the British owner fled to Shamian but his American co-owner was captured.[67] The incident hardened foreign interventionists. Brenan warned Chen Youren that

---

team stalled in the hope that Northern Expedition successes would strengthen their hand.

62. "Shenggang bagong weiyuanhui zhi quanguo tongbao daidian," August 5, 1926; *FO* 405/252a [F3932/1/10], p. 235, Enclosure 2, extract from *Canton Gazette*, August 7, 1926.

63. "Shenggang bagong weiyuanhui zhi Chen Shuren," August 1926.

64. *FO* 405/252a [F3562/71/10], p. 188, weekly summary, August 27, 1926.

65. *Kuomintang Publicity Department*, vol. 1, #2 (September 17, 1926): 6, included in *ZWDL-YS* (October 19, 1926); *FO* 405/252a [F4211/1/10], p. 260, Enclosure 1, Brenan to Clementi, Guangzhou, August 29, 1926.

66. *FO* 405/252a [F4257/1/10], p. 267, Brenan to Macleay, Guangzhou, August 31, 1926. Naval threats against Wuzhou broke another stalemate after GMD officials refused to pilot British ships past defenses so they could investigate the murder of a British national. *FO* 405/252a [F2959/71/10], p. 39, weekly summary, July 17, 1926; *FO* 405/252a [F3932/1/10], p. 233, Enclosure 1, Brenan to Macleay, Guangzhou, August 16, 1926.

67. *FO* 405/252a, pp. 188-189, acting consul-general to Macleay, Guangzhou, August 28, 1926; *FO* 405/252a [F4257/1/10], p. 266, Enclosure 1, Brenan to Macleay, Guangzhou, August 31, 1926; *FO* 405/252a [F4326/1/10], p. 272, events of Guangzhou Boycott, October 13, 1926.

Britain would protect trade and take forcible action against the GSC if attacks continued.[68] Chen claimed that the GMD regime *had* genuinely tried to curb picket excesses, but he persuaded no one.[69]

On September 4, dynamics changed dramatically when British troops attacked and seized Guangzhou wharves and facilities leased to British firms and cleared the waterways of interfering picket launches. Picket lines blockading British vessels and the flow of British goods were scattered. Naval escorts and British steamers restored traffic between Hong Kong and Guangzhou. As the pickets lost their grip on the waterways, Brenan issued threats of more force should the Nationalists or pickets try to restore the lines or fail to resume settlement talks within a "reasonable" amount of time.[70]

To avoid further escalation, both sides opted for prudence. British authorities decided against dispersing the pickets blocking Shamian's bridges since that would mean encroaching on Chinese soil. Meanwhile, the Nationalist Government replaced unruly pickets with police and troop patrols. Nevertheless, larger developments kept relations strained and volatile. Along the Yangzi, Nationalist troops fired at British ships.[71] Near Hankou, GMD forces engaged the British gunboat *H.M.S. Scarab*. Two days later, on September 7, British gunboats exchanged naval and artillery fire with Sichuan troops under General Yang Sen, an ally of the southern regime, killing hundreds (or perhaps thousands) and setting the Sichuan town of Wanxian ablaze. Erupting anti-imperialism forced British nationals in Yichang, Chongqing and Wanxian to flee to Hankou.[72]

Riding the wave of anti-imperialist sentiment that swept Guangzhou, Sun Ke publicly proclaimed government support for the GSC and divulged alleged plans to inflict more damage on Hong Kong and spread the boycott through all China. British authorities took Sun's threats seriously and decided to stand fast lest the party "interpret any relaxation of our naval activities

---

68. Possible military actions included: (1) seizing and disabling all picket boats, (2) placing gunboats next to boycott examination stations and the strike headquarters, (3) blockading all Chinese shipping, (4) landing forces to destroy the strike headquarters, and (5) blockading Guangzhou. *FO* 405/252a [F3932/1/10], p. 235, Enclosure 3, Fitzgerald to the Commodore, Guangzhou, August 13, 1926.

69. *FO* 405/252a [F4211/1/10], pp. 260-261, Brenan to Clementi, Guangzhou, August 29, 1926.

70. *FO* 405/252a, p. 202, Commander-in-Chief to Admiralty, September 4, 1926; *FO* 405/252a, pp. 189-190, Chamberlain to Brenan, August 31, 1926; *FO* 405/252a [F3622/71/10], p. 200, weekly summary, September 3, 1926; *FO* 405/252a, p. 201, Macleay to Chamberlain, Beijing, September 4, 1926; *FO* 405/252a, p. 216, Brenan to Chamberlain, Guangzhou, September 12, 1926; *FO* 405/252a, p. 217, Hong Kong governor to secretary of colonies; *CWR* 38 (September 18, 1926): 78.

71. *FO* 405/252a, p. 217, Hong Kong governor to secretary of colonies; *FO* 405/252a, p. 216, Macleay to Chamberlain, Beijing, September 13, 1926.

72. *CWR* 38 (September 11, 1926): 55; *CWR* 38 (September 18, 1926): 84; *CWR* 38 (October 2, 1926): 138; *FO* 405/252a [F4913/3623/10], pp. 502-504, chronology of the Wanxian Affair, November 15, 1926.

before removal of the land boycott as demonstrating that we shrink from the consequences of such activities." On September 10, Brenan wrote the GMD foreign affairs minister, demanding to know if Sun's speech reflected the southern regime's official policy. Meanwhile, British circles endorsed new calls by Governor Clementi for a blockade of Guangzhou and Shantou. Sir Ronald Macleay, Britain's minister to China, added that Britain should offer aid to anti-GMD warlords such as Sun Chuanfang. On September 12, British ships landed marines in Hankou to shore up concession defenses there.[73]

As relations with Britain deteriorated and forceful measures became more commonplace, the CEC found itself caught between Scylla and Charybdis: British intervention on one side and anti-imperialist agitation on the other. Just six months earlier, party leaders would have dodged culpability for anti-imperialist incidents by claiming neutrality and denying responsibility for popular activism. That line no longer worked, however. As Brenan summarized in August, "If we want a change, the Canton [Guangzhou] Government must be made to feel that things will not be allowed to go on as they are, and that *unless they deal with the Strike Committee themselves, there will be unpleasant reprisals on the part of the British.*"[74] [Emphasis added.] With Nationalist liability unquestioned and the GSC actively provoking British intervention, "unpleasant reprisals" loomed.[75] The only thing stalling Clementi's blockade was Foreign Office interest in learning whether or not Guangzhou would repudiate Sun Ke's outbursts.[76]

Cornered, the CEC adjusted its tactics. On September 14, it issued a series of mixed messages to agitative forces. On one hand, party leaders encouraged popular anti-imperialism to reinforce official protests against British gunboat diplomacy. Labor Ministry officials sent agitators to distribute anti-British handbills supporting government protests that accused Britain of plotting to weaken the Northern Expedition's rear, engage in gunboat diplomacy, and disrupt negotiations via "massacres" as occurred in Wanxian.[77] Energized by regime statements, anti-imperialist energies

---

73. *FO* 405/252a, p. 217, Hong Kong governor to secretary of colonies; *FO* 405/252a, p. 219, Macleay to Chamberlain, Beijing, September 15, 1926; *CWR* 38 (September 18, 1926): 83-84.

74. *FO* 405/252a [F3932/1/10], p. 233, Enclosure 1, Brenan to Macleay, Guangzhou, August 16, 1926.

75. As a CEC report bluntly put it, "Most everyone outside the party says that the Guomindang [directs] the workers movement and all strikes. Truthfully speaking that is about right." "Zhongyang dangwu baogao," *ZWDL-YS* (October 16, 1926).

76. *FO* 405/252a, p. 222, Tyrrell to Macleay, September 17, 1926.

77. (Discussion item #5), *2-ZXWH*, vol. 4 (September 14, 1926); *CWR* 38 (September 25, 1926): 111; "Zhongyang zhixing weiyuanhui changwuhui zhi zhongyang gongrenbu han," September 15, 1926; "Zhongyang zhixing weiyuanhui mishuchu zhi zhongyang gongrenbu han," September 15, 1926; *CWR* 38 (September 18, 1926): 83; *Kuomintang Publicity Department*, vol. 1, #2 (September 17, 1926): 3-5, included in *ZWDL-YS* (October 19, 1926).

swelled from Guangdong to Hubei. On the other hand, the CEC tried to restrain escalation, telling popular forces that agitation was but one way to manage imperialism and that all demonstrators should "make the utmost effort to avoid conflict." Explicit directives declared that all speeches had to be cleared by central authorities before being delivered publicly and that government officials must exercise extreme caution when commenting on foreign relations, thus limiting further loose-cannon damage by Sun Ke or others.[78] Propaganda produced in English for foreign consumption, meanwhile, revealed the party's new approach:

> Had it not been for the promptness of the Nationalist Government in controlling the incensed people, the policy of the British Navy to provoke a bloody massacre would have achieved its purpose. Although the people had in view the greater aim of the victory of the Army in the field, therefore bending all their efforts to avoid trouble with the English at this juncture, *it is not to be supposed that they cannot eventually use effective means of retaliation to show the English their proper place.*[79] [Emphasis added.]

Rather than hiding its ties to anti-imperialist agitation, the Guomindang now openly highlighted them while representing itself as the only force preventing China's "incensed people" from hurtling headlong into conflict with British interests. The subtext was clear; if Britain hoped to avoid conflict with China's populace, it needed warm relations with Guangzhou.

Openly assuming responsibility for Chinese nationalism, however, was also a gamble. With both agitative and British forces straining to get at each other, the ground between them became quite hazardous. The British called pickets "pirates" and swore that they would be treated as such. NRA forces along the Yangzi complained that British gunboats purposely orchestrated incidents to induce exchanges of gunfire. Meanwhile, outraged at British offenses, students demanded arms with which to destroy the foreign threat.[80]

Something had to give. Surprisingly, it was CEC support for agitative forces. The GMD Foreign Affairs Ministry declared that it would meet British imperialism with diplomacy and negotiations while the party reinforced police patrols to ensure that pickets and bluejackets had no opportunity to test each others' resolve. On September 18, Chen Youren informed Brenan that immediate orders had been issued to stop GMD troops from

---

78. (Discussion item #5), *2-ZXWH*, vol. 4 (September 14, 1926).

79. *Kuomintang Publicity Department*, vol. 1, #2 (September 17, 1926): 3-5, included in *ZWDL-YS* (October 19, 1926).

80. *CWR* 38 (September 18, 1926): 78-79; *CWR* 38 (September 25, 1926): 111, vi. On the other hand, U.S. Minister to China John Van A. MacMurray announced that the U.S. would not support intervention. "MacMurray Opposes Intervention, Supports Extrality!," *CWR* 38 (September 25, 1926): 92.

firing at British ships along the Yangzi. That same day, the Guomindang renounced Sun Ke's speech and declared that officials could no longer comment on foreign affairs without government consent. Even more astonishing to British authorities, however, was a unilateral announcement from Guangzhou that the Anti-British Boycott would end on October 10. Putting the ball in Britain's court, Chen Youren declared, "To what extent this step will lead to a restoration of Chinese-British trade relations must depend on British policy and action and on British comprehension of Chinese Nationalism."[81]

Impressed by Guangzhou's sudden change of heart, British officials reciprocated. Brenan reversed his calls for intervention and aid to Nationalist enemies while British military officials abandoned blockade plans in favor of giving Guangzhou a chance to demonstrate its sincerity. Macleay agreed. Shortly thereafter, Chamberlain vetoed all interventionist plans.[82] (Only Clementi, perhaps unhappy at losing his spot in the limelight, continued to lobby for a blockade.[83]) Even the *China Weekly Review*, generally quite critical of GMD policy, unabashedly praised Guangzhou:

> Whatever may be one's final judgment upon the Russians and their sinister economic, social and political propaganda, it must be granted that in some respects they have been a unifying and conserving element in Canton [Guangzhou], as witness the firm stand which their chief, Mr. Borodin, took against the anti-Christian disturbance which had been long planned for Christmas week. They have helped create a better trained, better disciplined and more intelligent body of troops than Kwangtung [Guangdong] has ever had previously, and their influence in civil affairs has been for a well-ordered administration.[84]

Other foreign reports lauded Nationalist reforms in Hunan and Hubei while blaming labor and banditry for limiting effectiveness.[85]

Continued British patience, of course, required evidence that the party would actually restrain anti-imperialist agitation. Chen Youren tried to win

---

81. *CWR* 38 (September 18, 1926): 79; *CWR* 38 (October 2, 1926): 130.
82. *FO* 405/252a, p. 226, Macleay to Chamberlain, Beijing, September 18, 1926; *FO* 405/252a, p. 227, Brenan to Chamberlain, Guangzhou, September 18, 1926; (doc. nos. 124-126); *FO* 405/252a, pp. 239-240, Macleay to Chamberlain, Beijing, September 20, 1926; *FO* 405/252a, p. 231, Tyrrell to Macleay, September 20, 1926; *FO* 405/252a, p. 242, Macleay to Chamberlain, Beijing, September 22, 1926; *FO* 405/252a, p. 262, Chamberlain to Macleay, October 7, 1926; *FO* 405/252a, p. 263, Chamberlain to Brenan, October 7, 1926.
83. *FO* 405/252a, pp. 228-229, Hong Kong governor to secretary for colonies, September 20, 1926; *FO* 405/252a, p. 241, Hong Kong governor to secretary of colonies, September 22, 1926; *FO* 405/252a, p. 230, Hong Kong governor to secretary for colonies, September 20, 1926.
84. Griggs, "Canton's Contribution to the Chinese Revolution," pp. 92-93.
85. *CWR* 38 (September 25, 1926): 110; Griggs, "Canton's Contribution to the Chinese Revolution," pp. 92-93.

some British sympathy by making the case that "anti-British feeling fostered by a year's propaganda cannot be stopped in a day."[86] Moving beyond mere rhetoric, party authorities officially ended the Anti-British Boycott on October 10, 1926. Pickets were disbanded, shipping restrictions were repealed, and communication between Hong Kong and Guangzhou was restored. British agents reoccupied the Bund and leased facilities, British steamers moored off Guangzhou, and Chinese merchants resumed contact. The CEC and GSC both publicly announced the boycott's end while breaking up inspection sheds used by pickets to examine confiscated goods.[87] Relations with Britain warmed. Nationalist authorities again promised to stop troops from firing on British ships plying Yangzi waters.[88] The CEC even formalized ties with London and Berlin news agencies so party views could reach the international community.[89] Pleased with signs of progress, the British Foreign Office ordered measures "to remove all the causes of friction with the Chinese, to abandon such rights and privileges as were galling to them but were of no real benefit to the British themselves, and to keep on the minimum that was essential for British trade."[90] Admiration from sympathetic missionaries and other foreigners aided general warming and whetted Nationalist hopes that recognition might follow.[91]

In sharp contrast to the positive shift in foreign relations, the Guomindang's ties to mass organizations looked quite different. Strikers took developments hard. Many of the GSC's two hundred leaders complained bitterly when government authorities announced that the boycott would end. Unions tied to Sun Ke accused the GSC of caving to foreign pressure or accepting merchant bribes. Others questioned the party's resolve. Eager to calm striker concerns and preempt a striker reaction, the CEC sent Chen Qiyuan and Gan Naiguang to explain the government's decision. Still malcontent, many strikers refused to accept that the boycott was over. Some petitioned for permission to renew it while others formed a new striker society committed to continuing the struggle despite CEC opposition.[92]

---

86. *FO* 405/252a, p. 242, Macleay to Chamberlain, Beijing, September 22, 1926; *FO* 405/252a, p. 262, Chamberlain to Macleay, October 7, 1926; *FO* 405/252a, p. 263, Chamberlain to Brenan, October 7, 1926; *FO* 405/252a, pp. 246-247, Brenan to Chamberlain, Guangzhou, September 24, 1926.

87. *CWR* 38 (October 23, 1926): 219; *FO* 405/252a, p. 269, Brenan to Chamberlain, Guangzhou, October 13, 1926.

88. *FO* 405/252a, p. 217, Hong Kong governor to secretary of colonies; *FO* 405/252a, p. 226, Macleay to Chamberlain, Beijing, September 18, 1926.

89. "Xuanchuan zhuyao zhi cailiao," *2-ZXWH*, vol. 4 (September 7, 1926); (Discussion item #17), *2-ZXWH*, vol. 5 (October 30, 1926); "Xuanchuanbu ti'an," *2-ZXWH*, vol. 5 (November 13, 1926).

90. Fung, *The Diplomacy of Imperial Retreat*, p. 90.

91. "The So-called "Red Menace" in China," *CWR* 38 (November 6, 1926): 257-259.

92. *CWR* 38 (September 25, 1926): iv; *CWR* 38 (October 2, 1926): 130; *CWR* 38 (October 23, 1926): 219; *FO* 405/252 [F1233/144/10], p. 174, Enclosure, Guangzhou political report;

The party tried to pacify labor, acknowledging its right to conduct anti-British activities and release pent-up steam, but officials hardened considerably when labor feuding again flared out of control. Unemployed workers with GMD credentials attacked street cleaning coolies with ties to the Guangzhou Board of Health because, as non-party workers, the latter was exempt from paying union dues. Near the silk market, conflicts destroyed 118 buildings. In Foshan, labor factions kidnapped rivals and engaged in street wars. In November, Guangzhou rivalries turned ugly. A fight in early November killed and injured thirty-five workers while another at the hog market killed two and wounded forty. Losing control, Guangzhou police called on the Garrison Commissioner for help, leading to joint warnings and threats that rioting pickets would be shot. Wuzhou military officials simply capitulated, announcing that unionized workers could murder each other if they insisted but would be punished if they continued to attack non-workers.[93] Meanwhile, Foshan and Shantou merchants shut markets to counter labor agitation.[94]

To improve British ties, CEC leaders cashed in labor ties. In some ways, this move was just as perilous as maintaining the boycott would have been. Labor was a powerful force and did not heed orders simply because government leaders had spoken. Common sentiment that they had been betrayed meant that strikers and GSC leaders required some reward if positive relations with the GMD regime were to be salvaged. At the same time, however, rivalries between Guangzhou's two major labor factions added complications. In August, Guomindang authorities had been pressured to arrest eight Central Labor Union (Mechanics Union) leaders and publicly side with the Workers' Delegates after the latter threatened a general strike. Once the boycott abruptly ended on October 10, with no sign of the promised striker compensation, party officials had even greater reason to build political capital with the Workers' Delegates. If sufficiently aggravated, workers could easily turn their agitative impulses against party rule.

Before month's end, Nationalist officials moved to heal ties by unionizing shop assistants, creating Guangzhou's largest union and increasing Workers' Delegates membership to three hundred thousand—three times that of the Central Labor Union. In Shantou, meanwhile, party officials closed the local Central Labor Union branch.[95] Some interpreted these steps, which

(Discussion item #10), *2-ZXWH*, vol. 5 (September 28, 1926); "Linshi baogao, Aozhou zongzhibu laidian 臨時報告, 澳洲之部來電," *ZWDL-YS* (October 22, 1926).

93. *CWR* 38 (October 2, 1926): 132; *CWR* 38 (October 30, 1926): 247; *CWR* 38 (November 13, 1926): 302-303; *CWR* 38 (November 20, 1926): 332.

94. *CWR* 39 (December 11, 1926): 47.

95. Accusing the Central Labor Union's Shantou branch "sowing seeds of disaffection," the party announced that only pickets in Guangzhou Strike Committee uniforms could be armed. Milking regime blessing, the GSC—dominated by the Workers' Delegates—quickly declared that it would increase its uniformed pickets from three to five thousand. *CWR* 37 (August 28,

clearly favored the more radical Workers' Delegates, as a way to keep the anti-foreign weapon sharp.[96] From another perspective, however, the move was shrewder, assuaging, *quid pro quo*, frustration among Workers' Delegates leaders by advantaging them in their struggle with rivals. Hoping to win favor among common strikers, party authorities also sought to free up economic incentives in the form of jobs and fiscal support.[97] Landlords, for example, were offered a chance to regain properties long occupied by striker squatters in exchange for a lump fee payment of $100,000 for "agitative expenses." More funds became available in late October when the party announced a customs surtax of 2.5 percent on imported regular goods and 5 percent on luxury items, ostensibly netting some $2.5 million a year to support many of the forty thousand unemployed strikers still on GSC rolls.[98]

Perhaps more than any other, this step stabilized relations. Since the foreign Diplomatic Corps in Beijing controlled China's customs service, the GMD's new surtax tied striker compensation—necessary if stability was to be maintained—to British cooperation. In one move, the party forced the foreigners to help calm labor unrest by "contributing" to striker support.[99] Although every other imperialist power protested the levies because they violated treaty guarantees, the British signaled their desire to improve ties with Guangzhou by remaining silent.[100]

Weighing Priorities: The Youth Movement Checked

Meeting with top CEC and provincial leaders in October 1926, General Tan Yankai explained why the boycott had to end: pickets could not succeed without military backing. In the quote opening this chapter, Tan noted, "We were doomed to fail . . . because diplomacy is highly dependent on military

1926): 326, 327; *CWR* 38 (September 11, 1926): 49; *CWR* 38 (October 30, 1926): 247.

96. *FO* 405/252 [F535/144/10], pp. 47-48, Enclosure 2, Brenan to Macleay, Guangzhou, September 30, 1926.

97. *CWR* 38 (October 30, 1926): 247; Tan, "Tan Yankai tongzhi zhongyang zhengzhi baogao," *ZWDL-YS* (October 15, 1926).

98. *CWR* 38 (October 23, 1926): 219; *CWR* 38 (October 30, 1926): 247-248; *CWR* 38 (November 13, 1926): 303; *CWR* 38 (November 20, 1926): 330; *CWR* 38 (November 27, 1926): 359; *CWR* 39 (January 15, 1927): 188.

99. Guangzhou trumpeted the new taxes as a key victory in the revolution's defiance of the unequal treaties. *FO* 405/252a, pp. 258-259, Macleay to Chamberlain, Beijing, October 3, 1926; *CWR* 38 (October 30, 1926): 248. Distribution of the funds began on November 20, and within three days some 4,612 workers had received their first installments of $10 each. *CWR* 39 (December 4, 1926): 20.

100. Iriye, *After Imperialism*, p. 99. *FO* 405/252a, pp. 244-245, Macleay to Chamberlain, Beijing, September 23, 1926; *FO* 405/252a, p. 245, Tyrrell to Macleay, September 24, 1926; *FO* 405/252a, pp. 246-247, Brenan to Chamberlain, Guangzhou, September 24, 1926; *FO* 405/252a, pp. 248-249, Macleay to Chamberlain, Beijing, September 27, 1926 (nos.147-148); *FO* 405/252a [F4072/71/10], pp. 250-251, weekly summary, September 27, 1926; *FO* 405/252a, p. 269, Brenan to Chamberlain, Guangzhou, October 13, 1926 (#170).

force. Without this 'last resort' we could not have continued the strike." The British, he warned, had already broken picket lines and would have invaded had not the strikers been disbanded.[101] Only broad-based popular agitation and deepened diplomatic efforts could counterbalance British aggression and allow the revolution to proceed.

Tan's confidence in the party's dual-prong combination of agitation and diplomacy, however, neglected one vital element—state checks on agitative disruption. Unfortunately for the Guomindang, just as its leaders openly acknowledged their influence over agitative forces, central control was declining. Hastily erected administrations in newly conquered territories relied heavily on popular organizations, favoring the latter in matters of sheer power. Wary of slipping control, the CEC had already tightened discipline over party officials. In September, it announced: (1) severe punishment for unlawful acts or oath-breaking, (2) expulsion of those abusing their office, (3) death to any individual engaged in currency manipulation, embezzlement, counter-revolutionary activities, or the instigation of internal strife, and (4) warnings that punishments would be carried out regardless of impact.[102] Measures aimed at leashing agitative forces were presented with more subtlety but sought to augment central control nonetheless. On October 26, CEC and provincial leaders passed five resolutions explaining the link between agitation, the state, and foreign relations. The first identified new treaties as the primary objectives of GMD foreign policy. The second lionized the "alliance between the vast masses and [their] revolutionary might under the party's guiding banner." From there, however, attention focused on state dominance. Resolution three asserted the right of party leaders to employ non-agitative methods when dealing with imperialists, such as exploiting tensions between the powers. Resolution four soothingly promised the masses that the party had "not changed or fundamentally altered its foreign policy position of liberating China from its semi-colonial status." In sterner language, meanwhile, resolution five warned that "GMD foreign policy should be managed through the Ministry of Foreign Affairs. . . . It cannot be handed over to any other organ or person to exercise it."[103]

Debates between CEC authorities over the final wording of these resolutions betray deep state-building concerns. Worried about provoking the imperialists, one official suggested excising resolution three because it revealed GMD intentions to manipulate the foreign powers. Concerned that foreigners would identify the link between agitation and foreign relations,

---

101. Tan, "Tan Yankai tongzhi zhongyang zhengzhi baogao," *ZWDL-YS* (October 15, 1926).
102. *Kuomintang Publicity Department*, vol. 1, #2 (September 17, 1926): 12, included in *ZWDL-YS* (October 19, 1926).
103. The original document was presented on September 22. "Lianxi huiyi ti'an chengshi ji yi'an 聯席會議提案程式及議案," *ZWDL-QC* (September 22, 1926). Discussion took place on October 26. See "Zhongyang zhixing weiyuanhui tichu yi'an," *ZWDL-YS* (October 26, 1926).

another called for scratching *all* references to the powers. Sun Ke muted concern by arguing that the resolutions were intended for party members only and that the foreigners would never see them. He then shifted the topic of debate by announcing that resolution five was the most important of the five resolutions because, unless the party could maintain central control over foreign relations, foreigners would sow divisions among the revolution's ranks. At all costs, the party had to guard against direct or indirect "consultations" *(xieshang)* with imperialists outside of central channels.

Sun's warnings suggest, as many modern historians have correctly concluded, that the CEC sought to discourage Chiang Kai-shek from opening his own negotiations with the imperialists. Nevertheless, more was involved. Before it was changed, the original draft of resolution five specifically targeted another group. As initially written, it began, "In order to prevent misunderstandings among party members *and the people*." [104] In short, as initially written, the resolution was intended to warn party members *and the people* that foreign policy was off limits to all but central authorities. Given the fact that anti-imperialist agitation directly impacted foreign relations, the CEC had good reason to worry that popular forces might take matters into their own hands.

In this context, the Anti-Christian Movement was particularly problematic. Student agitation rose dramatically through mid-1926 and was becoming strong enough to command the attention of foreign and revolutionary leaders alike. The Youth Ministry and provincial youth bureaus actively promoted anti-Christian demonstrations, spread propaganda, and transferred mission school students to government schools. [105] In January 1926, the Second National Congress added an additional boost and extended revolutionary reach to even Hong Kong students. [106]

Everywhere, student organizations reshaped the landscape of China's educational world. Throughout the country, campus strikes and disruption targeted unsympathetic principals and administrators—pejoratively called "traitors" or "education tyrants" *(xuefa)*. Some youth activists left mission schools and formed their own institutions, such as Dongnan University, which was founded by former students of Yadong Medical University. Others agitated in secret. Banished CEC member Zou Lu opened a new

104. "Zhongyang zhixing weiyuanhui tichu yi'an," *ZWDL-YS* (October 26, 1926).
105. (Discussion item #28), *1-ZXWH*, vol. 5 (October 30, 1925); (Discussion item #28), *2-ZXWH*, vol. 5 (November 30, 1926); "Zhongguo Guomindang Guangxisheng zhixing weiyuanhui qingnianbu wuyuefen gongzuo baogao," June 5, 1926; "Sichuan linshi sheng zhixing weiyuanhui shang zhongyang zhixing weiyuanhui cheng," June 17, 1926.
106. *2QDD*, p. 125; "Shisinian yiyuefen gongzuo baogao," January 31, 1925; "Zhongyang qingnianbu zhi geming qingnian lianhehui han," December 24, 1925; "Xianggang qingnianbu qingnian yundong jihua," December 15, 1925.

school in the hope of avoiding student revolutionaries, but he miscalculated because the Shanghai Youth Bureau quickly enrolled GMD agents so "some day they will be able to continue the work of the party." Some were advised to stay put and endure the discomfort of mission school life rather than form a new school "because revolutionaries are not supposed to abandon the battlefield of their enemies."[107]

Anti-Christian Movement energies swelled in large part due to the widespread adoption of inclusive tactics. The CCP Central Committee ordered agitators to drop anti-Christian prejudice and unite with all students "without discrimination on the basis of religion, party, or ideology." Agitators were encouraged: to invite and embrace Christian student participation; to stop branding Christians "reactionary" or "counter-revolutionary" in order to cultivate friendships; and to target the evils of religious education rather than the students *per se*.[108] The Great Alliance Against Cultural Aggression formed joint executive committees with mission school student organizations while the National Student Union hosted lectures and study groups specifically designed to recruit mission school students.[109] The Hunan Student Union publicly reversed its discrimination against mission school students and Hunan's GMD Youth Bureau prepared over ten thousand leaflets emblazoned with the slogan "We welcome students of mission schools to join in the battle front of revolution!" The Anti-Christian Federation produced its own circulars, exclaiming, "Save the oppressed! Christian school students! Leave those schools where you suffer!"[110] Eager to prove their nationalistic zeal, revolutionized mission school students amplified anti-foreign sentiment.

The anniversary of the May Thirtieth Incident also contributed. In 1926, Shanghai youth bureaus were preparing to commemorate its first anniversary when leaders discovered that Sun Chuanfang and foreign authorities planned to quash all student activities. Meanwhile, field reports also complained that schools were expelling student leaders by the dozens while foreigners actively "bribed" Chinese officials, educators, businessmen, and nationalistic societies with coveted Boxer indemnity educational grants. Seizing on these

---

107. "Zhongguo Guomindang Shanghai tebieshi dangbu qingnianbu liuyuefen gongzuo baogao shu," July 20, 1926.

108. "Resolutions on the Student Movement," in Wilbur and How, *Documents on Communism*, pp. 311-312. Also see "Qingnian yundong jueyian," *2QDD*, pp. 131-132; "Zhaoji dierci quanguo daibiao dahui xuanyan," *1-ZXWH*, vol. 5 (December 11, 1925).

109. One committee linked the Hubei Student Union to the Former Mission School Student Alliance. The Great Alliance Against Cultural Aggression, with executive offices in Changsha, coordinated 120 organizations, including the Hunan GMD Party Office, the Hunan Teachers Association, student and labor unions, peasant associations, and the Merchants Alliance. Lutz, *Chinese Politics and Christian Missions*, p. 222; Li, *Cong ronggung dao qingdang*, p. 651.

110. Lutz, *Chinese Politics and Christian Missions*, p. 222; Yip, *Religion, Nationalism, and Chinese Students*, p. 70.

critical points, propagandists contacted over 420 different youth organizations and asked Shanghai students to boycott classes. On May 30, some seventy to eighty thousand students participated in parades and other demonstrations, some of which here held in the foreign concessions. As one GMD activist reported, "[we] concentrated on the foreign concessions because we considered the May Thirtieth Movement to be an anti-imperialist movement and it was our duty to fearlessly speak out there."[111]

In June, the inception of the Northern Expedition added a new wave of intensity. Anti-Christian agitators captured Chinese ministers and laymen, adorned them with dunce caps and paraded them through streets as "traitors." Others tore down crucifixes and hung pictures of Sun Yat-sen in their place.[112] Propaganda from the GMD's Fourth Army's political department equated missions with a disease which had stolen China's authority and produced slaves. Guangxi leaders even tried to change the weekly holiday to Monday so as to avoid Christian connotations portraying Sunday as a day of rest.[113] Anti-Christian Federation branches spread to schools everywhere.

Stimulated by the exciting events of mid-1926 and swelling with each stage of the NRA push into central China, anti-Christian agitation began to overwhelm mission institutions. Events in Hunan were particularly intense. In August, for example, when students in Liuyang protested church attendance at the Wesleyan Boarding School for Boys, school authorities threatened to revoke their scholarships. As relations deteriorated, missionaries decided to close the school, whereupon agitators conspired to arrest and hold them for a "public trial." Forewarned by friendly students, the seven missionaries escaped, but only after they abandoned all personal belongings and left school facilities to be seized and converted into a propaganda school. That same month, student agitators demanded that Yale-in-China fire all foreign teachers, hire Nationalist teachers for all social science courses, build a tiled swimming pool, and limit study to four hours a day. Nursing students agitated to oust non-GMD Chinese members of the Medical Board to open room for others more sympathetic to the revolutionary cause. Yale-in-China middle school students took over their school.[114] In Nanxian, students attacked the barricaded doors of the China Inland Mission offices several times before breaking through, destroying and looting the chapel and residences, and driving the missionaries out of the city. According to reports, demon-

---

111. "Zhongguo Guomindang Shanghai tebieshi dangbu qingnianbu wuyuefen gongzuo baogao," June 21, 1926.

112. *The North China Herald* (September 18, 1926): 534.

113. Lutz, *Chinese Politics and Christian Missions*, p. 227. The CEC rejected the Guangxi petitions. (Discussion item #4), *2-ZXWH*, vol. 5 (October 30, 1926).

114. Dailey, "The Red Wave on the Yangtze," p. 345; *FO* 405/252 [F1520/2/10], pp. 241-242, Enclosure, Jones to O'Malley, Changsha, December 13, 1926; Lutz, *Chinese Politics and Christian Missions*, pp. 226-227; Yip, *Religion, Nationalism, and Chinese Students*, p. 68; Dailey, "Bolshevizing the Yale-in-China College," p. 116; Giles, *Chaos in China*, p. 40.

strations assailed almost every mission school in Changsha, including Yale-in-China, the Hunan Bible Institute, various girls schools, the Presbyterian mission schools, and Hunan University.[115]

The scale of destruction—or more specifically its ability to implicate the Nationalist regime with foreign interests—aroused passionate debates among top party leaders worried about flagging control. Meanwhile, related problems deepened CEC concern about the youth movement. Operating in scattered locations, student organizations were easily compromised by outside agendas. Nationalist reports through 1926 repeatedly warned of infiltration by "false-revolutionary" or "counter-revolutionary" interests such as the Nationalist Comrade Club *(Guomindang tongzhi jülebu)*, a GMD splinter group seeking to "mislead" *(yaoluan)* society's conceptions and "shake the party's foundations" *(dongyao bendang zhi jichu)*.[116] In October, CEC authorities uncovered an alleged plot by "false" *(wei)* party officers to penetrate Sun Yat-sen University and overthrow the Guangzhou Student Federation as a first step toward undermining the Guangzhou regime. Later investigations once again implicated Sun Yat-sen University, this time for harboring heretical Nationalism Faction *(Guojia zhuyi pai)* influence.[117] Still other Guangzhou student organizations had to be examined because of rumored ties to Sun Chuanfang.[118] In Wuzhou, party authorities also struggled with so-called "reactionary" faction members.[119] Repeated complaints about the Association for the Study of Sun Yat-sen Ideology *(Sun Wen zhuyi xuehui)* eventually compelled the CEC to close all chapters except for the one in Guangdong which was already under GMD control.[120] In each case, authorities revoked the membership of implicated party members and ordered all others to avoid further contact with tainted associations or face expulsion themselves.[121] Repeated directives, meanwhile, mandated that party members sacrifice individual freedom to "absolutely maintain strict discipline and solid unity."[122]

Factionalism complicated regime concerns about the student activism.

---

115. *FO* 405/252 [F1520/2/10], p. 242, Enclosure, Jones to O'Malley, Changsha, December 13, 1926; Dailey, "Bolshevizing the Yale-in-China College," p. 116.

116. "Shengli dierzhong xuexiao xueshenghui daibiao dahui minggu er gong xuegun Li Yueting diyici xuanyan," August 29, 1926; "Tonggao diyisiqihao," *1-ZWQH* (May 23, 1925); (Discussion item #10), *ZWDL-YS* (October 28, 1926).

117. "Anhui sheng linshi sheng dangbu baogao (siwuyuefen)," May 31, 1926; (Discussion item #9), *ZWDL-YS* (October 28, 1926); (Discussion item #5), *2-ZXWH*, vol. 5 (October 12, 1926).

118. "Guangzhou jingcha tebie dangbu zhuansong gefenbu jianyi chengban Shen Hongci an," *ZWDL-YS* (October 28, 1926).

119. "Wuzhou gejie dangyuan quchu fandongpai weiyuanhui xuanyan," December 14, 1926; "Wuzhoushi zhixing weiyuanhui zhi zhongyang dangbu deng daidian," January 1927.

120. (Discussion item #11), *2-ZXWH*, vol. 2 (April 23, 1926).

121. "Tonggao diyisiqihao," *1-ZWQH* (May 23, 1925).

122. "Xunling cao'an," *1-ZWQH* (May 22, 1925); "Tonggao diyisiqihao,"*1-ZWQH* (May 23, 1925).

While unable to compete in the same league as labor feuds, student rivalries enflamed tensions and undermined revolutionary discipline. In April 1926, different Guangzhou schools accused each other of breaking the law, disrupting the Nationalist Revolution, disobeying party directives, and heeding imperialist efforts to destroy student unity. Since all belonged to the Guangzhou Student Union, each side demanded that the Nationalist regime decide in its favor.[123] Divisions within a single student union could also spawn violent attacks. At Guangzhou Vocation School, a faction seized control of the student union, had a chop made, issued declarations without permission, and disrupted elections. As elsewhere, rivals insisted that justice be meted out and punishments follow.[124] Excessive personalities intensified rivalries. For example, after the student union of Xinhui County Middle School publicly denounced one of its members, the maligned individual—Zhao Renchang—sought support from the county youth and political bureaus, forcing the student union to approach the county student union and the Youth Ministry. Both sides denounced the other as "reactionary" before a violent melee involving pipes and sticks injured some thirty people. Appeals to the CEC and provincial authorities produced an investigation but no outright decision, likely because both groups were headed by party members.[125]

The youth movement also suffered from fundamental failings related to GMD partyization *(danghua)* efforts. Although the term *danghua* implied that expanding party influence would translate to party control, that was not always the case. In the fall of 1925, for example, the Guangdong University Student Union refused to follow party direction and denounce teacher protests against *danghua* reforms. A split ensued when unhappy students condemned the union, claiming that it had "many times disregarded the orders of party central headquarters."[126] As one Second National Congress delegate

123. "Guangzhou xuesheng lianhehui daibiao dahui zhongyao xuanyan," April 11, 1926; "Guangzhou xuesheng lianhehui shang zhongyang qingnianbu cheng," April 14, 1926; "Guangdong quansheng xuelianhui daibiao dahui duiyu pohuai xuesheng tongyi yundong de fandong fenzi xuanyan," April 15, 1926; "Guangdong gedi xuesheng daibiao lianhehui shang zhongyang dangbu deng daidian," April 23, 1926; "Guangdong xuesheng lianhehui shang zhongyang zhixing weiyuanhui cheng," May 1926; "Zhongyang mishuchu zhi qingnianbu," April 29, 1926; *Hunan Changdeshi dangbu zhiweihui Chen Baoxiang ershifan can'an zhenxiang, GHGZ*, April 1926.
124. "Jiaozhong xueshenghui dui Guangzhou xuelianhui fengchao xuanyan," April 16, 1926; "Shili zhiye xuexiao xueshenghui zhongyao xuanyan," April 17, 1926.
125. Zhao was accused of beating and knifing another student, destroying the school telephone system, and blockading classes with bands of toughs. "Xinhui xuesheng lianhehui dui xinzhong fengchao disici xuanyan," July 5, 1926; "Xinhui xianli zhongxue xueshenghui zhixing weiyuanhui shang zhongyang qingnianbu daidian," June 7, 1926. To avoid personnel problems, authorities often relied on letters of introduction and recommendation. "Zhongyang qingnianbu zhi Ding Chaowu han," August 8, 1926.
126. "Shiyue sanshiyiri quanti xuesheng dahui xuanyan," November 2, 1925. Problems arose

complained, "Guangdong University is a party school, but it is not revolutionary."[127]

In relation to problems with the youth movement in general, *danghua* measures were also disparaged for dividing revolutionary ranks. Guangdong activists were generally party members, so their contributions could easily be considered "partyized." Outside Guangdong, however, most revolutionary youth had not been inducted. As a result, their contributions could not technically count as "partyized" because such youth did not belong to the party in the first place.[128] Underlying this trivial semantic debate, of course, was the unhappy recognition that many revolutionary organizations operated outside the channels of party control. If students in *danghua* schools failed to heed party directives, Guomindang underwriting and "party fraction *(dangtuan)*" infiltration notwithstanding, then students in non-partyized institutions had even less cause to do so.[129] *Danghua*, in short, did not translate into party control.[130] As CEC official Cai Yichen reported, slack coordination and laggard direction meant the Youth Ministry retained only loose ties with even Guangdong youth bureaus.[131]

To expand revolutionary might and rectify problems with control, the CEC moved to fully "partyize" education and the youth movement. In July 1926, the party convened its First Educational Conference. Noting that educational progress had lagged behind political advances, leaders promised better direction. Championing *danghua* ideals, delegates called for bans on "superstitious" *(mixin)* materials such as almanacs, fortune telling manuals, and divination charts while describing enforcement with warnings such as "completely forbidden" *(yilü jinshou)*, "severely punished" *(yanzhong chufa)*, and "all burned" *(yilü fenhui)*. Discussion topics ranged from *How Party Thought Should Be Inculcated* to orthodox curricula for courses such as *A Brief History of Imperialist Encroachment in China*, *Guomindang History*, and *The Three Principles of the People*. Resolutions called for stricter regu-

---

elsewhere as well. Students at Guangdong Women's Normal School admitted that, "In the past, [we] refused to follow the ideas of party headquarters. From now on, however, [we'll] move to accept all direction of party headquarters and unite under the Nationalist flag." "Guangdong shengli nüzi shifan xuexiao gexin xueshenghui tongmenghui jieshu xuanyan," 1926.

127. *2QDD*, p. 125. In December 1926, Sun Yat-sen University administrators organized the Office of Political Education to oversee political indoctrination, student activities, and morality. It reported directly to the CEC. Yeh, *The Alienated Academy*, p. 174.

128. As a solution, delegates expanded terminology to include "revolutionization" *(geminghua)* and "massification" *(pingminhua)* as descriptions of the transformation of education. "Qingnian yundong jueyian," *2QDD*, pp. 131-132; "Zhaoji dierci quanguo daibiao dahui xuanyan," *1-ZXWH*, vol. 5 (December 11, 1925).

129. (Discussion item #2) and "Yinianlai quanguo xuesheng yundong zhi gaikuang," *2-ZXWH*, vol. 3 (July 17, 1926); *2QDD*, p. 125.

130. *2QDD*, p. 126.

131. (Report #9), *2-ZXWH*, vol. 2 (April 23, 1926).

lation over traditional academies *(sishu)* and mutual aid society schools, and more government county, municipal, and township schools to take up the slack. Alongside teacher qualifications and accreditation standards, delegates identified party principles *(dangyi)* as the fundamental basis for educational reform.[132]

In Nationalist territories *danghua* reforms spread. Shantou officials set up seventeen new schools incorporating GMD theory and practice.[133] The Youth Ministry's Mass Education Committee was ordered to institute mass or commoner *(pingmin)* schools in every district to cultivate "general revolutionary knowledge and revolutionary thought, awaken the masses, and bring about the quick success of the Nationalist Revolution."[134] To expand the reach of party principles, Women's Ministry leaders asked provincial educational officers to inspect schools and license only teachers who had passed tests on GMD thought. Despite the challenge of operating in secret, *danghua* advanced even outside GMD territory. In Sun Chuanfang's Anhui, for example, party agents set up *pingmin* schools for peasants and workers. Meanwhile, surveys kept the party apprised and ready for opportunities.[135]

As Northern Expedition advances enlarged the Guomindang base, new provincial authorities threw their weight behind partyizing measures. In July 1926, Hunan's provincial government redefined education's primary objectives: the fulfillment of Sun Yat-sen's Three Principles of the People and the union of Chinese heritage and science. To achieve this goal, Hunan education officials began initiating reforms and asserted, "Educators at primary schools—the foundation of national universal education—must be made to understand party principles and must, moreover, sincerely accept party training in order to help realize education's *danghua*." Prescriptions included:

(1) All schools must hang a portrait of Sun Yat-sen and use the Guomindang flag, a square of blue sky with a white sun on a field of red; (2) every Monday, during the first hour, a memorial service commemorating Sun Yat-sen must be held at which the will of Sun Yat-sen must be read and a patriotic address delivered; (3) when teaching civics all teachers must use only material found in Sun Yat-sen's most famous books, including *Plans for National Reconstruction, Fundamentals of*

---

132. "Guomin zhengfuxia zhi jiaoyu xingzheng huiyi," *Jiaoyu zazhi* 18:8 (August 1926): 5.
133. *CWR* 39 (December 25, 1926): 103.
134. "Zhongyang qingnianbu banli pingmin jiaoyu jingguo ji jinhou zhengli dagang," and "Zhongguo Guomindang zhongyang qingnianbu pingmin jiaoyu weiyuanhui zongzhang caoan," 2-*ZXWH*, vol. 4 (September 14, 1926).
135. "Xuexiao jiaoyuan ying shou dang de xunlian," October 20, 1926; "Anhui sheng linshi sheng dangbu baogao," May 31, 1926; "Guangzhou lingnan daxue gongren shenghuo zhi diaocha," 1926.

National Reconstruction, and *The Three Principles of the People.*[136]

In October, Hubei provincial authorities added their own interpretation of *danghua*, claiming, "Students of private schools [Chinese and foreign], must be taught additional courses on Guomindang principles and policy. In regards to training, students of private schools must accept orders from party headquarters, allow the observation of Premier Sun Yat-sen Commemorative Meetings, and participate in mass movements." Hubei leaders also mandated that all private middle and elementary school teachers and principals register for and graduate from a Party Principles Research Institute or other comparable party school.[137] When Zhejiang joined the bandwagon in March 1927, its Provincial Party Office quickly announced that "absolute *danghua* education principles must be carried out in all schools."[138]

Noncompliant schools faced retribution while uncooperative educators were replaced. Student activists policed curriculum and policy to ensure that school officials followed regulations. Even modest negligence risked student attacks and reports to Central Headquarters. Sun Yat-sen University students, for example, denounced their president as "reactionary" when he failed to implement *danghua* reforms. When students of Meixian's Fifth Middle School and Guangzhou Normal College failed to participate in demonstrations, local leaders asked the CEC to close both institutions because otherwise, "students at other schools will surely imitate them, destroying the unity of the student movement."[139]

Alongside educational reforms, the CEC took steps to unify and subjugate youth organizations to greater party oversight. As early as July 1926, the party conducted a detailed study of student organizations as the basis of streamlining the youth movement and identifying leaders of questionable allegiance.[140] Findings gave some cause to celebrate. In general, the party directed and influenced most of the thirteen formally established provincial student unions. Nevertheless, a short list of specific problems also plagued progress. Some provincial unions remained outside GMD circles. *Dangtuan* provided leverage, but not enough in many cases. Generalized propaganda detached from local concerns struggled to capture popular attention. Unity

---

136. "Guomin zhengfuxia zhi Hunan quansheng jiaoyu jihua," *Jiaoyu zazhi* 18:10 (October, 1926): 2; Dailey, "The Red Wave on the Yangtze," pp. 344-345.

137. "Qudi sili xuexiao zhanxing tiaoli—Hubei zhengwu weiyuanhui faling," in *Guonei jinshinian lai zhi zongjiao sichao,* comp. Zhang, pp. 374-375; "Guomin zhengfuxia zhi Esheng jiaoyu," *Jiaoyu zazhi* 18:12 (December, 1926): 3.

138. "Zhesheng zhenggangzhong zhi jiaoyu yu xuesheng," *Jiaoyu zazhi* 19:4 (April, 1927): 6.

139. "Shengli dierzhong xuexiao xueshenghui daibiao dahui minggu er gong xuegun Li Yueting diyici xuanyan," August 29, 1926; "Guoli zhongshan daxue gongye zhuanmenbu xueshenghui quzhu Xiao Guanying xuanyan," October 27, 1926; "Meixian zhixing weiyuanhui zhi zhongyang zhixing weiyuanhui dian," May 1926.

140. (Discussion item #3), *2-ZXWH,* vol. 3 (July 13, 1926); (Untitled report), *2-ZLQ* (July 6, 1926).

was undermined when union leaders failed to report to higher authorities. Too often, students found themselves minorities within their own organizations and exploited by outside agendas. Finally, religious beliefs divided student organizations and compromised their ability to conduct anti-imperialist activities.[141]

In August, CEC leaders acted on this information by issuing new directives governing student *dangtuan*. As expected, policy reemphasized central control and stern disciplinary action against failure to follow policy.[142] The Youth Ministry went further, ordering special commissioners *(tepaiyuan)* to attend all student union *dangtuan* meetings and all party bureau discussions concerning the youth.[143] Ministry leaders also banned county party offices from directly organizing or reorganizing National Student Union branches in order to "clarify authority limits and avoid conflicts."[144] The Propaganda Ministry, meanwhile, sought to "unite and centralize" *(yizhi er jizhong)* its message to ensure that "standard" *(biaozhun)* information could correct "errors" *(cuowu)* by party members.[145] That same month, the Youth Ministry sent agents to Shanghai to conduct a full-scale investigation so revolutionary youth there could be unified and concentrated.[146] Student leaders complained bitterly but to no avail.[147]

On September 2, Youth Ministry officials announced to all provincial and municipal party offices new regulations governing the formation of *dangtuan* and student unions, emphasizing that protocol *must* be followed and that all youth organizations and federations *must* report to their supervising party organs. Clear youth movement objectives were defined and passed to all student union leaders: (1) implementation of *danghua* education, (2) mass(ifying) education; (3) expulsion of "opiate" *(mazui)* teachers; (4) improved communication; (5) reformation of student life; and (6) the rejection of "opiate" books.[148] If student groups produced more trouble than they were worth, the party simply dissolved them.[149] In October 1926, the Guangzhou Student Federation reported to the Youth Ministry that certain student unions had to be shut down because of unrest. When a propaganda

---

141. "Yinianlai quanguo xuesheng yundong zhi gaikuang," *2-ZXWH*, vol. 3 (July 17, 1926).
142. "Xueshenghui dangtuan zuzhi xiuzheng an," *2-ZXWH*, vol. 4 (August 28, 1926).
143. "Zhongyang qingnianbu tepaiyuan tiaoli," *2-ZXWH*, vol. 5 (November 13, 1926).
144. (Discussion item #14), *2-ZXWH*, vol. 5 (November 30, 1926).
145. "Xuanchuanbu jihua dagang cao'an," Shanghai (June 15, 1926).
146. "Zhongyang qingnianbu zhi quanguo xuesheng zonghui dangtuan zhixing weiyuanhui han," August 31, 1926.
147. See *Guangxi shengli dier zhongxuexiao xueshenghui fandui Wuzhou fayuan yazhi xuesheng yundong qingxing, GHGZ*, August 12, 1926.
148. "Zhongyang qingnianbu tonggao," September 2, 1926; "Zhongyang qingnianbu zhi mishuchu han," September 3, 1926; "Hongying xueshenghui gaizu diyici quanti dahui gexin xiaowu xuanyan," September 11, 1926.
149. The Youth/Soldier Alliance Association was disbanded once its leadership could no longer be trusted. "Zhongguo qingnian junren lianhehui daidian," Guangzhou, 1926.

team from the Jianguo Propaganda School tried to illegally raise funds by soliciting contributions in North River districts, the school was closed and public notice circulated so it would not happen again.[150] On November 1, 1926, meanwhile, factional strife between student groups at Sun Yat-sen University got so bad that Guomindang leaders ordered the Youth Ministry to form Committees for Dissolving the Student Tide within all youth bureaus down to the municipal level. Weeks later, the committees were disbanded when the Political Conference determined that the "student tide has been quelled."[151]

The CEC also took strong steps to curb agitative violence against mission institutions. Even so-called left-wing leaders voted to institute restraining controls over students in order to preserve warming relations with the powers. The CCP Central Committee refused to grant agitative forces *carte blanche* freedom, resolving, "We must not at this time create any opportunity of actual conflict with the Church. This condition is imposed by our present situation (the Church is allied with militarists everywhere under the pretext of treaty protection)."[152]

CCP leaders even went as far as to dismiss Communist Youth Corps members, removing them from positions of leadership in the youth movement because they could not be trusted to maintain a moderate course.[153] GMD officials, meanwhile, took special care to improve foreign relations, inviting missionaries and Chinese Christians to accept government sovereignty and support its efforts to strengthen the country. Sun Ke appealed to Christian sensitivities, declaring that the religion's survival in China would be determined by "whether Christians and the Christian church stand with or against the people."[154] Playing on Christian beliefs, he equated "true Christianity" with the Nationalist Revolution since both sought to improve the lives of the people. At the same time, in late August, just as relations with Britain began to warm, Guangzhou authorities loudly declared their intent to restore the Stout Memorial Hospital and the Guangzhou Hospital to mis-

---

150. "Guangzhou xuesheng lianhehui zhixing weiyuanhui dishisici changhui jilu," October 16, 1926; "Zhongyang zhixing weiyuanhui tonggao diereryihao," November 16, 1926.
151. "Zhongyang zhengzhi huiyi mishuchu zhi zhongyang qingnianbu han," November 1, 1926; "Zhongyang qingnianbu zhi zhongyang zhengzhi huiyi mishuchu han'gao," November 2, 1926; "Zhongyang qingnianbu zhi zhongshan daxue weiyuanhui han'gao," November 5, 1926; "Zhongyang qingnianbu fu zhongshan daxue Li Xiuran han'gao," November 5, 1926; "Zhongyang zhengzhi huiyi mishuchu zhi jiejue xuechao weiyuanhui han," November 20, 1926; "Zhongyang zhengzhi huiyi mishuchu zhi zhongyang qingnianbu han," November 22, 1926; "Jiejue xuechaoweiyuanhui zhi zhongyang zhengzhi huiyi han'gao," November 26, 1926; "Zhongyang zhengzhi huiyi mishuchu zhi jiejue xuechao weiyuanhui han," November 26, 1926; "Jiejue xuechaoweiyuanhui zhi Xu Chongqing deng han'gao," November 27, 1926.
152. "Resolutions on the Peasant Movement," in Wilbur and How, *Missionaries of Revolution*, pp. 748.
153. Lutz, *Chinese Politics and Christian Missions*, p. 220.
154. Yip, *Religion, Nationalism, and Chinese Students*, p. 66.

sionary control, blaming agitators for the seizures and issuing orders that missionaries were *not* to be disturbed.[155]

Guangzhou's efforts to accommodate missionaries during the early Northern Expedition very much impressed the foreign community. Those most optimistic applauded the party's stabilizing influence, announcing that Nationalist leaders could not be anti-Christian if Chiang Kai-shek could get a tooth pulled at the Yale-in-China Hospital. Foreign attitudes softened. The party had been sharply denounced for hospital takeovers in Wuzhou, but in July the foreign press produced a revisionist account which acquitted the government and vilified anti-Christian agitators, arguing that: "the local Chief of Police tried to help and protect, but Bolshevism knows nothing of law and order, and the mass of strikers and pickets seemed to have entire control. Outnumbered by the national movement, the *police could not afford to clash with the sentiment of the populace as expressed in their agitation and hatred in numerous demonstrations.*"[156] [Emphasis added.] Other reports defended the southern regime from allegations of harboring anti-foreign or anti-Christian aims, noting that while foreigners were not immune to agitation, they were not specifically targeted either. Missionaries noted that Guangzhou authorities routinely tried to restrict anti-foreign agitation—except in cases involving Britain—and that foreigners too often complained to consular authorities or the press about things which Chinese endured without complaint. Even the death of an American missionary and the kidnapping of Catholic priests were declared to be the result of robbery and not revolutionary anti-foreignism.[157] The International Missionary Council, an interdenominational federation of mission societies, went further, proposing that mission board leaders: (1) petition that foreign gunboats and troops be withdrawn from China, (2) request that new treaties be formed, (3) register mission schools with Chinese authorities, and (4) indigenize the Christian church.[158]

In Hankou, a major center of agitative disruption, missionaries anxiously awaited a Guomindang victory, believing it would improve conditions and bring respite from agitative "mobs."[159] When NRA troops overran Wuchang after a month-long siege, foreigners gave glowing reports about soldier interactions with the civilian population in general, and missionaries and Christians specifically. As one witness recorded,

The [GMD troops] are fine looking, good-tempered and a very orderly

155. *CWR* 38 (September 11, 1926): 54.
156. Daily, "How the "Reds" Drove American Missionaries From Wuchow," p. 158.
157. "Facts regarding Anti-Americanism in South China," *CWR* 37 (August 28, 1926): 317-318; Wong, "There is no Anti-Americanism in South China!," pp. 319-320.
158. *FO* 405/252 [F51/2/10], pp. 10-11, Enclosure 3, situation in China, November 16, 1926.
159. "The Cantonese Victory and the Future," *CWR* 38 (September 18, 1926): 59-60; Breslin, *China, American Catholicism, and the Missionary*, p. 55.

lot of men. The scenes which took place as they entered this city are vastly different from those which were witnessed when northern troops and their reinforcements arrived here. The appearance a few days before of General Chin Yun-ao's [Jin Yun'e] forces in Hankow [Hankou] created a reign of terror. The arrival of these southern forces inspired a wave of confidence and security.[160]

Circulated stories about the experience of foreigners at Wuchang's Church General Hospital confirmed positive assessments. To avoid aerial bombardment, northern warlord officers had set up their headquarters directly adjacent to the hospital grounds. When defenses broke, northern troops looking to hide scaled the courtyard walls, bringing Nationalist troops into the hospital compound. Much to the surprise of the missionaries, "nothing was touched nor was anything else about the premises injured or interfered with." Similar accounts highlighted the fact that when NRA forces entered the Church of St. Michael and All Angels, packed with two hundred women and children refugees, the soldiers examined the premises and left without disturbance—a pleasant experience in contrast to the looting and extortion exercised by warlord troops.[161]

Under this cover of missionary praise, party leaders moved—albeit cautiously—to extend influence over mission schools. Progress toward an articulated policy had been building. Resolutions from the Educational Conference of July banned foreign involvement in elementary and normal school education and demanded that mission schools register with the government.[162] On October 10, Chiang Kai-shek unveiled the GMD's determination to regulate all foreign education and institutions.[163] Nevertheless, it was not until November—two full years after the National Federation of Provincial Educational Associations meeting in Kaifeng and one year after Guangdong provincial educational authorities called for mission school registration—that the Nationalist Government finally adopted an official policy vis-à-vis mission schools. According to the government's Education Administrative Committee, all private Chinese and foreign schools were ordered to: (1) accept GMD supervision; (2) insert the word "private" *(sili)* in school names; (3) appoint an accountable board of directors to deal with the regime; (4) appoint a Chinese principal; (5) follow directives governing school times, teachers, and coursework; (6) drop mandatory religious classes and classroom proselytizing; and, (7) abandon compulsory attendance at

160. Schwartz, "The Siege of Wuhan: From Day to Day," p. 76.
161. "The Dramatic Story of the Capture of Wuchang," *CWR* 38 (October 23, 1926): 204-205; Lutz, *Chinese Politics and Christian Missions*, p. 21.
162. The resolutions were mandated by the Central Education Executive Committee. "Guomin zhengfuxia zhi jiaoyu xingzheng huiyi," *Jiaoyu zazhi* 18:8 (August 1926): 5.
163. *Minguo ribao* (October 10, 1926); *FO* 405/252 [229/229/10], pp. 72-73, Annex 2, GMD programme, January 11, 1927.

religious ceremonies. The final article stated clearly and bluntly that "schools found not in compliance with these statutes will be dissolved."[164]

Collectively, the regulations promised to uproot the missionaries' Christianizing agenda by swapping Christian content for *danghua* curriculum, and thereby co-opt foreign institutions for nationalistic purposes. At the same time, the measures seemed anti-climactic. The Guangzhou regime's new standards governing mission schools looked just like those of the Beijing government and even closely resembled comparable directives regulating private Chinese schools.[165] Far from destroying mission schools as the "claws" of imperialism, the party folded them into the "nation" alongside Chinese institutions—albeit on GMD terms. With so many missionaries celebrating advances by the Northern Expedition and Nationalist reconstruction, the Christian enterprise seemed to scarcely notice.

From the perspective of the southern government, dual-prong tactics based on bifurcated nationalism worked remarkably well. As NRA triumphs liberated new territory, popular agitative and state-building interests rushed in to fill the vacuum. Both encountered entrenched localist and foreign interests and formulated new relationships with each. Agitative forces weakened localist and foreign resistance to Nationalist authority while state-building interests offered accommodation, instituted official policy, and initiated *danghua* reforms. Success required delicate balance. Top CEC and provincial officials had to slide back and forth along a spectrum bounded on one end by support for anti-imperialist agitation and on the other end by accommodative negotiations with localist and foreign interests. Required agility notwithstanding, the system effectively move revolutionary rivals to embrace party policy.

At the same time, symbiosis between the two prongs depended on the ability of top decision-making officials to keep agitative escalations in check. As both agitative and state-building interests rushed into newly acquired territories, they did not just encounter revolutionary enemies—they also encountered each other. By the fall of 1926, however, restricting widespread anti-imperialist fire among China's mass organizations was not enough. With central control thinning as the Guomindang expanded its reach over vast tracts of south and central China, top party leaders found their position disturbingly vulnerable should either foreign or agitative forces decide to press their advantage. Few denied that British truculence had pushed

---

164. "Sili xuexiao guicheng—Guomin zhengfu jiaoyu xingzheng weiyuanhui bugao," in *Guonei jinshinian lai zhi zongjiao sichao*, comp. Zhang, pp. 372-373; "Guomindang de zuixin zhenggang," *ZWDL-YS* (October 22, 1926).

165. "Quanguo shengjiaoyuhui lianhehui yijue an," in *Guonei jinshinian lai zhi zongjiao sichao*, comp. Zhang, pp. 339-342; "Quanguo jiaoyuhui lianhehui dishijie nianhui gailue," *Jiaoyu zazhi* 16:12 (December 1924): 1-9; "Sili xuexiao guicheng—Guomin zhengfu jiaoyu xingzheng weiyuanhui bugao," in *Guonei jinshinian lai zhi zongjiao sichao*, comp. Zhang, p. 372.

Guangzhou officials to suddenly end the Anti-British Boycott and had forced Shantou officials to apologize to Consul Kirke. Should either anti-imperialist or foreign forces surge at the other, GMD officials playing the middle ground stood just as likely to get crushed between the two as they were to wrest some advantage from the situation.

7. Agitation Unleashed
—Defying Anti-Revolutionary Intransigence, November 1926 - January 1927

The method of campaign seems to be that a force of professional labor agitators always precedes the Kuomintang [Guomindang] military forces and paves the way for Kuomintang occupation by promising the laborers higher wages and improved working conditions just as soon as the Kuomintang comes into power. Then after the Kuomintang comes in the laborers are encouraged to organize and strike for betterment of conditions. Owing to the uneducated character of Chinese laborers, who really constitute the bulk of the population, liberty usually runs to license, so that a state of anarchy often results. Something approaching this has prevailed at Hankow [Hankou] since the Kuomintang occupation, the chief trouble being due apparently to the fact that the newly formed labor unions have fallen into the control of unscrupulous agitators bent upon doing all the damage possible.

That this situation has become embarrassing to the Kuomintang itself, was indicated in news from Canton [Guangzhou] last week to the effect that the Kwangtung [Guangdong] provincial government had finally announced regulations for the control of labor agitations, the enforcement of arbitrations, and the prohibition of strikes and lockouts, prohibition of labor parades and so on. This naturally has raised a storm in labor circles the responsibility for the new regulations being laid at the door of Gen. Chiang Kai-shek. . . . Officials in many cases are powerless to control the labor unions which the Kuomintang and Soviet officials have created.[1]

—*China Weekly Review, December 25, 1926*

Shortly after noon on January 16, 1927, two foreign missionaries—Misses Crabbe and Holbrook—sat inside the compound of Fuzhou's Anglo-Chinese Girls' School. While they enjoyed their lunch and conversation, shouts and chants began to echo through the buildings, indicating the approach of a large and raucous crowd. The noise focused the attention of the two women, but it did not necessarily arouse panic, despite the fact that they were alone.

Even before NRA troops arrived in Fuzhou, anti-Christian demonstrations, lectures, and parades were common. Since "liberation" in November 1926, they had become familiar occurrences, attracting mission school

---

1. *CWR* 39 (December 25, 1926): 108.

students as well as those of government schools. Restless students at Fujian Christian University demanded a three-day holiday to spread party principles *(dangyi)*, agitate for the recovery of educational rights, and urge the university to register with the government. From Jiujiang spread rumors that the party was planning to coordinate attacks on all foreigners to avenge the death of a local Chinese demonstrator killed by British troops there.[2] In Fuzhou, revolutionary students expanded anti-imperialist activity when Fujian Christian University's board of managers refused to register with the government and rejected university president John Gowdy's attempt to resign in favor of a Chinese head. Despite the frequency of anti-foreign demonstrations and the magnitude of revolutionary fervor, disruptions were closely monitored by government authorities eager to stabilize conditions. Indeed, Guomindang efforts to curb anti-imperialism prompted high praise from Fuzhou and Changzhou missionaries.[3]

In mid-December, however, Guomindang leaders suddenly lifted all restraints on agitation, releasing a torrent of anti-foreign activity. The Fuzhou Propaganda Bureau published sensationalized stories of murder and cannibalism at the local Spanish Dominican orphanage. Photographs of dead infants, news of dissected corpses, and sightings of burial services fueled rumors and spawned agitator calls for a massacre of missionaries and Chinese Christians. On January 15, crowds and Nationalist Seventeenth Army troops attacked and looted the orphanage, driving out orphans, novices, and missionaries.[4]

The very next day, Misses Crabbe and Holbrook found their conversation cut short by angry crowds bursting through the compound gates. Looting and smashing, the throng swarmed the school grounds. Discovering the startled women, rioters stripped them of their dresses before turning to other plunder. Seizing a chance to escape, the two raced into the streets in their under clothes and made their way hurriedly to the shelter of a nearby Catholic orphanage. There, however, they encountered an even larger and more menacing gathering. Noticing their plight, a GMD officer ordered his troops to push the demonstrators back and usher the women into the compound. After locating shoes and Chinese clothing, he called for an automobile and an armed guard to convey the missionaries safely away from the "howling" crowd.[5]

2. *FO* 405/252 [F915/2/10], p. 170, Enclosure 1, Ogden to O'Malley, Jiujiang, December 11, 1926.
3. Lutz, *Chinese Politics and Christian Missions*, pp. 214-215.
4. Some escaped but were later again captured and "mistreated" by popular forces at Xiamen. *FO* 405/252 [F2714/1/10], p. 457, Enclosure, Moss to Lampson, Fuzhou, January 21, 1927; Lutz, *Chinese Politics and Christian Missions*, p. 216; Yip, *Religion, Nationalism, and Chinese Students*, p. 67; *FO* 405/253 [F4176/144/10], p. 112, Enclosure, Fuzhou political report for March quarter 1927.
5. *FO* 405/252 [F2714/1/10], p. 460, Enclosure 2, Bishop Hind to Barclay, Fuzhou, January 18,

In just days, anti-Christian agitators and Nationalist troops—sometimes former northern warlords and bandits who had defected to the revolutionary side—systematically looted all mission properties in Fuzhou, including the YMCA, the Central Institutional Church, three mission hospitals, the Girl's School, the Dominican orphanage, and the homes of missionaries associated with the American Board Mission. General He Yingqin—the military authority of the region—promised to issue strict orders enjoining the protection of foreign lives and property in surrounding territories. Nevertheless, foreign confidence was deeply shaken. American leaders evacuated families to the Philippines while British missionaries seeking some degree of security congregated in the treaty ports.[6]

Spiking anti-Christian and anti-foreign violence from mid-December through mid-January marked a dramatic shift in Guomindang foreign relations. Just before the outbreaks, all indicators had pointed to *rapprochement* or even recognition for the Nationalist regime. Foreign portrayals of GMD administration contrasted favorably to those depicting the "decrepit" northern regime. Optimistic reports in late November claimed that the U.S. minister, the Japanese minister, and Hong Kong's Governor Clementi had all met with party officials to discuss new ties. Northern press releases reported that British and Japanese recognition was imminent.[7] In England, the National Labour Party urged treaty revisions while the London Labour Party specifically praised Britain's transition from a policy of "diplomatic inactivity, supplemented by threatening naval demonstrations" to one that aimed to "remove present ill-will and secure friendship" with the southern regime.[8] Meanwhile, Japanese consul authorities reported that GMD leaders planned to suspend agitation and pursue moderate policies in order to court friendly relations with the powers and "induce" recognition.[9]

Guomindang statements confirmed that party interest in improving relations was genuine. In late November, General Deng Yanda, the head of the political division of the Nationalist army, reported to a foreign journalist:

> You must realize that when the revolutionary movement has become a success, and when the people are free, equal and independent, that the economic condition of the people of China will be improved. And so you

---

1927; *FO* 405/253 [F4176/144/10], p. 112, Enclosure, Fuzhou political report for March quarter 1927.

6. *FO* 405/252 [F2714/1/10], pp. 457-459, Enclosure, Moss to Lampson, Fuzhou, January 21, 1927, 1927; *FO* 405/253 [F4176/144/10], p. 112, Enclosure, Fuzhou political report for March quarter 1927.

7. *CWR* 38 (November 27, 1926): 364; *CWR* 38 (November 27, 1926): 366. Reports claimed that the Beijing government failed to collapse only because Zhang Zuolin refused to accept President Gu Weijun's (V. K. Wellington Koo) resignation. *CWR* 39 (December 4, 1927): vi.

8. *FO* 405/252 [F217/122/10], pp. 74-75, Enclosure, China situation, London, January 4, 1927.

9. *CWR* 38 (November 27, 1926): vi.

foreigners must realize also that in those circumstances you will not lose but will enjoy even greater economic benefits from the better living conditions of the people and their greater purchasing power. It has been asserted that we are anti-foreign. This is an untrue statement and circulated chiefly by those interested in the continuance of the present feudal system. The Kuomintang [Guomindang] and the Nationalist Army have not at any time shown any attitude of anti-foreignism, but there has been a certain foreign hostility towards us, and this has brought about a natural resentment. Even this is being cleared up as our motives are becoming more clearly understood and less credence given to the misleading statements poured into the ears of the foreigners by the militarists and their tools in Peking [Beijing]. *Let me assure you that when the Nationalist government achieves success everybody will enjoy the benefits to which they are entitled, you citizens of foreign powers as well as the Chinese people.*[10] [Emphasis added.]

Positive foreign assessments mounted when Nationalist authorities announced that both the Nationalist Government and party headquarters would abandon facilities in Guangzhou for new offices in Wuchang and Hankou, respectively. (Along with Hanyang, the three nearby cities are collectively called Wuhan.) The move to Wuhan offered undeniable advantages: safe distance from Hong Kong interventionists, a chance to link with ally militarist Feng Yuxiang in the north, dominance of the rich middle Yangzi region, control of Yangzi traffic, and ready access to Beijing. The move and its accompanying military successes also gave the southern regime new prestige and legitimacy as a viable competitor for domestic and international recognition as China's rightful government.

Foreign officials were impressed. As Chen Gongbo reported, within the first few days of the revolutionary government's arrival in Wuhan, the foreign consuls of Japan, Britain, and the U.S. all visited with party officials and demonstrated a "very friendly" attitude.[11] Basking in its new popularity, the Nationalist regime boldly announced that it would only respond to foreign inquiries about tariffs and foreign vessel rights after the Diplomatic Corps recognized it as China's only legitimate government.[12] Unfortunately for the party's international hopes, however, warming relations and the opportunity they presented collapsed just weeks later. As a result, in the place of accommodation and negotiation, Guomindang foreign relations came to reflect the type of anti-foreign and anti-Christian violence encountered by Misses Crabbe and Holbrook in Fuzhou.

---

10. Dailey, "The Red Wave on the Yangtze," p. 345.

11. Chen, "Chen Gongbo tongzhi waijiao caizheng baogao," *ZGLH*, vol. 1 (December 17, 1926).

12. *CWR* 38 (November 27, 1926): 360.

Restraining Agitation: Autumn 1926

Through the autumn of 1926, Nationalist leaders carefully cultivated warm relations with the powers and limited popular forces to cement the relationship. Checking mass organizations, however, was becoming increasingly difficult. Dramatic shifts in China's political landscape excited revolutionary spirit, pushing activism to new heights.

Northern Expedition advances fired popular forces and opened to them virgin territory. When NRA forces defeated Wu Peifu's armies and took Wuhan in September, revolutionary agitators poured into the new base. Many were leaders of the Guangzhou Strike Committee and Shanghai's General Labor Union which moved its national headquarters to Hankou. Under the direction of mass organizers, unions proliferated. Within two months, the Hubei branch of the General Labor Union encompassed three hundred thousand workers in sixty participating organizations. By the three-month mark it had grown by five times to include over three hundred unions.[13] Throughout Wuhan, professional agitators abounded; indeed, so many had left Guangzhou for Wuhan that anti-imperialist demonstrations in the southern port had to be cancelled because no one remained behind to lead them. In Wuhan, armed pickets, strikes, and coordinated demonstrations became the norm.[14] Unions justified the disruption on nationalistic grounds, but most activity aimed to secure economic advantage. General Labor Union advice and assistance meant that strikers risked little while pursuing benefits. Union encouragement, in turn, pushed over thirty unions to strike within four weeks of the party's arrival in Wuhan.[15] Factories and other enterprises often faced four or five strikes in succession as different labor organizations sought their share. Severe strikes hit foreign institutions such as the British-American Tobacco Company, various Japanese factories, and the foreign concessions. Nevertheless, disruptions also impacted vital Chinese institutions—including the Chinese Post Office, Chinese telegraph offices, and the telephone administration—greatly inconveniencing Nationalist operations.[16]

In Hunan, with its weak CEC presence and strong local authorities, agitation enjoyed an even freer hand. After defeating Governor Zhao Hengti's regime in July, NRA forces dissolved the provincial assembly and instituted a revolutionary government under General Tang Shengzhi.

---

13. Jordan, *The Northern Expedition*, p. 220; Chesneaux, *The Chinese Labor Movement*, p. 323. Peasant organizations expanded as well, comprising some 287,000 members in Hubei and 1.2 million in Hunan by year's end. Wilbur and How, *Missionaries of Revolution*, p. 342; "Canton Has Three Political Factions," *CWR* 40 (March 5, 1927): 8.
14. See *CWR* 39 (February 19, 1927): 319; Wilbur and How, *Missionaries of Revolution*, p. 341.
15. Chen, *Han feng ji*, pp. 103-104; Jordan, *The Northern Expedition*, p. 220.
16. *FO* 405/252 [F2145/67/10], p. 353, Asiatic Petroleum Oil Company to London headquarters, Shanghai, January 28, 1927; *CWR* 39 (December 18, 1926): 81-82; *CWR* 39 (December 25, 1926): 109-110.

Short-handed party officials, however, gave district power to lower-tiered labor and peasant organizations—pejoratively called "Soviets and radicals" by the foreign press—which began advancing the agitative agenda. In some cases, central party authority expanded as non-party interests and mass organizations were replaced by others supposedly under CEC supervision.[17] Nevertheless, in other ways, central control was compromised. With military and police might unavailable, provincial authorities struggled to enforce their mandates, leaving popular organizations to run unchecked. In Changsha, the Hunan Commissioner of Foreign Affairs resigned after failing to curb anti-foreign agitation. Chinese merchants first welcomed the Nationalists but then begged General Tang Shengzhi, who had left for the front, to return to Hunan and moderate excessive mass organizations. According to reports, peasant and labor bureau officials dominated local and provincial administration. To augment its muscle, the Changsha Labor Bureau set up armed labor units. Changsha organizers unionized virtually all trades and pressed all workers into joining while ordering obligatory participation in strikes, demonstrations, and parades.[18] Anyone unwilling to embrace the new order was shot.[19] Religious and educational institutions faced intense disruption as did older guilds and chambers of commerce. Peasant militias confronted *mintuan* and, if provoked by efforts to restrict their power, even engaged Guomindang troops in pitched battles, including one that reportedly killed 150 and left five thousand homeless.[20]

Agitation was also energized by party efforts to transfer party and government headquarters to Wuhan. From late November through December 1926, vacating officials left a power vacuum in Guangdong in addition to the many others created when warlord regimes abandoned south and central China. Unable to adequately fill the void, state authority gave way to agitator might. In November, Guangdong reports warned that depleting central control would soon free popular disruption to "turn for the worse."[21] As factional feuds and attempts to revive the Anti-British Boycott set popular

---

17. *FO* 405/252 [F1520/2/10], p. 240, Enclosure, Jones to O'Malley, Changsha, December 13, 1926; *FO* 405/252 [F989/2/10], pp. 143-144, Enclosure 2, Asiatic Petroleum Oil Company letter, Changsha, December 17, 1926.

18. *CWR* 38 (November 27, 1926): 364, 366; *CWR* 39 (December 11, 1926): 51, 53-54; *FO* 405/252 [F989/2/10], pp. 143-144, Enclosure 2, Asiatic Petroleum Oil Company letter, Changsha, December 17, 1926.

19. The British consul expressed astonishment at the power wielded by labor leaders, noting that government authority could not even touch criminals when they enjoyed labor's support. The General Labor Union, for example, included both robber and prostitute guilds. *FO* 405/252 [F1520/2/10], p. 240, Enclosure, Jones to O'Malley, Changsha, December 13, 1926.

20. *FO* 405/252 [F1329/144/10], p. 209, Enclosure, Hunan political report, December 31, 1926; *FO* 405/252 [F1520/2/10], p. 240, Enclosure, Jones to O'Malley, Changsha, December 13, 1926; Wilbur and How, *Missionaries of Revolution*, pp. 339, 342.

21. *FO* 405/252 [F229/229/10], p. 68, Brenan memorandum, Guangzhou, November 23, 1926; *FO* 405/252 [F1233/144/10], pp. 174-175, Enclosure, Guangzhou political report.

interests against each other, conditions became tense, despite stern CEC calls for unity.

Stretched to breaking point, central control deteriorated. Immature local authorities, often workers or peasants, proved unreliable guardians of central authority. Student leaders in a district north of Guangdong complained about "party bandits *(dangzei)*" who rigged elections to win seats on local GMD executive committees, attacked student demonstrators, and even tore up a party flag. Angered over these and other abuses, the students complained to the CEC: "Even as [district] executive committee members, they went as far as to follow the example of the imperialist Shaji and May Thirtieth Massacres, demonstrating a complete disregard for party principles."[22] Elsewhere, local leaders showed comparable failings. In Sichuan, party officials sought posts to enhance their own political power.[23] Reporting on Jiangxi conditions in mid-December, even Chen Gongbo—an ardent champion of agitation—had to announce,

> The executive committee members in the Jiangxi party office are quite naïve. Most graduated from mid-level and preliminary normal schools. Senior comrades are politically defective. Although hardworking, the younger students are still naïve and receive no respect or recognition from the people. Even senior comrades are reluctant to cooperate with them. I suggest reform to strengthen the party. It would be very dangerous if politics cannot develop along with the military. The party will die if we absorb speculators into the party. *At present the party cannot unite the masses because we lack talented people and the mass movements are frequently in conflict with party policy.*[24] [Emphasis added.]

Next to the rising influence of mass organizations, stirred by military and political changes, local party authorities looked tenuous, presenting central officials with a challenge when troubling reports began to appear. Agitators seemed anxious to provoke conflict with the powers. In Guling, propaganda posters announced a coming war between Britain and a Russian/Chinese alliance. Guangzhou propaganda claimed that war would be directed against all foreigners and begin as soon as Chiang Kai-shek took Shanghai.[25] Fuzhou

---

22. "Dangzei Kang Zhunian Tan Yaoming Hu Xingqun shida zuizhuang," December 1, 1926; "Dangzei Kang Zhunian cansha xunxing qunzhong canju," December 1926; "Yingdexian liusheng xuehui wei Kang Zhunian Tan Yaoming Hu Xingqun deng goushuai wulai ouda xunxing qunzhong shu xuanyan," December 1926.
23. "Handian baogao 13, Liu Xiang lai dian 函電報告 13, 劉湘來電," *ZGLH*, vol. 1 (December 24, 1926).
24. Chen, "Chen Gongbo tongzhi Jiangxi zhengwu baogao," *ZGLH*, vol. 1 (December 17, 1926).
25. *FO* 405/252 [F777/2/10], p. 120, Enclosure, Ogden to Macleay, Jiujiang, November 29, 1926; *FO* 405/252 [F903/20/10], p. 123, Enclosure 2, Captain Karetsky to King, November 3, 1926.

agitators attacked foreigners and burned buildings.[26] Meanwhile, local party squabbles in Shanghai got so bad that the CEC sent agents to institute reform.[27] No doubt it was conditions such as these that led Clementi to disagree with his more optimistic compatriots and report that prospects for friendly relations with the Nationalists looked grim.[28] From his perspective, too much power resided in the hands of mass organization and lower-tier party leaders.

Other problems followed. In Wuhan, agitation's new muscular presence aroused localist ire, prompting merchants, bankers, and exchange brokers to leave for Shanghai. Remaining localists tried to manage labor unrest by forming a commission through the Wuhan Chamber of Commerce and announcing that workers had to get approval before striking. Merchants threatened market closures unless the government slowed disturbances. Concerned foreign interests in Hankou, meanwhile, met with British minister Miles W. Lampson to discuss possible responses to rising agitation.[29]

Outwardly, the GMD regime supported the strikers, warning British-American Tobacco Company executives to increase wages or lose their factory, for example. Nevertheless, as in Guangzhou, siding with labor exacted a heavy price: inflated costs, reduced productivity, lost revenues, and disrupted transportation and communications—all of which jeopardized the revolution's base. Party leaders funneling support to NRA troops were particularly upset when strikes broke out at the Hanyang Arsenal and the Chinese Telegraph Administration—well after Wuhan's liberation.[30] In the reminiscing words of Chen Gongbo,

> Nothing influenced the order and finances of the rear more than strikes. What the GMD needed was stability, but what the CCP needed was strikes. . . . The base of the CCP at Wuhan during this first stage was very weak so this tactic and strategy was necessary. Local order, stability, and revenues were the affairs of the GMD, not the concern of the CCP. As a result, because of the needs of the CCP . . . Wuhan, with its depressed markets and its workers parading and petitioning all day, clearly represented the disruption of order.[31]

Chen's analysis—written in hindsight years later—distinguishes between CCP and GMD needs, highlighting the factional split showcased in modern Chinese history's dominant paradigm. His own habit of pressing loans from

---

26. *CWR* 39 (December 11, 1926): 54.

27. "Fujian wenti an," *ZGLH*, vol. 1 (December 22, 1926).

28. *FO* 405/252 [F903/20/10], pp. 121-122, Clementi to Amery, Hong Kong, November 14, 1926.

29. *CWR* 39 (December 11, 1926): 51, 53; *CWR* 39 (December 18, 1926): 81; *CWR* 39 (December 25, 1926): 110.

30. *CWR* 39 (December 11, 1926): 51, 54.

31. Chen, *Han feng ji*, pp. 103-104.

merchants at bayonet point makes his analysis somewhat disingenuous, and his attempt to differentiate between GMD and CCP interests falls apart on closer inspection. Nevertheless, it still nicely illuminates how mass agitation undermined state-building efforts by threatening social order, torpedoing international prospects, and weakening central control.

Top revolutionary authorities tried to dull agitation's sharpest edges. Karachev—Soviet political advisor to the Central Military and Political Academy—criticized aggressive activity in Guangdong. Mass organizations, he argued, had moved beyond anti-warlordism and anti-imperialism to embrace selfish agendas rooted in the peasant and labor problems. The Guangdong Provincial Council banned all strikes involving military manufacturing, finance, communications, public services, and necessity industries. [32] Council authorities denounced "bad elements" heading labor organizations and announced a series of regulations prohibiting union leaders from making arrests, staging demonstrations, carrying weapons, closing factories and shops, and confiscating goods. [33] Workers protested and denounced Chiang Kai-shek. When six instances of weapons hoarding and other illegal actions were discovered among activists, however, party leaders justified even heavier intervention. From the foreign perspective, Guomindang troops performed "admirably" in restraining agitation, and by mid-December Guangzhou's situation showed "distinct improvements." [34]

Under government pressures, disruptions faded elsewhere as well. In Hunan, foreigners reported that, "The strictest orders must . . . have been issued by whatever power is controlling the situation that no [anti-foreign] violence is to be permitted." [35] On December 7, at Lushan, top party authorities—including Chiang Kai-shek, Song Qingling, Sun Ke, Song Ziwen, Xu Qian, Chen Youren, and Borodin—voted to curb labor disruption. CCP leaders decided on December 13 to curtail peasant and labor agitation lest it precipitate a reaction. Comintern concurred, resolving at the Seventh Enlarged Plenum in Moscow to restrain mass movements. What agitation was necessary, stated the resolution, must be carried out through the Nationalist Government rather than through mass organizations themselves. [36]

---

32. *FO* 405/252 [F1020/20/10], p. 152, Enclosure 1, Brenan to Lampson, Guangzhou, December 23, 1926; Wilbur and How, *Documents on Communism, Nationalism, and Soviet Advisers in China*, p. 377; *CWR* 39 (December 25, 1926): 104.

33. *CWR* 39 (December 25, 1926): 109-110; "New Kuomintang Rules Regulating Strikes," *CWR* 39 (January 22, 1927): 206; *FO* 405/252 [F1233/144/10], pp. 174-175, Enclosure, Guangzhou political report; *FO* 405/252 [F2400/2142/10], p. 375, Clementi to Amery, Hong Kong, January 15, 1927.

34. *CWR* 39 (December 25, 1926): 110; *CWR* 39 (December 25, 1926): 104; *FO* 405/252 [F1020/20/10], p. 151, Enclosure 1, Brenan to Lampson, Guangzhou, December 23, 1926.

35. *FO* 405/252 [F989/2/10], p. 144, Enclosure 2, Asiatic Petroleum Oil Company letter, Changsha, December 17, 1926.

36. Wilbur and How, *Documents on Communism, Nationalism, and Soviet Advisers in China*, pp.

Simultaneous regime efforts sought to stabilize relations with localist interests, repair merchant morale, and end the flight of Wuhan's intellectual and business classes.[37] On December 15, Song Ziwen, Borodin, and Xu Qian proposed measures allowing the regime to temporarily seize the personal estates of anyone who left. At the same time, Song invited Hankou merchants to a special conference to solicit their fiscal support and promised to protect private property. His assurances seemed to have an impact. On December 24, merchants wined and dined party leaders for five hours, giving Borodin, Song Ziwen, Sun Ke, Xu Qian, and Jiang Zuobin further chance to strengthen merchant confidence in the GMD.[38] Reciprocating, the party passed mediation rules which granted labor leverage in setting working hours and benefits, but which also allowed employers the right to hire and fire union members.[39]

CEC interests and intervention notwithstanding, success at minimizing disruption all depended on the agitators and whether they would let themselves be restrained or not. The wave of strikes sweeping Wuhan were still pursuing economic benefit, needed more time to play their hand, easily flared out of control, and enjoyed undeniable leverage vis-à-vis the Guomindang. As one report noted, "The officials in the Hankow [Hankou] district, anxious to make [a] good impression for the administration, have tried to prevent serious labor trouble from developing, but they have been powerless against the radical elements in the Guomindang [Kuomintang] who are bent upon causing all of the havoc possible, even to the institution of a communistic regime."[40]

Significantly, "possible havoc" did not exclude open defiance of government mandates. In early November, for example, after a labor strike went awry at Hankou's British-American Tobacco Company, angry pickets kidnapped five foreign employees and seized control of the factory. Intervention by Chen Gongbo, chair of the GMD Hubei Finance Bureau, eventually secured the hostages' release, but did not end hostilities.[41] In mid-December, Political Ministry officials tried to defuse the standoff by ordering the strikers to return tobacco stores that they had confiscated. On December 17, however, Song Ziwen had to report to the CEC that not only had Central Labor Union officers refused to return the tobacco, they had even seized the company

374, 376-377, 380-381.
37. *FO* 405/252 [F1199/2/10], p. 156, Enclosure, Tsuyee Pei statement, December 30, 1926.
38. (Discussion item 14), *ZGLH*, vol. 1 (December 15, 1926); "Taolun shixiang 7, Wuhan ming yinhangzhong diren cunkuan wenti 討論事項 7, 武漢名銀行中敵人存款問題," *ZGLH*, vol. 1 (December 17, 1926); *CWR* 39 (December 25, 1926): vi; *CWR* 39 (January 1, 1927): 137.
39. "Laozi wenti baogao," *ZGLH*, vol. 1 (December 22, 1926).
40. *CWR* 38 (November 27, 1926): 364.
41. Chen, promised that the government would confiscate the factory and operate it for the benefit of the workers. When he reneged, however, the workers threatened violence until he paid off the picket leaders. *FO* 405/252 [F550/2/10], p. 108, Enclosure 1, Goffe to Macleay, Hankou, November 19, 1926.

representative sent to receive it. Borodin demanded that the union explain itself, but there was little else he could do.[42] Meeting with the British consul, apologetic foreign affairs officials could only blame union leaders and promise to keep trying to settle the dispute.[43] In Wuhan, at least, agitative might could still defy Guomindang authority.

Unleashing Popular Anti-British Forces

Party struggles to minimize popular disruption enjoyed more success in some places and less in others. When agitation did overshadow central authority, it often did so because party leaders refused to risk stronger measures that might alienate the masses. In late December, however, CEC restrictions and limits on agitation suddenly gave way.

The change came when shifts in China's political landscape dissolved all incentive for restraining popular forces. Impetus came from the impotent north. Alarmed at Wuhan's developing foreign prospects, northern militarist leaders set aside their differences and joined forces to roll back NRA advances. Northern stirrings, in turn, roused anti-GMD British officials committed to warlord Zhang Zuolin. Some British leaders continued to favor a pro-party stance, including Sir James Jamieson and J. F. Brenan (consul-generals in Guangzhou), Herbert Goffe (consul-general in Hankou), and Sir Austen Chamberlain (British foreign secretary). Nevertheless, others such as F. W. Wilkenson (consul-general in Shenyang), Bertram Giles (consul-general in Nanjing), Owen O'Malley (Beijing Legation), and Sir Ronald Macleay (Britain's minister to China) staunchly opposed overtures to the south.[44] With Zhang showing life and promising to destroy revolutionary influence via incursions from Zhili and Shandong, the anti-GMD cohort became increasingly vocal.

Hoping to tip the balance in favor of the Nationalists and avoid more civil war, Chamberlain replaced Macleay with Miles W. Lampson, a friend with pro-GMD leanings. The foreign secretary then offered to revise China's treaties as soon as a regime could legitimately represent all of China. The proposition, called the "December Memorandum" or Britain's "New Policy," likely represented a genuine attempt to accommodate Guomindang demands for treaty revision, open the door for recognition of the GMD regime should it successfully unify China, and exchange old unequal treaty rights for assurances of British economic security in China's budding order.[45] Cham-

---

42. "Taolun shixiang 7, Wuhan ming yinhangzhong diren cunkuan wenti," *ZGLH*, vol. 1 (December 17, 1926).

43. *FO* 405/252 [F550/2/10], p. 109, Enclosure 2, Extract from the *Central China Post*, Hankou; *FO* 405/252 [F550/2/10], p. 109, Enclosure 1, Goffe to Macleay, Hankou, November 19, 1926.

44. Fung, *The Diplomacy of Imperial Retreat*, pp. 90-92; *FO* 405/252 [F1330/2/10], pp. 194-204, Lampson to Chamberlain, Beijing, December 31, 1926.

45. According to Fung, Chamberlain assumed that the memorandum would be taken as a sign of

berlain also desperately wanted peace. To pave its way, he arranged talks with Wuhan leaders in the hope that his proposal would be well received by the party. As he revealed to Lampson, "The Great War still haunts every household. . . . Far away from England . . . you can have no conception how profoundly pacific our people now are. Yet I must bear this fact constantly in mind, for I must not embark you on any struggle I cannot see through. It is for this reason that I was so patient—weak you would say."[46]

Well intended or not, however, Chamberlain's conciliatory gesture failed to have the desired effect, largely thanks to a series of developments that had already begun to chill GMD-British relations. One point of contention occurred on November 23 when police raided a secret meeting in the British concession at Tianjin. Arrested in the dragnet were more than a dozen local Guomindang branch officials who were then handed over to northern China's Fengtian authorities. Infuriated, Wuhan retaliated, accusing Britain of violating international law and threatening: "The Nationalist Government takes this opportunity to warn the British Government against its apparent policy of antagonism towards the Nationalist movement. . . . For its consequences, the Nationalist Government will hold the British Government to strict accountability."[47] Chiang Kai-shek was even blunter: "The Imperialists, seeing the opportunity to control our financial arteries, are making desperate efforts to satisfy themselves and to lengthen the duration of their hold."[48] Frustrated, Chiang swore that the revolution would bury imperialism in China and everywhere else.[49]

In December, relations cooled further after speculation circulated that Beijing would send Zhang Zongchang's Shandong troops south to shield the lower Yangzi region and drive the Nationalists from Hubei. Britain was implicated when newspapers reported that Hong Kong interests had offered Zhang Zuolin and Sun Chuanfang £5,000,000 to finance this Southern Expedition. Rising tensions prompted Britain to land marines in Hankou to guard the concessions. Meanwhile, the U.S. minister to China (Shi Zhaoji or Alfred Sao-Ke Sze) announced that Washington would not recognize the Wuhan regime after all.[50]

By the time the "December Memorandum" negotiations between Lampson and GMD foreign affairs minister Chen Youren opened on December 8, tensions were already rising. Chen fervently sought recognition as

---

good faith. Fung, *The Diplomacy of Imperial Retreat*, pp. 102-103.

46. See Chan, *China, Britain, and Hong Kong*, p. 225.

47. *FO* 405/252 [F292/292/10], pp. 76-77, Enclosure, copy of GMD protest; *FO* 405/252 [F1019/292/10], p. 149, Enclosure 1, Brenan to Chen, Guangzhou, December 23, 1926.

48. Dailey, "Canton's Promise and Performance," p. 88.

49. *FO* 405/252 [F934/934/10], pp. 138-139, Enclosure 4, extract from Hong Kong's *South China Morning Post* (November 25, 1926).

50. *CWR* 39 (December 4, 1926): 25-26, vi; *CWR* 39 (December 18, 1926): 81; *FO* 405/252 [959/959/10], p. 250, Lampson to Chamberlain, Beijing, January 11, 1927.

well as the customs revenues of south China, claiming that the party would seize them if Britain would not concede. The party, he noted, had already added strike relief surtaxes and could do it again.[51]

When Lampson refused, the party turned to its trump: dual-prong tactics. On December 15, Borodin outlined his stratagem to the CEC. First he argued for continued negotiations to prevent a complete break and to better assess Britain's attitude. As a peace offering, he ordered the Foreign Affairs Ministry to guarantee the protection of British lives and property. At the same time, however, Borodin also asked party leaders to excite popular forces by declaring that Britain had not changed its policy and really only aimed, "to protect its special rights and develop its commerce without giving any actual concessions." Borodin then concluded his motion: "The Foreign Affairs Ministry must ensure that the people of China and Britain understand the mutual benefit of Sino-British relations and the fact that *the British government has rejected an understanding that would benefit both sides in favor of escalating danger.*"[52] [Emphasis added.] As it usually did when facing a looming imperialist threat, the party turned to popular forces—including, this time, popular labor organizations in Britain—to reshape foreign relations.

When talks broke down completely on December 17, Borodin pushed for even stronger action. Chastising CEC members, the chief Soviet advisor firmly argued, "Our enemies are seeking alliances to encircle us. If you had only read the speech by Zhang Zuolin, you would have realized how urgent and serious the situation is. . . . It is always better to be overly conscientious than to lose because of carelessness." Insisting on stronger ties with the people, Borodin demanded more propaganda, nightly lectures, better media coverage, and new periodicals to spread and explain the foreign policy views and announcements of the Nationalist regime.[53] That same day, NRA troops began marching through the foreign concessions in Hankou. British barricades diverted the soldiers through back roads and thus temporarily avoided an incident. Nevertheless, the move gave popular anti-imperialism further cause for offense.

Poised and ready, anti-imperialist agitative organizations did not need to be prompted twice. On December 16, in Hanyang, a hastily arranged meeting of the newly organized Anti-British and Anti-Fengtian Movement attracted no less than 150 organizations. After discussing a laundry list of possible directions, delegates formed propaganda corps to acquaint Chinese "with the insulting tactics of the British Imperialists in enticing the Fengtien [Fengtian] troops southward, to raise funds to support striking workers from British

---

51. *CWR* 39 (December 18, 1926): vi.
52. "Yijue'an 1: waijiao wenti an 議決案: 外交問題案," *ZGLH*, vol. 1 (December 15, 1926).
53. "Taolun shixiang 8, Bao guwen xuanchuan baogao 討論事項 8, 鮑顧問宣傳報告," *ZGLH*, vol. 1 (December 17, 1926). Responsibility for a propaganda club was given to the Hankou mayor. (Untitled document), *ZGLH*, vol. 1 (December 22, 1926).

companies, and to actively seek help from British labor unions, the Labour Party, and so forth against British gunboat diplomacy."[54]

Given a green light by regime authorities, anti-foreign agitation erupted. Huge anti-British demonstrations appeared in Hankou on December 19 and 20. Borodin and Sun Ke delivered violent anti-British speeches, indignantly denouncing British imperialism.[55] Meeting with foreign journalists, Chiang Kai-shek iterated the party's foreign policy objectives: nullify the unequal treaties, expel all foreign troops and naval forces, cancel all port leases to foreigners, regain sovereignty over tariffs, and take control of mission institutions.[56] In Changde, Guomindang officials demanded Tls. 30,000 from foreign merchants, arrested Chinese employees of foreign firms, and closed a Japanese match factory. In Tianjin, anti-British accusations by Borodin and Sun Ke goaded agitation to explosive fervor. In Hankou, agitators representing the Grand Alliance of Peasants, Workers, Merchants and Students began coordinating anti-British activities. In the British concessions at Jiujiang, strike announcements and the arrest of a propagandist sparked massive demonstrations that forced the British to land marines to shore up concession defenses.[57]

With GMD/British talks stymied, Lampson left Hankou for Beijing to meet with Zhang Zuolin. Meanwhile, the Diplomatic Corps announced that it had decided allow the southern regime to keep customs collected from southern ports and would raise the customs tariff limit from 5 to 25 percent.[58] From the perspective of the Guomindang, the announced change was both good and dreadful. The move gave the party access to revenues, but also granted Zhang an enormous fiscal advantage. He and his allies controlled most of China's import revenues, including Shanghai, the greatest prize of all. If applied equally in all ports, the Beijing regime was projected to gain some $22.5 million a year while the southern regime could expect only $7.5 million at best. The total impact was far greater, however, because the north used the new customs receipts as collateral for immediate foreign loans of $100 million.[59]

54. *CWR* 39 (January 1, 1927): 133-134.
55. *FO* 405/252 [F2359/2/10], p. 302, Enclosure 2, memorandum, December 27, 1926; *CWR* 39 (January 1, 1927): 136; "Handian baogao 2, Wuchang shimin fan Ying yundong dahui choubei chu han 函電報告 2, 武昌市民反英運動大會籌備處函," *ZGLH*, vol. 1 (December 17, 1926).
56. Dailey, "Canton's Promise and Performance," p. 89; *FO* 405/252 [229/229/10], pp. 72-73, Annex 2, GMD programme, January 11, 1927.
57. *CWR* 39 (January 1, 1927): 133-134, 136-138; *CWR* 39 (January 8, 1927): 165-166; *FO* 405/253 [F4905/144/10], p. 325, Enclosure, intelligence notes.
58. *CWR* 39 (December 25, 1926): 110; *CWR* 39 (January 1, 1927): 136; Chapman, *The Chinese Revolution*, p. 121. Tokyo officials complained about Britain's unilateral decision and refused to acknowledge Zhang's right to raise the taxes, but they could do little else except pressure the northern leader to resist the temptation. *CWR* 39 (December 25, 1926): vi.
59. *CWR* 39 (January 8, 1927): 164.

Taking advantage of his good fortune, Zhang set up a new cabinet and announced a platform designed to attract maximum foreign interest: (1) formation of a stable government, (2) moderate principles of diplomacy, (3) retention of the treaties between China and the powers, (4) recognition of China's debts to the powers, (5) opposition to "Bolshevism," and (6) a ban on all anti-imperialist and pro-strike propaganda. Concluding his proclamation, Zhang expressed the hope that foreign interests would support his fight against "Bolshevism."[60] The Beijing regime, which had long hung by a thread, could not have asked for a timelier windfall than December's new customs policy. Infused with new revenues, the north looked to revive itself.

Nationalist authorities in Wuhan, meanwhile, were outraged. The change in the customs structure severely challenged party plans to take the lower Yangzi. In retaliation, the CEC encouraged agitative leaders to condemn the north and the imperialists. Cai Yuanpei's Three Provinces Association, an organization dedicated to revolutionary success in the lower Yangzi region, denounced the surtaxes and Beijing's decision to issue $24 million in treasury bonds, claiming that the money would only prolong the war.[61] In Jiujiang, the site of Chiang Kai-shek's temporary headquarters, General Labor Union leaders organized enormous demonstrations, a general strike, and a series of meetings condemning Beijing's actions. In Shanghai, agitators blasted Sun Chuanfang for selling out to the north while a mass meeting of twenty thousand laborers and students protested the proposed British loan and the arrival of Fengtian troops in Xuzhou and Pukou. Although angry with the north, revolutionary leaders ultimately blamed Britain for conspiring to revitalize Beijing and terminate the revolution.[62]

By December 22, frightening rumors circulated that northern warlord authorities had brutally executed seven of the GMD leaders arrested in Tianjin, convincing party leaders in Wuhan to show a stronger hand. Sun Ke announced that if Britain would not take responsibility for the safety of party members residing in its concessions, then the Guomindang certainly would not take responsibility for the protection of British lives and property in its territories. Borodin, Xu Qian, Chen Youren, and others called for "retaliation" *(baofu)* before Borodin quickly outlined a strategy once again showcasing anti-foreign agitation. As he explained, the party should remain behind the scenes but "make demands on the British through the people" *(you minzhong tichu yaoqiu)*. The best approach, he continued, was to spread popular propaganda threatening British economic interests and to launch a mass movement protesting recent developments in Tianjin. In order to avoid

60. *CWR* 39 (January 1, 1927): 138.
61. *CWR* 39 (December 25, 1926): vi; *FO* 405/252 [F2026/144/10], p. 332, Enclosure, Shanghai political report for December quarter, 1926.
62. *CWR* 39 (December 18, 1926): 81-82; *CWR* 39 (December 4, 1926): 26, vi; Fung, *The Diplomacy of Imperial Retreat*, p. 111.

implicating the Nationalist Government, Borodin insisted that this latest anti-foreign wave emerge as a series of independent demonstrations headed by local authorities rather than a nationwide movement directed by the center. Local leaders were also specifically charged to "avoid activities that might lead to conflict" or provoke skirmishes. Finally, Borodin argued that propaganda and demonstrations should alert Chinese everywhere to the vital role played by the foreign concessions: *"the foreign concessions have become the headquarters of anti-revolution and therefore represent a trap. . . . The people's revolution must destroy this trap. Therefore, there is an increasing need to recover the concessions."*[63] [Emphasis added.]

For agitators, in short, open season had been declared on the foreign concessions—the foundation of British imperialism. Some restrictions still applied. Borodin tried to create the illusion of popular spontaneity and avoid escalating conflict. Thus he ordered Fujian party leaders, for example, to restrict anti-foreign agitation lest it provoke hostilities with the Japanese navy.[64] Nevertheless, agitative forces enjoyed fuller party support and blessing than ever before. On December 26, a group called the Citizens of Wuhan Anti-British Movement—a federation of over two hundred organizations representing some one hundred thousand people—announced its resolve to support the Guomindang and destroy Britain's "conspiracy of disruption and destruction" *(raoluan pohuai zhi yinmou).*[65] (CEC leaders remained closely apprised and were given full reports of activities.) Hankou agitators formed the Christmas Anti-Christian Society which called for boycotts on British goods and services and the seizure of the British concessions. On December 29, the GMD press published scathing criticisms of the December Memorandum and British imperialism. On January 1, the day that the Nationalist Government mandated Wuhan as Nationalist China's new official capital, Nationalist papers continued their onslaught, accusing the British of conceiving policy in an "aggressive spirit" and blaming British, American, and Japanese imperialists for "digging their own graves."[66]

On January 3, angry crowds and some eighty to one hundred NRA troops gathered to demonstrate before a row of British marines guarding the concession in Hankou. Anti-British Society agitators tried to break through the line, threw stones, and crossed bamboo poles with British bayonets. Violence left two Chinese and one marine injured. British authorities asked the Nationalist Government for help controlling the crowds and received assurances that police reinforcements would come, but none did. Equally concerned that blood might be spilt, the Hubei General Labor Union made

---

63. "Tianjin dangwu baogao," *ZGLH*, vol. 1 (December 22, 1926).
64. "Fujian wenti an," *ZGLH*, vol. 1 (December 22, 1926).
65. "Wuhan shimin fan Ying yundong dahui chengwen," *ZGLH*, vol. 2 (December 27, 1926).
66. *CWR* 39 (January 1, 1927): 137-138; *CWR* 39 (January 8, 1927): 165-166; *FO* 405/253 [F3553/2/10], p. 51, Enclosure 4, Rear-Admiral at Hankou report, Yangzi, January 1, 1927.

the same appeal, asking the regime to "quickly devise a way to regain control" before the situation escalated into a "great conflict" *(da chongtu)*. Although CEC and government officials were meeting when the Union's report was delivered, their initial response betrays a calculating coolness. Chairmen Xu Qian merely ordered that someone be sent to investigate.[67]

As other concerned reports about the developing confrontation poured in from the Wuhan Union of Staff at Foreign Enterprises, the General Headquarters Political Department, the mayor of Wuchang, and the Security Bureau—which complained that police protection was too light—CEC discussion became more animated. Chen Youren suggested surrounding the concession with troops to separate the demonstrators from British troops. Xu Qian argued that unarmed agitators should not be left vulnerable to armed marines. Borodin then posited four possible responses: (1) ask the crowds to disperse, informing them that the government would settle the affair within twenty-four hours; (2) send police cordons to separate the two sides, (3) strengthen police lines with union muscle, and (4) tell the British to withdraw its troops, otherwise the party would not accept responsibility for any resulting injury and destruction.[68]

In the end, the CEC opted for the first and the last options, but not before letting the British twist in the wind. At dusk, the crowds dispersed, marines returned to their ships, and the Hankou Volunteers—a foreign defense corps formed for such crises—assumed the task of guarding the concession gates. The next morning, however, another large rally assembled. Agitative leaders announced that a protestor had been martyred the previous day and demanded that the Volunteers disarm. As enraged crowds again surged, concession police tried to maintain the barricade, but they were overwhelmed. British marines again landed, the Volunteers again mobilized, and violence again threatened.

As the crowds descended and British troops braced for conflict, however, Nationalist troops and officials representing the Political Ministry suddenly appeared. In exemplary mediating fashion, Xu Qian and Jiang Zuobin validated the agitators' demands before asking the protesters to leave for their own safety. The party, Xu added, had prepared a resolution which would be announced later.[69] At the same time, British concession authorities were asked to withdraw their troops with assurances that Guomindang officials would disperse the demonstrators. Hesitant to use force, which would only

---

67. Xu, "Hubei quansheng zonggonghui mishuzhang Xu Baihao baogao," *ZGLH*, vol. 2 (January 3, 1927).

68. Tu, "Wuhan yangwu zhiyuan gonghui zhixing weiyuanzhang Tu Zonggen baogao," *ZGLH*, vol. 2 (January 3, 1927); Zhang, "Zongsilingbu zhengzhibu Zhang Bojun baogao," *ZGLH*, vol. 2 (January 3, 1927).

69. See discussion and decisions related to the document "Gonganju Zhang juzhang baogao," *ZGLH*, vol. 2 (January 3, 1927).

inspire more demonstrations, and yet unable to maintain the concession without it, the British had little choice. Marines returned to their ships, taking the concession's weapons stores with them, and British police stood down. Nationalist forces then proceeded to occupy the concession premises while protesters began to calmly remove the barricades. That evening, Chinese were allowed into the concession, occupying the Customs House, the Municipal Building, and several business houses. Shortly thereafter, some 450 refugees, comprised mostly of the families of British and U.S. missionaries and businessmen, fled *en masse* to Shanghai, prompting talk that mission boards should begin ordering all missionaries to leave their posts.[70] Three days later, anti-foreign agitators overran the evacuated British concession in Jiujiang as well, looting and burning the consulate in the process.[71]

Full Throttle Anti-Christianity

The swift collapse of British power in Hankou and Jiujiang captured headlines around the globe. Popular revolutionary might had reached a new milestone, proving that it could sweep foreign influence aside if simply allowed. Foreign concessions had faced pressures before. A preview to the Hankou concession takeover occurred in 1925 when warlord Xiao Yaonan encouraged mass demonstrations using propaganda and techniques similar to that employed by the Guomindang.[72] The party succeeded where Xiao failed, however, largely due to the full spectrum backdrop of anti-foreignism sweeping central and south China and the threat it posed against imperialist targets everywhere. Unrestrained by party fiat, popular anti-imperialism could not be parried—not by the defenders of the foreign concessions and certainly not by more vulnerable targets.

Concessions generally featured police, troops, or volunteers to blunt the anti-imperialist tempest. Missionaries had nothing. In late December, Nationalist media reports vilified mission schools as houses of prostitution that hid illegitimate births and abused young girls, unleashing a fierce wave of anti-Christian violence. In Hunan, Christian middle school students led destructive rallies in Liling, Yuezhou, Yiyang, Liuyang, and Xiangtan. Agitators and troops in Changsha seized Yale-in-China facilities, forcing the Chinese head and all foreign staff to flee. In Hankou, rioters stormed Christmas celebrations at the Wesleyan Methodist Mission and delivered blasphemous speeches. Anti-Christians disrupting the David Hill School for the Blind dragged out and beat a missionary who tried to stop them. New

---

70. "The Hankow Crisis and the Lessons Involved!," *CWR* 39 (January 15, 1927): 169-171; "More than 400 Refugees Arrive in Shanghai from Hankow," *CWR* 39 (January 15, 1927): 172.
71. Munro-Faure, "The Kiukiang Incident of 1927," pp. 68-71; *FO* 405/252 [F1227/2/10], pp. 167-169, Enclosure 1, Ogden to O'Malley, Jiukiang, December 11, 1926; *FO* 405/253 [F4183/4183/10], pp. 115-118, Admiralty to Foreign Office, April 29, 1927.
72. *FO* 405/250 [F38/38/10], pp. 1-7, Macleay to Chamberlain, Beijing, November 11, 1925.

organizations such as the Christmas Anti-Christian Society and The Association for the Destruction of Foreign Religious Institutions sacked churches and schools as symbols of British imperialism.[73]

On Christmas Day, agitators swarmed Hankou's Christian institutions, breaking up celebrations and disrupting functions. Propaganda alleged that Catholic orphanages dug out the eyes of children for use as medicine, spawning violence that forced the Wuchang dispensary to close. NRA troops in Wuchang seized the Catholic mission's high school, church, and convent; others in Huangshi took the convent, school, and hospital while the local peasant association seized Franciscan properties. In Nanchang, Jiujiang, and Wuhu, Nationalist troops and agitators ransacked and looted missionary institutions and residences. Marchers in Ningbo savaged mission properties while agitators wrecked churches, burning and tearing up Bibles and hymnals in the process.[74] Field reports from Jiujiang noted that friendly NRA troops suddenly turned so hostile that British and American Catholics had to be smuggled out by trusted converts to avoid injury.[75] As showcased at the beginning of this chapter, anti-Christian crowds in Fuzhou cleared out virtually every missionary institution in the city, including the YMCA, the Central Institutional Church, three mission hospitals, the Dominican orphanage, the homes of American Board Mission officers, and Misses Crabbe and Holbrook's Anglo-Chinese Girls' School. Responding to the rising threat, foreign consuls and mission officials evacuated women and children from Sichuan, Hunan, and Jiangxi. Elsewhere, missionaries left along with their families.[76]

In sharp contrast to the perilous conditions facing foreign missionaries, Chinese Christians enjoyed warmth and accommodation. They described top Guomindang leaders as "very friendly" toward Christian schools and Christianity in general.[77] In December, CEC leader Wei Que—representing both the Guangzhou Education Bureau and the Foreign Affairs Bureau—promised that the Nationalist regime harbored no anti-Christian agenda and that Christian schools would be welcomed if they conformed to government

---

73. Dailey, "Bolshevizing the Yale-in-China College," p. 116; "YueXiang shouhui jiaoyuquan yundong zhi jijin," *Jiaoyu zazhi* 19:2 (February 1927): 2; Yip, *Religion, Nationalism, and Chinese Students*, pp. 68, 71; *FO* 405/253 [F3553/2/10], p. 52, Enclosure 4, Rear-Admiral at Hankou report, Yangzi, January 1, 1927.

74. *CWR* 39 (January 1, 1927): 136; Breslin, *China, American Catholicism, and the Missionary*, p. 54; Yip, *Religion, Nationalism, and Chinese Students*, p. 68.

75. *FO* 405/252 [F777/2/10], pp. 119-120, Enclosure, Ogden to Macleay, Jiujiang, November 29, 1926; *FO* 405/252 [F915/2/10], pp. 169-170, Enclosure 1, Ogden to O'Malley, Jiujiang, December 11, 1926.

76. *FO* 405/252 [F915/2/10], pp. 170-171, Enclosure 1, Ogden to O'Malley, Jiujiang, December 11, 1926. Also see *FO* 405/252 [F915/2/10], p. 172, Enclosure 2, Ogden to missionaries, Jiujiang, December 13, 1926; *CWR* 39 (January 1, 1927): 137.

77. *CWR* 39 (January 1, 1927): 133.

regulations.[78] The CEC even invited Chinese believers to help draft the regulations for governing Christian institutions in China.[79] On December 18, Song Qingling, Song Ziwen, Sun Ke, and Xu Qian attended a special dinner with Chinese Christian leaders to discuss issues facing them in central China.[80]

With missionaries grappling with popular agitative hostilities and Chinese Christians enjoying accommodative overtures, rifts in the Christian enterprise widened into gaping chasms. By year's end, a number of Chinese Christians had severed foreign ties and pledged their full support for the revolution. A former reverend of Hong Kong's Renji (Yan Chai) Street Church headed the anti-Christian Nationalist League of Workers, Peasants, Students and Merchants.[81] Strikes at a Liuyang middle school were led by a pastor's son. Changsha's mayor resigned as the finance campaign chief of the YMCA, forcing it to close when Chinese cancelled memberships, refused to attend meetings, and withheld contributions. At the same time, staff of the YMCA Bible Institute organized Changsha's anti-Christian campaign. Meanwhile, Wuhan mission school girls became Guomindang propagandists, enrolling at the Wuhan Political Institute and organizing the Wuhan Women's Union.

Many Chinese Christians proved their revolutionary zeal by turning on their former missionary allies. Mission school students in Yancheng led anti-Christian crowds to their school to conduct agitative exercises. In Yanzhou, Southern Baptist Mission Hospital employees donned Nationalist badges and confiscated the church before handing it over to NRA troops for use as a military headquarters. Even leaders of the National Christian Council signaled their allegiance to the revolution by distributing posters that portrayed Chinese Christians attacking "aggression, cruelty, and ignorance"—each represented by caricatures of foreign missionaries. On January 1, 1927, the Wuhan Christians Reform Movement severed all ties with imperialism and declared full support for the Guomindang, its principles, mission school registration, and indigenization. The reformists then demanded the expulsion of all missionaries who continued to resist the revolution and failed to put Christ before their home countries.[82]

Pressured by extensive portions of their Chinese constituencies, many missionaries openly declared sympathy for the revolution and China's nationalistic desires. Educators at Nanchang's Methodist Episcopal Mission were among the few to avoid activist disruptions thanks to their policy, as one

78. Lutz, *Chinese Politics and Christian Missions*, p. 213.

79. Lee, "Registration of Christian Schools in Canton," *CWR* 39 (January 8, 1927), p. 156.

80. *CWR* 39 (January 1, 1927): 133.

81. *CWR* 37 (August 7, 1926): 246; Lee, "Registration of Christian Schools in Canton," p. 156.

82. Lutz, *Chinese Politics and Christian Missions*, pp. 222-223; Yip, *Religion, Nationalism, and Chinese Students*, p. 68.

foreign critic described it, "of pandering to the Southerners [GMD] in every way."[83]

Other missionaries, however, became increasingly defensive and denounced the Anti-Christian Movement as a Nationalist invention created explicitly to usurp missionary influence and seize their institutions.[84] In December, after reporting that mission properties had been forcibly taken in fifty-one different incidents, American consul-general Frank P. Lockhart presented an explanation: "The plan of occupation was so systematized and so widespread that one cannot escape the conclusion that it was a fixed policy of the Nationalist Government . . . to permanently [drive] the missionary from the field, or at least [curb] his influence, if such could be done."[85] The party had certainly stacked the deck in its favor. Foreign reports from Changsha complained that the GMD Commissioner of Foreign Affairs (the office fielding missionary grievances and petitions for help) was headed by Dong Weijian, who concurrently acted as the acting Superintendent of Education (the office charged to register mission schools) and the Director of Propaganda (the office producing anti-Christian publications). According to foreign critics, this was evidence enough that the party aimed to steal mission property, bleach Christianity from mission schools, politicize education and Christian students, destroy religious freedom, and poison China's future.

Foreigners inimical to the revolution were particularly maddened by the alleged hypocrisy of the Guomindang's anti-imperialism. They portrayed party ties to Soviet Russia as manacles binding China to a darker, more insidious variety of imperialism. What party leaders called "partyization" *(danghua)*, foreigners called "red-ization" *(chihua)*—a pejorative reference to Bolshevik-inspired changes in China's sociopolitical order. Juxtaposing their own foreignness, described in positive, democratic, Christian terms, to that of the "godless" Soviets, critics of the Anti-Christian Movement argued that good Christians would never support a "Soviet plot" to destroy religion in China. Describing the Anti-Christian Movement as a distinctly politicized and anti-religious event, one reporter noted, "[the party has sought] to drive the missionary and the Bible from the field. The Christian missionaries in Central China are taking stock over the long Christmas and New-Year holidays . . . and for the most part have come to the conclusion that the spread of the Bolshevist-aided Nationalist government . . . is distinctly non-Christian and that the present onslaughts against Christianity are but the prelude."[86]

Chinese believers generally rejected such blackened portrayals of the Anti-Christian Movement, pointing out that mission schools had long been

---

83. *FO* 405/252 [F915/2/10], p. 170, Enclosure 1, Ogden to O'Malley, Jiujiang, December 11, 1926.
84. Dailey, "Bolshevizing the Yale-in-China College," p. 116.
85. Varg, *Missionaries, Chinese, and Diplomats*, pp. 191-192.
86. Dailey, "Bolshevizing the Yale-in-China College," p. 116.

politicized by consistently supporting the foreign powers. Efforts by missionary administrators to prevent student participation in politics were themselves a political expression that favored the powers-dominated *status quo*. To Chinese Christian leaders, registration was the best way to ensure that mission schools did *not* get caught up in revolutionary China's political *milieu*. On December 25, even as anti-Christian agitation flared throughout central and south China in conjunction with Christian celebrations, Li Yinglin (Y. L. Lee)—outspoken head of the Guangzhou YMCA—explained:

> It has to be admitted that there is a radical group within the Party which is not very friendly to the Christian schools. Party workers are every where [sic] among the students and laborers. However this is not as critical as it looks. Both the Kuomintang [Guomindang] and the Communist Party have a bigger program to tackle. Christianity is not so important to them as we think. They are anti-Christian only as they are anti-imperialist. If Christianity does not seek the protection of the foreign gunboats or the unequal treaties and foreign Christian workers preach more on Christian principles instead of about nations they represent, Christianity will be left free to exist in China.[87]

The question asked by many Chinese Christians was not *Will registration politicize Christian education?* but *Which political agenda should we support?* Registration would allow Christian schools to fall in line with the Nationalist Revolution and gain inclusion within its emerging "nation" while non-registration implied solidarity with imperialism and Christianity's alienation. In short, by January 1927, the pressure on Chinese Christians to abandon imperialist ties and join the "nation" had dramatically increased and the arguments in its favor had become irresistible. CEC member Xu Qian, a Christian who once taught at Lingnan University, even found ways to employ Christian dogma as leverage. As Xu explained to students at Boone College, since Christianity was itself a revolutionary belief system, any Christian unwilling to support the Nationalist Revolution deserved condemnation for failing to fulfill their religious obligations.[88]

In the end, polemics mattered little. Revolutionary and missionary supporters presented rhetorical and historical arguments using nationalistic sentiment and religious doctrines equally well. In pure ideological terms, neither side enjoyed an overwhelming advantage. In organization terms, however, the missionary position was crumbling. Through December and January, the ability of China's foreign missionaries to disseminate their message via institutions and churches could not compete with Guomindang propaganda, agitative networks, and centralized coordination. Indeed, be-

---

87. Lee, "Registration of Christian Schools in Canton," p. 156.
88. Yip, *Religion, Nationalism, and Chinese Students*, p. 66.

cause they had always sought to shield Chinese students, nurses, and so forth from political involvement, missionaries could not but fail to mobilize popular support. Party success at peeling away Chinese Christian loyalties and identities proved a *coup de grace* to which the missionaries had little response. Deserted by their Chinese followers—the very people that the foreign community had hoped would Christianize the country—missionaries could only make academic arguments against registration. Some foreign principals expelled perceived trouble makers, dispersed their student bodies, or closed schools as a last ditch attempt to turn the tide, but many others, including those heading Changsha's Yale-in-China School of Medicine and Yale-in-China College, determined to accept government registration.[89]

Triangular Politics: Agitators, State-Builders, and the British

In terms of strategic advantage, the violent events spanning late December through mid-January did much more than disrupt mission institutions and seize a foreign concession or two. They realigned GMD-British relations and revolutionary dynamics. Judging from the particulars of his planning, that was Borodin's intent. Agitation deftly forced British officials, hoping to maintain some claim over the lost concessions, to enter into negotiations. Indeed, as one report put it, that was what gave popular agitation its power. Like nothing else, it possessed the ability to "bring ... everybody ... to the table."[90]

At the same time, however, ties to popular mobilization also bound the party's fate to agitative disruption. British minister Lampson nicely summarized the party's predicament: "[Chen Youren] realizes fully [the] weakness of our position vis-à-vis labour agitation, etc., and is prepared to use [it as a] weapon to drive a hard bargain with us; at the same time he realizes . . . *the danger of letting things go too far and getting out of control* and the advantages of reaching some early settlement with us."[91] [Emphasis added.]

The danger Lampson warned about extended far beyond simple socio-economic disruption or regime inconvenience. Events at Hankou and Jiujiang outraged British authorities who opted to strengthen the British hand before anti-foreign organizations tried their luck elsewhere. Even Lampson and Chamberlain, who generally supported Nationalist state-building efforts, resolved that no other British concessions would be so easily relinquished. In Lampson's words,

> The only way to deal with [Chinese], be they north or south, is to show them that we are perfectly prepared to be fair with them and even to go to great lengths to meet their legitimate national aspirations, but simulta-

89. Dailey, "The Red Wave on the Yangtze," p. 344.
90. *CWR* 39 (December 25, 1926): 108.
91. *FO* 405/252a, p. 700, Lampson to Chamberlain, December 22, 1926.

neously to make it absolutely clear that we will not allow our rights to be trampled upon by methods of violence and that where we are in a position to do so (as at Shanghai and Canton [Guangzhou]), we will in fact defend our rights if driven to it.[92]

Conditions in Shanghai—the crown jewel of Britain's economic enterprise in China—aroused deep concern. Stability had been guaranteed by warlord Sun Chuanfang: a close British ally who tirelessly suppressed anti-imperialist activity.[93] Sun, however, had been backpedaling since NRA forces took Jiangxi and Fujian and no longer commanded respect as an able defender of British interests.

With the Shanghai concession overshadowed by both mushrooming anti-foreign agitation and NRA troops poised to invade the lower Yangzi, the British decided to take action. On January 7, Admiral Sir Reginald Y. Tyrwhitt left Hong Kong for Hankou to confer with British officials there. Soon thereafter, although the Yangzi River's seasonally low waters prevented larger cruisers from making the journey, gunboat reinforcements followed. Meanwhile, British troops converged on Hong Kong and Shanghai from posts all around the globe.[94] Hong Kong's entire Punjabi Regiment left for the lower Yangzi. From Calcutta came another brigade while reports broke that the Devonshire Regiment, the Bedfordshire and Hertfordshire Regiments, the Border Regiment, the Middlesex Regiment, the Cameroonians, and the Green Howards had all been given similar orders. By January 22, thirty-five foreign warships, from river gunboats to battle cruisers, waited near Hankou while another forty-two vessels rested at Shanghai, part of a massive 171-vessel foreign fleet adorning Chinese waters. In early February, the Second Suffolk Regiment from Singapore reached Hong Kong and was joined by portions of the Durham Regiment's Second Battalion. In all, over twenty thousand British troops were summoned to China, along with tanks, airplanes, artillery, Indian cavalry, hospital units, and support. Japan added two cruisers—the *H.I.J.M.S. Isuzu* and *H.I.J.M.S. Sendai*—with five hundred marines.[95]

On the diplomatic front, Lampson tried to coordinate a united front with the French, Japanese, and Americans but with no success. Washington clung to non-intervention, leading to emotionally charged volleys between British and U.S. newspapers. Tokyo officials sent destroyers but artfully evaded

---

92. Fung, *The Diplomacy of Imperial Retreat*, p. 121.

93. *CWR* 39 (December 18, 1926): 81-82; *CWR* 39 (January 1, 1927): 137-138; *CWR* 39 (January 8, 1927): 165.

94. *CWR* 39 (January 22, 1927): 212; *CWR* 39 (January 29, 1927): 244; Lü, "Beifa shiqi Yingguo zengbing Shanghai yu dui Hua waijiao di yanbian," pp. 204-207.

95. *CWR* 39 (January 29, 1927): 244; *CWR* 40 (March 12, 1927): 54; "The Destination of British Troops," *CWR* 39 (February 12, 1927): v; Chapman, *The Chinese Revolution*, pp. 124-125.

British's calls for solidarity.[96] Even without international collaboration, however, the buildup was intimidating and prompted loud protests from officials in both Wuhan and Beijing.[97] With China already embroiled in civil war, few saw the move as a bluff.

With British military might pouring into China, Wuhan officials took careful steps to slow anti-foreign violence and dampen anti-imperialist fire. Shortly after the Hankou concession fell to Chinese control, agitative leaders excitedly requested government permission to launch a "spontaneous general strike by the people" to carry the revolution to the next level. On January 5, however, Borodin rejected the petition. Explaining his position to CEC and other Nationalist leaders he exclaimed, "No general strike should be launched at this time for should the concession fall into our hands it would be tantamount to opposing ourselves. *If we cannot secure it, then we can reconsider at that point.*" [Emphasis added.] Betraying his sensitivity to British relations, he then argued that a strike would refute Guomindang claims that it had things under control. Evidently convinced, CEC leaders agreed and ordered labor and merchant organizations to return to business as usual.[98] On January 7, the CEC then directed all provincial officials to protect British lives and property. Three days later, official party pronouncements urged restraint, using slogans such as "Rigorous people's discipline!" *(Yanmi de qunzhong jilü!).*[99]

On January 12, revolutionary military and civil officials—including Tang Shengzhi, Chen Youren, He Xiangning, Xu Qian, Song Qingling, Gu Mengyu, Peng Zemin, Deng Yanda, Jiang Zuobin, Mikhail Borodin, and General Galen (a Russian military advisor)—greeted enormous and enthusiastic crowds at the Hankou Race Course. Speaking to the throng, Chiang

---

96. *FO* 405/252 [F1652/2/10], p. 266, Howard to Chamberlain, Washington, February 11, 1927; *FO* 405/252 [F1441/156/10], p. 229, Enclosure, Howard to Secretary of State, Washington, January 26, 1927; *FO* 405/252 [F334/156/10], p. 80, Chamberlain to Tilley, January 13, 1927; *FO* 405/252 [F706/2/10], p. 111, Chamberlain to Tilley, January 24, 1927; *FO* 405/252 [F1041/2/10], p. 148, Tilley to Chamberlain, Tokyo, December 9, 1926; *FO* 405/253 [F3808/1530/10], p. 80, Enclosure, Kellogg to Howard, Washington, April 7, 1927; "British Advertisers Threatening Boycott Tientsin American Paper," *CWR* 39 (January 15, 1927): 172; *CWR* 39 (January 29, 1927): 244.

97. *FO* 405/252 [F944/156/10], pp. 133-134, Enclosure, China Foreign Relations Ministry to British Minister, January 31, 1927; *FO* 405/252 [F1093/2/10], pp. 154-155, Hankou telegram, February 2, 1927; *FO* 405/252 [F1275/2/10], p. 181, extract from the *Times* (February 8, 1927); *FO* 405/252 [F1336/1278/10], p. 189, Balfour speech in House of Lords, February 9, 1927; *FO* 405/252 [F1389/1278/10], p. 223, Chamberlain speech in House of Commons, February 10, 1927; *FO* 405/252 [F2041/67/10], pp. 350-351, Enclosure, minutes of meeting between Chen, Wu, O'Malley, and Teichman, January 23, 1927.

98. See discussion item #6 of the morning session as well as the discussion minutes and Borodin's response to Li Wuyun and Li Lisan, "Dui Ying weiyuanhui daibiao Li Wuyun Li Lisan baogao," *ZGLH*, vol. 2 (January 5, 1927).

99. (Untitled document), *ZGLH* (January 7, 1927); "'Yisan' can'an zhi xuanchuan dagang," *ZGLH*, vol. 2, (January 10, 1927).

Kai-shek urged all present to (1) unite to better support the revolution and government; (2) obey government mandates; and (3) join and follow the Guomindang. Russian leaders echoed the themes of unity and obedience.[100] It soon became clear, however, that what Chiang and others meant by both "unity" and "obedience" was lower levels of popular disruption. In Fujian, authorities trying to protect foreign property shot a dozen agitators for robbery and rumor-mongering, quickly reducing anti-foreign molestations.[101] In Guangdong, General Li Jishen was appointed Labor Bureau chief in place of Chen Shuren because party leaders felt that military power could better keep labor agitators under control. Committed to stopping unrest, Li posted Huangpu cadets to guard key junctures. In Changsha and Jiujiang, meanwhile, troop intervention noticeably slowed anti-British activity.[102]

Significantly, CEC interest in restoring order was not based on fear as much as diplomatic opportunity. On January 12, talks opened in Hankou between GMD and British representatives to determine the fate of Britain's former concessions and to outline a new relationship. Representing Wuhan, foreign affairs minister Chen Youren promised socioeconomic stability if Britain would reciprocate by offering support for the revolutionary regime. On the first day of talks, Chen swore that the party harbored no plans to overrun the Shanghai concessions and promised that if Britain would just trust the party, it would protect foreign lives and property, compensate damages, and let foreigners continue their "good works."[103]

Despite Chen's assurances, British negotiators Owen O'Malley and Eric Teichman remained suspicious, primarily because the party consistently portrayed its ties to popular agitation in mutually exclusive ways. On one hand, Chen consistently maintained that the GMD did not control anti-foreign agitation and *had not* incited the masses during the Hankou and Jiujiang concession takeovers; as presented by Chen, both incidents were spontaneous popular responses to imperialist offenses.[104] When O'Malley contended that the Wuhan regime should return the concessions since they had been taken without government consent, Chen countered that any such

---

100. Guomindang leaders also appealed to other "oppressed" peoples, including those of Vietnam, Korea and India, and persuaded sixteen British Indians to parade through the British concession singing revolutionary songs. *CWR* 39 (January 22, 1927): 216.
101. *FO* 405/252 [F2714/1/10], pp. 458-459, Enclosure, Moss to Lampson, Fuzhou, January 21, 1927; *FO* 405/4176/144/10], p. 112, Enclosure, Fuzhou political report for March quarter, 1927.
102. *CWR* 39 (January 8, 1927): vi; *CWR* 39 (January 22, 1927): 212; *CWR* 39 (January 29, 1927): vi.
103. *FO* 405/252 [F2036/67/10], pp. 335-336, Enclosure, minutes of meeting between Chen, Wu, O'Malley, and Teichman, January 12, 1927.
104. *FO* 405/252 [F2129/67/10], p. 370, Enclosure, minutes of meeting between Chen, Wu, O'Malley, and Teichman, January 24, 1927; *FO* 405/252 [F2038/67/10], p. 340, Enclosure, minutes of meeting between Chen, Wu, O'Malley, and Teichman, January 18, 1927.

move would so enrage the "people" that no amount of regime intervention could stop the resulting hostilities; after all, Chen exclaimed, the party could not resort to shooting its own people.[105]

On the other hand, Chen also insisted that the Guomindang *could* control anti-foreign agitation. When O'Malley defended troop buildups as a way to defend against further "spontaneous" agitation, Chen retorted that the presence of foreign soldiers on Chinese soil unnecessarily provoked the "people" and that the troops were not necessary because the Nationalist Government could guarantee the protection of British lives and property.[106] In contrast to popular forces, Chen claimed, the Nationalist regime sought warm relations with Britain, had ordered agitation to cease, and told mass organizations to support the talks.[107]

British negotiators were not persuaded, especially once Chen revealed the connection between mass agitation and state authority by threatening to worsen anti-foreign activity. Any British attempt to regain the Hankou concession by force, he warned, and *"we shall make it a deadweight on your hands. By boycotts, strikes, pickets, and the stoppage of food supplies, we shall make the situation intolerable for you,* up to such a point that you will give us back the concession."[108] [Emphasis added.] On January 22, Chen left no doubt about the Guomindang's willingness to exploit popular anti-foreign agitation to secure foreign policy advantages:

Today the effective protection of foreign life and property in China does not stand, and can no longer rest, on foreign bayonets and foreign gunboats, *because "the arm" of Chinese Nationalism—the economic weapon—is more puissant than any engine of warfare that a foreigner can devise.* It is, however, the view of the Nationalist Government that the liberation of China from the yoke of foreign imperialism need not necessarily involve any armed conflict between Chinese nationalism and the foreign Powers. For this reason the Nationalist Government would prefer to have all questions outstanding between Nationalist China and the foreign Powers settled by negotiation and agreement. To prove that this is no idle statement of policy, the Nationalist Government hereby declares its readiness to negotiate separately with any of the Powers for a

---

105. *FO* 405/252 [F2038/67/10], p. 340, Enclosure, minutes of meeting between Chen, Wu, O'Malley, and Teichman, January 18, 1927; *FO* 405/253 [F3633/67/10], p. 76, Enclosure 5, minutes of meeting between Chen, Wu, O'Malley, and Teichman, March 2, 1927; *FO* 405/252 [F2036/67/10], p. 335, Enclosure, minutes of meeting between Chen, Wu, O'Malley, and Teichman, January 12, 1927.
106. *FO* 405/252 [F2036/67/10], p. 335, Enclosure, minutes of meeting between Chen, Wu, O'Malley, and Teichman, January 12, 1927; *FO* 405/253 [F3553/2/10], p. 49, Enclosure 3, political assessment, January 18, 1927.
107. *FO* 405/252 [F2036/67/10], p. 335, Enclosure, minutes of meeting between Chen, Wu, O'Malley, and Teichman, January 12, 1927.
108. *FO* 405/253 [F3553/2/10], p. 49, Enclosure 3, political assessment, January 18, 1927.

settlement of treaty and other cognate questions on the basis of economic equality and mutual respect for each other's political and territorial sovereignty.[109] [Emphasis added.]

Chen's claim that the party *had not* manipulated popular forces in the past but *could* control them in the future struck O'Malley as a Nationalist ploy to strengthen the party's negotiating hand; others bluntly called it a Janus-faced "double game."[110]

Despite their own cynicism, however, the British employed the same logic in their own diplomatic position. On one hand, O'Malley and others genuinely believed that party leaders had long enflamed anti-imperialism. As summarized in one report, "It is upon this weapon of public opinion, incited by propaganda, that the Nationalist Government have all along relied . . . to gain their . . . great object of abolition of foreign treaty rights."[111] Chamberlain claimed that there was "no doubt" that anti-foreign forces had been directed by top party authorities to seize the British concessions in Hankou and Jiujiang.[112] Hankou consul Goffe and the British Rear-Admiral agreed, noting that popular violence was orchestrated to force Britain to request Nationalist assistance and to secure the moral high ground for Wuhan.[113] Declarations made by the GMD only confirmed British suspicions by invariably crediting the party with organizing, unifying, and empowering the people. Government slogans relating to the Hankou concession takeover, meanwhile, added more proof by exclaiming: "The people extended might, the government provided direction" *(Minzhong chuli, zhengfu zhidao)*; "The government and people cooperate!" *(Zhengfu yu minzhong hezuo!)*; and "Revolutionary success depends on the people's strength!" *(Geming de chenggong yao kao minzhong de liliang!).*[114] In short, by January 1927, British officials almost universally assumed that the Nationalist regime *did* indeed encourage and manipulate agitative disruptions.

---

109. *FO* 405/252 [F708/2/10], p. 114, telegram from Nationalist News Agency, Hankou, January 23, 1927. Also see Chapman, *The Chinese Revolution*, p. 124.

110. *FO* 405/252 [F543/482/10], pp. 98-99, Enclosure 1, Affleck to Macleay, Chengdu, October 26, 1926.

111. *FO* 405/252 [F2145/67/10], p. 344, General Macdonogh memorandum, March 4, 1927.

112. *FO* 405/252 [F982/2/10], p. 132, extract from the *Times* (January 31, 1927); *FO* 405/252 [F1085/27/10], pp. 60-61, weekly summary, Hankou, January 7, 1927; *FO* 405/252 [F1203/115/10], p. 176, Chamberlain to Drummond (League of Nations), February 8, 1927; *FO* 405/252 [F1389/1278/10], p. 222, Chamberlain speech in House of Commons, February 10, 1927.

113. In Goffe's words, the Nationalists wanted to "force us to call upon them for military assistance to deal with a situation which we were no longer able to control." *FO* 405/252 [F1722/67/10], pp. 270-271, Enclosure 1, Goffe to the Minister, Hankou, January 7, 1927; *FO* 405/252 [F2145/67/10], p. 353, Asiatic Petroleum Oil Company to London headquarters, Shanghai, January 28, 1927; *FO* 405/253 [F3553/2/10], p. 46, Enclosure 2, Rear-Admiral at Hankou to Commander-in-Chief, Yangzi, January 8, 1927.

114. "'Yisan' can'an zhi xuanchuan dagang," *ZGLH* (January 10, 1927).

On the other hand, the British defended troop buildups because they also presumed that the Nationalist Government *could not* control disruptions in the future. Conditions during the takeover of Britain's Jiujiang concession validated this conclusion. When hostilities first broke out, CEC official Song Ziwen, who happened to be meeting with British authorities in the concession at the time, promised government help to protect foreign lives and property. General He Yaozu sent twenty military police, but after just a few hours only two remained. One hundred government troops arriving later not only failed to contain anti-foreign disruption, they actually participated alongside popular forces in looting and destroying foreign homes. Later still, a squad of Nationalist police sent to calm the violence was overrun and lost several of its members to injury. When asked to use more forceful measures, General He refused because, as his secretary explained, the general had been viciously denounced as a "foreign slave" for suppressing anti-imperialist agitation in earlier incidents and could not go as far again.[115] Even if and when they wanted to stem anti-foreignism, O'Malley noted, party officials could not repress their own people. On this argument, the British continued augmenting their forces, asserting that foreign lives and property needed something more solid than Nationalist promises on which to depend.[116]

Views about how to act next, however, proved divisive.[117] Some British authorities wanted to arm the remaining concessions against popular agitation and signal the Wuhan government that British interests would be defended "at all costs." Non-action, hawk-minded interventionists contended, had allowed popular disruptions to reach insufferable levels while force secured results; after all, it was force, the hawks argued, that had ended the Anti-British Boycott. Any armchair general could see that a blockade or troop action in Hankou, Shanghai, or Guangzhou would seriously undermine the Nationalist Government and slow NRA advances. The only response that had *ever* compelled the GMD to drop its duplicity and stop agitation, they claimed, was the threat of "imminent" intervention.[118]

---

115. *FO* 405/253 [F3553/2/10], p. 46, Enclosure 2, Rear-Admiral at Hankou to Commander-in-Chief, Yangzi, January 8, 1927; *FO* 405/253 [F3098/67/10], pp. 174-183, Lampson to Chamberlain, Beijing, March 15, 1927; *FO* 405/253 [F3098/67/10], p. 177, Enclosure 1, Ogden to Lampson, Jiujiang, January 15, 1927.
116. *FO* 405/252 [F2145/67/10], p. 347, General Macdonogh memorandum, March 4, 1927; *FO* 405/253 [F3403/1278/10], p. 23, Secretary for Foreign Affairs speech to House of Commons, April 6, 1927; Chapman, *The Chinese Revolution*, p. 128; *FO* 405/253 [F3628/67/10], pp. 53-54, O'Malley to Lampson, Hankou, February 12, 1927; *FO* 405/253 [F3629/67/10], pp. 54-58, O'Malley to Lampson, Hankou, February 15, 1927; *FO* 405/253 [F3632/156/10], pp. 70-71, O'Malley to Lampson, Hankou, February 27, 1927; *FO* 405/253 [F3633/67/10], pp. 71-77, Teichman to Lampson, Hankou, March 3, 1927.
117. Niu, "Yingguo di liangshou zhengce yu shenggang bagong zhi shoushu," pp. 45, 49-51.
118. *FO* 405/252 [F827/156/10], p. 124, Enclosure, British Embassy to Ministry of Foreign Affairs, Paris, January 26, 1927; also see *FO* 405/253 [F3553/2/10], p. 49, Enclosure 3, political assessment, January 18, 1927; *FO* 405/252 [F934/934/10], pp. 135-136, Enclosure 2, Clementi

Dove-minded arguments, meanwhile, emphasized Britain's weak hand vis-à-vis the lost concessions and sought to salvage future security via negotiations. Urging caution, those favoring conciliation and diplomacy claimed that troop concentrations forced the party to embrace agitative options while reversing troop movements and continuing talks would encourage Wuhan to moderate its policy.[119] Strong international calls supported conciliation over force. England's Labour Party condemned British troop movements and applauded GMD nationalistic ambitions. In January, the Joint National Council—London labor's representative body—telegraphed Chen Youren saying, "We will do everything we can to procure such a settlement as will place China on a footing of national independence in the fullest meaning of the term."[120] In Washington, a movement spearheaded by New York Congressman Stephen G. Porter sought a new Sino-American Treaty and expressed interest in recognizing the Nationalist Government. Meanwhile, labor unions in Japan also lobbied for Wuhan's recognition.[121]

External pressures notwithstanding, Guomindang and British negotiators broke the deadlock by offering to meet halfway. Chen insisted that negotiations alone would determine the fate of the Shanghai concessions while O'Malley promised to use troops only as a last resort and offered to hold new arrivals aboard their transports rather than landing them on Chinese soil. Explaining the balance, Chamberlain noted, "There is no intention on our part to hold Shanghai if we can obtain satisfactory assurances that what has happened at Hankow [Hankou] will not be repeated there. The military movements, therefore, which fill our papers and supply them with pictures for the picture page . . . are all a precaution, a necessary precaution, and nothing but a precaution."[122]

As trust rose, progress followed. On January 24, British banks and firms in Hankou voluntarily reopened their doors, ending a financial freeze.[123] Three days later, Britain suggested to both the Beijing and Wuhan govern-

to Amery, Hong Kong, November 27, 1926; *FO* 405/252 [F934/934/10], p. 138, Major Johnson memorandum; *FO* 405/252 [F1085/27/10], pp. 60-61, weekly summary, Hankou, January 7, 1927; *FO* 405/253 [F3563/959/10], p. 33, Lampson to Chamberlain, Beijing, February 28, 1927; *FO* 405/252 [F535/144/10], pp. 42-43, Enclosure 1, memorandum; *FO* 405/252 [F543/482/10], pp. 98-99, Enclosure 1, Affleck to Macleay, Chengdu, October 26, 1926; *FO* 405/252 [F543/482/10], pp. 104-105, Enclosure 5, Commissioner for Foreign Affairs interview, Chongqing, November 3, 1926; *FO* 405/252 [F543/482/10], pp. 105-106, Enclosure 6, General Liu Hsiang interview, Chongqing, November 3, 1926.

119. *CWR* 39 (February 12, 1927): 292.

120. *FO* 405/252 [F836/122/10], p. 126, British labour and China, January 28, 1927.

121. *CWR* 39 (February 12, 1927): 288; "Congress Debates the China Question," *CWR* 40 (March 12, 1927): 37; *CWR* 40 (March 12, 1927): 54.

122. "The Destination of British Troops," *CWR* 39 (February 12, 1927): v; *FO* 405/252 [F982/2/10], p. 132, extract from the *Times* (January 31, 1927).

123. British businesses had refused to open until negotiations were fully concluded. *CWR* 39 (January 29, 1927): 244.

ments that the time had come to modify the treaties. The British even promised to accept Chinese law (civil and commercial) and judicial authority, pay Chinese taxes, model all British concession administrations on the new Hankou concession agreement, and "accept the principles that British missionaries should no longer claim the right to purchase land in the interior, and Chinese converts should look to Chinese law and not to treaties for protection, and that missionary educational and medical institutions will conform to Chinese laws and regulations applying to similar institutions."[124]

To CEC leaders, the offer could not have been better. The British Foreign Office even went as far as to suggest dissolving all other concessions outright if the Nationalist Government would protect British interests.[125] Chamberlain explained his position to the House of Commons:

> We are ready to negotiate, as circumstances make it possible, to meet Chinese national aspirations and to remove the special conditions which were rendered necessary by past Chinese history, as soon as China can protect the foreigner within its gates and give him the kind of justice and the same security for life, and, I add, for property, as the Chinaman can obtain here, or as we can obtain in any civilized country.[126]

Needless to say, never had the Guomindang's diplomatic prospects looked so good.

The only loose end was agitation itself and how popular forces would respond to the negotiations. Since no representatives of China's vast array of mass organizations had been invited, both British and Nationalist officials reduced them to mere game pieces. Nationalist authorities spoke for the "people" with fluid ease. Chen Youren, for example, claimed that the concession takeovers had occurred because the Chinese people were "enraged" by British actions.[127] Similarly, on January 3, Borodin and the CEC ordered that all official demands *must* be made "through the people" *(you renmin)* rather than through the party. As a result, it was the "people" who threatened a general anti-British boycott unless Britain paid indemnities, offered apologies, and punished perpetrators. According to the party, it was also the "people" who demanded that Britain abolish the Volunteer Corps, withdraw

---

124. *FO* 405/252 [F953/2/10], p. 125, O'Malley to Chen, Hankou, January 27, 1927; Chapman, *The Chinese Revolution*, pp. 122-123.

125. *FO* 405/252 [F1389/1278/10], p. 224, Chamberlain speech in House of Commons, February 10, 1927; *FO* 405/252 [F268/67/10], pp. 85-86, Pratt memorandum, January 15, 1927; *FO* 405/252 [F1719/67/10], pp. 276-277, Enclosure 1, Brenan to the Minister, Guangzhou, January 17, 1927; *FO* 405/252 [F2144/2144/10], p. 374, memorandum concerning British concession, Amoy, March 4, 1927.

126. *FO* 405/253 [F3403/1278/10], p. 19, Foreign Affairs secretary speech in House of Commons, April 6, 1927.

127. "The Hankow Crisis and the Lessons Involved!," *CWR* 39 (January 15, 1927): 170.

gunboats, disarm British police, and expand Chinese political rights in the concession. And, it was the "people" who insisted that the Nationalist Government protest, send police and two brigades of troops to maintain order, and establish a garrison in the concession.[128] As thus choreographed, the "people" led the way; the party merely *accepted* the order-keeping responsibilities pressed upon it. Speaking for the "people" and standing behind the notion of popular will, the Wuhan regime legitimized its new control of the former British concessions.

British spin, meanwhile, depicted agitative forces as "practically . . . synonymous with [party] control," portraying the "people" as little more than puppets manipulated by Guomindang authorities for political purposes.[129] Organized and dangerous, the "people" were selfish, emotional, childish "mobs" requiring strict supervision. According to the British view, they also represented the Nationalist regime's greatest liability. As one critic reported,

> The best thing that can happen, from the foreign point of view, is that disorders should break out. . . . Noisy demonstrations by radical groups shouting their slogans of "Take the Foreign Settlements," "Down with the Imperialists," and the usual appeals to prejudice and patriotism, cannot help but bring on a mob attack upon the Settlement. This would mean the opening of fire by the foreign troops. The Chinese troops, a hundred chances to one, would take the side of the mob, and then the fat would be in the fire.[130]

Confident that His Majesty's troops could handily defeat Chinese forces, hawkish Hong Kong and Shanghai observers welcomed unbridled disruption because they believed it would justify military retaliation by the powers.

Concern about this very scenario, the danger that hostilities might provoke British intervention and torpedo diplomatic gains, prompted CEC authorities to "look askance at any move on the part of the radical element to create disorder." [131] As a result, Wuhan again placed restrictions on anti-foreign activity.

The collective enthusiasm of China's vast array of popular, agitative forces, however, was still climbing. Many mass organizations found themselves entangled in struggles with localist interests. In Guangzhou, for example, merchants had begged Guomindang authorities for the traditional right to hire and dismiss workers without union interference at least one day a year. When the party accepted their petition in February, most of Guang-

---

128 . "Hankou nonggong shangxue gejie daibiao lianxi huiyi jinji huiyi jinji huiyi dui Yingzhengfu zhi jiangyuan tiaoyuan," *ZGLH* (January 3, 1927); *CWR* 39 (January 15, 1927): 192, vi.
129. *CWR* 39 (December 25, 1926): 108.
130. "U.S. Attitude Unchanged Despite Nanking!," *CWR* 40 (April 2, 1927): 118.
131. "U.S. Attitude Unchanged Despite Nanking!," *CWR* 40 (April 2, 1927): 118.

zhou's 455 labor unions boycotted, disrupting over eight hundred shops and factories before snail-paced arbitration gave way to more effective police and military action aimed at dispersing strike pickets. Meanwhile, Guangdong silk producers complained of losing $10 million, owing to "labor troubles" and interference. In Fuzhou, labor faction rivalries produced widespread unease while Jiujiang peasant clashes with labor unions precipitated martial law.[132] Sometimes agitation seemed to exist for its own sake. In Hankou, inmates at the Wesleyan Methodist Mission's David Hill School for the Blind struck without making any particular demands while prostitutes seeking tax exemptions stormed the Municipal Council Chambers. Tenants formed a Pay-no-rent Society which fixed its own rates and compelled landlords to accept them. Even Buddhist priests agitated for higher fees, boycotting all prayers for the dead until their demands were met.[133]

Far more frightening to CEC officials, however, was a sharp spike in anti-foreign agitation. Excited by the concession takeovers, British troop buildups, and NRA troop advances on Shanghai, brewing anti-imperialist sentiment in China's greatest port city had become increasingly potent. On January 22, local strikers anticipating the arrival of General Bai Chongxi (General Commander of the Eastern Division of the Northern Expeditionary Army) clashed with police and Sun Chuanfang troops. From February 19 to 24, hundreds of thousands of Shanghai General Labor Union members launched a general strike.[134]

By the end of February, energies were still building. On February 28, the All-China General Labor Union protested foreign troop buildups by organizing a one-hour general strike that attracted two million workers in seven provinces.[135] In Wuhu, a crowd of thirty thousand welcomed NRA troops with fiery speeches that denounced the presence of British and Japanese troops, provoking attacks against foreign establishments and driving off foreigners before NRA troops dispersed the crowds.[136] In Guangzhou, protestors raged against foreign-controlled institutions, such as the Chinese Post Office, which still employed a half-foreign, half-Chinese administrative system. Lingnan University and the American Presbyterian Pei Ying (Pui Ying) School endured agitative hostilities, but other institutions, including

---

132. *CWR* 40 (March 5, 1927): 18; *CWR* 40 (March 19, 1927): 86; *CWR* 40 (March 26, 1927): vi. Hong Kong, Guangzhou, and Macao merchants began to organize in their defense. As labor disruption and demands rose, some 30,000 Guangzhou merchants and shopkeepers threatened to launch a market strike of their own unless authorities allowed them the right to fire employees at least one day a year. *FO* 405/252 [F2574/2/10], p. 416, Enclosure 1, Brenan to Lampson, Guangzhou, February 16, 1927.

133. Chapman, *The Chinese Revolution*, pp. 30-31.

134. *CWR* 39 (January 29, 1927): vi; *CWR* 39 (February 26, 1927): 346; *CWR* 40 (March 5, 1927): 18; Wilbur and How, *Missionaries of Revolution*, p. 328.

135. Chesneaux, *The Chinese Labor Movement*, p. 347.

136. *CWR* 39 (February 19, 1927): 319; *CWR* 40 (March 19, 1927): 87.

John G. Kerr Hospital for the Insane, the Hua Ying (Wah Ying) Middle School of Foshan, and the Trinity College of Guangzhou, simply closed.[137]

Anti-foreign pressures in Guangzhou reached breaking point when press reports inflated accounts of the events leading to the seizure of the Hankou and Jiujiang concessions, describing both as "massacres" against Chinese that required vengeance.[138] Eager for retribution, anti-foreign troops and labor organizations began making preparations to attack the Shamian concession before local GMD police broke up the planning meetings. Alarmed, British and French authorities loudly warned that any move by agitative forces against the concession would be met with "vigorous defense" and that "Hankou tactics" would not work in Guangzhou. American and Japanese authorities concurred, issuing warnings of their own that an attack against Shamian would end their "neutrality."

When anti-foreign agitators planned a massive anti-British rally for January 15, therefore, the GMD Foreign Affairs Ministry ordered that the rally be postponed while assuring foreign consuls that no disturbances would be allowed. The rally was held on January 16, but it passed quietly because the demonstrators were not allowed to approach Shamian and were prevented from creating any anti-imperialist disruption. Reporting to his superiors, Brenan offered three explanations for this "fortunate" turn of events: (1) British vows to defend Shamian and plentiful naval support; (2) intimations by the Americans and Japanese that they would not stand idly by; and (3) Nationalist Government orders that local officials "allow no trouble with the foreigners."[139]

A showdown in Guangzhou was averted because the Guomindang possessed the troop and police strength needed to squelch anti-imperialist activity. Nevertheless, as NRA forces readied the final push into the lower Yangzi, top party officials in other provinces had to rely on less effective mechanisms. CEC and provincial officials instructed all military and political leaders to urge restraint and "exert every possible effort to prevent untoward events" that might give British troops cause to act.[140] Control, however, could not always be assured. Among British circles, anti-imperialist activity justified defensive forces to protect British nationals and interests. Foreign troops in turn played into the hands of agitators anxious to stir up anti-imperialist sentiment. With both forces provoking the other, GMD

---

137. *CWR* 39 (February 12, 1927): 288; *CWR* 39 (February 19, 1927): 319.
138. *FO* 405/252 [F1719/67/10], p. 275, Enclosure 1, Brenan to the Minister, Guangzhou, January 17, 1927; *FO* 405/252 [F1720/2/10], p. 280, Enclosure, Brenan to Lampson, Guangzhou, January 18, 1927.
139. *FO* 405/252 [F1719/67/10], pp. 275-276, Enclosure 1, Brenan to the Minister, Guangzhou, January 17, 1927; *FO* 405/252 [F1720/2/10], p. 280, Enclosure, Brenan to Lampson, Guangzhou, January 18, 1927.
140. *CWR* 39 (February 12, 1927): 288, 292; Chesneaux, *The Chinese Labor Movement*, p. 351.

state-builders found themselves scrambling to keep the two sides apart, creating deep rifts within the revolutionary camp. From his vantage point in Hankou, one foreign observer described the division as follows:

> As evidence of the two opposing principles interacting within the Government, a Gilbertian episode was occasionally to be seen on the Hankow [Hankou] streets. Some mornings, bands of official bill-stickers from one of the Government departments would plaster the walls of the principal thoroughfares with abusive and inflammatory anti-foreign posters: a few hours later other bands from another Government department would go round and carefully tear them all down.[141]

Seething with anti-foreign ardor and struggling to advance their own interests, mass organizations proved a difficult challenge for CEC authorities trying to maintain the appearance, if not actuality, of centralized control.

---

141. Chapman, *The Chinese Revolution*, pp. 130-131.

8. State versus Nation
—Silencing Popular Revolutionary Agitation, January 1927 - October 1928

The whole of the Yang-tse [Yangzi] Valley has now been submerged in the advancing wave of revolutionary and militant nationalism, and as the wave increases in size the puny figures of the Nationalist Government, riding like froth upon its crest, become, it seems to me, less and less able to control the storm and turmoil they have created. Labour runs riot, propaganda rages, and masterless armies overrun the countryside under the red flag of the Kuo Min-tang [Guomindang]. It is a strange and incalculable mixture of revolution, Bolshevism, youthful idealism and crime. Mr. Eugene Chen . . . tossed from side to side and for the moment thrown into the arms of the extremists, does, I believe, his best to carry out his undertakings; and I have recently had proof of the efforts he made to meet our representations and remedy matters at Changsha and Ichang [Yichang], with no success at all at the former and with some effect at the latter port. But neither he nor anyone else here can for the moment control the forces of disorder let loose on the lower river.[1]
—Eric Teichman, British consular officer, April 7, 1927

On April 13, 1927, Lingnan University's president James M. Henry and Earl Swisher, a Lingnan teacher, began preparing to move nine cows off school premises to a safer location. Located on Henan island, across the river from Shamian, the campus had been racked with strikes and picket blockades for weeks. Normal operations froze, reducing living conditions to the point that the school was unfit for people or cows. Ironically, disruptions arose because Lingnan authorities had announced that the school would soon complete the paperwork and steps necessary to fully register with the Nationalist Government.

Maintaining liberal and nondenominational views, Lingnan administrators had long showed unusual sensitivity to Chinese nationalism and thus decided early to comply with Guomindang educational policy. Shortly after the May Thirtieth and Shaji Incidents of 1925, for example, Lingnan au-

---

1. *FO* 405/253 [F4906/1530/10], p. 315, Enclosure, Teichman to Lampson, Hankou, April 7, 1927.

thorities abolished all mandatory religious instruction and worship. In the fall of 1926, when the Nationalists announced their registration regulations, three members of the school's board of trustees visited from New York to convey institutional control to a Chinese board of directors based in Guangzhou. Retaining only fiscal responsibility for the property and foreign staff, the trustees agreed to lease all school resources to the Chinese for a mere one dollar a year. Subsequent registration measures followed as Lingnan made ready to receive its new Chinese administrators.

Conciliation notwithstanding, Lingnan still faced severe disruptions. Paralyzing labor strikes broke out in November 1926 when union organizers sought wage and benefit increases. Borodin and Chen Youren both offered sympathy but then excused themselves from greater involvement because, as Swisher wrote, they "dared not turn a finger" against labor organizations as long as the Northern Expedition depended on agitative support. Lacking any other recourse, Lingnan authorities met the strikers' demands and offered them unusually good contracts. The following March, however, once it became clear that the registration process was nearly complete, the workers struck again. This time union leaders feared that Lingnan's incoming Chinese administrators would initiate sweeping layoffs to avoid paying out on the recently acquired contracts. The latest general strike, therefore, aimed to secure an agreement with Henry that would obligate the new Chinese president to maintain jobs.

Conflict raised all stakes, however, when irritated and inconvenienced students ejected a young labor union advisor from their dormitory and labor pickets cut food and electricity. The first casualties were American women and children who left for Hong Kong. Anticipating a permanent leave of absence, foreign faculty shipped their belongings home. Chinese students volunteered to cover duties usually handled by the striking workers, but school administrators thought it was too risky and decided instead to temporarily close the school. Once the student body was discharged, therefore, only about twenty men and nine cows remained on campus grounds.

Lingnan administrators repeatedly asked government authorities to help mediate a solution but could secure only a promise that troops would be sent to help escort the cows through the picket lines. While Henry and Swisher waited for their bovine guards, however, a commotion erupted at the front gate. An elderly Chinese professor and his son were trying to wheelbarrow some personal items through the pickets. Strikers blocked the way and began to insult and push the two. Believing he could help, Swisher approached the jostling mass, scooped up a basket of dishes on his shoulder, and proceeded to wend his way through the crowd. He had miscalculated, however. Shifting their aggression, the angered pickets pressed in before unceremoniously shoving him into a muddy ditch nearby, dashing the dishes to pieces in the process.

Before Swisher's humiliating and soggy encounter with a ditch, Nationalist leaders had been too preoccupied to bother with a few strikers trying to protect their jobs. Just one day earlier, Chiang Kai-shek had launched a *coup d'état* designed to purge revolutionary ranks of all communists. Bloody and swift, the attacks massacred thousands of revolutionaries with CCP ties. Because many of the arrested or executed had headed or advised popular organizations, the bold and violent move greatly strained party relations with agitative forces, compelling Guomindang leaders to tread lightly lest the masses interpret the campaign as an anti-mass event. Trying to account for the Guomindang's reluctance to intervene, Swisher explained in his journal: "The government still had the delicate problem of putting down Communists and, at the same time, *convincing the peasants and workmen at large that the Kuomintang [Guomindang] still represented their interests. Therefore, [it] could not antagonize any faction.*"[2] [Emphasis added.]

As implied by the above observation, Chiang's mid-April purge transformed the party's relationship with popular organizations and foreigners alike, inextricably intertwining state-building and agitative interactions with a second set of dynamics—rivalry between the revolution's left-wing and right-wing factions. As factional competition became more pronounced, the basic physics governing bifurcated nationalism and revolutionary action changed, forcing individual interests and actors to adapt and adjust to a strikingly new revolutionary order.

The Two Prongs Diverge

Through February 1927, problems with revolutionary bifurcated nationalism were tolerated because they were overshadowed by its astonishing successes and the leverage it provided. Top leaders of Nationalist Revolution manipulated the triangular interplay between state-building, agitative, and foreign interests with near perfect agility, producing undeniable results. Payoff came on February 19 when Britain signed agreements transferring the Hankou concession to Chinese administration.[3] On March 15, the old British Municipal Council handed concession keys to a new Council of British and Chinese Ratepayers, headed by a government-appointed Chinese director.[4] In Jiujiang, British negotiators went even further, agreeing to dissolve the concession outright and transfer its assets to the government.[5]

---

2. Rea, ed., *Canton in Revolution*, pp. 50-56, 70, 73-74.
3. According to settlement terms, the Nationalist Government would first return the concession to British authorities who would then voluntarily relinquish control to a joint British-Chinese administrative committee, thus preserving face for both sides. *FO* 405/252 [F1671/67/10], pp. 267-270, Hankow and Jiujiang concession agreements, February 19, 1927; *FO* 405/253 [F3265/67/10], pp. 16-18, Southborough to Foreign Office, London, April 5, 1927.
4. Chapman, *The Chinese Revolution*, p. 124.
5. *CWR* 40 (March 12, 1927): 54-55; *FO* 405/253 [F3633/67/10], pp. 71-77, Teichman to

According to terms agreed upon by Britain, however, all arrangements depended on CEC promises to restrain anti-foreignism, a task that Northern Expedition successes and nationalistic euphoria made virtually impossible. By February, even as party leaders stood on the threshold of state-building triumph, the primary defects of revolutionary bifurcated nationalism became readily apparent to all. The timing was not just an inconvenience, however. In key ways, it was agitation's very success that made it problematic.

One major failing was the party's inability to monopolize nationalism. China's vast anti-imperialist network intersected a host of popular organizations, many of which enjoyed complete autonomy. This decentralized structure gave revolutionary anti-imperialism its strength, both by substantiating claims that it was strictly of the "people" and by amplifying the popular response to imperialist offenses; an incident occurring at any point in China's vast anti-imperialist grid could ignite a firestorm of activity throughout the entire system. The problem, from the CEC's perspective, was that almost any interest could trigger this response. Anyone could tap anti-imperialism's power—including Guomindang political rivals such as Shanghai civilian groups, Sun Chuanfang, or Beijing authorities, all of whom denounced British troop buildups and stood poised to capitalize on Chinese patriotism.[6] Nationalism, in short, was not strictly limited to the Nationalists.

Riding a wave of popular enthusiasm generated by the Hankou concession takeover, for example, militarist Zhang Zuolin loudly warned the British that a counter-offensive against Wuhan would "not be advisable." Another Fengtian general declared that his troops would fight *alongside* the GMD if Britain tried to retake the former concession by force.[7] Beijing then went as far as to copy the revolutionary tactics used at Hankou by initiating agitations against the British concession in Tianjin. As the Fengtian declaration noted,

> While Fengtien [Fengtian] is opposed to the steps the Nationalist Government has taken at Hankow [Hankou] . . . the desire to restore the foreign concession is unanimous among the Chinese people. Therefore we advise the British to voluntarily take the initiative in surrendering the British Concession at Tientsin [Tianjin] to the Chinese in order that the territory can be converted into a 'special area' and in the future leave the maintenance of order in the hands of the Chinese Peace Preservation Forces, so that more friendly relations may be promoted between Great Britain and China.[8]

Lampson, Hankou, March 3, 1927; *Hankou Jiujiang Yingzujie shouhui, GZD* 165:1404-1429.

6. *CWR* 39 (February 12, 1927): 292; *CWR* 39 (February 19, 1927): 323; *CWR* 40 (March 12, 1927): 54.

7. *CWR* 39 (January 22, 1927): 216; "Congress Debates the China Question," *CWR* 40 (March 12, 1927): 38.

8. *CWR* 39 (January 22, 1927): 216.

Britain rejected the Zhang's proposal, claiming that conditions in Hankou and Tianjin were "different."[9] Nevertheless, the northerners had shown that Wuhan possessed no exclusive right to popular anti-imperialism.

Throughout China, northern posturing excited popular forces thrilled to see Beijing authorities stand up to British imperialism. From the perspective of CEC leaders, however, northern toyings with nationalistic sympathies looked suspiciously like an attempt to capture popular attention, hijack agitative influence, and undermine Wuhan's fragile control. Northern militarists had turned the tables on party officials accustomed to maneuvering popular sentiment for their own purposes. British might was arrayed against southern targets, not northern ones. Therefore, any effort to stimulate the China-wide anti-imperialist network at a time when the Nationalists wanted to quiet it must have seemed an attempt to provoke foreign retaliation against revolutionary forces. Having stirred up mass patriotism in warlord territories to destabilize rival militarist regimes, party leaders could not have taken pleasure in seeing the same tactic used against them.

Another flaw in bifurcated nationalism—once again a product of agitation's autonomy—appeared when mass action ran contrary to state-building need. Sometimes popular forces pursued their own self-interest. Sometimes, they followed a mandate oriented toward confrontation and disruption. Either way, the divergence split revolutionary unity. As early as December 1926, mass leaders accused the Guomindang of betraying the revolution (at least, their version of it) by curbing agitation in order to placate the powers. Restrictions drew formal complaints from Guangzhou and Wuhan labor unions as well as denunciations from Shanghai student groups. Foreign newspapers heightened popular mistrust by reporting that the party exploited labor for its own political purposes, raising CEC worries that the powers were trying to break up revolutionary solidarity.[10] International labor leaders visiting Guangzhou in February widened the gap. When asked if the labor movement would coordinate its activities with the Nationalist Government's broader state-building objectives, a delegate from the Red International of Labor Unions retorted, "The government. To hell with the government. We don't care. Our only interest is for the laborers. Shorter hours, shorter hours, shorter hours. More leisure, more leisure, more leisure."[11]

A third shortcoming, the most frightening of all, was the very real possibility that empowered and energized popular forces could turn on the regime. Mass sensitivities required delicate handling. In late 1926, a report to

---

9. *CWR* 40 (March 12, 1927): 54.

10. "Handian baogao 17, Guangdong wenti 函電報告 #17, 廣東問題," *ZGLH*, vol. 1 (December 24, 1926).

11. Rea, ed., *Canton in Revolution*, p. 48; Chesneaux, *The Chinese Labor Movement*, p. 346; *FO* 405/253 [F4267/144/10], p. 163, Enclosure 2, Guangzhou political report for March quarter 1927.

the CEC warned, "The workers in Wuhan think the workers in Guangdong face government oppression and thus question the government. *They will probably hold meetings to oppose us. . . . The party will be deeply impacted if the workers begin to doubt the party.*" [Emphasis added.] Irritated that labor dissatisfaction had been allowed to rise to such threatening levels, Borodin exclaimed, "Restrictions on workers are justifiable during times of war because finance, transportation, and food are of critical importance and workers in those industries must not go on strike. But now the war is going well and there is no disruption in the rear base. . . . Had the party sided with the masses, this development would not have occurred." Borodin then berated party authorities in Guangzhou, contending that they should have reported problems to higher officials more experienced in soothing labor concerns—i.e., himself. As it was, he continued, deteriorating ties required drastic measures: greater freedoms and expanded striker rights.[12]

Earlier in the revolutionary experience, weak central control over popular forces generated little concern. Agitation plowed ahead without adversely affecting Nationalist administration because the party gained mediating status when imperialists and localists were forced to the negotiating table. As the Northern Expedition expanded party reach and authority, however, the regime could no longer afford to grant mass organizations such license. Preserving political capital vis-à-vis the powers meant that Nationalist administrators had to make good on promises of stability and control. Indeed, it was the party's primary bargaining chip, the only thing that the CEC could offer foreigners in exchange for new treaties and recognition. Steps aimed at securing that control, however, strained CEC/agitator ties to a degree inversely proportional to regime efforts to accommodate the powers. Wedged between the demands of both sides, top party leaders found their ability to either balance the two or play one off the other greatly compromised.

It is into this context that left-wing/right-wing factional disputes made their grand entrance, adding another thick layer of complexity to an already complicated scenario. Rising tensions, originating from deep-seated factional disagreements and distrust, profoundly realigned dynamics between agitative, state-building, and foreign interests. Factional rivalries amplified the inherent failings within the Guomindang's bifurcated approach. At the same time, the revolution's two prongs exacerbated factional differences.

Renowned scholars such as C. Martin Wilbur, Lloyd Eastman, Conrad Brandt, Jiang Yongjing, Li Yunhan and many others, have carefully tracked factional rivalries from their earliest beginnings in 1923. Initially, revolutionaries hid festering acrimony and breaches from outside view in order to

---

12. "Handian baogao #17, Guangdong wenti," *ZGLH*, vol. 1 (December 24, 1926).

preserve images of solidarity.[13] By early 1927, however, a rift had become plainly visible. In January, Borodin and Chiang Kai-shek quarreled over leadership, alleged plots against each other, the location of party headquarters, and Chiang's role as commander-in-chief, among other things. The rupture forced party leaders high and low to side with one or the other, drawing a clear line between the CCP/GMD left-wing, led by Borodin in Wuhan, and the GMD right-wing, headed by Chiang from his base in Nanchang. The left feared Chiang's growing power while the right criticized "communist" designs to seize the revolutionary helm.[14] By early March, both sides were positioning for advantage.

The rising preeminence of factional disagreements did more than spawn bitter feelings. It completely retooled the bifurcated approach, converting both the agitative and state-building prongs into weapons of internecine strife. Before 1927, Chiang and Borodin had generally voted in unison to curb or unleash popular forces as needed to secure diplomatic objectives. In early March, at the Third Plenum of the Second CEC, however, Borodin and other left-wing leaders in Wuhan broke from standard procedure and systematically realigned their approach to foreign relations, agitation, and state-building. First, Wuhan signaled disassociation from the powers by condemning Britain's "trivial concessions" *(buzhongyao de rangbu)*, troop buildups, aid to the north, and efforts to "devastate China's masses" *(cuican Zhongguo minzhong)*. Relying on aggressive terminology, CEC declarations warned that Britain's "latest strategy is to claim that it supports the expectations of China's people and [will] cooperate with the backbone of the Nationalist Revolution while only opposing the radicals. Obviously, this is a strategy to break up our revolutionary forces."[15] Next, the left deepened its commitment to the masses, calling them the only firm foundation for fighting imperialism and announcing plans to improve mass living standards, raise support for peasants, expand cooperation with Soviet Russia, and embrace even the "most radical" *(zui jijin)* communist party elements.[16] Lastly, the Wuhan CEC repudiated state-building fundamentals such as negotiating with foreigners and limiting anti-imperialist agitation:

> *We oppose those who are tired of revolution and who have compromised with imperialists. They are the enemies of the revolution. We shall point out their mistakes and crimes and overthrow them.* . . . [Mass organizations] do not oppose the interests of the Nationalist Revolution but

---

13. Wilbur and How, *Missionaries of Revolution*, pp. 330-331, 364; Jiang, *Baoluoting yu Wuhan Zhengquan*, p. 258.
14. *CWR* 36 (March 12, 1927): 54.
15. "Zhongguo Guomindang dierjie zhongyang zhixing weiyuanhui disanci quanti huiyi dui quan Zhongguo renmin xuanyan," *2-ZWQH* (March 1927).
16. "Dierjie zhongyang zhixing weiyuanhui disanci quanti huiyi dui quanti dangyuan xunling," *2-ZWQH* (March 1927).

strengthen revolutionary efforts to overthrow imperialists, warlords, and all other reactionaries. . . . *We must oppose efforts aimed at weakening mass movements so they can develop rapidly. . . .* It is wrong for some people to believe that we can still succeed without helping the masses and without the support of oppressed people in other countries. . . . Those who believe this are in fact helping the imperialists and reactionaries.[17] [Emphasis added.]

Before March 1927, CEC foreign policy announcements featured an irrefutable state-building backdrop: warnings against provoking anti-foreign incidents, support for negotiations, and state promises to deal with imperialism in its own time frame. Third Plenum directives, however, noticeably discarded almost all state-building qualifications. No doubt Wuhan officials aimed to reverse labor's growing sense of alienation and perhaps undercut Beijing's incipient agitative tinkering. Nevertheless, the *raison d'être*—as historians of Republican China have long argued—grew from factional strife. Wuhan hoped to isolate Chiang and prevent him from reaching clandestine agreements with the powers by declaring any unsanctioned contact with foreign or warlord interests an act of treason. As explained by Third Plenum pronouncements, "individual will" *(geren yizhi)* had supplanted "party will" *(dang de yizhi)* and politics had fallen *"more under the control of the army than under the control of the party."*[18] [Emphasis added.] Three groups were blamed: (1) "individual autocrats" *(geren ducai)* who challenged CEC authority, such as NRA commanders, (2) "opportunist gentry" *(tushen touji fenzi)* leaders in branch party offices, and (3) "muddleheaded geezer" *(hunyong laoxiu fenzi)* party heads who allowed the other two to function. To combat these threats, Wuhan authorities promised to align more closely with the masses and fully centralize all political, military, financial, and foreign affairs.[19] Foreign affairs regulations still threatened to expel any Guomindang member who expressed opinion about foreign policy or contacted foreigners without CEC permission.[20] Nevertheless, the purpose behind the rules had shifted. Now they aimed to support agitative, left-wing objectives rather than state-building goals.

---

17. "Zhongguo Guomindang dierjie zhongyang zhixing weiyuanhui disanci quanti huiyi dui quan Zhongguo renmin xuanyan," *2-ZWQH* (March 1927).
18. "Benhui jingguo gaikuang," and "Dierjie zhongyang zhixing weiyuanhui disanci quanti huiyi dui quanti dangyuan xunling," *2-ZWQH* (March 1927).
19. "Dierjie zhongyang zhixing weiyuanhui disanci quanti huiyi dui quanti dangyuan xunling," *2-ZWQH* (March 1927).
20. Supporters of the motion included: Sun Ke, Tan Yankai, Xu Qian, and Song Ziwen. The proposal was first presented in late 1926 and suggested: (1) expelling all party members who expressed foreign affairs opinions or contacted imperialists without CEC approval, (2) removing all Guomindang officers who contacted or negotiated with imperialists in secret without party permission, and (3) directly appointing all foreign affairs staff through the national government, not regional administrative units. "Tongyi waijiao tiyi an," *2-ZWQH* #2 (March 1927).

The right-wing tended to believe that Wuhan leaders aligned with agitation and painted the revolution in red hues in order to discredit the right-wing with the powers. Chiang certainly believed this, asserting that the communists hoped to provoke a British backlash against his exposed forces in Shanghai.[21] If Wuhan authorities did seek to isolate Chiang, however, they failed. Chesneaux, Wilbur, and others assert that CEC radicalism only gave Chiang further incentive to secure what the left-wing feared most: right-wing alliances with Shanghai commercial interests, the powers, and even Fengtian forces.[22] In short, while the left-wing more fully embraced the masses, Chiang more fully turned against them. He was already impatient with the fruits of popular agitation. Visiting Wuhan for conferences in early March, he expressed disgust at signs of social disorder and economic stagnation.[23] By April, quieting popular forces was made doubly necessary in order to avoid embarrassing anti-foreign incidents and to shorten Wuhan's reach.

With Wuhan officials and Chiang pulling in different directions, bifurcated nationalism's state-building and agitative functions separated along factional lines, destroying their symbiosis and exposing revolutionaries to foreign and domestic challenges formerly kept in equilibrium. In other words, abandoning a balanced stance between the two prongs and closely aligning with just one of them meant that both the left and right-wing struggled to manage excesses previously softened by the opposite prong.

In CCP/left-wing areas, for example, without state-building oversight to check agitative expansion, socioeconomic disturbances rose to acute levels. Hubei reports claimed that "business was practically dead" with all foreign banks, newspapers, and most local industrial plants, all closed on account of "labor troubles."[24] Trade froze, debt-ridden banks and shops closed, merchants fled, and revenues fell to the point that the finance minister could not even pay NRA troops. (Fourth and Eighth Army regulars resentfully asked why they had not been paid in five months while agents with the propaganda bureau had never been asked to wait on a paycheck.[25]) Unable to sell government zinc and lead ores elsewhere, Hunan authorities begged a British firm to set up a different—less noticeably foreign—name so transactions could occur without attracting the attention of anti-foreign agitators.[26] In his

21. Chiang, *Soviet Russia in China*, p. 50.
22. Wilbur and How, *Missionaries of Revolution*, p. 394; FO 405/253 [F4170/2/10], p. 115, Enclosure, Brenan to Lampson, Guangzhou, March 21, 1927.
23. FO 405/252 [F2145/67/10], pp. 348-349, General Macdonogh memorandum, March 4, 1927.
24. FO 405/253 [F4906/1530/10], p. 314, Enclosure, Teichman to Lampson, Hankou, April 7, 1927.
25. FO 405/252 [F2145/67/10], pp. 348-349, General Macdonogh memorandum, March 4, 1927; FO 405/253 [F3553/2/10], p. 52, Enclosure 4, Rear-Admiral report, Yangzi, January 1, 1927.
26. FO 405/253 [F4901/1654/10], p. 296, Enclosure 1, Jones to Lampson, Changsha, April 3, 1927.

study of the Northern Expedition, Donald Jordan nicely summarizes Wuhan's economic situation:

> With the success of unionization based on economic labor strikes, labor costs spiraled followed by prices in general as the supply of needed goods slumped due to the strikes. The loss of income in commerce, industry, and wages cut deeply into the Wuhan government's sources of revenue. Boycotts and strikes against "imperialist" factories, stores, and goods greatly decreased vital tariff revenues. Most unusual was that this regime, so engrossed in fighting a war, permitted such widespread strikes and economic dislocation at home.[27]

Anti-Christian violence also soared. Hunan agitators seized the YMCA and arrested six secretaries. In Yichang and Chongqing, the agitative Inspection Brigade of Workers Unions arrested mission employees and confiscated mission property. Further south in Huazhou, three to four hundred agitators sacked the Maryknoll Catholic Mission headquarters. Wuhan authorities intervened to stop the destruction but then could only ask missionaries and Chinese Christians to accept agitator demands. Sun Ke wrote a public letter acknowledging the past contributions of mission schools and promising a role for them in the future if they accepted government oversight and sided with the people. Meanwhile, Chen Youren and Borodin met with missionary leaders and offered comparable assurances.[28] In general, foreigners accepted Wuhan's assurances and accommodating gestures as sincere.[29] Nevertheless, the GMD Foreign Office—the foreign community's point of contact with party authority—had become impotent and could extend little assistance. As one observer in Hankou noted,

> The Foreign Office was practically powerless to influence the Government to arrest or even restrain the destructive and disorderly forces that they had deliberately let loose for the purpose of arousing the people and pushing forward the Revolution. In spite of Foreign Office assurance, and official caveats issued by them, the seizing and occupying of foreign Missionary Societies' property in the country, and the paralyzing of foreign business in Hankow [Hankou] by unreasonable strikes and intimidation continued.[30]

---

27. Jordan, *The Northern Expedition*, p. 221.
28. Chao, "The Chinese Indigenous Church Movement," p. 192; Breslin, *China, American Catholicism, and the Missionary*, p. 52; Lutz, *Chinese Politics and Christian Missions*, pp. 251, 231, 342.
29. Chapman, *The Chinese Revolution*, p. 25. Before the Nanjing Incident, foreign refugees trying to avoid anti-foreign agitation in Sichuan, Hunan, and Hubei routinely fled to Wuhan even though the city was a major center of mass activism and even though the Hankou concession was already under partial Chinese management.
30. Chapman, *The Chinese Revolution*, p. 130.

Currying mass-organization favor may have offered Wuhan officials a modest counterweight to right-wing military power, but it also meant that they could not take stronger action against agitative abuses. Siding with the masses meant that CCP/left-wing leaders had no choice except to endure socioeconomic disintegration and dwindling central control.

Meanwhile, in right-wing territories where mass organizations often faced repression, authorities had to grapple with fading popular support. Mass enthusiasm skyrocketed when NRA troops in Fuzhou, Jiujiang, Nanchang, Wuhu, and Ningbo helped ransack mission institutions, but it then plunged when party officials opposed further disruptions.[31] In early March, for example, the Association to Restore Educational Rights demonstrated against Fujian Christian University. Most faculty members had voted to pursue government registration, but they were opposed by a few radical teachers who wanted the school nationalized. When local Fuzhou officials sided with the radicals and insinuated that a party takeover was imminent, moderate faculty turned to the higher-ranked GMD Education Commission which denied any such plans. Stymied, Association agitators joined forces with the Great Alliance Against Cultural Aggression, faculty and students from mission schools, Fujian Christian University activists, and NRA troops in a massive anti-Christian rally held on March 24. Throngs of demonstrators marched on local Guomindang offices and demanded that the Nationalist Government confiscate all of Fuzhou's Christian institutions. Thus pressured, Fujian Christian University's foreign president and other foreign principals resigned. Nevertheless, higher party officials rejected agitator calls. Even after Fujian Christian University's board of managers renounced faculty calls to register with the government and fired radical teachers, regional party heads still refused to consider agitator petitions or even convey them to central headquarters. Instead, the provincial education commissioner assured foreign missionaries that he would curtail further anti-Christian activity and soften registration requirements. Making good on his pledge, he transferred all anti-Christian leaders and students out of town. Without top-level support, the Anti-Christian Movement in Fuzhou lost steam and died.[32]

Popular forces in Guangzhou found even less sympathy from government authorities. Police banned all demonstrations against Christian churches or missions. Authorities refused agitator requests to take over the John G. Kerr Hospital for the Insane, the last hospital in Guangzhou still under foreign control. Failing to secure regime blessing, anti-Christian activity dropped precipitously to the point that reports of "no attacks" began to appear in the foreign press.[33]

31. *FO* 405/252 [F2714/1/10], p. 457, Enclosure, Moss to Lampson, Fuzhou, January 21, 1927; Yip, *Religion, Nationalism, and Chinese Students*, p. 68.
32. Lutz, *Chinese Politics and Christian Missions*, pp. 217-218.
33. *CWR* 39 (February 12, 1927): 287.

Writing to his various commanding officers, Chiang issued strict orders that anti-foreign agitation be restrained and that his troops safeguard foreign lives and property, including hospitals, churches, and schools.[34] As one Chinese soldier wrote,

> There are a small number of soldiers in our forces who looted church property freely along the way and engaged in assault and battery in the name of the anti-Christian movement. These acts affect nothing as far as the imperialists are concerned, but have brought a significantly bad name for our Party. . . . During this time there should no longer be any further anti-Christian activities. Should any one violate this prohibition, he shall be strictly stopped. . . .[35]

In Ganzhou, NRA troops dispersed agitators planning anti-Christian activities.[36] Continued anti-foreign and anti-localist activism among the masses, however, quickly produced a stronger right-wing response. On March 11, a subordinate of Chiang executed the head of the Ganzhou General Labor Union and scattered union members.[37] Six days later other attacks followed in Ganzhou and Nanchang. On March 19, Chiang crushed Jiujiang's labor unions and closed the municipal party office for its pro-agitative stance before ordering his supporters three days later to engage popular forces in Anqing, Chongqing, Xiamen, Fuzhou, Hangzhou, Ningbo, Wuhu, and elsewhere.[38] Those who resisted fared poorly against the union breakers, secret police, and right-wing troops recruited to destroy them.

Repression fueled animosity toward Chiang, weakened his legitimacy, and alienated mass organizations, allowing Wuhan to better claim their loyalty. Nevertheless, the right wing was lucky. To avoid a power struggle, Wuhan leaders refused to support popular calls for retaliation.[39] Instead, mass organizations were ordered to fixate on foreign and warlord targets, ready themselves to usher NRA forces into Shanghai, and disregard right-wing suppression for the time being.

Agitation and State-Building vis-à-vis Factional Rivalry

By March 1927, factionalism had turned the two visions of bifurcated nationalism against each other. Both were still headed in the same general direction—toward a strong, independent, and modern China—but each interpreted "modernity" in very different ways, confusing revolutionary objectives just as NRA forces were set to take Shanghai. In early March,

---

34. "Baohu waiqiao ji jiaohui zhi gaowen," *Zhenguang zazhi* 26.4 (April 1927): 73.
35. Wang, "Qingtian bairi chixia di Jidujiao," p. 7.
36. Breslin, *China, American Catholicism, and the Missionary*, p. 55.
37. The union chief was a communist. Wilbur and How, *Missionaries of Revolution*, p. 398.
38. Chesneaux, *The Chinese Labor Movement*, p. 365.
39. Chesneaux, *The Chinese Labor Movement*, p. 354.

Anhui generals Chen Tiaoyuan and Wang Pu defected to the revolutionary cause, neutralizing a Fengtian counterstrike from the west. When reports indicated that warlord general Yan Xishan of Shanxi also contemplated joining the revolutionaries, Zhang Zuolin withdrew troops from central China to bolster Beijing's defenses, allowing NRA troops to fill the vacuum in Suzhou and southern Anhui. Attacks on railway junctures by NRA infiltrators and a subordinate's defection also forced Zhang Zongchang's army northward, raising speculation that the Nationalists would soon take all of Jiangsu province.[40] Quickly taking advantage of the opening, Guomindang troops marched on Shanghai. With the gap between the left-wing and right-wing factions widening, however, the approaching struggle represented far more than just a battle between revolutionary and militarist forces. Warlord armies, right-wing troops, left-wing agitators, and foreign naval forces all had stakes in the port city and the muscle to defend them.

Foreign observers were most concerned about anti-imperialist agitation. Everywhere were signs that what had occurred in Hankou and Jiujiang might be repeated in Shanghai—especially in light of the party's latest factional divide. The Wuhan left-wing loudly declared its intent to destroy British influence in China and exercised considerable leverage over Shanghai's mass organizations. Outspoken CCP leader Tan Pingshan described them as proletariat forces armed to prevent the "bourgeoisie" from "slowly liquidat[ing] the revolution by means of compromise." Fiercely anti-foreign, Tan pushed student and labor agitators to rise up and shatter the prestige of the foreigners so the unequal treaties could be torn to shreds.[41] The All-China General Labor Union, based in Shanghai, also denounced compromise and urged resistance against imperialist threats.[42]

Meanwhile, Hangzhou labor agitators closed a British hospital before putting British nationals to flight. Ten thousand Chongqing paraders forced foreigners to hide indoors. Guangzhou workers called for another anti-British boycott. Right-wing Nationalist leaders sat in middle—but not neutral—ground. They appreciated the masses' potential against warlords but not their provocative actions against the foreigners—especially since popular organizations seemed to be following Wuhan's direction. Repression slowed agitation in Guangzhou and elsewhere but not in Shanghai since a right-wing presence had not yet arrived to put it in check.[43]

---

40. *CWR* 40 (March 12, 1927): 54-55; *FO* 405/252 [F934/934/10], p. 137, Enclosure 3, Major Johnson memorandum.

41. *FO* 405/252 [F2359/2/10], p. 306, Enclosure 4, confidential memorandum, January 5, 1927; *FO* 405/252 [F439/28/10], p. 83, extract from *International Press Correspondence*, December 30, 1926.

42. Chesneaux, *The Chinese Labor Movement*, p. 347.

43. *CWR* 40 (March 12, 1927): 54-55; *CWR* 40 (March 5, 1927): 18; *FO* 405/253 [F4170/2/10], p. 113, Enclosure, Brenan to Lampson, Guangzhou, March 21, 1927; *FO* 405/253 [F4267/144/10], p. 163, Enclosure 2, Guangzhou political report for March quarter 1927.

On March 12, as NRA troops approached the Yangzi delta, Shanghai-Nanjing Railway mechanics launched a strike in Wusong, disrupting Sun Chuanfang's communications. Three days later, Shanghai-Hangzhou Railroad engineers joined as well. On March 21, vanguard NRA units reached the outskirts of Shanghai, triggering a general strike by the All-China General Labor Union, worker uprisings directed against northern troops, and sabotage campaigns that cut electricity and phone lines, seized the Jiangnan arsenal, released jailed prisoners, and so forth.[44] Armed popular forces attacked police stations and the northerners' headquarters in Zhabei—the district directly adjacent to the foreign concessions. Fierce fighting lasted through the night, raising foreign alarm that violence might breach concession defenses. To make sure that did not happen, NRA General Bai Chongxi issued strict orders that his troops protect foreign lives and property. Not satisfied, the Japanese landed fifteen hundred soldiers while the Americans added fourteen hundred marines. Fires burned out of control in Zhabei and stray bullets from the melee there peppered the International Settlement.[45]

When mass organization units gained the upper hand, panicked northern (Shandong) troops tried to flee into the concessions. British guards responded with gunfire, killing some sixty-five warlord soldiers and wounding scores more before taking about two thousand prisoners.[46] In spite of the tinderbox conditions, however, no major anti-foreign incident occurred before General Bai took control of Shanghai the next day. Agitative forces had indeed engaged in pitched battles near the concessions and foreign armies had indeed intervened, but neither had attacked the other as feared. Rather, both had confronted the northerners' Fengtian troops.

In Nanjing, however, events played out very differently. On March 24, while revolutionary forces routed Sun Chuanfang's armies, soldiers in Nationalist uniforms systematically attacked foreign nationals, killing several. Those that escaped did so only after U.S. and British ships shelled the city. Spreading rapidly, details about this latest attack—soon identified as the Nanjing Incident—spawned general panic among missionaries who quickly fled.[47] Approximately five thousand left China for good while another 2,500 gathered in the concessions of Shanghai or elsewhere. Within just a few weeks, only about five hundred missionaries remained in China's interior.[48]

The exodus represented a stunning blow to Guomindang state-building. Missionary institutions represented a valuable resource; U.S. investments alone amounted to over US$21 million. More importantly, missionaries

---

44. Chesneaux, *The Chinese Labor Movement*, pp. 356-357; *CWR* 40 (March 26, 1927): 116.
45. *CWR* 40 (March 26, 1927): vi.
46. *CWR* 40 (March 26, 1927): vi.
47. Breslin, *China, American Catholicism, and the Missionary*, p. 56.
48. Latourette, *A History of Christian Missions in China*, p. 820; Breslin, *China, American Catholicism, and the Missionary*, pp. 51-52.

played a valued role in augmenting Nationalist foreign policy claims. Missionary reports to consular authorities verified Guomindang efforts to protect foreign interests.[49] Before the Nanjing Incident, Nationalist officials had asked missionaries to trust the government and promised to protect property, rights, and lives.[50] Afterwards, however, no amount of persuasion could keep missionaries at their stations. Missionary support, in short, collapsed.

The crisis also raised the indignation of interventionists who demanded that British troops forcibly retake the Hankou concession.[51] In the words of one shrill editorial, "It is time the Powers acted swiftly and severely to punish the wrong done at Nanjing and to teach Mr. Eugene Chen [Chen Youren] and his fellows that if we cannot prevent them from ruining their own countrymen, we can at least avenge the crime committed against ours."[52] Angered that the Nationalist Government had not kept its word, others called for direct action against it. Even if such action stimulated more anti-foreign agitation, they argued, it would at least reestablish British prestige.[53]

Historians have never been able to clearly establish who initiated the anti-foreign attacks in Nanjing and why. Nevertheless, whether it was northern warlords pulling a page from the Guomindang playbook, Wuhan officials hoping the powers would retaliate against Chiang, communists seeking to instigate another May Thirtieth Incident, or just anti-imperialism running amok is not as important here as the fact that all implicated parties denied involvement. Representing Wuhan, Chen Youren blamed an unnamed "counter-revolutionary" interest seeking to embarrass the party by instigating an anti-foreign incident.[54] Exposed to British armies amassed at Shanghai, right-wing Guomindang forces went further. Chiang Kai-shek immediately drove to the Shanghai concession to assess foreign attitudes which one reporter described as "nervousness closely bordering on panic."[55] General Bai Chongxi, meanwhile, held a press interview at the Shanghai Bureau of Foreign Affairs, meticulously expressing the hope that "foreigners of Shanghai will respect the aspirations of the Chinese people and will meet us in a conciliatory manner. After all, we are not up against individual foreigners but against the imperialistic system."[56]

---

49. "Congress Debates the China Question," *CWR* 40 (March 12, 1927): 40; "U.S. Attitude Unchanged Despite Nanking!," *CWR* 40 (April 2, 1927): 118-119.
50. *CWR* 39 (February 12, 1927): 288; *CWR* 39 (February 19, 1927): 319.
51. *FO* 405/252 [F2954/1530/10], p. 477, House of Commons inquiries, March 28, 1927; Yip, *Religion, Nationalism, and Chinese Students*, p. 74.
52. *North China Daily Herald* (April 2, 1928).
53. *FO* 405/253 [F5171/67/10], p. 353, memorandum, Foreign Office, May 31, 1927; *FO* 405/253 [F5115/67/10], p. 345, Enclosure 2, Teichman to Chen, Hankou, April 16, 1927.
54. *FO* 405/253 [F4842/1530/10], p. 291, Enclosure 1, Teichman to Lampson, Hankou, April 2, 1927.
55. Powell, "Nationalists Take Over Shanghai—The Present Situation," p. 121.
56. Powell, "Nationalists Take Over Shanghai—The Present Situation," pp. 121-123.

Accommodating statements by Nationalist leaders helped calm the situation, but foreigners withheld their fury primarily because a far greater test of party sincerity was still unfolding. In Shanghai, labor forces celebrated their victory over warlord forces and expanded the general strike, all under the shadow of NRA armies busily consolidating right-wing power and foreign forces trying to determine how to best preserve their interests. Tensions remained high. Even a small spark could ignite a war. Foreign attention, therefore, quickly shifted from the recent, but already past, events in Nanjing to looming and far more consequential possibilities in Shanghai. At General Bai's press conference, foreign reporters asked far more questions about the general labor strike in Shanghai than about the attacks in Nanjing. After confessing that he could not call the strike off, Bai offered assurances that labor had agreed to cooperate, that the party would form arbitration boards to limit disturbances, and that the army would prohibit extremism. Three days later, Bai and Chiang again fervently denied claims that they harbored an anti-foreign agenda and repudiated suggestions that the Nanjing Incident constituted part of a larger anti-imperialist strategy. Both also pledged that agitation would not overrun Shanghai's International Settlement but that its fate would be determined through diplomatic channels.[57]

Meanwhile, party assurances could not erase the hard reality that anti-imperialist potential was rapidly expanding. Agitative forces included hundreds of thousands of workers, ran a military training center in Zhabei, wielded enormous stocks of weapons captured from northern troops, and added seventy-five new unions between March 22 and April 12. Labor leaders also set up a Shanghai Provisional Municipal Government through which they hoped to further the labor agenda.[58] From the perspective of Chiang and other right-wing authorities, the defeat of the northerners meant that mass organizations were no longer needed and once again represented a greater liability than a benefit.

To preclude another anti-foreign incident and to weaken his Wuhan rivals, Chiang moved against popular forces with unprecedented ferocity.[59] Perpetrators behind the Nanjing Incident may have remained obscure, but agitative leaders in Shanghai were not. Thus they caught the brunt of right-wing repression. Chiang first ordered workers to give up their arms and organized an anti-communist labor organization called the Federated Association of Labor Unions. On April 12, fifteen thousand troops and police moved to break the back of agitative might and crush communist influence in the process.[60] Unions lashed back, declaring a general strike on April 13 and besieging military headquarters with thousands of unarmed workers before

---

57. Powell, "Nationalists Take Over Shanghai—The Present Situation," pp. 121-123.
58. Chesneaux, *The Chinese Labor Movement*, pp. 359, 362.
59. *FO* 405/252 [F706/2/10], p. 112, Chamberlain to Tilley, January 24, 1927.
60. *FO* 405/253, p. 436, Barton to Chamberlain, Shanghai, April 15, 1927.

gunfire scattered them, killing and wounding many. Troops loyal to Chiang closed the General Labor Union headquarters, arresting some union leaders and executing others. On April 15, while the purge continued, Chiang formed his own Nationalist Government in Nanjing, challenging the party's official government in Wuhan.

In Guangdong, anti-agitative attacks followed suit. Local British reports claimed that anti-imperialist organizations planned to assail the Shamian concession on April 16 in order to secure another concession takeover or produce another Nanjing Incident that would, in Brenan's words, "involve local [right-wing GMD] authorities with the Powers." Early in the morning of April 15, however, one day after local commander General Li Jishen returned from meeting Chiang Kai-shek in Shanghai, NRA troops, police, and armed Mechanics Union forces (anxious for revenge against rivals), attacked Guangzhou agitative strongholds: the headquarters of the Hong Kong Strike Committee, the All-China General Labor Union, the Guangzhou Workers Delegates Conference, the All-China General Railwaymen's Union, Sun Yat-sen University, and the offices of *Nationalist News (Guomin xinwen)* and *Republican Daily (Minguo ribao).*[61] Declaring martial law, Li and the chief of police ordered their men to disarm all labor pickets and arrest all "dangerous elements."[62] That evening, right-wing forces swept Guangzhou, arresting student leaders and closing labor unions. Those with CCP ties were executed. The local party office, which had supported Wuhan, was closed.[63] By the following morning, thousands had been caught in the dragnet. Raids in Shantou also sealed sources of agitative unrest: the local GMD office, the General Labor Union headquarters, and schools. Meanwhile, in Changsha, Chengdu, Chongqing and a host of other cities, student union offices and schools were "cleansed."[64]

During the anti-agitative sweeps, strict precautions were taken to ensure the safety of foreigners. Chinese were not allowed on Shaji Street, directly across the river from the concession on Shamian. Hong Kong steamers were told to anchor away from the wharves, out of the reach of mass organizations.[65] When finished with the purge, right-wing Nationalist leaders lost no time assuring foreign authorities that order had been restored. On April 16,

---

61. *FO* 405/253 [F5103/2/10], pp. 346-347, Enclosure 1, Brenan to Lampson, Guangzhou, April 20, 1927.

62. *FO* 405/253 [F5103/2/10], p. 348, Enclosure 2, Police Bureau proclamation, Guangzhou, April 15, 1927; *FO* 405/253 [F5103/2/10], p. 349, Enclosure 3, Martial Law Headquarters proclamation, Guangzhou, April 15, 1927.

63. Li, *Cong ronggong dao qingdang,* pp. 629, 666, 669, 702.

64. *FO* 405/253 [F5103/2/10], pp. 346-347, Enclosure 1, Brenan to Lampson, Guangzhou, April 20, 1927; *FO* 405/253 [F5816/2/10], p. 481, Enclosure 1, Kirke to Lampson, Shantou, May 24, 1927; Li, *Cong ronggong dao qingdang,* pp. 629, 666, 669, 702.

65. *FO* 405/253 [F5103/2/10], p. 347, Enclosure 1, Brenan to Lampson, Guangzhou, April 20, 1927.

Chen Youren—now representing Nanjing—reported to the Guangzhou British consul that the Nationalist Government had swept away "disorderly elements planning unlawful activities" and that it could finally take full responsibility for the protection of foreign life and property. Concluding his report, he asked consul-general Brenan to pass the word so all British subjects could return to their normal occupations.[66]

True to their word, right-wing leaders showed little tolerance for anti-foreign or anti-Christian activity. On May 16, 1927, the British ship *S.S. Longshan* fell under a rifle salvo as it passed by Huangpu fortifications, taking some fifty shots before it steamed out of range. Dozens of similar attacks had occurred on the Yangzi River during the Northern Expedition, but this particular incident challenged the new order and thus represented a true test of Guomindang commitments. The British demanded that the Nationalist Government punish the responsible officer and pay two hundred dollars for damages within five days or face "retaliation"—a threat taken by most to mean a naval attack on Huangpu fortifications. By May 21, local party authorities had not only fully complied, they even exceeded British demands, imprisoning the private to first fire his weapon, cashiering his two superior officers, and dismissing ten other implicated soldiers. [67] Anti-foreignism had limits, and the consequences for crossing them were severe.

Bifurcated Nationalism Torn Asunder

Before Chiang's coup, Shanghai had been the flash point of a strained triangular standoff between agitative, state-building, and foreign interests. As conditions there stabilized, however, the spotlight swung west to Wuhan. Before April 15, Chiang helped direct this shift in foreign attention by shrewdly refusing to respond to questions about foreign policy, claiming that Wuhan was responsible for politics and that he was just a military commander.[68] Spring runoff also helped, raising Yangzi water levels to the point where heavy foreign battle cruisers could again proceed up river. The threat of riots in the Japanese Hankou concession on April 3 had already convinced Japanese naval forces to make the journey. Even more ships came after Chiang's anti-agitative attacks quieted Shanghai; on April 21, the British sent two armored cruisers while the U.S. added another.

The arrival of large warships tested the Wuhan regime. They added little additional protection to foreign lives and property since a long row of gunboats was already anchored there. The extra firepower seemed all the more

---

66. *FO* 405/253 [F5103/2/10], p. 351, Enclosure 6, Chen to Brenan, Guangzhou, April 16, 1927.
67. *FO* 405/253 [F5813/4638/10], pp. 471-472, Enclosure 1, Brenan to Lampson, Guangzhou, May 20, 1927.
68. Powell, "Nationalists Take Over Shanghai—The Present Situation," pp. 121-122.

pointless because the Wuhan government had set itself up in the foreign concession to discourage bombardment. Intimidation seems to have been the cruisers' principal intent and ultimately their primary effect.

With foreign scrutiny and pressure now bearing down on Wuhan, both factions adjusted their tactics. Wuhan's communist and GMD left-wing leaders quickly resumed a state-building mien. On April 23, the Wuhan CEC issued a manifesto denouncing Britain's "imperialistic" posturing, but then it dramatically reversed its Third Plenum pronouncements by warning Chinese to avoid—at all costs—any measure that might provoke foreign intervention or provide a pretext for war. The next day the Hubei General Labor Union issued a declaration of its own, iterating major points of the CEC announcement while adding a series of strongly worded regulations and penalties for disobedience. To minimize the chance that hostilities might break out accidentally, the regime set up a Committee of Public Safety charged with seeking out and repressing "counter-revolutionary activities"—now defined as agitative efforts that might implicate the regime. Strict regulations governed all mass organizations and their conduct. Wuhan papers, meanwhile, published articles explaining the value of capitalism and repudiating rumors that the regime sought to implement a communist system. Leaders even met with representatives from missionary societies to arrange the return of schools, churches, and residences seized in earlier anti-imperialist episodes while the Hankou Bureau of Foreign Affairs expelled troops from foreign-owned buildings. [69] Under a cloud of government disapproval, anti-Christian and anti-foreign energy dissipated.

The need to stabilize relations with the powers—as well as a host of related factors fully explained by Wilbur and other scholars of Republican China—gradually forced a rift between CCP/Soviet leaders and GMD left-wing authorities, once again reshaping the revolutionary camp. On May 10, the Wuhan CEC formed its own Central Purification Committee to purge all "communists, local bullies and evil gentry, corrupt officials, speculators, and all rotten and evil elements" *(gongchan fenzi tuhao lieshen tanguan wuli touji fenzi ji yiqie fuhua ehua fenzi).* [70] Regulations steering the process warned against "anti-revolutionaries creating trouble and interfering with party purification *(qingdang)* activities."[71]

Wuhan's anti-communist crackdowns never approached the levels of bloodshed witnessed in right-wing areas and avoided the heavy suppression of mass organizations. Nevertheless, left-wing leaders still showed the same degree of sensitivity to foreign interests. That same month, Wuhan circulated notice to all party members arguing for the protection of missionary schools

---

69. Chapman, *The Chinese Revolution*, pp. 133-136.
70. "Zhongyang qingdang weiyuanhui zuzhi dagang," *2-ZXWH*, vol. 6 (May 10, 1927).
71. "Qingdang tiaoli," *2-ZXWH*, vol. 6 (May 10, 1927).

and churches, noting that such institutions "have their own value," that "religion is permitted by law," and that "the government protects Catholic and Protestant churches."[72]

Again muzzled and prevented from engaging enemy targets, revolutionary anti-imperialism in Wuhan became an empty exercise without vigor or drive. Wuhan authorities kept alive a few slogans and state-sponsored activities, but formalization only dampened enthusiasm. Explaining conditions, one observer recorded,

> The attendance of the demonstrators at many of these processions was compulsory: for example, it might be ordered that all the shops in a district should send 20 percent of their employees, or that the whole of the scholars of certain schools should attend on a particular day. Under intimidation from the pickets the shopkeepers would be compelled to pay their men as if they had been working, and the school-teachers to grant leave; and the individual who failed to attend the parade would be liable to a beating or other punishment. By the time the hot weather in May began it was obvious that the Government had overdone this method of propaganda. The procession had become such a commonplace that hardly anyone in a crowded street even turned his head to look; the demonstrators themselves began to appear rather spiritless; and more and more of this work was left to boys, they being evidently more easily procured than their elders. At last even schoolboys themselves, and many of them, began to complain that they were spending far more time in processions than in school classes and that they were tired of it.[73]

While Wuhan patched up relations with the powers, right-wing leaders found themselves trying to regain the trust of China's people. Efforts to limit disruption notwithstanding, the right went out of its way to assure labor leaders that popular mobilization still comprised an integral part of the revolution, that routine strikes or boycotts were still allowed, and that labor unions still enjoyed the "right to exist and organize" as long as they avoided "extremist measures."[74] General Bai and other right-wing leaders were not simply concerned about protecting rights, however. Guangzhou consul Brenan explained that right-wing officials disliked agitative "lawlessness" but genuinely feared that suppression might inspire anti-regime hostility and inflame more strikes and boycotts.[75] Given the severity of Chiang's brutal crackdown against popular forces, the right-wing had even greater cause to try to appease the masses.

---

72. Wan, "Zuijin Wuhan minzhong ji zhengfu duiyu Jidujiao di taidu, pp. 5-6.

73. Chapman, *The Chinese Revolution*, p. 25.

74. Powell, "Nationalists Take Over Shanghai—The Present Situation," p. 123

75. *CWR* 40 (March 5, 1927): 18; *FO* 405/252 [F2574/2/10], p. 416, Enclosure 1, Brenan to Lampson, Guangzhou, February 16, 1927.

Besides validating agitator rights, right-wing officials also tried to channel popular energies into less disruptive occupations. Efforts were made to encourage mass organizations to pursue self-interest at the local level rather than grander anti-imperialist objectives. Before Chiang's coup, anti-Christian activists hailed educational rights or defied cultural imperialism with demonstrations, such as anti-Christmas week, that swept the entire country. Afterwards, however, agitation came to focus on the narrow and specific conditions at local schools or factories. Thus, students at Changsha's Yale-in-China College demanded lower tuition and room fees, participation at faculty meetings, a voice over library additions, veto power over the expulsion of students, subsidies for the student union, and better recreational facilities.[76] With mass mobilization concentrating energies on localized objectives, it lost much of its cumulative revolutionary weight.

The right-wing also tried to heal relations with popular forces by justifying their suppression as a prerequisite to stamping out communism. Illuminating Comintern plots to seize the revolutionary helm and China's sovereignty, Chiang and others identified an enemy more insidious than even the imperialists—one that necessitated the bloody purges of mid-April and continued restraints thereafter. In the long run, communism provided the perfect scapegoat for ejecting revolutionary agitation altogether. In the short run, however, anti-communist arguments struck many in China's thousands of mass organizations as unconvincingly shallow. To them, Chiang's coup was an attack against labor and the masses as much as an anti-communist purge. Some retaliated. On April 22, the Guangzhou Seamen's Union organized a general strike to protest regime repression. Suppression came shortly thereafter, but not before sympathetic railway workers interrupted all three railway lines, derailed locomotives, and destroyed telegraph lines.[77]

Among Guangzhou's forty thousand former Anti-British Boycott strikers still on the government dole, the potential for trouble was even greater.[78] As Brenan explained, Chiang's officials "cannot afford to alienate the whole body of labour, and there is no indication that they intend to do so."[79] Gan Naiguang, a high provincial official in Guangzhou, concurred:

> The position of Chiang Kai-shek and the government now is very delicate. They are getting rid of Communists but their success in the Northern Expedition and the unification of China depends upon keeping the support of the common people. They must get rid of the destruc-

76. Lutz, *Chinese Politics and Christian Missions*, pp. 226-228.
77. *FO* 405/253 [F5108/2/10], p. 352, Enclosure, Brenan to Lampson, Guangzhou, April 26, 1927.
78. *FO* 405/253 [F5814/2/10], p. 477, Enclosure, Brenan to Lampson, Guangzhou, May 20, 1927.
79. *FO* 405/253 [F5103/2/10], p. 348, Enclosure 1, Brenan to Lampson, Guangzhou, April 20, 1927.

tive . . . radicals and demagogues, but at the same time convince the peasants and laborers that the government is going to help them. Of course, it is with these lower classes of people that the Communists have their influence and on whom their propaganda has been poured out. Therefore the government . . . has to be very careful not to openly oppose any group of laborers for fear of losing its grip on them.[80]

In order to avoid further alienating the masses, the right-wing decided against dissolving Shanghai's powerful labor unions. Instead, it opted to "reorganize" them.[81]

Partyization Redefined: Revolutionization Abandoned

Through the post-purge months of 1927, politics in revolutionary China simplified. Foreigners sought security, agitators pursued self-interest, and the Nationalists tried to avoid offending either. Left-wing Wuhan subordinated itself to right-wing Nanjing while localist interests submitted to Guomindang rule. Bloodletting against missionaries during the Nanjing Incident and against agitators during Chiang's purge stunned both groups and put them on their heels, allowing the Nationalist Government to seize initiative. It still faced foreign gunboats but had earned a respite thanks to its anti-communist stance and pro-foreign accommodation. Party leaders moved to centralize control, improve foreign relations, and stabilize socioeconomic conditions—all hallmark state-building objectives.

With Nationalist political dominance expanding through south and central China, the time had come to enhance sociocultural influence. Education in south and central China had not fared well through late 1926 and early 1927. Fighting during the Northern Expedition had damaged facilities, drained funding, and filled classrooms with billeting NRA troops. In December 1926, Borodin reproved such practices, ordered troops off school premises, and met with students to explain the government's financial plight. With CEC support, most primary schools reopened, but other schools remained closed, stranding thirty thousand students in Hubei alone.[82] Similar problems in Jiangxi led Chen Gongbo to complain in late December that operations had not yet recovered.[83] Popular activism aggravated problems. Even private schools fully registered and staffed by Chinese faced debilitating strikes and boycotts.[84] Chiang's purge only added to the chaos plaguing education, closing radical schools such as Dongnan University and

---

80. Rea, ed., *Canton in Revolution*, p. 66.
81. *FO* 405/253 [F5816/2/10], p. 482, Enclosure 1, Kirke to Lampson, Shantou, May 24, 1927.
82. "Hubei jiaoyu baogao," *ZGLH*, vol. 1 (December 22, 1926).
83. Chen, "Chen Gongbo tongzhi Jiangxi zhengwu baogao," *ZGLH*, vol. 1 (December 17, 1926).
84. Lutz, *Chinese Politics and Christian Missions*, pp. 227-228.

Shanghai University.[85] In Hunan and Hubei, *all* schools were shut for six months to rid them of agitative and communist influence.[86] Students were not happy. National Student Union branch officers in Wuhan denounced Chiang and the CCP alike for derailing the revolution while National Student Union leaders in Nanjing condemned their Wuhan rivals for being "tools of Russia" *(Sue zhi gongju).*[87]

Educational disruption, however, had its advantages. Optimistic reports from Hubei noted that NRA advances and mass agitation had opened the way for full reform by forcing schools to align with the Guomindang, closing those with questionable connections, and putting "reactionary forces" to flight.[88] Collapse of the *status quo*, in short, meant that Nationalist officials could begin earnestly pursuing their two primary objectives vis-à-vis education: (1) subjugating mission schools to party regulations, and (2) refitting Chinese schools to *danghua* standards.[89]

Regarding the first task, progress came quickly. After Chiang established a new regime in Nanjing, missionary educators sought registration in droves. They did not acquiesce, however, simply because they felt more secure as GMD protections rose and popular disruptions declined. In strange ways, the new position of Chiang's government actually made agitation worse. Anti-imperialist activism was not tolerated, but mass organizations were still allowed to mobilize for their own benefit. Since mission institutions were simultaneously localist and foreign, it was often impossible to differentiate between "legitimate" and "illegitimate" anti-Christian activity, leaving missionaries on shaky ground.

Events surrounding Earl Swisher's muddy encounter with a ditch illuminate some of the peculiar challenges facing Christians in China's new order. Before Swisher's upending by angry strikers, Nationalist authorities had refused to offer Lingnan University any assistance beyond guarding the transfer of its cows. As soon as party headquarters received word of the assault against Swisher, however, police and troops were promptly dispatched to arrest the perpetrators, clear away the pickets, and guard the campus. An anti-foreign incident, even a small, wet one, was met swiftly and decisively.

Nevertheless, once the immediate crisis had been averted, the party refused to intervene any further. Most Lingnan workers simply crossed the

---

85. Yeh, *The Alienated Academy*, pp. 164-165.
86. Yip, *Religion, Nationalism, and Chinese Students*, p. 75.
87. "Zhonghua Minguo xuesheng lianhui zonghui gaizu weiyuanhui yonghu zhongyang dangbu guomin zhengfu tongdian," 1927; "Zhongguo xuesheng zonghui dijiuhui daibiao dahui kaimuri fouren Wuhan weixue zonghui," 1927.
88. "Hubei zhengwu baogao," *ZGLH*, vol. 1 (December 17, 1926).
89. "Quansheng dangwu zong baogao jueyian," *J3QD* (n.d., early 1927).

river to Dongshan where they continued their strike with General Labor Union and Labor Ministry support, confident, in the words of Swisher, "that if they hold out long enough they can get everything they ask from the college." Unwilling to risk a backlash by challenging labor's right to strike, officials kept their distance, ensuring that virtually every matter referred to labor and peasants bureau chiefs was decided in favor of the strikers.[90]

Other changes proved equally troublesome to missionaries. Chiang's new order swept aside the most zealous and extreme anti-Christian leaders, but it also removed the most active state-building authorities on whom missionaries had long depended. In a letter dated June 10, 1927, Swisher recounted:

> In [forming Lingnan's] new Board of Directors . . . an attempt was made to keep in close touch with the government by placing one or two prominent government officials on the Board. Sun Fo [Sun Ke] . . . was made a member—but now [he] is advertised in everyday's [sic] newspaper with a price on his head. "Execute Sun Fo, the leader of the anti-Kuomintang [Guomindang] Communists." George Hsu [Xu Qian], who was on the staff here at Lingnan just a few years ago as a professor of Chinese literature and more recently the head of the Department of Justice in the Nationalist government, is now denounced. In yesterday's Chinese newspaper, I read in characters three inches high: "Execute the anti-party leaders, George Hsu and Eugene Chen [Chen Youren]." And Eugene Chen is the clever, Oxford man whom [Henry] Brownell and I had such a long talk with last fall. He was sympathetic toward our strike then but helpless to do anything about it. A year ago if anyone wanted a favor from the government, he went to Borodin. . . . If his favor was gained, the consent of the government was surely forthcoming. But now M. Borodin is also wanted for execution.[91]

With Borodin, Chen, Sun, and Xu in disgrace, missionaries lost valuable contacts within the regime and struggled when incoming replacements proved relatively weak.[92]

Mission school administrators also complained about uncertainties that complicated the registration process. Hankou mission schools, for example, faced separate regulations from the CEC, the provincial government, and the local municipal government.[93] Even simple interactions with the party often

---

90. Rea, ed., *Canton in Revolution*, pp. 61, 63, 73-74.

91. Rea, ed., *Canton in Revolution*, p. 65.

92. Lingnan's new incoming Chinese President, Zhong Rongguang, sat on the Nationalist Government's Education Commission, but missionaries feared that he might not have wielded much influence. Rea, ed., *Canton in Revolution*, p. 65.

93. Lutz, *Chinese Politics and Christian Missions*, pp. 226, 228; Yip, *Religion, Nationalism, and Chinese Students*, p. 76.

failed because affairs of state had become a highly politicized venture filled with unpredictable "political intricacies."[94]

Despite these challenges, the registration of mission schools proceeded. Missionaries were finally ready to submit to Chinese authority.[95] In late 1924, when the Beijing regime first issued regulations, missionaries refused to concede because they believed that registration would destroy Christian education's "reason for being."[96] Instead, the China Christian Education Association retorted, "Government efforts to restrict the teaching of religion do not reflect the freedom of religion promised and impede the moral foundation and contributions already established."[97] After the May Thirtieth Incident of 1925, Chinese Christian demands for indigenization brought some missionaries around, but the Christian Colleges Alliance Association still rejected the government's ban on proselytizing.[98] By late 1926, the Northern Expedition and Anti-Christian Movement had melted all but the most stalwart defiance. It was the Nanjing Incident of March 1927, however, that brought missionaries to their collective knees. Their flight produced *de facto* indigenization when the administration of abandoned institutions fell to Chinese Christians. Facing the prospect of losing everything, foreigners stopped arguing about whom should head mission schools or Christianize China and began wondering if they would have any role at all. On April 20, 1927, D. Willard Lyon summarized the general mood among missionary refugees huddled in Shanghai:

> The future which we now confront is quite a different one. Policies which have for decades been accepted as sound must now be restudied. Neither the missionaries, nor the societies which sent them, can any longer take these policies for granted. A missionary revolution has taken place. The functions of the mission and of the missionary call for radical redefinition. It is plainly obvious that the missionary cannot return to a position similar to the one he has previously occupied, nor ply his trade with the same implements he has used in the past.[99]

By the spring of 1927, most missionaries had to concede that only registration and indigenization would allow their institutions a respectable

---

94. Rea, ed., *Canton in Revolution*, p. 65.
95. *FO* 405/253 [F5261/3210/10], p. 355, Lampson to Chamberlain, Beijing, April 14, 1927.
96. As Lutz notes, most missionaries "contended that the inculcation of religion and morality was what distinguished parochial education from public and was its reason for being." Lutz, *Chinese Politics and Christian Missions*, p. 158.
97. "Zhonghua Jidu jiaoyuhui zhi xuanyan," *Jiaoyu zazhi* 17:5 (May 1925): 9.
98. The 180 members deliberated for four days in February 1926. "Beijing jiaoyubu bugao dishiliu hao," in *Guonei jinshinian lai zhi zongjiao sichao*, comp. Zhang, pp. 370-371. The issue of indigenization divided delegates, however, and forced them to seek further input. "Jidujiao jiaoyuhui zhi zhengqiu yijian," *Jiaoyu zazhi* 18:5 (May, 1926): 6.
99. Lyon, "Should the Missionary Be Discouraged?" p. 313.

place in Chinese society. Yanjing University was the first to register with the Beijing regime. In August 1927, Lingnan University became the first to comply with the Nationalist Government. Conformity had its advantages. Guomindang officials presided over celebrations marking Lingnan's official registration and congratulated school authorities with friendly overtures about the future. Immensely satisfied, Swisher recorded in his diary, "It really seems that there is an increasing number of men in the government who really want the college to continue its work in the best way possible. All of them are very impressed with the fact that we are the first school to register with the Nationalist Government and the first to turn over the school to the Chinese."[100]

Other institutions followed and, by April 1929, about 70 percent of China's two hundred Christian middle schools had begun or completed the registration process; virtually all also hosted a Chinese principal and a Chinese majority on their boards of directors.[101] In most, mandatory Bible study and religious services had been supplanted by obligatory classes on the Three Principles of the People *(Sanmin zhuyi)* and weekly memorials honoring Sun Yat-sen. By the close of 1932, all Christian colleges and universities had registered except for St. John's in Shanghai, which waited until 1947.[102]

The party's second educational task—that of expanding "partyization" *(danghua)*—proceeded even more readily than the first. As revolutionary influence spread during the Northern Expedition, educators in rival systems found themselves besieged. The Youth Ministry designed front organizations and Northern Expedition Youth Work Groups to extend student agitation behind enemy lines and drum up Chinese support while evading warlord police.[103] Through these and other means, popular forces assailed "education tyrants" *(xuefa)* who emphasized national salvation through self-cultivation rather than through revolutionary activism.[104]

Once NRA forces arrived on the scene, education's partyization only accelerated. In Jiangxi, for example, youth bureau leaders announced with celebration that the "era of secrecy" *(mimi shiqi)* had finally ended and that the youth movement could at last step into the open.[105] New party provincial officers intervened with the full weight of the new state, augmenting popular efforts to destroy "education tyrant" influence, punish corrupt officials,

---

100. Rea, ed., *Canton in Revolution*, pp. 9, 18, 75.

101. *China Christian Year Book*, vol. 1931, p. 250.

102. Yip, *Religion, Nationalism, and Chinese Students*, p. 77.

103. "Zhongguo Guomindang zhongyang zhixing weiyuanhui qingnianbu gongzuo fangzhen ji jihua cao'an," April 1927; "Beifa qingnian gongzuotuan zuzhi dagang," 1927; "Zhongguo Guomindang Shanghai tebieshi dierqu dangbu qingnianbu gongzuo jihua," 1927.

104. "Zhongguo Guomindang Shanghai tebieshi dierqu dangbu qingnianbu gongzuo jihua," 1927.

105. "Guanyu qingnian yundong jueyian," *J3QD* (n.d., early 1927).

dismantle evil gentry and local bully power, and dissolve all people's corps *(mintuan)* and merchant corps *(shangtuan).*[106] In no time *xuefa* organizations, such as the Jiangsu Provincial Educational Association, were disbanded and their members prohibited from steering educational policy.[107]

Problems hampered a smooth transition to partyized education. Standards had to be established. Investigations were needed to determine which non-party teachers deserved the *xuefa* label and which did not.[108] Officials worried that students had become a new class of intellectual elites rather than revolutionaries.[109] Even under good conditions, party fractions *(dangtuan)* remained inert when overly passive students or excessively elitist faculty failed to work together.[110] In response, the Youth Ministry prescribed political training *(zhengzhi xunlian)* and deeper oversight.[111]

Chiang's seizure of power, however, replaced worries about revolutionary effectiveness with concerns about communist infiltration, forcing youth organizations to reorganize and heighten vigilance against communist spies.[112] As a result, the drive to partyize education transformed and central Guomindang officials replaced mass organizations as the primary engine behind partyization. Directing change from the top, the government duplicated the Sun Yat-sen University system—the model of *danghua*—in Hangzhou by forming the Number Two Sun Yat-sen University and again in Nanjing by founding the Number Three Sun Yat-sen University. Through Dai Jitao, the president of Guangzhou's Sun Yat-sen University since late 1925, the GMD gradually moved to fashion *all* schools after the same standard.[113] In her study of China's educational world, Wen-hsin Yeh explains the party's intent:

> In central and southern provinces, the Nationalists took control of established institutions in city after city. The major regional universities of the Nanjing decade—Zhongyang University in Nanjing, Zhejiang University in Hangzhou, Wuhan University in Wuhan, and Sichuan University in Chengdu, in addition to the original Zhongshan [Sun Yat-sen] University in Guangzhou—were all assembled from former provincial higher normal schools and other specialized institutes, given a Party

---

106. "Quansheng dangwu zong baogao jueyian," *J3QD* (n.d., early 1927); "Zhongyang zhixing weiyuanhui," *1-ZXWH*, vol. 4 (June 2, 1925).
107. Yeh, *The Alienated Academy*, p. 167.
108. "Hubei zhengwu baogao," *ZGLH*, vol. 1 (December 17, 1926).
109. "Guanyu qingnian yundong jueyian," *J3QD* (n.d., early 1927).
110. "Zhongguo Guomindang Shanghai tebieshi dierqu dangbu qingnianbu gongzuo jihua," 1927.
111. "Zhongguo Guomindang zhongyang zhixing weiyuanhui qingnianbu gongzuo fangzhen ji jihua cao'an," April 1927.
112. "Zhongguo Guomindang zhongyang zhixing weiyuanhui qingnianbu gongzuo fangzhen ji jihua cao'an," April 1927.
113. Yeh, *The Alienated Academy*, pp. 168-169, 174.

superstructure, put under the command of a new leadership, and propelled in the direction prescribed by the Guomindang in 1927.[114]

Under regime direction, the partyization movement formalized and extended its reach. Youth Ministry officials set up night schools for uneducated adults aimed at inculcating party principles *(dangyi)* and realigning mass loyalties.[115] Literacy programs taught students to understand basic party principles and read party announcements, slogans, and letters. General education was couched in pro-party terms. Standards mandated that textbooks—closely edited and approved by Guomindang officials—included 50 percent party principles and 50 percent general knowledge. For every ten hours of instruction, at the hand of GMD teachers, students were obligated to attend two hours of instruction on party issues.[116]

With *danghua* proceeding under the micromanaging care of central authorities, it came to mean something other than a process of reforming institutions so they could better revolutionize China's youth.[117] CEC directives ordered the Youth Ministry to teach party principles, policy, and objectives to ensure that China's youth could be molded into disciples of Sun Yat-sen's Three Principles of the People and to ready party fractions *(dangtuan)* to "act in absolute compliance with Guomindang authority and implement government resolutions."[118] Youth bureau officials were instructed to maintain central control by "providing the youth with sufficient guidance and telling them what is *correct thought and proper action.*"[119] [Emphasis added.]

As central oversight expanded, youth organizations transformed. Instead of acting as agents of agitative change, they became targets of political purity campaigns. The Youth Ministry ordered surveys of *dangtuan* in all youth organizations to ensure that none opposed party objectives.[120] Top CEC

114. Yeh, *The Alienated Academy*, p. 169.
115. "Zhongguo Guomindang Shanghai tebieshi dierqu dangbu qingnianbu gongzuo jihua," 1927.
116. "Zhongyang qingnianbu xianren zhiyuan ji guicheng yilan," April 1927; "Zhongyang nongminbu zhi Jiangsu jiaoyuting han," November 27, 1927.
117. "Guanyu qingnian yundong jueyian," *J3QD* (n.d., early 1927); "Zhongguo Guomindang zhongyang zhixing weiyuanhui qingnianbu gongzuo fangzhen ji jihua cao'an," April 1927.
118. "Zhongguo Guomindang zhongyang zhixing weiyuanhui qingnianbu gongzuo fangzhen ji jihua cao'an," April 1927.
119. "Zhongguo Guomindang Shanghai tebieshi dierqu dangbu qingnianbu gongzuo jihua," 1927.
120. "Zhongguo Guomindang zhongyang zhixing weiyuanhui qingnianbu gongzuo fangzhen ji jihua cao'an," April 1927. Even Boy Scout leaders were ordered to receive training in *danghua* courses. Topics of study included: military science, party principles, Guomindang history, the unequal treaties, world revolutionary history, the history of social evolution, the history of imperialist invasion, class analysis, peasant and labor union organization, child psychology, mass psychology, and propaganda techniques. "Guangxisheng qingnianbu shang zhongyang qingnianbu cheng," January 14, 1927.

authorities kept close watch over all partyization activity.[121] Reports about educational and youth movement reform poured into central headquarters, relaying information about individual schools, principals, student unions, and—most importantly—the general attitude of each toward "revolutionary objectives."[122]

Danghua, in short, became its opposite: a process that sought to depoliticize students rather than prepare them to make revolution. In February 1928, CEC leaders justified the shift, warning that, "Educational institutions everywhere have been endangered by military disaster and political change from the outside and disrupted by the student movement influence . . . on the inside. As a result, not a single student could study in peace and not a single school could maintain itself efficiently." Condemning schemes that had transformed students into "commodities of political strife" *(zhengzheng huopin)*, the CEC declared that students belonged in school and not in politics.[123] Primary and secondary school students were banned from engaging in political activity while college students were prohibited from joining politicized organizations.[124] In May, CEC authorities folded the five mass-organization ministries—Youth, Women's, Peasant, Labor, and Commerce—into the single Committee for Mass Training which worked with officials from the Secretariat, Organization Ministry, Propaganda Ministry, Training Ministry, and the CEC to prevent students and other mass organizations from engaging in "selfish" struggles.[125]

By the time that the Third National Congress opened in March 1929, student activism had become little more than another way to prop up regime authority. Nationalist leaders Dai Jitao and Cai Yuanpei favored dismantling the youth movement entirely and instituting a pure educational experience washed clean of any political involvement. Chen Guofu, on the other hand, sought continued youth engagement with national affairs but only under the tight control of the party.[126] Educators supported Dai and Cai's position. Mass organizations supported Chen, calling Dai and Cai's proposal "boiling the hound after capturing the rabbit" *(tusi goupeng)*. In contrast, Wang Jingwei supported agitation's original function as an independent and autonomous branch of the revolution, but only because he feared that squelching activism would hand students to communists operating underground. Differences notwithstanding, all Guomindang authorities moved to

---

121. "Jiangsu quansheng xuelianhui gebu gongzuo jihua," 1927; "Zhongyang qingnianbu zhi zhonghua minguo daxueyuan han," October 31, 1927.
122. A few examples include: "Gesheng shixian xuesheng lianhehui zuzhi yilan biao," 1927; "Hangzhou zhongdeng yishang xuexiao zuzhi biao," 1927; "Zhejiang quansheng qingnian yundong gaikuang tongji biao," 1927. Also see *Jiaoyuhui fa an, GZD* 168:895.
123. Lü, *Cong xuesheng yundong dao yundong xuesheng*, pp. 399-400.
124. Israel, *Student Nationalism in China*, pp. 16-17.
125. Lü, *Cong xuesheng yundong dao yundong xuesheng*, pp. 400, 405.
126. Lü, *Cong xuesheng yundong dao yundong xuesheng*, p. 401.

pacify students with the same "book learning" arguments long employed by
missionaries and "education tyrants," press them under tight state control,
and divert their energies into less disruptive channels. On October 9, 1929,
the party essentially signaled the official end of the youth movement by
ordering the National Student Union to discontinue plans for its Eleventh
National Congress and to cease all activities.[127]

Party interest in popular forces had changed. Rather than expand popular
forces as a potent weapon against new enemies, such as communism or
Japanese militarism, Chiang's regime stripped the masses of their autonomy
and co-opted their organizations before dissolving many of them outright.
Revolutionary agitation, in short, was treated just like the allies of imperialism that it had helped bring down. To be sure, the party did not completely
eliminate all mass organizations. Chiang required their blessing to maintain
claims of popular support, even if he could not tolerate any independent
mobilization. Their primary role, however, had shifted from active agents of
revolutionary change to passive supporters of the state-building *status quo*.
Thus, even while CEC authorities continued to validate popular organizations as legitimate parts of Chinese society and national life, pronouncements
reaffirmed the fact that the masses were also barred from political activity. As
a result, student agitation lost its spontaneity and agitation in all its forms
stopped functioning as an autonomous revolutionary prong, withdrawing
instead into a cocoon of self-interest. Stripped of any legitimate role within
China's new political order, true agitation could only exist outside that same
order. Lamenting the fate of popular mobilization, Lin Yutang—one of
China's greatest social commentators—penned the following in 1936:

> Since 1927, and the dissolution of Chinese labour unions, such mass
> action and even ordinary popular demonstrations are practically un-
> known. Boycott organizations have been suppressed everywhere, and
> even the economic war at present going on between China and Japan
> through the wholesale smuggling of goods, grave enough to cripple the
> Chinese national finance, has failed to arouse in any newspaper even a
> suggestion of a boycott, the natural economic reprisal against illegal
> economic aggression. *The Chinese people have forgotten, or have been
> intimidated into forgetting, the use of a weapon which they have learnt to
> wield with terrible effectiveness in the last three decades.*[128] [Emphasis
> added.]

In some respects, the demise of agitation was unavoidable. Worried that
communists might revive popular activism and infiltrate mass organizations,

127. Yeh, *The Alienated Academy*, p. 230; Lü, *Cong xuesheng yundong dao yundong xuesheng*,
pp. 411-414.
128. Lin, *A History of the Press and Public Opinion in China*, p. 123.

the Nanjing regime could not help but view them as a threat.[129] Nevertheless, the reverse could also be argued. Revolutionary state-building impulses had long coexisted uneasily with agitative forces. The two agendas opposed each other in fundamental ways, producing friction along with symbiosis. Examining the Nanjing regime from this perspective, Chiang's suppression of communism did more than simply close a chapter on revolutionary factional politics. It also provided the perfect moment to jettison a fundamental revolutionary component that had outlived its usefulness. Like an ancient dynastic founder eager to slay the lieutenants that had ushered him into power, top Nationalist leaders turned against the revolution's agitative prong, using the communist specter as the *raison d'être*. Tainted by CCP associations, agitation could not justify any further role for itself, allowing state-building to prevail.

Until the end of his life, Chiang Kai-shek blamed Borodin and the CCP for trying to divide the revolution and steal the revolutionary helm.[130] What his anti-communist stance refused to acknowledge, and sought to erase from memory, however, was the fundamental observation that the Nationalist Revolution had only succeeded because it *was* divided (bifurcated) and that Borodin *had* steered it from the very beginning. Despite all that Lin Yutang presumed in 1936, even a decade of anti-communist rhetoric could not erase from memory the basics of popular revolution. All that the Chinese people needed was a cause great enough to awaken them again.

---

129. Lü, *Cong xuesheng yundong dao yundong xuesheng*, p. 417.
130. Chiang, *Soviet Russia in China*, p. 50; *FO* 405/253 [F5763/2/10], p. 465, Enclosure 3, report of meeting at governor's yamen, Guangzhou, May 10, 1927.

9. Conclusion
—Inclusive Nation, Exclusive State

Fellow Labourers: the Nationalist Revolution has already eliminated the militarists of Guangdong; has already overthrown the capitalists who rob us. At the present time, amongst those who oppress us, apart from the militarists, imperialists and capitalists, there are still the labour thieves. These labour bandits adopt false disguises and mix with our labour bodies, pretending to be our leaders. Actually, the labour bandits are taking the opportunity to deceive us and oppress us, swallowing up the funds which we have earned with our sweat and blood, and which we have contributed to the union. These labour bandits have gone even further, and in the guise of workmen have tried to destroy the Northern Expedition, have tried to destroy the Guomindang, have opposed [Chiang Kai-shek], the man of a hundred battles and a hundred victories, have opposed the loyalty and unity of the Guomindang, and have opposed the Three Principles of the People. . . . These kinds of people are our worst enemies. If we do not rise up and clear out these labour bandits, their oppression of the workers will become worse than that of the capitalists, worse than that of the imperialists, worse than that of the militarists. Fellow-workers! Rise up quickly! . . . If we workers are to set ourselves free, if the Chinese people are to seek liberty and equality, it is all the more important that we should rise up quickly.[1]

—All-China General Labor Union, All-China General Railwaymen's Union, Guangzhou Workers' Delegates Conference, April 15, 1927

On October 13, 1927, a young educator hailing from Guangzhou but teaching in Shanghai penned a letter to the Youth Ministry. Zhu Naibin needed funding and therefore wrote with purpose. He first explained how his Jianguo Propaganda School had started as a fully "partyized" *(danghua)* institution committed to attacking imperialist and landlord influence in Guangzhou, but had later been forced to close by local "communists." Avoiding these rivals, who sought to "try to destroy" his institution, Zhu moved it to Shanghai.

Once Chiang Kai-shek purged the communists, however, Zhu recommitted his resources to education's partyization, this time in the lower Yangzi.

---

1. *FO* 405/253 [F5103/2/10], pp. 349-350, Enclosure 4, Guangzhou labor unions pamphlet. (The British translation inaccurately identifies Zhang Zuolin as the "man of a hundred battles." Context and slogans indicate that the original Chinese refered to Chiang Kai-shek.)

In July, for example, he and others proposed a *Danghua* Education Curricula Institute. To recruit propagandists, directors conducted a series of open house events, featuring performances by the *Danghua* Theater Society, the Chinese Music Association, the Chinese Music and Dancing School, and the Chinese Women's Public School. The response was overwhelming. On August 27 alone, over nine hundred students participated, recruiting hundreds more to help further propaganda work.

With building enthusiasm, Zhu's petition then outlined further plans to establish a massive propaganda network incorporating over one hundred Shanghai schools. Most had not yet been folded into the party educational system and still required "partyizing" reforms. Eager to spearhead that effort, Zhu sought permission to promote his Jianguo Propaganda School as the flagship institution and make it a model of both party principles and partyization. Guomindang support, Zhu promised, would allow him to recruit and educate students so all would fall "subject to party direction."[2]

For all its political *savoir-faire*, Zhu's presentation was somewhat disingenuous. Efforts to impugn the communists failed to mention that CEC leaders in Guangzhou had actually closed his school in 1925 because over-zealous fund raisers had incurred heavy gambling debts.[3] Nevertheless, Zhu's eagerness to distance himself from "hated" communism nicely confirms how far he was willing to stretch in order to align with China's new regime.

Zhu's letter also showed how popular notions of partyization had changed. Before April 1927, the term *danghua*—as used by Zhu—meant preparing revolutionary students to undermine imperialists and landlords. Afterwards, however, it sought obedience and state control. Passé revolutionary goals of anti-imperialism and agitative fervor had given way to strict allegiance to anti-communist and state-building objectives. Nowhere did Zhu's letter seek support for further anti-imperialism, celebrate student activism, or call for the training of agitative agents. Schools and education now sought to enhance party control. Propaganda bypassed the old targets of imperialism and warlordism in favor of "labor bandits," "disorderly elements," and "secret conspirators." As the labor pronouncement opening this chapter proclaimed, communists had risen as a new enemy that was worse than the capitalists, worse than the imperialists, and worse than the militarists.[4]

---

2. "Hu jianguo xuanchuan xuexiao xiaozhang shang zhongyang qingnianbu cheng," October 13, 1927.

3. The offense was reported by Chen Gongbo—one of the founding members of the CCP and likely one of the "communists" Zhu's petition condemned. After Chen's report, the CEC voted unanimously to shut the school down. (Discussion item #25), *1-ZXWH*, vol. 5 (October 30, 1925). Also see "Zhongyang zhixing weiyuanhui tonggao diereryihao," November 16, 1926.

4. *FO* 405/253 [F5103/2/10], pp. 349-350, Enclosure 4, Guangzhou labor unions pamphlet.

On the international front, anti-imperialist agitation had completely given way to appeasement. On April 11, 1927, British authorities responded to the Nanjing Incident by claiming an earnest "desire to continue and improve relationships of goodwill and co-operation" with China. At the same time, they demanded the suppression of any influence eager to "break up existing friendship and to enflame Chinese people to distrust, hatred and violence toward people of friendly Powers."[5] After Chiang's strike against communists and popular forces, party leaders complied with these demands one hundred percent, ordering that "all civil and military officials shall refrain from giving official support in any form to any violence or agitation directed against foreign lives and property and endangering the public peace and order."[6]

Perhaps the greatest change in revolutionary dynamics, however, was the end of popular autonomy. Under Chiang's rule, institutions and organizations pursuing inclusion within China's new sociopolitical milieu had to make the same commitments as individuals seeking membership in the GMD. The very first article of the Guomindang General Regulations *(zongzhang)*, adopted at the First National Congress in January 1924, stated, "Any Chinese citizen, irrespective of sex, if willing to accept the party's constitution, carry out the party's resolutions, join party organs overseen by the party, and pay party dues, will be accepted as a party member."[7] Any Chinese could join the Nationalist Party as long as he or she submitted to its authority, followed its line, paid its fees, and implemented its directives. Those hoping to become party members adjusted their behavior to meet expectations. By mid-1927, institutions and organizations desiring to participate in the new GMD-defined nation had to follow the same basic formula. National unity demanded conformity—not autonomy.

Changes notwithstanding, the new order shared a striking resemblance to the old one. The Nanjing regime's quickness to abandon agitation and institute state-building as the *modus operandi* caught many by surprise, but it should not have. Signs portending the eventual supremacy of state-building, although subtle, had steadily accumulated since 1924. As Michael Tsin nicely summarized:

> It was not that the Guomindang-led government faced a simple dichotomy between mobilization and control in terms of its strategy. . . . Rather, it was that the process of mobilization itself was in many respects a disciplinary exercise. The social foundationalism of the

5. *Nanjing shijian—zhongying*, document #5, 155:1480, *GZD* 155:1421.
6. C. H. Wang, GMD Minister of Justice, to British consul Barton," *Nanjing shijian—zhongying*, document #3, 155:1465, *GZD* 155:1421.
7. "Diyici quanguo daibiao dahui tongguo Zhongguo Guomindang zongzhang," *Geming wenxian*, vol. 70, p. 44.

Guomindang-led government meant that it would inevitably have to negotiate such tension in its mobilization of society."[8]

As Tsin implies, popular mobilization had a purpose—and it was far greater than agitation's simple anti-imperialist, pro-mass agenda could have foreseen. In key ways, therefore, Chiang's coup was not necessarily the reactionary, anti-communist, anti-mass "reversal" historians on both sides of the Taiwan Straits have described. Instead, it represented the logical culmination of a steady stream of CEC decisions that had long steered popular activism in order to secure state-building ends. Even if obscured by dual-prong duplicity, state-building had called the shots from the beginning. All Chiang did was drop the pretext of CEC interest in an autonomous agitative agenda in favor of open and transparent acknowledgement of state-building principles.[9]

Contradiction as Power: Inclusion

Perhaps it was a twist of fate that, even as Chiang's regime sought new levels of government control, the party's primary means for securing the submission of other groups was gone. Efforts to extend conformity and universalize national culture could no longer depend on dual-prong machinations or the levers of decentralized centralism. Both had been shelved. With mass organizations demobilized and popular agitation just a shadow of its former self, the Nationalists had discarded one of their most powerful tools.

Before factionalism and Northern Expedition advances set the revolution's two prongs against each other, contradictions between them produced remarkable flexibility and power, enough to undermine foes and expand revolutionary might at the same time. Bifurcated nationalism—a vision embracing both state-building and agitative objectives—and decentralized centralism—a system linking tightly controlled Leninist structures to independent and even non-party popular organizations—greatly expanded revolutionary options. Rhetorics of "awakening" and supplementary political, economic, social, and cultural levers helped subjugate rivals, but they never would have succeeded without the synergy produced when the contradictory yet symbiotic parts of bifurcated nationalism and decentralized centralism combined in dual-prong tactics. Agitative strikes, boycotts, demonstrations, and so forth demoralized localist and foreign interests and threatened to deny them a place within China's budding national sociocultural spectrum. As disruption mounted, top party officials offered mediatory and accommodative relief on the condition that those targeted accept regime oversight.

---

8. Tsin, *Nation, Governance, and Modernity in China*, p. 144.
9. This was the unavoidable fate of popular agitation. Even the CCP, ostensibly far more linked and committed to popular mass activism than Chiang Kai-shek's government, could not tolerate its autonomy or interference with state-building once Mao Zedong and others seized the country in 1949.

Pressured groups could yield, flee, or fight, but more often than not chose the first option, tempted by the benefits of inclusion and discouraged by a withering *status quo*. Pushing and pulling, the revolution gradually processed localist and foreign organizations, institutions, and individuals for inclusion within its new order.

When conditions were ideal, top CEC leaders could direct all pieces on the board. By encouraging or discouraging agitative forces, opening or closing negotiations with foreign and localist leaders, and intervening against popular disruption or standing by quietly, top revolutionary leaders surreptitiously manipulated enemy and popular forces alike. Exploiting tensions often meant directing agitation to undermine imperialist institutions. Nevertheless, stern warnings against activities that might provoke foreign intervention could just as easily be used to *restrain* impulsive agitators.

Either way, the CEC was advantaged. Responding to changing conditions, it adjusted the relative ratio of agitative or state-building ingredients to create new revolutionary mixtures. Between 1924 and early 1925, Guangzhou's weakness necessitated a cautious defensive stance with Nationalist officials publicly denying any linkage to popular agitation and focusing on "safe" missionary targets. By mid-1925, better stability and control over the base area meant dual-prong efforts could assume a more visible and assertive line, employing the Anti-British Boycott and Anti-Christian Movement to peel Chinese loyalties away from imperialist institutions. By mid-1926, advances made during the Northern Expedition ensured that CEC leaders could openly champion either state-building or agitation to meet foreign and northern warlord threats, depending on opportunity and need. As evidenced by the carefully orchestrated events surrounding the Hankou concession takeover, Borodin and others knew exactly what they were doing, and the British knew they knew.

Although fraught with contradiction, the actions of the Nationalist Revolution's top leaders were not irrational. Incorporating mutually exclusive revolutionary approaches provided flexibility enough to overcome even the worst paradoxical requirements demanded by warlord China's unusually complex sociopolitical system. It allowed revolutionary leaders to champion a popular anti-imperialist agenda while simultaneously negotiating for foreign recognition and new treaties. It offered a way to extend decentralized popular influence behind enemy lines on the national level while also centralizing state authority within its base of Guangdong. It ensured that the Guomindang could pursue a single, unifying centralist vision even while coloring that vision with the specific demands of various regional, local, class, and localist interests. It provided a way to preserve central control, unity, and discipline over party forces while also expanding broad-based support among non-party organizations. All requisite bases—control and support, regional and national, anti-imperialist and pro-foreign—were covered. Success ultimately depended on military might. Nevertheless, long before the party's military power solidified, bifurcated nationalism and its derivatives preserved momentum and allowed party influence to expand under the most malevolent conditions.

Inconsistency as Weakness: Exclusion

CEC leaders benefited as long as they could maintain some degree of control over the revolution's varied parts. Nevertheless, that was easier said than done. Harboring both state-building and popular agitative interests, each of which pursued mutually exclusive objectives, the revolution struggled under its own inconsistencies. State-building designs were thwarted when agitation stimulated reactive alliances between anti-revolutionary interests. Popular forces could follow their own agendas. Anti-imperialist disruption justified foreign intervention and concentrated foreign pressure on the Nationalist Government itself. While the CEC enjoyed considerable influence over them, mass organizations proved perfectly willing to defy its authority. Sun Yat-sen, Mikhail Borodin, Chiang Kai-shek, and others managed to steer the chaos sufficiently well to accomplish major objectives, but only with the same precision as firefighters trying to manage a forest fire in shifting cross winds.

Revolutionary participants at every level, both individual and collective, possessed a will of their own and organically responded to opportunities as they arose. At the lowest grassroots plane, unions and associations often sought to advance narrow economic or political benefit. Higher up the collective ladder, organization alliances and federations marching in the same general direction were less motivated by a monolithic understanding of singular purpose than a few shared perceptions, assumptions, and interests. Participants generally believed they were working toward something revolutionary, but then imagined that future in their own specific terms. Student activists rallying against imperialism viewed the revolution very differently from merchants supporting the Anti-British Boycott or military leaders engaging warlord armies or GMD foreign affairs officers pursuing new treaties with Britain.

When shifts in China's political landscape necessitated a tactical change, as they often did, the revolution's top-most leaders had to reconcile its adjustment to bewildered and frustrated lower-level forces. If the cost proved too prohibitive, the party turned to more exclusive measures. Indeed, large segments of revolutionary forces were routinely jettisoned, including Chen Jiongming's provincialists in 1922, Labor Corps troops in 1924, Sun Yat-sen's guest armies in 1925, Anti-British Boycott strikers in 1926, and the CCP in 1927.[10] Indeed, by mid-1927, the entire agitative prong had been

---

10. After the Merchant Corps was defeated in October 1924, GMD authorities disbanded the Labor Corps. Tsin, *Nation, Governance, and Modernity in China*, p. 112.

disengaged and dissolved. Sometimes interests were expelled because their loyalties were suspect, their utility had faded, or they were insufficiently revolutionary. Sometimes specific groups were expelled because they were *too* revolutionary. In each case, however, the decision was justified on the premise that state control would be compromised otherwise.

In some respects, exclusion was the unavoidable fate of almost all participants in the Nationalist Revolution. It did not march ahead as much as stagger forward under the combined steam of a variety of distinct and often mutually exclusive agendas. As long as revolutionary tasks remained undone and the "nation" existed only in the imagination of each individual actor, the revolution's various agendas, interests, and approaches cooperated, welcomed new-comers, and focused on assailing enemies.[11] As soon as military triumphs began to mount, however, top party leaders had to choose between the myriad of possible national "visions" represented in their ranks.

Despite its success as a revolutionary model, bifurcated nationalism could never serve as the basis of the rising GMD state. The same contradictions that gave the bifurcated approach strength against enemies also made it horribly ill-suited for the needs of modern nationalistic order. A formal state apparatus required a national definition to shape institutions, policy, and systems. Since the agitative and state-building visions differed dramatically on each count, only one of them could endure. By mid-1927, state-building won. CEC leaders predictably opted for stability and began to jealously guard what power they had accumulated. Chiang's White Terror purge of the communists, as a result, sought more than the destruction of Russian or CCP influence; it had to disenfranchise all mass agitation for reasons beyond simple factional rivalry or ideological orientation. National unity required it. Factional plotting between the left and right precluded a clean, quick break between state-building and agitative might, but could not prevent it.

The Origins of the Bifurcated Approach

While filled with references to bifurcated nationalism's two opposing visions and the components of decentralized centralism, party documents do not place either in any long-term strategy. Nor do they specifically articulate the inner workings of dual-prong tactics. Nothing was mapped out in advance. If anything, this study has shown that CEC decision-making and policy followed opportunity on an *ad hoc* basis. Identifying the origins of the Nationalist Revolution's particular approach, therefore, is problematic.

As faction-centered interpretations have long claimed, some evidence suggests a factional correlation that juxtaposes the CCP/GMD left-wing's penchant for agitation and the GMD right-wing's preference for state-building. According to this line of reasoning, the revolution's bifurcated

---

11. Anderson, *Imagined Communities*.

approach thus appeared as an accidental byproduct of interactions between the two parties' radically differing agendas. While revolutionary dynamics at the grassroots level may support this assertion, politics at the highest levels of revolutionary power defy it. Sun Yat-sen himself stumbled into dual-prong tactics long before the CCP arrived on the scene. More significant, both left-wing and right-wing CEC members emphasized state-building's foreign relations advantages and domestic control when prudent, but could be equally aggressive in stirring up agitative forces when required. Sun, Borodin, Chiang, and other representatives of either faction played both roles equally well.

Factional predilections may have leaned in favor of one approach over the other, but did not change the overall game plan. Four months after Sun Yat-sen's death in March 1925, for example, leftists headed by Wang Jing-wei assumed control of the party and alienated conservative right-wing members. Despite Wang's alleged radical agenda and an explosion of agitative energy following the May Thirtieth Incident, however, the CEC continued to accommodate foreign interests in dual-prong fashion just as when Sun was alive. After Chiang Kai-shek drove leftists like Wang out of power in March 1926, the regime did not abandon support for popular forces but maintained it. Indeed, until the spring of 1927, foreign critics called Chiang the "ultra-red" general because of his loud encouragement for anti-foreign agitation and anti-imperialist statements. Except for a few zealous individuals, factional alignment had less bearing on whether the CEC would advocate a state-building or agitative course than the pragmatic opportunities present at any given moment. Borodin, after all, proved a champion to missionary petitioners while popular forces overran the Jiujiang concession right under Chiang Kai-shek's nose.

Other evidence implies that functional differentiation served as the basis of the revolution's bifurcated nature. Specialty naturally predisposed some party and government units to more closely align with agitation and others with state-building. Foreign affairs officers generally sought accommodative ties with foreigners, for example, while youth and labor bureaus preferred mass-based interactions. Nevertheless, at the highest levels of revolutionary decision-making, again, analyses based on functional distinctions quickly break down. They may explain the existence of the agitative and state-building modes, but not how these were then used in tandem. Nor can they explain why functionaries so readily betrayed their specialty.

Foreign Affairs spokesman Chen Youren, for example, proved perfectly comfortable playing the agitation card, threatening British negotiators with further disruption should foreign troops attempt to retake the Hankou concession. Meanwhile, the Labor Ministry and even labor union officials could order pickets and demonstrators to stay away from foreign residences. By themselves, obvious and unavoidable functional differences cannot explain the revolution's bifurcated variety of nationalism any better than factional divisions. The CEC, after all, operated above the specialty associated with function by overseeing all branches of administration—both party and government. Functionality was exploited by dual-prong tactics; it was not the source of them.

The problem of "origin" may be that inquiries into the source of bifurcated nationalism miss the point. The primary objective of the First National Congress was power. Long before January 1924, Sun Yat-sen demonstrated singular creativity in his quest for it and employed even wildly disjointed means to get it. He could wine and dine Japanese imperialists and immediately thereafter solicit funds from anti-Japanese nationalists. Perhaps it is not a stretch, therefore, to assert that bifurcated nationalism was simply an institutionalized reflection of Sun's unrestrained penchant for combining multiple ideas, approaches, systems, and allies. By extension, therefore, it is also a reflection of warlord China's sociopolitical climate. Sun's elasticity did not appear in a vacuum, but evolved through years of struggle in a political environment that routinely sent him back to the drawing board. By 1924, he was no longer concerned with consistency or even principle. Any who stood by these—such as Chen Jiongming—did not last. In Sun's mind, power by any means necessary would, in the end, be justified by his superior vision.

Most likely, therefore, the bifurcated approach arose neither by accident nor design but evolved somewhat on its own in response to the specific demands of the era and as revolutionary leaders ingeniously made the most of what the political environment allowed into their arsenal. Partha Chatterjee's Indian revolutionaries employed national culture because that is what British imperialists forfeited to them. China's revolutionaries had to make do with far less.

Despite alleging access to some mysterious fountain of sagely knowledge, Sun was no prophet. Neither he nor Borodin could pretend to know how all would work out. Little wonder, therefore, that revolutionary leaders left unexplained how all the pieces would fit together and failed to identify a master strategy beyond vague assertions about destroying enemies, seizing national power, and unifying China. Forecasting specifics outside of military concerns was impossible. Too much depended on how events would unfold, how enemies and the people alike would respond, and which inclusive and exclusive tools would prove most useful at any given point in time. At the First National Congress in January 1924, when the revolutionary system was framed, no one could have predicted the answer to any of these questions. The best party leaders could do, therefore, was strive for maximum flexibility and hope they could respond to challenges as they arose.

The Architecture of Historical Memory

If the leaders of the Nationalist Revolution did possess an elaborate general strategy, they kept it well hidden—and for good reason. Naturally, they would not have wanted revolutionary participants to know where it all would end. Had popular forces guessed that the party would eventually begin acting just like the enemies they had only recently vanquished, motivation and energy would have immediately deflated. Sun first discovered dual-prong tactics in the spring of 1922 when he pitted the Seamen's Union strike against British Hong Kong. Five years later NRA troops suppressed that exact same union because it was protesting anti-agitative measures. In the sociocultural realm, meanwhile, redefined notions of partyization generated the same kind of depoliticizing education for which missionaries and education tyrants *(xuefa)* educators had just recently been attacked. In short, some participating interests found their revolutionary hopes and dreams disappointed.

While very effective at securing power in the short-term, bifurcated nationalism's long-term impact required dexterous handling, particularly within the realm of national memory. Inherent contradictions within the revolutionary movement must have appeared quite unbecoming when the state made ready to partyize historical accounts of the Nationalist Revolution. By definition, a nation's official history or master narrative aims to strengthen unity, obscure differences within the people, enhance loyalty, cement national pride, and legitimize the state—all hallmark features of the "imagined community" pursued by basic state-building. For officials in both the Republic of China and the People's Republic of China, forming a useful version of history that could legitimize state power was easy when dealing with the revolution's laudable achievements: the defeat of warlordism, the capitulation of imperialism, and the unification of China. Accounting for the means by which those triumphs came about, however, was another story. Whether implied or actual, all hint of intrigue, duplicity, deception, misdirection, inconsistency, redirection, exploitation, deceit, or betrayal undermined national legacy because revolutionary leaders did not just manipulate warlord and imperialist enemies. They played and betrayed revolutionary organizations, the "people" of China, and nationalistic movements (i.e., the Anti-British Boycott and the Anti-Christian Movement) as well.

Official memory, as presented through the master narratives of both the ROC and PRC, therefore, came to reflect the political dynamics of China's subsequent political order. The best way to obscure unpleasant revolutionary inconsistencies and sordid manipulation of the "people" was to deflect attention to a narrative not less encumbered with intrigue, but one featuring a conflict that authorities were eager to acknowledge, one wherein the villains—be they communists or reactionaries—continued to serve as a vivid enemy "other." The results were impressive. Official history in both the ROC and PRC not only justified state suppression of "communists" or "class enemies," respectively, it simultaneously laid all blame for the revolution's sticky inconsistencies at their feet. Blaming the other as the source of all intrigue, deception, and machination, both the GMD and CCP could drape their own legacy of participation in a cloak of undefiled purity.

By the time partyizing editors were finished and the final cut readied, the state's portrayal of the Nationalist Revolution showed it surging ahead under the guidance of whitewashed heroes, such as Sun Yat-sen, in spite of traitorous "false revolutionaries" who sought their own selfish designs. In the end, the revolution itself came out portrayed as a natural, predestined extension of popular anti-warlord and anti-imperialist nationalism, stopped short of full success by the "traitor Chiang Kai-shek" *(Jiangzei)* or "communist bandits" *(gongfei)*, depending whether one was reading the official PRC or the ROC version. Left out was any mention of Borodin's state-building efforts, the selectivity of revolutionary anti-imperialism, CEC efforts to mollify foreigners, early regime limits on popular forces, Chiang Kai-shek's "ultra-red" support of agitation, CCP/GMD cooperation within the CEC, and so forth.

The issue here is not whether the faction-centered paradigm is sufficiently objective or accurate, but where historical focus has been directed. Factional discord certainly characterized the Nationalist Revolution. For decades, assumptions driving faction-based interpretations have allowed scholars to explore and identify fundamental tensions dividing revolutionary ranks. These presumptions were not arbitrary but derived from *real politick* examples of GMD/CCP that continued to mount throughout the twentieth century. Driving official history, they also helped cement popular nationalism in both the PRC and ROC and produced standardized typologies, labels, and classifications describing how individual figures fit in tidy historical narratives. At the same time, however, official histories also allowed a relatively minor subplot to overshadow the larger picture of the Nationalist Revolution. During the 1920s, compared to the sweeping changes associated with the Guomindang's digestion and incorporation of non-revolutionary interests and the impossible drive toward China's reunification and independence, factional tensions seemed trivial. Embalmed by official memory, however, the inner dynamics of Chinese nationalism became off-limits. Interparty bickering stole the limelight from the revolution itself and rendered it insignificant or worse.[12] Like all other elements that had outlived their usefulness, memory of the tactics and systems by which the Nationalist Revolution garnered success was also purged.

---

12. Harold Isaacs called it a "tragedy." See Isaacs, *The Tragedy of the Chinese Revolution.*

Glossary

Anhui 安徽
Anqing 案慶

ba dang fangzai guoshang 把黨放在國
  上
Bai Chongxi 白崇禧
ban zhimindi zhi diwei 半殖民地之地位
Baodingfu 保定府
baofu 報復
baoweiju 保衛局
baoweituan 保衛團
Beihai 北海
Beijing 北京
Beiyang 北洋
bendihua 本地化
biaozhun 標準
buliang fenzi 不良份子
buzhongyao de rangbu 不重要的讓步

Cai Yuanpei 蔡元培
Cai Yichen 蔡以忱
Changde 常德
Changsha 長沙
Changzhou 常州
Chen Bingsheng 陳炳生
Chen Bolin, See Chen Lianbo
Chen Duxiu 陳獨秀
Chen Gongbo 陳公博
Chen Guofu 陳果夫
Chen Jiongming 陳炯明
Chen Lianbo 陳聯伯
Chen Qitian 陳啓天

Chen Qiyuan 陳其瑗
Chen Shuren 陳樹人
Chen Tiaoyuan 陳調元
Chen Youren (Eugene Chen) 陳友仁
Cheng Jingyi 誠靜怡
Chengdu 成都
Chenghai 澄海
chengyi 誠意
chihua 赤化
Chongqing 重慶
chubu 處部
chufenbu 處分部
chunxi wudang tongzhi 純係吾黨同志
cuican Zhongguo minzhong 摧殘中國民
  眾
cuowu 錯誤

da chongtu 大衝突
da de gongxiao 大的功效
Da Mingguo 大明國
Da Qingguo 大清國
Dai Jitao 戴季陶
Dalian 大連
dang de yizhi 黨的意志
dang xuexiao 黨學校
dang zhi jingshen de zhongxin 黨之精神
  的中心
dang zhuyi zhi daoshi 擋主義之道師
dangbu 黨部
danggang 黨綱
danghua 黨化
dangtuan 黨團

291

dangyi 黨義
dangyi puji 黨義普及
dangzei 黨賊
dangzhang 黨章
Daxue 大學
dayuanshuai 大元帥
Deng Xiaoping 鄧小平
Deng Yanda 鄧演達
Dong Weijian 董維鍵
Dongguan 東莞
Dongnan 東南
Dongshan 東山
dongyao bendang zhi jichu 動搖本黨之
　基礎
Duan Qirui 段祺瑞
duban 督辦
dui 隊

fan geming 反革命
*fan geming jia geming bu geming zhong-
　zhong fenzi* 反革命假革命不革命種
　種分子
Fan Jidujiao tongmeng 反基督教同盟
Fan Shisheng 范石生
Fan Yuanlian 范源廉
fandong 反動
fandui Jidujiao 反對基督教
Fei Jidujiao 非基督教
feichang da zongtong 非常大總統
Feng Yuxiang 馮玉祥
fengchao 風潮
fengjian 封建
Fengtian 奉天
Foshan 佛山
Fu Bingchang 傅秉常
Fujian 福建
fulao xiongdi 父老兄弟
Fuzhou 福州

Gan Naiguang 甘乃光
Ganzhou 贛州
Gao Erbo 高爾柏

*Geming de chenggong yao kao minzhong
　de liliang* 革命的成功要靠民眾的力
　量
Geming qingnian 革命青年
Gemingdang 革命黨
geminghua 革命化
geren ducai 個人獨裁
geren yizhi 個人意志
*gongchan fenzi tuhao lieshen tanguan
　wuli touji fenzi ji yiqie fuhua ehua fenzi*
　共產份子土豪劣紳貪官污吏投機份
　子及一切腐化惡化份子
Gongchandang 共產黨
gongfei 共匪
gonghui 工會
gongtuan 工團
Gongyi (Kong Yee) 公醫
Gongyi (Taishan) 公益
Gu Mengyu 顧孟餘
Gu Weijun (Wellington Koo) 顧維鈞
Guangdong 廣東
Guanghua 光華
Guangning 廣寧
Guangxi 廣西
Guangzhou 廣州
Guangzhou renmin ribao 廣州人民日報
guanliao 官僚
Guilin 桂林
Guizhou 貴州
Guling 牯嶺
guo 國
guofu 國父
guojia 國家
Guojia zhuyi pai 國家主義派
guomin 國民
Guomin xinwen 國民新聞
guomin xuexiao 國民學校
Guomindang 國民黨
Guomindang tongzhi jülebu 國民黨同
　志俱樂部
guxi 姑息
guzhi 姑置

Haifeng 海豐
Hainan 海南
Han 漢
Hangzhou 杭州
Hankou 漢口
Hanren 漢人
Hanyang 漢陽
Harbin 哈爾濱
He Xiangning 何香凝
He Yaozu 賀耀祖
He Yingqin 何應欽
Henan (island) 河南
Henan (province) 河南
Heping huiyi pai 和平會議派
houdun 後盾
houshe yu zhuaya 喉舌與爪牙
Hu Hanmin 胡漢民
Hu Shi 胡適
Hua Ying (Wah Ying) 華英
huan bu jiji de 緩不濟急的
Huang Renjun 黃仁君
Huang Xing 黃興
Huanggang 黃岡
Huangpo 黃坡
Huangpu 黃埔
Huangshi 黃石
Huazhou 化州
Huazi ribao 華字日報
Hubei 湖北
Huifeng 匯豐
Humen (Bocca Tigris) 虎門
Hunan 湖南
hunmi 昏迷
hunyong laoxiu fenzi 昏庸老朽份子
huzun 互尊

Jiang Menglin 蔣夢麟
Jiang Yongjing 蔣永敬
Jiang Zuobin 蔣作賓
Jiangmen 江門
Jiangnan 江南
Jiangsu 江蘇

Jianguo 建國
Jianguo lianjun 建國聯軍
Jiangxi 江西
Jiangzei 蔣賊
jianshe guojia 建設國家
jiaoyu ji xunlian 教育及訓練
Jiaoyu zazhi 教育雜誌
Jidujiao 基督教
jifen shili 幾份勢力
Jimei 集美
Jin Yun'e 靳雲鶚
Jinan 濟南
Jiujiang (Guangdong) 九江
Jiujiang (Jiangxi) 九江
Jiulong 九龍
juewu 覺悟
juexing 覺醒
junfa 軍閥
junxian 郡縣

Kaifeng 開封
kaobuzhu de 靠不住的
kejun 客軍
Kong Xiangxi (H.H. Kung) 孔祥熙

laojia 老家
li 禮
Li Chunfan 李春蕃
Li Fulin 李福林
Li Huang 李璜
Li Jishen 李濟深
Li Yinglin (Y. L. Lee) 李應林
Li Yuanhong 黎元洪
Li Yunhan 李雲漢
Liang Qichao 梁啟超
Liang Shuming 梁漱溟
Liansheng zizhi pai 廉省自治派
Liao Zhongkai 廖仲凱
lijin 厘金
Liling 醴陵
Lin Yutang 林語堂
Lingnan 嶺南

Liu Xiang 劉湘
Liu Zhan'en 劉湛恩
Liu Zhenhuan 劉震寰
Liuyang 瀏陽
Lixian pai 立憲派
Longzhou 龍州
Lu Rongting 陸榮廷
Lufeng 陸豐
Luogang 蘿崗
Lushan 廬山

maiban 賣辦
maiguo wangmin 賣國罔民
Mao Zedong 毛澤東
mazui 麻醉
Meixian 梅縣
mimi shiqi 秘密時期
Ming 明
Minguo ribao 民國日報
mintuan 民團
Minzhong chuli, zhengfu zhidao 民眾出力, 政府指導
mixin 迷信
mu 畝

Nanchang 南昌
Nanguan 南關
Nanhua 南華
Nanjing 南京
Nankai 南開
Nanning 南寧
Nantong 南通
Nanxian 南縣
Nanyang 南洋
Ningbo 寧波
nongmin xiehui 農明協會
nongtuan 農團
nuchao 怒潮
nuli jiaoyu 奴隸教育

Pei Ying (Pui Ying) 培英
Peng Pai 彭湃

Peng Zemin 彭澤民
pingmin 平民
pingminhua 平民化
pingtianxia 平天下
pouxin geshang 剖心割傷
pubian de xuanchuan 普遍的宣傳
Pukou 浦口

Qianshan 前山
Qiaokou 橋口
qieyao 切要
qijia 齊家
Qing 清
qingdang 清黨
Qingdao 青島

raoluan pohuai zhi yinmou 擾亂破壞之陰謀
renge de mofan 人格的模範
Renji (Yan Chai) 仁濟

sanda zhengce 三大政策
sanman 散漫
Sanmin zhuyi 三民主義
Sanshui 三水
Shaanxi 陝西
Shaji 沙基
Shamian 沙面
shanchu 芟除
Shandong 山東
Shanghai 上海
Shangren zhengfu pai 商人政府派
shangtuan 商團
Shantou 汕頭
Shanxi 山西
Shaoguan 韶關
Shaoxing 紹興
Shenyang 瀋陽
Shi Zhaoji (Alfred Sze) 施肇基
Shiqi 石岐
shouxiao bu shenda 收效不甚大
Shuangshijie 雙十節

Shunde 順德

Sichuan 四川

sili 私立

sishu 私塾

Song Qingling (Madame Sun Yat-sen)
宋慶齡

Song Ziwen (T. V. Soong) 宋子文

Su Zhaozheng 蘇兆徵

Sue zhi gongju 蘇俄之工具

Sun Chuanfang 孫傳芳

Sun Ke 孫科

Sun Wen zhuyi xuehui 孫文主義學會

Suzhou 蘇州

Taibei 台北

Taiping 太平

Taishan 泰山

Taiwan 台灣

Taiyuan 太原

Tan Pingshan 譚平山

Tan Yankai 譚延闓

Tang 唐

Tang Gongxian 唐公憲

Tang Jiyao 唐紀堯

Tang Shaoyi 唐紹儀

Tang Shengzhi 唐生智

Tangren 唐人

Tao Xingzhi 陶行知

tepaiyuan 特派員

Tianjin 天津

tianxia 天下

Tianzhujiao 天主教

Tong'an 同安

Tongmenghui 同盟會

tuan 團

tuanfangju 團防局

tuhao 土豪

tuidao xuefa 推倒學閥

tushen touji fenzi 土紳投機份子

tusi goupeng 兔死狗烹

Wang Jingwei 汪精衛

Wang Pu 王普

Wang Zhengting (C.T. Wang) 王正廷

Wanguo ribao 萬國日報

Wanxian 萬縣

wei 偽

Wei Que (Sidney Kok Wei) 韋慤

Wen Hua 文化

Wenzhou 溫州

Wu Chaogang (C. C. Wu) 伍朝樞

Wu Peifu 吳佩孚

Wu Tiecheng 吳鐵城

Wu Tingfang 伍廷芳

Wu Zhenchun 吳震春

Wu Zhihui 吳稚暉

Wuchang 武昌

Wuhan 武漢

Wuhan pinglun 武漢評論

Wuhu 蕪湖

Wujingfu 五經富

wujuewu 無覺悟

wuli de lueduo yu jingji de yapo 武力的
掠奪與經濟的壓迫

Wusong 吳淞

Wuzhou 五洲

Xiamen 廈門

Xi'an 西安

xiang 鄉

Xiangdao zhoubao 向導週報

Xiangshan 香山

Xiangtan 湘潭

Xiangyang 襄陽

Xiao Yaonan 蕭耀南

Xiaolan 小欖

Xiaoyu shangtuan wufu he panni 曉諭商
團勿附和叛逆

xieshang 協商

Xiguan 西關

Xin jiaoyu 新教育

Xingshi zhoubao 醒獅週報

Xinhui 新會

xiushen 修身

xiuyang shengxi 休養生息

Xiwan 西灣
Xu Chongqing 許崇清
Xu Chongzhi 許崇智
Xu Hengyao 徐恆耀
Xu Qian 徐謙
Xu Shiying 許世英
xuefa 學閥
xuehui 學會
xunhui jiaoshou 巡迴教授
Xuzhou 徐州

Yadong 亞東
Yan Xishan 閻錫山
Yan Yangchu (James Yen) 晏陽初
Yancheng 鹽城
Yang Sen 楊森
Yang Ximin 楊希閔
yangnu 洋奴
Yangzi 揚子
Yanjing 燕京
Yanmi de qunzhong jilü 嚴密的群眾紀律
yanzhong chufa 嚴重處罰
Yanzhou 兗州
yaoluan 淆亂
Ye Ju 葉舉
Yichang 宜昌
yilü fenhui 一律焚燬
yilü jinshou 一律禁售,
yixing nanzhi 易行難知
Yiyang 益陽
yizhi er jizhong 一致而集中
yizhi nanxing 易知難行
you minzhong tichu yaoqiu 由民眾提出要求
you renmin 由人民
youjian shangfei 有奸商匪
Yuan Shikai 袁世凱
Yuezhou 岳州
Yunnan 雲南
zaisuo bichu 在所必除
Zeng Qi 曾琦

Zhabei 閘北
zhandou 戰鬥
Zhang Qiuren 張秋人
Zhang Renjie 張人傑
Zhang Shizhao 章士釗
Zhang Taiyan 章太炎
Zhang Zongchang 張宗昌
Zhang Zuolin 張作霖
Zhao Hengti 趙恆惕
Zhao Renchang 趙仁長
Zhejiang 浙江
zhengfu 政府
Zhengfu yu minzhong hezuo 政府與民眾合作
zhengquan 政權
zhengxin 正心
zhengzheng huopin 政爭貨品
zhengzhi shang zhi qinlue 政治上之侵略
zhengzhi xunlian 政治訓練
Zhengzhi zhoubao 政治週報
Zhengzhou 鄭州
Zhenli 真理
zhenzheng de ziyou yu duli 真正的自由與獨立
zhiguo 治國
Zhili 直隸
Zhong Rongguang 鐘榮光
Zhongguo guojia zhuyi qingnian tuan 中國國家主義青年團
Zhongguo nongmin 中國農民
Zhongguo qingnian 中國青年
Zhongguo qingnian dang 中國青年黨
Zhonghua jiaoyu jie 中華教育界
Zhongshan 中山
Zhongyang 中央
Zhou Enlai 周恩來
Zhou Yinren 周蔭人
Zhu Naibin 朱乃斌
ziyou ji quanli 自由及權利
zongjiao zhi xuanchuan 宗教之宣傳
zongli 總理

zongli zhi 總理制
zongzhang 總章
Zou Lu 鄒魯
zu 組
zui jijin 最急進
zui zhongyao zhiwu 最重要職務
zuihou shengli 最後勝利
zuihui guo 最惠國

References

Archival Materials

Guangzhou he Hankou guomin zhengfu 廣州和漢口國民政府. Fifteen microfilm reels. Zhongguo dier lishi dang'an guan. 中國第二歷史檔案館. Nanjing, China, 1986. [Abbreviated *GHGZ*.]

Guomin zhengfu dang'an 國民政府檔案. Guoshiguan 國史館. Taipei, Taiwan. [Abbreviated *GZD*.]

Zhongyang diyi, erji zhixing weiyuan dang'an 中央第一, 二屆執行委員檔案. Zhongguo Guomindang zhongyang weiyuanhui dangshi weiyuanhui 國民黨中央委員會黨史委員會. Taipei, Taiwan. [Abbreviated *ZXWD*.]

Zhongyang qian wubu dang'an 中央前五部檔案. Guomindang zhongyang weiyuanhui dangshi weiyuanhui 國民黨中央委員會黨史委員會. Taipei, Taiwan. [Abbreviated *QWBD*.]

Zhongyang zhengzhi huiyi dang'an 中央政治會議檔案. Guomindang zhongyang weiyuanhui dangshi weiyuanhui 國民黨中央委員會黨史委員會. Taipei, Taiwan.

Chinese Language Materials

"Anhui sheng linshi sheng dangbu baogao (siwuyuefen) 安徽省臨時省黨部報告 (四五月份)." May 31, 1926. *QWBD* 11155.

"Anmin gaoshi 安民告示." In *Chen Jiongming ji*, eds. Duan Yunzhang and Ni Junming, 500. Guangzhou: Zhongshan Daxue chubanshe, 1998.

"Baohu waiqiao ji jiaohui zhi gaowen 保護外僑及教會之告文." *Zhenguang zazhi* 26.4 (April 1927): 73.

"Beifa qingnian gongzuotuan zuzhi dagang 北伐青年工作團組織大綱." 1927. *QWBD* 1804.

Beifa tongyi liushi zhounian xueshu taolun ji 北伐統一六十周年學術討論集. Taipei: Beifa tongyi liushi zhounian xueshu taolun jibianji weiyuanhui, 1988.

"Beijing jiaoyubu bugao dishiliu hao 北京教育部佈告第十六號." In *Guonei jinshinian lai zhi zongjiao sichao*, comp. Zhang Qinshi, 370-371.

Beijing: Yenching School of Chinese Studies, 1927.

"Beijing Zhongguo Jidutu Hu'an houyuanhui xuanyan 北京中國基督徒滬案後援會宣言." *Shengming yuekan* V-9 (July 1925): 35.

"Bendang ge zhixingbu difang dangbu duiwai taidu wenti an 本黨各執行部地方黨部對外態度問題案." *Geming wenxian*, vol. 79, pp. 14-15.

"Bendang muqian zhengce zhi xuanchuan dagang 本黨目前政策之宣傳大綱." *1-ZXWH*, vol. 5 (July 23, 1925). *ZXWD* 1.3/2.5.

"Benhui jingguo gaikuang 本會經過概況." *2-ZWQH*. Hankou: March 1927. *ZXWD* 2.4/9.1.

Cai Yuanpei 蔡元培. "Beijing feizongjiao dahui yanjiang zhi yi 北京非宗教大會演講之一." In *Guonei jinshinian lai zhi zongjiao sichao*, comp. Zhang Qinshi, 199-201. Beijing: Yenching School of Chinese Studies, 1927.

Chen Gongbo 陳公博. "Chen Gongbo tongzhi Jiangxi zhengwu baogao 陳公博同志江西政務報告." *ZGLH*, vol. 1. Hankou: December 17, 1926. *ZXWD* 2.4/1.1.

_____. "Chen Gongbo tongzhi waijiao caizheng baogao 陳公博同志外交財政報告." *ZGLH*, vol. 1. Hankou: December 17, 1926. *ZXWD* 2.4/1.1.

_____. *Han feng ji* 寒風紀. Shanghai: Association of Local Government, 1945. Reprinted in *Minguo congshu* 民國叢書, vol. 99, part 1. Shanghai: Shanghai shudian, 1989.

_____. "Zhongyang dangbu qingnian yundong baogao 中央黨部青年運動報告." 1926. *QWBD* 10730-1.

Chen Dingyan 陳定炎. *Chen Jingcun (Jiongming) xiansheng nianpu* 陳競存 (炯明) 先生年譜. 2 volumes. Hong Kong: Guiguan tushu gongsi, 1995.

"Chouban shangmin yundong jiangxisuo yijianshu 籌辦商民運動講習所意見書." *1-ZXWH*, vol. 5 (July 23, 1925). *ZXWD* 1.3/2.5.

"Chuban ji xuanchuan wenti an 出版及宣傳問題案." *Geming wenxian*, vol. 76, pp. 13-14.

"Dangtuan ganshi weiyuan zhixing weiyuan huiyi shixiang 黨團幹事委員執行委員會議事項." August 5, 1926. *QWBD* 10457.

"Dangzei Kang Zhunian cansha xunxing qunzhong canju 黨賊康祝年殘殺巡行群眾慘劇." Issued by the Yingde student federation. December 1926. *QWBD* 6673.

"Dangzei Kang Zhunian Tan Yaoming Hu Xingqun shida zuizhuang 黨賊康祝年譚耀明胡醒群十大罪狀." Issued by the Yingde student federation. December 1, 1926. *QWBD* 6675.

Deng Zhongxia 鄧中夏. *Zhongguo zhi gong yundong jianshi, 1919-1926* 中國職工運動簡史, 1919-1926. Beijing: Renmin chubanshe, 1953.

"Dierjie zhongyang zhixing weiyuan disanci quanti huiyi dui quanti dangyuan xunling 第二屆中央執行委員第三次全體會議對全體黨員訓

令." *2-ZWQH*. Hankou: March 1927. *ZXWD* 2.4/9.1.

"Diyici quanguo daibiao dahui tongguo Zhongguo Guomindang zongzhang 第一次全國代表大會通過中國國民黨總章." *Geming wenxian*, vol. 70, pp. 47-48.

"Diyici quanguo daibiao dahui xuanyanzhong zhi Guomindang zhenggang 第一次全國代表大會宣言中之國民黨政綱." *Geming wenxian*, vol. 70, p. 383.

Dongfang zazhi 東方雜誌. Beijing.

Duan Yunzhang 段云章 and Ni Junming 倪俊明, eds. *Chen Jiongming ji* 陳炯明集. Guangzhou: Zhongshan Daxue chubanshe, 1998.

"Duiyu nongmin yundong zhi xuanyan 對於農民運動之宣言." *1-ZXWH*, vol. 2 (June 19, 1924). *ZXWD* 1.3/2.2.

"Fan diguozhuyi yu feichu bupingdeng tiaoyue zhi yundong 反帝國主義與廢除不平等條約之運動." *Dongfang zazhi* 22:6 (August 1924): 127-141.

"Fandui diguozhuyi ganshe wuguo neizheng zhi xuanyan 反對帝國主義干涉吾國內政之宣言." *Geming wenxian*, vol. 69, pp. 109-111.

"Foshanshu Nanpu nongtuan chengli zhuangkuang 佛山屬南浦農團成立狀況." *1-ZXWH*, vol. 2 (June 2, 1924). *ZXWD* 1.3/2.2.

"Fujian geming tongzhi qingniantuan zhi zhongyang qingnianbu han 福建革命同志青年團致中央青年部函." May 13, 1926. *QWBD* 1184.1.

"Fujian geming tongzhi qingniantuan zhi zhongyang qingnianbu han 福建革命同志青年團致中央青年部函." May 1926. *QWBD* 1184.2.

"Fujian Tong'anxian dangbu qingnianbu zhuren shang zhongyang qing-nianbu han 福建同安縣黨部青年部主任上中央青年部函." June 9, 1926. *QWBD* 11659.

"Fujian wenti an 福建問題案." *ZGLH*, vol. 1. Hankou: December 22, 1926. *ZXWD* 2.4/1.1.

"Gan Naiguang deng tichu guanyu mintuan wenti jueyi cao'an 甘乃光等提出關於民團問題決議草案." *ZWDL-YS* (October 28, 1926).

"Gao yue fulao xiongdi shu 告粵父老兄弟書." In *Chen Jiongming ji*, eds. Duan Yunzhang and Ni Junming, 504-505. Guangzhou: Zhongshan daxue chubanshe, 1998.

Geming wenxian 革命文獻. Continuing multi-volume series. Taipei: Zhongguo Guomindang dangshi weiyuanhui, 1973-.

"Gesheng dangwu jinxing jihua jueyian 各省黨務進行計畫決議案." *Geming wenxian*, vol. 79, pp. 7-8.

"Gesheng shixian xuesheng lianhehui zuzhi yilan biao 各省市縣學生聯合會組織一覽表." Compiled by the Organization Ministry. 1927. *QWBD* 12357.

"Gonganju Zhang juzhang baogao 公安局張局長報告." *ZGLH*, vol. 2.

Hankou: January 3, 1927. *ZXWD* 2.4/1.2.

"Gonghui fa cao'an 工會法草案." *1-ZXWH*, vol. 3 (August 7, 1924). *ZXWD* 1.3/2.3.

"Gongren daibiao dahui kaihui jingguo baogao 工人代表大會開會經過報告." *1-ZXWH*, vol. 2 (May 12, 1924). *ZXWD* 1.3/2.2.

"Gongren yundong jihua cao'an 工人運動計畫草案." Shanghai, 1926. *ZXWD* 2.5/5.5.

Guangdong daxue jieshou gongyi xuexiao jingguo qingxing 廣東大學接收公醫學校經過情形. *GHGZ* 19:275, July 1925-August 1926.

Guangdong dazhong xuexiao qiu li'an 廣東大中學校求立案. *GHGZ* 19:274, September 1925-October 1926.

"Guangdong dubo zhanxing zhizui zhangcheng 廣東賭博暫行治罪章程." In *Chen Jiongming ji*, eds. Duan Yunzhang and Ni Junming, 521. Guangzhou: Zhongshan Daxue chubanshe, 1998.

"Guangdong gedi xuesheng daibiao lianhehui shang zhongyang dangbu deng daidian 廣東各地學生代表聯合會上中央黨部等代電." April 23, 1926. *QWBD* 7830.

"Guangdong quansheng xuesheng lianhehui changwu weiyuanhui shang zhongyang qingnianbu han 廣東全省學生聯合會常務委員會上中央青年部函." August 22, 1926. *QWBD* 13760.

"Guangdong quansheng xuesheng lianhehui daibiao dahui duiyu pohuai xuesheng tongyi yundong de fandong fenzi xuanyan 廣東全省學生聯合會代表大會對於破壞學生統一運動的反動份子宣言." April 15, 1926. *QWBD* 12781.

"Guangdong shengli diyi zhongxuexiao xueshenghui zhongyao qishi 廣東省立第一中學校學生會重要啓事." December 19, 1924. *QWBD* 1050.

"Guangdong shengli nüzi shifan xuexiao gexin xueshenghui tongmenghui jieshu xuanyan 廣東省立女子師範學校革新學生會同盟會結束宣言." Guangzhou, 1926. *QWBD* 1065.

"Guangdong xinxueshengshe deng shang zongli deng daidian 廣東新學生社等上總理等代電." October 29, 1924. *QWBD* 13235.

"Guangdong xuesheng lianhehui shang zhongyang zhixing weiyuanhui cheng 廣東學生聯合會上中央執行委員會呈." May 1926. *QWBD* 7835.

"Guangdong Zhonghua jidutu jiuguo dalianhehui shang zhongyang gon-grenbu daidian 廣東中華基督徒救國大聯會上中央工人部代電." June 26, 1925. *QWBD* 13138.

Guangxi shengli dier zhongxuexiao xueshenghui fandui Wuzhou fayuan yazhi xuesheng yundong qingxing 廣西省立第二中學校學生會反對梧州法院壓制學生運動情形. *GHGZ* 19:239, August-September, 1926.

"Guangxisheng qingnianbu shang zhongyang qingnianbu cheng 廣西省青年

部上中央青年部呈." January 14, 1927. *QWBD* 11122.

"Guangzhou gexiao yilan biao 廣州各校一覽表." Compiled by the Youth Ministry. 1924. *QWBD* 12580.

"Guangzhou jingcha tebie dangbu zhuansong gefenbu jianyi chengban Shen Hongci an 廣州警察特別黨部轉送各分部建議懲辦沈鴻慈案." *ZWDL-YS* (October 28, 1926).

"Guangzhou lingnan daxue diaocha biao 廣州嶺南大學調查表." Compiled by the Youth Ministry. October 7 and 10, 1924. *QWBD* 12569.

"Guangzhou lingnan daxue gongren shenghuo zhi diaocha 廣州嶺南大學工人生活之調查." 1926. *QWBD* 12504.

"Guangzhou lingnan daxue quanti xuesheng wei qingchu buliang fenzi xuanyan 廣州嶺南大學全體學生為清除不良份子宣言." April 6, 1926. *QWBD* 7753.

"Guangzhou 'shengsanyi' xuesheng tuixue xuanyan! 廣州 '聖三一' 學生退學宣言!" May 20, 1924. *QWBD* 13174.

"Guangzhou shi jiaoyuju zhi zhongyang qingnianbu han 廣州市教育局致中央青年部函." February 7, 1925. QWBD 12049.

"Guangzhou tebieshi zhixing weiyuanhui qingnianbu eryuefen gongzuo jinguo baogao 廣州特別市執行委員會青年部二月份工作進過報告." March-April, 1926. *QWBD* 11119.

"Guangzhou xuelianhui zhixing weiyuanhui dierci changhui jilu 廣州學聯會執行委員會第二次常會紀錄." July 11, 1926. *QWBD* 4616.

"Guangzhou xuesheng lianhehui daibiao dahui zhongyao xuanyan 廣州學生聯合會代表大會重要宣言." April 11, 1926. *QWBD* 7856.

"Guangzhou xuesheng lianhehui gaizu xuanyan 廣州學生聯合會改組宣言." April 1924. *QWBD* 1049.

"Guangzhou xuesheng lianhehui shang zhongyang qingnianbu cheng 廣州學生聯合會上中央青年部呈." April 14, 1926. *QWBD* 3008.

"Guangzhou xuesheng lianhehui zhixing weiyuanhui dishisici changhui jilu 廣州學生聯合會執行委員會第十四辭呈會紀錄." October 16, 1926. *QWBD* 4617.

"Guangzhoushi diyiqi chouban yiwu jiaoyu jihua shu 廣州市第一期籌辦義務教育計畫書." In *Yisui zhi Guangzhoushi*, comp. Huang Yanpei, 70-75. Shanghai: Commercial Press, 1922.

"Guangzhoushi shixing yiwu jiaoyu zhanxing guicheng 廣州市實行義務教育暫行規程." In *Yisui zhi Guangzhoushi*, comp. Huang Yanpei, 65-70. Shanghai: Commercial Press, 1922.

"Guangzhoushi xuesheng tongyi yundong jueyian 廣州市學生統一運動決議案." *1-ZXWH*, vol. 1 (March 12, 1924). ZXWD 1.3/2.1.

"Guanyu Guomindang yu Jidujiao di taolun 關於國民黨與基督教的討論." *Shengming* (January 1926): 1-2.

"Guanyu jiancha weiyuanhui zhi jueyian 關於監察委員會之決議案." *Geming wenxian*, vol. 79, p. 3.

"Guanyu mintuan wenti jueyian 關於民團問題決議案." In *Zhongguo Guomindang zhongyang weiyuan gesheng getebie qushi haiwai gezong zhibu daibiao lianxi huiyi xuanyan ji jueyian*, 40-41. Guangzhou: Zhongyang zhixing weiyuanhui, November 1926.

"Guanyu qingnian yundong jueyian 關於青年運動決議案," *J3QD* (n.d., early 1927). *ZXWD* 2.3/121.

Guanyu Yue Gui liangdi xuexiao xuesheng bake shijian yijiao jiaoyu xingzheng weiyuanhui banli zhi wenshu 關於粵桂兩地學校學生罷課事件議交教育行政委員會辦理之文書. *GHGZ* 19:240, April, 1926.

Guanyu zhengshou lijuan yanxijuan fangzujuan ji zhulujuan gexiang faling 關於征收釐捐筵席捐房租捐及築路捐各項法令. *GHGZ* 19:263, April 21, 1926.

"Guiding bendang zhi gongren zuzhi zhengce ji ci zhengce duiyu zhengfu zhi guanxi an 規定本黨之工人組織政策及此政策對於政府之關係案." *1-ZXWH*, vol. 2 (June 2, 1924). *ZXWD* 1.3/2.2.

Guofu quanji 國父全集. Three volumes. Zhonghua Minguo gejie jinian guofu bainian danchen zhoubei weiyuanhui, 1965.

"Guoli zhongshan daxue gongye zhuanmenbu xueshenghui quzhu Xiao Guanying xuanyan 國立中山大學工業專門部學生會驅逐蕭冠英宣言." October 27, 1926. *QWBD* 12783.

"Guomindang de zuixin zhenggang 國民黨的最新政綱." *ZWDL-YS* (October 22, 1926).

"Guomindang shixing dangjiaoyu zhengce 國民黨實行黨教育政策." *Jiaoyu zazhi* 17: 2 (February 1925): 16.

"Guomindang zhengzhi xuanchuan weiyuanhui tebie xuanchuanban kemu biao 國民黨政治宣傳委員會特別宣傳班科目表." *1-ZXWH*, vol. 5 (October 8, 1925). *ZXWD* 1.3/2.5.

"Guomin zhengfuxia zhi Esheng jiaoyu 國民政府下之鄂省教育." *Jiaoyu zazhi* 18:12 (December, 1926): 3.

"Guomin zhengfuxia zhi Hunan quansheng jiaoyu jihua 國民政府下之湖南全省教育計畫." *Jiaoyu zazhi* 18:10 (October, 1926): 2.

"Guomin zhengfuxia zhi jiaoyu xingzheng huiyi 國民政府下之教育行政會議." *Jiaoyu zazhi* 18:8 (August 1926): 5.

"Hangzhou zhongdeng yishang xuexiao zuzhi biao 杭州中等以上學校組織表." 1927. *QWBD* 1188.

Hankou Jiujiang Yingzujie shouhui 漢口九江英租界收回. *GZD* 165:1404-1429.

"Hankou nonggong shangxue gejie daibiao lianxi huiyi jinji huiyi dui Yingzhengfu zhi jiangyuan tiaowen 漢口農工商學各界代表聯席會議

緊急會議對英政府之講願條文." *ZGLH*. Hankou: January 3, 1927. *ZXWD* 2.4/3.1.

He Rizhang 何日章, ed. *Zhongguo tushu shijin fenleifa* 中國圖書十進分類法. Fourteenth edition. Taipei: Shijie shuju jingshou, 1972.

"Heyuan xuesheng lianhehui gaizu chengli xuanyan 河源學生聯合會改組成立宣言." October 16, 1926. *QWBD* 1064.

"Hongying xueshenghui gaizu diyici quanti dahui gexin xiaowu xuanyan 宏英學生會改組第一次全體大會革新校務宣言." September 11, 1926. *QWBD* 13177.

"Hu jianguo xuanchuan xuexiao xiaozhang shang zhongyang qingnianbu cheng 滬建國宣傳學校校長上中央青年部呈." October 13, 1927. *QWBD* 11665.

Huang Yanpei 黃炎培. *Yisui zhi Guangzhoushi* 一歲之廣州市. Second edition. Shanghai: Commercial Press, 1922.

Huazi ribao 華字日報. Hong Kong.

Hubei geming lishi wenjian huiji 湖北革命歷史文件彙集. Eleven volumes. Changsha: Hubei renmin chubanshe, 1985-1987. [Abbreviated *HGLW*.]

"Hubei jiaoyu baogao 湖北教育報告." *ZGLH*, vol. 1. Hankou: December 22, 1926. *ZXWD* 2.4/1.1.

"Hubei shengdangbu yinianban jingguo gaikuan 湖北省黨部一年半經過概況." *1-ZXWH*, vol. 5 (November 6, 1925). *ZXWD* 1.3/2.5.

"Hubei zhengwu baogao 湖北政務報告." *ZGLH*, vol. 1. Hankou: December 17, 1926. *ZXWD* 2.4/1.1.

Hunan Changdeshi dangbu zhiweihui Chen Baoxiang ershifan can'an zhenxiang 湖南常德市黨部執委會陳報湘二師範慘案真象. *GHGZ* 19:241, April 1926.

Jiang Yongjing 蔣永敬. *Baoluoting yu Wuhan zhengquan* 鮑羅廷與武漢政權. Taipei: Chuanji wenxue chubanshe, 1963.

_____. "Lun beifa shiqi de yige kouhao: 'Sanda zhengce' 論北伐時期的一個口號: '三大政策'." In *Beifa tongyi liushi zhounian xueshu taolun ji*, 438-454. Taipei: Beifa tongyi liushi zhounian xueshu taolun jibianji weiyuanhui, 1988.

Jiang Zhongzheng 蔣中正 [Chiang Kai-shek]. *Sue zai Zhongguo: Zhongguo yu E gong sanshinian jingli jiyao* 蘇俄在中國: 中國與俄共三十年經歷紀要. Reprint edition. Taipei: Zhongyang wenwu gongying she, 1983.

"Jiangsu quansheng xuelianhui gebu gongzuo jihua 江蘇全省學聯會各部工作計畫." 1927. *QWBD* 10456.

"Jiangsusheng qingnianbu siyuefen baogao 江蘇省青年部四月份報告." May 1926. *QWBD* 11147.

"Jianyi Dayuanshuai pixing nongmin xiehui zhangcheng gongwen 建議大元帥批行農民協會章程公文." *1-ZXWH*, vol. 2 (June 16, 1924). *ZXWD*

1.3/2.2.

"Jiaobu duiyu sili daxue zhi qudi 教部對於私立大學之取締." *Jiaoyu zazhi* 17: 11 (November 1925): 5.

Jiaokeshu bianshen weiyuanhui zhangcheng 教科書編審委員會章程, *GHGZ* 19:270, April-October, 1926.

Jiaoyu zazhi 教育雜誌. Shanghai.

Jiaoyuhui fa an 教育會法案. *GZD* 168:895-913.

"Jiaoyuju xunhui jiaoshou zhanxing zhangcheng 教育局巡迴教授暫行章程." In *Yisui zhi Guangzhoushi*, comp. Huang Yanpei, 75-79. Shanghai: Commercial Press, 1922.

"Jiaozhong xueshenghui dui Guangzhou xuelianhui fengchao xuanyan 教忠學生會對廣州學聯會風潮宣言." April 16, 1926. *QWBD* 7861.

"Jidujiao jiaoyuhui zhi zhengqiu yijian 基督教教育會之徵求意見." *Jiaoyu zazhi* 18:5 (May, 1926): 6.

"Jidujiao liangguang jinxinhui daibiao dahui xuanyan 基督教兩廣浸信會代表大會宣言." 1925. *QWBD* 12745.

"Jiejue xuechao weiyuanhui zhi Xu Chongqing deng han'gao 解決學潮委員會致許崇清等函稿." November 27, 1926. *QWBD* 1163.2.

"Jiejue xuechao weiyuanhui zhi zhongyang zhengzhi huiyi han'gao 解決學潮委員會致中央政治會議函稿." November 26, 1926. *QWBD* 1162.1.

"Jindu bugao 禁賭布告." In *Chen Jiongming ji*, eds. Duan Yunzhang and Ni Junming, 522. Guangzhou: Zhongshan Daxue chubanshe, 1998.

"Jinzhiwen Wei Tang Liang Liu siwei xuesheng de xuanyan 謹質問韋湯梁劉四位學生的宣言." April 13, 1926. *QWBD* 7857.

"Kaifeng neidihui quanti jiaoyou yin Hu'an yu Yingren wanquan juejiao xinzucheng `Kaifeng Zhonghua Jidujiaohui' zhi xuanyan 開封內地會全體教友因滬案與英人完全絕交新組成 '開封中華基督教會' 之宣言." *Shengming yuekan* V-9 (July 1925): 41-42.

"Laozi wenti baogao 勞資問題報告." *ZGLH*, vol. 1. Hankou: December 22, 1926. *ZXWD* 2.4/1.1.

Li Wuyun 李午雲 and Li Lisan 李立三. "Dui Ying weiyuanhui daibiao Li Wuyun Li Lisan baogao 對英委員會代表李午雲李立三報告." *ZGLH*, vol. 2. Hankou: January 5, 1927. *ZXWD* 2.4/1.2.

Li Yunhan 李雲漢. *Cong ronggong dao qingdang* 從容共到清黨. Taipei: Zhongguo xueshu zhuzuo jiangzhu weiyuanhui, 1966.

Liang Huijin 梁惠錦. "Beifa qijian Guomindang lingdaoxia de funü yundong 北伐期間國民黨領導下的婦女運動." In *Beifa tongyi liushi zhounian xueshu taolun ji*, 492-514. Taipei: Beifa tongyi liushi zhounian xueshu taolun jibianji weiyuanhui, 1988.

"Liangguang jinxinhui banshisuo zhi zhongyang gongrenbu daidian 兩廣浸信會辦事所致中央工人部代電." June 6, 1925. *QWBD* 13203.

"Lianxi huiyi ti'an chengshi ji yi'an 聯席會議提案程式及議案." *ZWDL-QC* (September 22, 1925).

"Lianyi haiwai jiaotongbu tebie dangbu shang zhongyang zhixing weiyuanhui cheng 聯議海外交通部特別黨部上中央執行委員會呈." April 25, 1926. *QWBD* 6676.

"Lingnan daxue tongxuehui duiyu muxiao yiye tongxue fasheng jiufen shi xuanyan 嶺南大學同學會對於母校肄業同學發生糾紛事宣言." April 1926. *QWBD* 7828.

"Linshi Shaanxisheng dangbu baogao diyihao 臨時陝西省黨部報告第一號." *1-ZXWH*, vol. 5 (December 25, 1925). *ZXWD* 1.3/2.5.

"Linshi zhongyang zhixing weiyuanhui baogao gaiyao 臨時中央執行委員會報告概要." *Geming wenxian*, vol. 76, p. 32.

Lü Fang-shang 呂芳上. "Beifa shiqi Yingguo zengbing Shanghai yu dui Hua waijiao di yanbian 北伐時期英國增兵上海與對華外交的演變." *Bulletin of the Institute of Modern History, Academia Sinica* 27 (1997): 185-229.

_____. *Cong xuesheng yundong dao yundong xuesheng* 從學生運動到運動學生. Taipei: Institute of Modern History, Academica Sinica, 1994.

Luo Jialun 羅家倫, ed. *Guofu nianpu* 國父年譜. Two volumes. Third expanded and revised edition. Zhongguo Guomindang dangshi weiyuanhui, 1985.

Luo Qiyuan 羅綺園. "Zhongshan xian shibian zhi jingguo ji xianzai 中山縣事變之經過及現在." *Zhongguo nongmin* 中國農民 no. 1 (January 1926): 39-58.

"Maping qingniantuan xuanyan 馬平青年團宣言." April 16, 1926. *QWBD* 1059.

"Meixian zhixing weiyuanhui zhi zhongyang zhixing weiyuanhui dian 梅縣執行委員會致中央執行委員會電." May 1926. *QWBD* 6663.

Minguo ribao 民國日報. Guangzhou.

Nanjing shijian—zhongying 南京事件—中英. *GZD* 155:1423-1562.

Niu Dayong 牛大勇. "Yingguo di liangshou zhengce yu shenggang bagong zhi shoushu 英國第兩手政策與省港罷工之收束." *Beijing daxue xuebao* 北京大學學報 2 (1991): 45-53.

"Nongmin yundong diyibu shishi fang'an 農民運動第一步實施方案." *1-ZXWH*, vol. 2 (June 30, 1924). *ZXWD* 1.3/2.2.

"Nongmin yundong jiangxisuo zuzhi jianzhang 農民運動講習所組織簡章." *1-ZXWH*, vol. 2 (June 30, 1924). *ZXWD* 1.3/2.2.

Peng Pai 彭湃. "Haifeng nongmin yundong baogao 海豐農民運動報告." *Zhongguo nongmin* 中國農民 no. 1 (January 1926): 59-69.

"Qingdang tiaoli 清黨條例." *2-ZXWH*, vol. 6 (May 10, 1927). *ZXWD* 2.3/121.

"Qingnian dangtuan zuzhi ti'an 青年黨團組織提案." *1-ZXWH*, vol. 1 (March 12, 1924). *ZXWD* 1.3/2.1.

"Qingnian yundong jueyian 青年運動決議案." In *Zhongguo Guomindang dierci quanguo daibiao dahui huiyi jilu*, sujike edition, 131-132. Guangzhou: Zhongyang zhixing weiyuanhui, 1926.

"Qingnian yundong zhengce jueyian 青年運動政策決議案." *1-ZXWH*, vol. 1 (March 12, 1924). *ZXWD* 1.3/2.1.

"Qingnianbu baogao pingmin xuexiao qingxing 青年部報告平民學校情形." *1-ZXWH*, vol. 2 (June 2, 1924). *ZXWD* 1.3/2.2.

"Qingnianbu baogao pingmin xuexiao qingxing 青年部報告平民學校情形." May 31, 1924. *QWBD* 10719.

"Qingnianbu bugao 青年部佈告." August 6, 1924. *QWBD* 15780.

"Qingnianbu gongzuo baogao 青年部工作報告." June 25, 1925. *QWBD* 10736.

"Qingnianbu pingmin jiaoyu yundong buzou 青年部平民教育運動步驟." February, 1925. *QWBD* 10734.

"Qingnianbu sanyuefen gongzuo jingguo baogao 青年部三月分工作經過報告." Prepared by the Guangxi Youth Bureau. April 1,1926. *QWBD* 11123.

"Qingnianbu siyuefen gongzuo jingguo baogao 青年部四月份工作經過報告." Prepared by the Guangxi Youth Bureau. May 20, 1926. *QWBD* 11125.

"Quanguo jiaoyuhui lianhehui dishijie nianhui gailue 全國教育會聯合會第十屆年會概略." *Jiaoyu zazhi* 16:12 (December 1924): 1-9.

"Quanguo shengjiaoyuhui lianhe huiyi jue an 全國省教育會聯合會議決案." In *Guonei jinshinian lai zhi zongjiao sichao*, comp. Zhang Qinshi, 339-342. Beijing: Yenching School of Chinese Studies, 1927.

"Quanguo xuesheng zonghui yijue an 全國學生會總會議決案." In *Guonei jinshinian lai zhi zongjiao sichao*, comp. Zhang Qinshi, 395-400. Beijing: Yenching School of Chinese Studies, 1927.

"Quansheng dangwu zong baogao jueyian 全省黨務總報告決議案," *J3QD* (n.d., early 1927). *ZXWD* 2.3/121.

"Qudi sili xuexiao zhanxing tiaoli—Hubei zhengwu weiyuanhui faling 取締私立學校暫行條例." In *Guonei jinshinian lai zhi zongjiao sichao*, comp. Zhang Qinshi, 374-375. Beijing: Yenching School of Chinese Studies, 1927.

"Shanghai zhixingbu qingqiu zengjia yusuan an 上海執行部請求增加預算案." *1-ZXWH*, vol. 2 (June 16, 1924). *ZXWD* 1.3/2.2.

"Shenggang bagong weiyuanhui zhi Chen Shuren buzhang daidian 省港罷工委員會致陳樹人部長代電." August 1926. *QWBD* 13955.2.

"Shenggang bagong weiyuanhui zhi quanguo tongbao daidian 省港罷工委

員會致全國同胞代電." August 5, 1926. *QWBD* 13955.1.

"Shengli dierzhong xuexiao xueshenghui daibiao dahui minggu er gong xuegun Li Yueting diyici xuanyan 省立第二中學校學生會代表大會鳴故而工學棍黎樾廷第一次宣言." August 29, 1926. *QWBD* 0140.

Shengming 生命. Beijing.

Shengming yuekan 生命月刊. Beijing.

"Shili zhiye xuexiao xueshenghui zhongyao xuanyan 市立職業學校學生會重要宣言." April 17, 1926. *QWBD* 7758.

"Shisi eryuefen gongzuo baogao 十四 二月份工作報告." Prepared by the Youth Ministry. February or March, 1925. *QWBD* 10725.

"Shisinian yiyuefen gongzuo baogao 十四年一月份工作報告." Prepared by the Youth Ministry. January 31, 1925. *QWBD* 10724.

"Shiyue sanshiyiri quanti xuesheng dahui xuanyan 十月三十一日全體學生大會宣言." Issued by the student union of Sun Yat-sen University. November 2, 1925. *QWBD* 1054.

Shou Hua 壽華. "Shou Hua zhi Zou Lu han 壽華致鄒魯函." September 2, 1924. *QWBD* 11421.

"Shuqi gongren xuexiao jihua 暑期工人學校計畫." *1-ZXWH*, vol. 5 (July 23, 1925). *ZXWD* 1.3/2.5.

"Sichuan linshi sheng zhixing weiyuanhui shang zhongyang zhixing wei-yuanhui cheng 四川臨時省執行委員會上中央執行委員會呈." June 17, 1926. *QWBD* 10462.

"Sili xuexiao guicheng—Guomin zhengfu jiaoyu xingzheng weiyuanhui bugao 私立學校規程－國民政府教育行政委員會佈告." In *Guonei jinshinian lai zhi zongjiao sichao*, comp. Zhang Qinshi, 372-373. Beijing: Yenching School of Chinese Studies, 1927.

"Sili xuexiao zhuce tiaoli zhi gongbu 私立學校註冊條例之公佈." *Jiaoyu zazhi* 17: 12 (December 1925): 9.

Su Qiming 蘇啓明. "Beifa shiqi de nonggong yundong 北伐時期的農工運動." In *Beifa tongyi liushi zhounian xueshu taolun ji*, 516-547. Taipei: Beifa tongyi liushi zhounian xueshu taolun jibianji weiyuanhui, 1988.

Sun Zhongshan 孫中山. "Zongli jiaoyi: jilü wenti jueyian 總理交議: 紀律問題決議案." *Geming wenxian*, vol. 76, p. 11.

_____. "Zongli jiaoyi: Zhongguo Guomindang diyici quanguo daibiao dahui xuanyan an 總理交議: 中國國民黨第一次全國代表大會宣言案." *Geming wenxian*, vol. 76, p. 2.

_____. "Zongli jiaoyi: zuzhi guomin zhengfu zhi biyao an 總理交議: 組織國民政府之必要案." *Geming wenxian*, vol. 76, pp. 18-22.

Tan Yankai 譚延闓. "Tan Yankai tongzhi zhongyang zhengzhi baogao 譚延闓同志中央政治報告." *ZWDL-YS* (October 15, 1926).

"Tianjin dangwu baogao 天津黨務報告." *ZGLH*, vol. 1. Hankou: December

22, 1926. *ZXWD* 2.4/1.1.

"Tonggao diyisiqihao 通告第一四七號." *1-ZWQH*. Guangzhou: May 23, 1925. *ZXWD* 1.2/12.

"Tongyi Guangdong gejie daibiaohui dagang 統一廣東各界代表會大綱." *1-ZWH*, vol. 5 (October 8, 1925). *ZXWD* 1.3/2.5.

"Tongyi waijiao tiyi an 統一外交提議案." *2-ZWQH* #2. Hankou: March 1927. *ZXWD* 2.4/10.2.

Tu Zonggen 屠宗根. "Wuhan yangwu zhiyuan gonghui zhixing weiyuan zhang Tu Zonggen baogao 武漢洋務職員工會執行委員長屠宗根報告." *ZGLH*, vol. 2. Hankou: January 3, 1927. *ZXWD* 2.4/1.2.

"Waibu duiyu xianzhi jiaohui xuexiao chuanjiao zhi yijian 外部對於限制教會學校傳教之意見." *Jiaoyu zazhi* 18: 4 (April 1926): 7.

Wan Fulin 萬福林. "Zuijin Wuhan minzhong ji zhengfu duiyu Jidujiao di taidu 最近武漢民眾及政府對於基督教地態度." *Zhenguang zazhi* 26.6 (June 1927), separate pagination, 1-9.

Wang Zhixin 王治心. "Qingtian bairi chixia di Jidujiao 青天白日旗下的基督教." *Wenshe yuekan* 2.6 (April 1927): 1-14.

"Wei Guangzhou shangtuan shijian duiwai xuanyan 爲廣州商團事件對外宣言." *Geming wenxian*, vol. 69, pp. 108-109.

"Wei 'Xianli ergao xuesheng bei yapo' xuanyan 爲'縣立二高學生被壓迫'宣言." April 27, 1926. *QWBD* 7831-0-2.

Wei Yan 畏喦, pseudo., ed. *Guangdong kouxie chao* 廣東扣械潮. Four *juan* 卷. Hong Kong: The Wah Tsz Yat Po, Ltd., 1924.

Wenshe yuekan 文社月刊. Shanghai.

"Wenzhou shengdaohui zili xuanyan 溫州聖道會自立宣言." *Shengming yuekan* V-9 (July 1925): 42-43.

"Wo ye tantan Sun zhengfu 我也談談孫政府." *Huazi ribao* (July 14, 1924). In *Jingcun (Jiongming) xiansheng nianpu*, ed. Chen Dingyan, vol. 2, 728-729. Hong Kong: Guiguan tushu gongsi, 1995.

Wu Leichuan 吳雷川. "Jiaohui xuexiao li'an yihou 教會學校立案以後." *Shengming yuekan* VI, 2 (November 1925): 1-3.

Wu Tiecheng. *Wu Tiecheng huiyilu* 吳鐵城回憶錄. Reproduced in *Yi-jiuersinian Guangzhou shangtuan shijian*, separate pagination. Hong Kong: Chongwen shudian, 1974.

"Wuhan shimin fan Ying yundong dahui chengwen 武漢市民反英運動大會程文." *ZGLH*, vol. 2. Hankou: December 27, 1926. *ZXWD* 2.4/1.2.

"Wuzhou gejie dangyuan quchu fandongpai weiyuanhui xuanyan 梧州各界黨員驅除反動派委員會宣言." December 14, 1926. *QWBD* 6408.

"Wuzhoushi zhixing weiyuanhui zhi zhongyang dangbu deng daidian 梧州市執行委員會至中央黨部等代電." January 1927. *QWBD* 6430.

Xiangdao zhoubao 向導週報. Shanghai.

"Xianggang qingnianbu qingnian yundong jihua 香港青年部青年運動計畫." December 15, 1925. *QWBD* 10463.

"Xiansheng dui xin xianzhang zhi xunshi 先生對新縣長之訓示," *Huazi ribao* (November 17, 1921). In *Jingcun (Jiongming) xiansheng nianpu*, ed. Chen Dingyan, vol. 1, 429. Hong Kong: Guiguan tushu gongsi, 1995.

"Xinhui xianli zhongxue xueshenghui zhixing weiyuanhui shang zhongyang qingnianbu daidian 新會縣立中學學生會執行委員會上中央青年部代電." June 7, 1926. *QWBD* 6665.

"Xinhui xuesheng lianhehui dui xinzhong fengchao disici xuanyan 新會學生聯合會對新中風潮第四次宣言." July 5, 1926. *QWBD* 6668.

Xu Baihao 許白昊. "Hubei quansheng zonggonghui mishuzhang Xu Baihao baogao 湖北全省總工會秘書長許白昊報告." *ZGLH*, vol. 2. Hankou: January 3, 1927. *ZXWD* 2.4/1.2.

Xu Songling 徐嵩齡. "Yijiuersi nian Sun Zhongshan de beifa yu Guangzhou shangtuan shibian 一九二四年孫中山的北伐與廣州商團事變." In *Yijiuersinian Guangzhou shangtuan shijian*, 1-11. Hong Kong: Chongwen shudian, 1974.

"Xuanchuan zhuyao zhi cailiao 宣傳主要之材料." *2-ZXWH*, vol. 4 (September 7, 1926). *ZXWD* 2.3/119.

"Xuanchuanbu jihua dagang cao'an 宣傳部計畫大綱草案." Shanghai, June 15, 1926. *ZXWD* 2.5/5.3.

"Xuanchuanbu ti'an 宣傳部提案." *2-ZXWH*, vol. 5 (November 13, 1926). *ZXWD* 2.3/120.

"Xuesheng dangyuan diaocha biao 學生黨員調查表." Compiled by the Youth Ministry. 1926. *QWBD* 12053 1-28.

"Xuesheng yundong jihua jueyian 學生運動計畫決議案." *1-ZXWH*, vol. 1 (March 12, 1924). *ZXWD* 1.3/2.1.

"Xueshenghui dangtuan zuzhi xiuzheng an 學生會黨團組織修正案." *2-ZXWH*, vol. 4 (August 28, 1926). *ZXWD* 2.3/119.

"Xuexiao jiaoyuan ying shou dang de xunlian 學校教員應受黨的訓練." Proposed by the Women's Ministry. October 20, 1926. *QWBD* 4389.

"Xunling cao'an 訓令草案." *1-ZWQH* . Guangzhou: May 22, 1925. *ZXWD* 1.2/11.

Yang Jiaming 楊家銘. *Minguo shiwunian Zhongguo xuesheng yundong gaikuang* 民國十五年中國學生運動概況. Shanghai: Guanghua shuju, 1927.

Ye Yaoqiu 葉耀述, et al. "Shengsanyi quanti bake xuesheng daibiao Ye Yaoqiu deng cheng zhongyang qingnianbu han 聖三一全體罷課學生代表葉耀述等呈中央青年部函." May 18, 1926. *QWBD* 15817.

"Yijue'an 1: waijiao wenti an 議決案: 外交問題案." *ZGLH*, vol. 1. Hankou: December 15, 1926. *ZXWD* 2.4/1.1.

Yijiuersinian Guangzhou shangtuan shijian 一九二四年廣州商團事件. Hong Kong: Chongwen shudian, 1974.

"Yingdexian liusheng xuehui wei Kang Zhunian Tan Yaoming Hu Xingqun deng goushuai wulai ouda xunxing qunzhong shu xuanyan 英德縣留省學會爲康祝年譚耀明胡醒群等勾率無賴毆打巡行群眾書宣言." December 1926. *QWBD* 6674.

"Yinianlai quanguo xuesheng yundong zhi gaikuang 一年來全國學生運動之概況." *2-ZXWH*, vol. 3 (July 17, 1926). *ZXWD* 2.3/118.

"'Yisan' can'an zhi xuanchuan dagang '一三' 慘案之宣傳大綱."*ZGLH*. Hankou: January 10, 1927. *ZXWD* 2.4/3.1.

"Yuejiaoting qudi jiaohui xuexiao zhi banfa 粵教廳取締教會學校之辦法." *Jiaoyu zazhi* 17: 7 (July 1925): 8.

"YueXiang shouhui jiaoyuquan yundong zhi jijin 鄂湘收回教育權運動之急進." *Jiaoyu zazhi* 19:2 (February 1927): 2.

"Zai zhanlingdinei zuzhi linshi dangbu zhouxu ji tiaoli 在佔領地內組織臨時黨部手續及條例." *2-ZXWH*, vol. 3 (July 17, 1926). *ZXWD* 2.3/118.

Zhang Bojun 章伯均. "Zongsilingbu zhengzhibu Zhang Bojun baogao 總司令部政治部章伯均報告." *ZGLH*, vol. 2. Hankou: January 3, 1927. *ZXWD* 2.4/1.2.

Zhang Qinshi 張欽十 (Neander C. S. Chang), comp. *Guonei jinshinian lai zhi zongjiao sichao* 國內近十年來之宗教思潮. Beijing: Yenching School of Chinese Studies, 1927.

"Zhaoji dierci quanguo daibiao dahui xuanyan 召集第二次全國代表大會宣言." *1-ZXWH*, vol. 5 (December 11, 1925). *ZXWD* 1.3/2.5.

"Zhejiang quansheng qingnian yundong gaikuang tongji biao 浙江全省青年運動概況統計表." 1927. *QWBD* 12605.

Zhenguang zazhi 真光雜誌. Shanghai.

"Zhesheng zhenggangzhong zhi jiaoyu yu xuesheng 浙省政綱中之教育與學生." *Jiaoyu zazhi* 19:4 (April, 1927): 6.

"Zhi Guangzhoushi zhengsuo jiaoyuju diaocha suoxia benshi gexuexiao han 致廣州市政所教育局調查所轄本市各學校函." September 15, 1924. *QWBD* 12571.

Zhong Rongguang 鍾榮光, et. al. "Jiaoyu xingzheng weiyuanhui weiyuan Zhong Rongguang deng fu zhongyang zhixing weiyuanhui han 教育行政委員會委員鍾榮光等復中央執行委員會函." April 23, 1926. *QWBD* 15852.

Zhongguo nongmin 中國農民. Guangzhou: Zhongguo Guomindang zhongyang zhixing weiyuanhui nongminbu, 1926.

"Zhongguo Guomindang dangli shangmin yundong jiangxisuo zhangcheng 中國國民黨黨立上民運動講習所章程." *1-ZXWH*, vol. 5 (July 23, 1925). *ZXWD* 1.3/2.5.

"Zhongguo Guomindang dangli xuanchuanyuan yangchengsuo zhangcheng 中國國民黨黨立宣傳員養成所章程." *1-ZXWH*, vol. 5 (July 7, 1925). *ZXWD* 1.3/2.5.

Zhongguo Guomindang dierci quanguo daibiao dahui huiyi jilu 中國國民黨第二次全國代表大會會議記錄. Sujike 速記科 edition. Guangzhou: Zhongyang zhixing weiyuanhui, 1926. [Abbreviated *2QDD*.] *ZXWD* 2.1/8.1.

"Zhongguo Guomindang dierci quanguo daibiao dahui xuanyan 中國國民黨第二次全國代表大會宣言." *Geming wenxian*, vol. 69, pp. 152-168.

Zhongguo Guomindang dierjie zhongyang zhixing weiyuanhui changwu weiyuanhui huiyi jilu 中國國民黨第二屆中央執行委員會常務委員會會議紀錄. Five volumes. Guangzhou, Nanchang, Nanjing: Zhongyang zhixing weiyuanhui, 1926-1927. [Abbreviated *2-ZXWH*.] *ZXWD* 2.3/116-121.

"Zhongguo Guomindang dierjie zhongyang zhixing weiyuanhui disanci quanti huiyi dui quan Zhongguo renmin xuanyan 中國國民黨第二屆中央執行委員會第三次全體會議對全中國人民宣言." Hankou: March 1927. [Abbreviated *2-ZWQH*.] *ZXWD* 2.4/9.1.

Zhongguo Guomindang dierjie zhongyang zhixing weiyuanhui disanci quanti huiyi xuanyan ji jueyian 中國國民黨第二屆中央執行委員會第三次全體會議宣言及決議案. Hankou, March 1927. [Abbreviated *2-ZWQH*.] *ZXWD* 2.4/9.1.

Zhongguo Guomindang dierjie zhongyang zhixing weiyuanhui linshi quanti huiyi jilu 中國國民黨第二屆中央執行委員會臨時全體會議紀錄. In *Zhongguo Guomindang dierjie zhongyang zhixing weiyuanhui changwu weiyuanhui huiyi jilu*, vol. 3. Guangzhou: July 6, 1926.

"Zhongguo Guomindang diyici quanguo daibiao dahui xuanyan 中國國民黨第一次全國代表大會宣言." *Geming wenxian*, vol. 69, pp. 91-92.

Zhongguo Guomindang diyijie zhongyang zhixing weiyuanhui disanci quanti weiyuanhui huiyi jilu 中國國民黨第一屆中央執行委員會第三次全體委員會會議紀錄. Guangzhou, May 1925. [Abbreviated *1-ZWQH*.] *ZXWD* 1.2/10-14.

Zhongguo Guomindang diyijie zhongyang zhixing weiyuanhui huiyi jilu 中國國民黨第一屆中央執行委員會會議紀錄. Five volumes. Guangzhou: Zhongyang zhixing weiyuanhui, 1924-1925. [Abbreviated *1-ZXWH*.] *ZXWD* 1.3/2.1-2.5.

"Zhongguo Guomindang dui Guangzhou bashi shijian xuanyan 中國國民黨對廣州罷市事件宣言." *Geming wenxian*, vol. 10, p. 50.

"Zhongguo Guomindang Guangxisheng zhixing weiyuanhui qingnianbu wuyuefen gongzuo baogao 中國國民黨廣西省執行委員會青年部五月份工作報告." June 5, 1926. *QWBD* 11126.

"Zhongguo Guomindang Guangzhou tebieshi zhixing weiyuanhui zhang-cheng 中國國民黨廣州特別市執行委員會章程." *1-ZXWH*, vol. 2 (May 29, 1924). *ZXWD* 1.3/2.2.

Zhongguo Guomindang Jiangxi disanci quansheng daibiao dahui jueyian 中國國民黨江西第三次全省代表大會決議案. In *Zhongguo Guomindang dierjie zhongyang zhixing weiyuanhui changwu weiyuanhui huiyi jilu*, [Abbreviated *J3QD*.] vol. 6. Nanchang: 1927.

"Zhongguo Guomindang Shanghai tebieshi dangbu qingnianbu liuyuefen gongzuo baogao shu 中國國民黨上海特別市黨部青年部六月份工作報告書." July 20, 1926. *QWBD* 11153.

"Zhongguo Guomindang Shanghai tebieshi dangbu qingnianbu wuyuefen gongzuo baogao 中國國民黨上海特別市黨部青年部五月份工作報告." June 21, 1926. *QWBD* 11152.

"Zhongguo Guomindang Shanghai tebieshi dierqu dangbu qingnianbu gongzuo jihua 中國國民黨上海特別市第二區黨部青年部工作計劃." 1927. *QWBD* 11175.

"Zhongguo Guomindang xuanyan 中國國民黨宣言." *Geming wenxian*, vol. 69, pp. 67-71.

"Zhongguo Guomindang zhongyang qingnianbu pingmin jiaoyu weiyuanhui zongzhang cao'an 中國國民黨中央青年部平民教育委員會總章草案," *2-ZXWH*, vol. 4 (September 14, 1926). *ZXWD* 2.3/119.

Zhongguo Guomindang zhongyang weiyuan gesheng getebie qushi haiwai gezong zhibu daibiao lianxi huiyi yian qicao weiyuan tanhua hui jilu 中國國民黨中央委員各省各特別區市海外各總支部代表聯席會議議案起草委員談話會紀錄. [Abbreviated *ZWDL-QC*.] *ZXWD* 2.0/2.2.

Zhongguo Guomindang zhongyang weiyuan gesheng getebie qushi haiwai gezong zhibu daibiao lianxi huiyi xuanyan ji jueyian 中國國民黨中央委員各省各特別區市海外各總支部代表聯席會議宣言及決議案. Guangzhou: Zhongyang zhixing weiyuanhui, November 1926. [Abbreviated *ZWDL-XJ*.] *ZXWD* 2.0/6.

Zhongguo Guomindang zhongyang weiyuan gesheng getebie qushi haiwai gezong zhibu daibiao lianxi huiyi yishilu 中國國民黨中央委員各省各特別區市海外各總支部代表聯席會議議事錄. Fifteen volumes. Guangzhou: October 1926. [Abbreviated *ZWDL-YS*.] *ZXWD* 2.0/4.1-15.

Zhongguo Guomindang zhongyang zhixing weiyuanhui guomin zhengfu weiyuanhui linshi lianxi huiyi jilu 中國國民黨中央執行委員會國民政府委員會臨時聯席會議記錄. Three volumes. Hankou: December 1926. [Abbreviated *ZGLH*.] *ZXWD* 2.4/1.1-1.3.

Zhongguo Guomindang zhongyang zhixing weiyuanhui guomin zhengfu weiyuanhui linshi lianxi huiyi jilu 中國國民黨中央執行委員會國民政府委員會臨時聯席會議記錄. One volume. Hankou: January 1927.

[Abbreviated *ZGLH*.] *ZXWD* 2.4/3.1.

"Zhongguo Guomindang zhongyang zhixing weiyuanhui qingnianbu gong-zuo fangzhen ji jihua cao'an 中國國民黨中央執行委員會青年部工作方針及計畫草案." April 1927. *QWBD* 1426.5.

"Zhongguo Guomindang zhongyang zhixing weiyuanhui xuanchuanbu banshi zhangcheng 中國國民黨中央執行委員會宣傳部辦事章程." *1-ZXWH*, vol. 1 (April 24, 1924). *ZXWD* 1.3/2.1.

"Zhongguo Guomindang zongzhang zhiding an 中國國民黨總章制定案," *Geming wenxian*, vol. 76, p. 10.

"Zhongguo qingnian junren lianhehui daidian 中國青年軍人聯合會代電." Guangzhou, 1926. *QWBD* 1055.

Zhongguo tushuguan shufenlei fa 中國圖書館書分類法. Beijing: Shumu wenxian chubanshe, 1980.

"Zhongguo xuexheng zonghui dijiuhui daibiao dahui kaimuri fouren Wuhan weixue zonghui 中國學生總會第九回代表大會開幕日否認武漢偽學總會." 1927. *QWBD* 12689.

"Zhonghua jiaoyu gaijin she chudeng jiaoyuzu yijue an 中華教育改進社初等教育組議決案." In *Guonei jinshinian lai zhi zongjiao sichao*, comp. Zhang Qinshi, 271-272. Beijing: Yenching School of Chinese Studies, 1927.

"Zhonghua Jidu jiaoyuhui zhi xuanyan 中華基督教育會之宣言." *Jiaoyu zazhi* 17:5 (May 1925): 9.

"Zhonghua Minguo xuesheng lianhui zonghui gaizu weiyuanhui yonghu zhongyang dangbu guomin zhengfu tongdian 中華民國學生聯會總會改組委員會擁護中央黨部國民政府通電." 1927. *QWBD* 12690.

Zhongshan Daxue gaikuang 中山大學概況. Guangzhou: Zhongshan Daxue chubanshe, 1994.

"Zhongyang qingdang weiyuanhui zuzhi dagang 中央清黨委員會組織大綱." *2-ZXWH*, vol. 6 (May 10, 1927). *ZXWD* 2.3/121.

"Zhongyang qingnianbu tepaiyuan tiaoli 中央青年部特派員條例." *2-ZXWH*, vol. 5 (November 13, 1926). *ZXWD* 2.3/120.

"Zhongyang qingnianbu tonggao 中央青年部通告." October 25, 1924. *QWBD* 15781.

"Zhongyang qingnianbu tonggao 中央青年部通告." September 2, 1926. *QWBD* 0059.

"Zhongyang qingnianbu xianren zhiyuan ji guicheng yilan 中央青年部現任職員及規程一覽." April 1927. *QWBD* 1426.1.

"Zhongyang qingnianbu yizhou gongzuo baogao 中央青年部一週工作報告." August 7, 1926. *QWBD* 10740.

"Zhongyang qingnianbu zhi Ding Chaowu han 中央青年部至丁超五函." August 8, 1926. *QWBD* 13771.

"Zhongyang qingnianbu zhi gedi xuexiao han 中央青年部致各地學校函." March 13, 1925. *QWBD* 3701.

"Zhongyang qingnianbu zhi geming qingnian lianhehui han 中央青年部致革命青年聯合會函." December 24, 1925. *QWBD* 12617.

"Zhongyang qingnianbu zhi Guangdong jiaoyu tingzhang han 中央青年部致廣東教育廳長函." September 15 1924. *QWBD* 12572.

"Zhongyang qingnianbu zhi Guangzhou gexuexiao tongqi 中央青年部致廣州各學校通啓." August 29, 1926. *QWBD* 15829.

"Zhongyang qingnianbu zhi jiaoyu tingju han 中央青年部致教育廳局函." January 21, 1925. *QWBD* 12048.

"Zhongyang qingnianbu zhi mishuchu han 中央青年部致祕書處函." September 3, 1926. *QWBD* 10747.

"Zhongyang qingnianbu zhi quanguo xuesheng zonghui dangtuan zhixing weiyuanhui han 中央青年部致全國學生總會黨團執行委員會函." August 31, 1926. *QWBD* 13759.

"Zhongyang qingnianbu zhi zhonghua minguo daxueyuan han 中央青年部致中華民國大學院函." October 31, 1927. *QWBD* 12544.

"Zhongyang qingnianbu zhi zhongshan daxue weiyuanhui han'gao 中央青年部致中山大學委員會函稿." November 5, 1926. *QWBD* 7874.

"Zhongyang qingnianbu zhi zhongyang zhengzhi huiyi mishuchu han'gao 中央青年部致中央政治會議秘書處函稿." November 2, 1926. *QWBD* 1159.

"Zhongyang zhengzhi huiyi mishuchu zhi jiejue xuechao weiyuanhui han 中央政治會議秘書處致解決學潮委員會函." November 20, 1926. *QWBD* 1161.

"Zhongyang zhengzhi huiyi mishuchu zhi jiejue xuechao weiyuanhui han 中央政治會議秘書處致解決學潮委員會函." November 26, 1926. *QWBD* 1163.1.

"Zhongyang zhengzhi huiyi mishuchu zhi zhongyang qingnianbu han 中央政治會議秘書處致中央青年部函." November 1, 1926. *QWBD* 1158.

"Zhongyang zhengzhi huiyi mishuchu zhi zhongyang qingnianbu han 中央政治會議秘書處致中央青年部函." November 22, 1926. *QWBD* 1162.2.

"Zhongyang zhixing weiyuan fenpei gedi wenti an 中央執行委員分配各地問題案." *Geming wenxian*, vol. 79, pp. 4-5.

"Zhongyang zhixing weiyuanhui 中央執行委員會." *1-ZXWH*, vol. 4 (June 2, 1925). *ZXWD* 1.3/2.4.

"Zhongyang zhixing weiyuanhui changwuhui zhi zhongyang gongrenbu han 中央執行委員會常務會致中央工人部函." September 15, 1926. *QWBD* 3384.

"Zhongyang zhixing weiyuanhui gebu zhiwu gaiyao 中央執行委員會各部

職務概要." *1-ZXWH*, vol. 1 (February 20, 1924). *ZXWD* 1.3/2.1.

"Zhongyang zhixing weiyuanhui gebu zuzhi wenti an 中央執行委員會各部組織問題案." *Geming wenxian*, vol. 79, pp. 1-2.

"Zhongyang zhixing weiyuanhui ji gedi zhixingbu zhijie guanxia quyu wenti jueyian 中央執行委員會及各地執行部直接管轄區域問題決議案." *Geming wenxian*, vol. 79, pp. 2-3.

"Zhongyang zhixing weiyuanhui ji Shanghai Beijing Haerbin deng zhixingbu zuzhi ji yusuan an 中央執行委員會及上海北京哈爾濱等執行部組織及預算案." *Geming wenxian*, vol. 79, p. 11

"Zhongyang zhixing weiyuanhui mishuchu zhi zhongyang gongrenbu han 中央執行委員會秘書處至中央工人部函." September 15, 1926. *QWBD* 3385.

"Zhongyang zhixing weiyuanhui tichu yi'an 中央執行委員會提出議案." *ZWDL-YS* (October 15, 1926).

"Zhongyang zhixing weiyuanhui tichu yi'an 中央執行委員會提出議案." *ZWDL-YS* (October 26, 1926).

"Zhongyang zhixing weiyuanhui tonggao diereryihao 中央執行委員會通告第二二一號." November 16, 1926. *QWBD* 1340.

"Zhongyang zhixing weiyuanhui zhi qingnianbu han 中央執行委員會至青年部函." December 29, 1925. *QWBD* 0065.

"Zhongyang zhixing weiyuanhui zhi Xu Chongqing han 中央執行委員會致許崇清函." April 16, 1925. *QWBD* 1139.

Zou Lu 鄒魯. "Zhongyang qingnianbu buzhang Zou Lu zhi Guangzhou gexiao tonghan 中央青年部部長鄒魯致廣州各校通函." May 1924. *QWBD* 15777.

_____. "Zou Lu zhi zhongyang qingnianbu han 鄒魯致中央青年部函." October 31, 1924. *QWBD* 13198.

English Language Materials

Alitto, Guy S. *The Last Confucian: Liang Shu-ming and the Chinese Dilemma of Modernity.* Berkeley: University of California Press, 1979.

"America's Policy: Dr. Schurman's Interview with Sun Yat-sen." *Peking and Tientsin Times* (January 18, 1924).

"An Unwelcome Guest." *Peking and Tientsin Times* (December 4, 1924).

Anderson, Benedict. *Imagined Communities: Reflections on the Origin and Spread of Nationalism.* Revised edition. New York: Verso, 1991.

Bastid, Marianne. *Educational Reform in Early 20th Century China.* Translated by Paul J. Bailey. Ann Arbor, MI: The University of Michigan, Center for Chinese Studies, 1988.

_____. "Servitude or Liberation: The Introduction of Foreign Educational

Practices and System to China from 1840 to the Present." In *China's Education and the Industrialized World: Studies in Cultural Transfer*, eds. Ruth Hayhoe and Marianne Bastid, 3-20. Armonk, NY: M. E. Sharpe, Inc., 1987.

Bergère, Marie-Claire. *Sun Yat-sen.* Translated by Janet Lloyd. Stanford: Stanford University Press, 1998.

Bhabha, Homi K. "DissemiNation: Time, Narrative, and the Margins of the Modern Nation." In *Nation and Narration*, ed. Homi K. Bhabha, 291-322. London: Routledge, 1990.

"Boxer Protocol Is Charter of Organized Imperialism in China." *Canton Gazette* (September 8, 1924).

Brandt, Conrad. *Stalin's Failure in China, 1924-1927.* Cambridge, MA: Harvard University Press, 1958.

Breslin, Thomas A. *China, American Catholicism, and the Missionary.* University Park, PA: Pennsylvania State University Press, 1980.

British Foreign Office, Confidential Prints, China. Great Britain. Public Records Office. [Abbreviated *FO*.]

"Canton Bolshevism." *Peking and Tientsin Times* (November 20, 1924).

Canton Gazette. Guangzhou.

"Canton Grievances: A Public Complaint." *Hong Kong Telegraph* (November 3, 1923).

"Canton House Seizures." *Hong Kong Telegraph* (October 17, 1923).

"Canton Land Sale." *Hong Kong Telegraph* (April 10, 1923).

"Canton Land Sale." *Hong Kong Telegraph* (April 11, 1923).

The Canton Times. Guangzhou.

"Canton War Taxes." *Peking and Tientsin Times* (January 15, 1924).

Chan, F. Gilbert. "Sun Yat-sen and the Origins of the Kuomintang Reorganization." In *China in the 1920s*, eds. F. Gilbert Chan and Thomas H. Etzold, 15-37, 198-205. New York: New Viewpoints, 1976.

Chan Lau Kit-ching. *China, Britain, and Hong Kong, 1895-1945.* Hong Kong: The Chinese University Press, 1990.

Chan, Ming Kou. "Labor and Empire: The Chinese Labor Movement in the Canton Delta, 1885-1927." Ph.D. dissertation. Stanford University, 1975.

Chang, Chun-shu, and Shelley Hsueh-lun Chang. *Crisis and Transformation in Seventeenth Century China.* Ann Arbor, MI: University of Michigan Press, 1992.

Chang, Sidney H., and Leonard H. D. Gordon. *All Under Heaven . . .: Sun Yat-sen and His Revolutionary Thought.* Stanford: Hoover Institutions Press, 1991.

Chao, Jonathan T'ien-en. "The Chinese Indigenous Church Movement,

1919-1927: A Protestant Response to the Anti-Christian Movements in Modern China." Ph.D. dissertation. University of Pennsylvania, 1986.

Chapman, Herbert Owen. *The Chinese Revolution, 1926-27.* London: Constable and Co., Ltd., 1928.

Chatterjee, Partha. *The Nation and Its Fragments: Colonial and Postcolonial Histories.* Princeton: Princeton University Press, 1993.

Chen, Leslie H. Dingyan [陳定炎]. *Chen Jiongming and the Federalist Movement: Regional Leadership and Nation Building in Early Republican China.* Ann Arbor, MI: University of Michigan, Center for Chinese Studies, 1999.

_____. comp. *A Collection of Historiographic Materials for a Biography of Chen Chiung-ming (1878-1933).* Twenty-one volumes. Unpublished manuscript deposited in the Brigham Young University, Harold B. Lee Library, 1988. [Abbreviated *BCCM*.]

_____. "A Tale of Two Cities: Canton (Guangzhou) in the 1920s." Unpublished paper presented at the 37th Annual Meeting of AACS, University of Nevada, 1995.

Cheng Ching-yi. "The Development of an Indigenous Church in China." *International Review of Missions* XII-3 (July 1923): 368-388.

Chesneaux, Jean. *The Chinese Labor Movement, 1919-1927.* Translated by H. M. Wright. Stanford: Stanford University Press, 1968.

_____. "The Federalist Movement in China, 1920-1923." In *Modern China's Search for a Political Form*, ed. Jack Gray, 97-137. Cambridge: Oxford University Press, 1969.

Chiang Kai-shek [蔣中正]. "Chiang Kai-shek's Letter to Bliukher." In *Missionaries of Revolution*, eds. C. Martin Wilbur and Julie Lienying How, 502-505. Cambridge MA: Harvard University Press, 1989.

_____. *Soviet Russia in China: A Summing Up at Seventy.* Revised and enlarged edition. Taipei: China Publishing Co., 1969.

China Christian Year Book. Multi-volume set. Shanghai: Christian Literature Society, 1926-1940.

"China Depends Upon Japan For Aid in Abolishing All Treaties Conferring Extraterritoriality." *Japan Times and Mail* (November 25, 1924).

The China Press. Shanghai.

China Weekly Review. Shanghai. [Abbreviated *CWR*.]

"Chinese Christian Education." *Chinese Recorder* (57): 340-344.

"Chinese Merchants and Politics." *Peking and Tientsin Times* (November 15, 1924).

The Chinese Recorder. Shanghai.

Cui, Dan. *The Cultural Contribution of British Protestant Missionaries and British-American Cooperation to China's National Development Dur-*

ing the 1920s. New York: University Press of America, 1998.

Dailey, Charles. "Bolshevik Students Put Check on American Donations." *CWR* 32 (May 30, 1925): 356-357.

_____. "Bolshevizing the Yale-in-China College." *CWR* 39 (January 1, 1927): 116.

_____. "Canton's Promise and Performance." *CWR* 39 (December 25, 1926): 88-89.

_____. "How the `Reds' Drove American Missionaries From Wuchow." *CWR* 37 (July 17, 1926): 156-158.

_____. "The Red Wave on the Yangtze." *CWR* 38 (November 27, 1926): 344-346.

DeAngelis, Richard C. "Jacob Gould Schurman, Sun Yat-sen, and the Canton Customs Crisis." *Bulletin of the Institute of Modern History, Academia Sinica* 8 (1979): 253-293.

Dennis, Rev. James S. *Christian Missions and Social Progress: A Sociological Study of Foreign Missions.* Two volumes. New York: Fleming H. Revell Co., 1897.

Dirlik, Arif. *The Origins of Chinese Communism.* New York: Oxford University Press, 1989.

"Disintegration in China: Dr. Schurman's Observations." *Peking and Tientsin Times* (January 19, 1924).

"Dr. Sun Denounces British Premier's Policy in China." *Canton Gazette* (September 24, 1924).

"Dr. Sun's Attack on Foreigners." *Shanghai Times* (November 18, 1924).

Duara, Prasenjit. *Rescuing History from the Nation: Questioning Narratives of Modern China.* Chicago: University of Chicago Press, 1995.

Fitzgerald, John. *Awakening China: Politics, Culture, and Class in the Nationalist Revolution.* Stanford: Stanford University Press, 1996.

_____. "The Nationless State: The Search for a Nation in Modern Chinese Nationalism." *The Australian Journal of Chinese Affairs* 33 (January 1995): 75-104.

Ford, Eddie. *The History of Educational Work in the Methodist Episcopal Church in China.* Fuzhou, 1938.

Friedman, Edward. *Backward Toward Revolution: The Chinese Revolutionary Party.* Berkeley: University of California Press, 1974.

Fung, Edmund S. K. *The Diplomacy of Imperial Retreat: Britain's South China Policy, 1924-1931.* Oxford: Oxford University Press, 1991.

Galbiati, Fernando. *P'eng P'ai and the Hai-Lu-feng Soviet.* Stanford: Stanford University Press, 1985.

Gannett, Lewis S. "Why Canton is Radical Center of Asia." *CWR* 37 (June 12, 1926): 29-31.

Giles, Herbert A. *Chaos in China.* Cambridge, Eng.: W. Heffer and Sons, 1924.

Goodman, Bryna. "The Locality as Microcosm of the Nation?: Native Place Networks and Early Urban Nationalism in China." *Modern China* 21:4 (October 1995): 387-419.

_____. *Native Place, City, and Nation: Regional Networks and Identities in Shanghai, 1853-1937.* Berkeley: University of California Press, 1995.

"The Government's Humiliation Day." *Peking and Tientsin Times* (May 13, 1925).

"Great Asia." *Peking and Tientsin Times* (December 6, 1924).

"The 'Great Asia' Stunt." *Peking and Tientsin Times* (December 8, 1924).

Griggs, John C. "Canton's Contribution to the Chinese Revolution." *CWR* 38 (September 25, 1926): 92-94.

Heeren, J. J. "Missionaries and Governments." *Chinese Recorder* (57): 112-113.

Holubnychy, Lydia. *Michael Borodin and the Chinese Revolution, 1923-1925.* Ann Arbor, MI: University Microfilms International, 1979.

Hong Kong Telegraph. Hong Kong.

Iriye, Akira. *After Imperialism: The Search for a New Order in the Far East, 1921-1931.* New York: Atheneum, 1969.

Isaacs, Harold R. *The Tragedy of the Chinese Revolution.* Second revised edition. Stanford: Stanford University Press, 1961.

Israel, John. *Student Nationalism in China, 1927-1937.* Stanford: Stanford University Press, 1966.

Jacobs, Dan N. *Borodin: Stalin's Man in China.* Cambridge, MA: Harvard University Press, 1981.

Japan Times and Mail. Tokyo.

Jordan, Donald A. *The Northern Expedition: China's National Revolution of 1926-1928.* Honolulu: University Press of Hawaii, 1976.

"Kuomintang's Declaration Regarding the Objects of The War." *Canton Gazette* (September 22, 1924).

Kuomintang Publicity Department. Guangzhou.

"Kuomintang Should Appeal to People for Support." *The Canton Times* (January 25, 1923).

Latourette, Kenneth S. *A History of Christian Missions in China.* New York: Macmillan Co., 1929.

Lee, Edward Bing-shuey. *Modern Canton.* Shanghai: The Mercury Press, 1936.

Lee, Feigon. *Chen Duxiu: Founder of the Chinese Communist Party.* Princeton: Princeton University Press, 1983.

Lee, Y. L. "The Anti-Christian Movement in Canton." *Chinese Recorder*

(April 1925): 220-226.

_____. "Registration of Christian Schools in Canton." *CWR* 39 (January 8, 1927): 156.

Legge, James. *The Four Books.* Four volumes. 1966.

Li, Lincoln. *Student Nationalism in China, 1924-1949.* Albany, NY: State University of New York Press, 1994.

Lin Yutang. *A History of the Press and Public Opinion in China.* Chicago: University of Chicago Press, 1936.

Lutz, Jessie G. *Chinese Politics and Christian Missions: The Anti-Christian Movements of 1920-28.* Notre Dame, IN: Cross Cultural Publications, Inc., Cross Roads Books, 1988.

Lyon, D. Willard. "Should the Missionary Be Discouraged?" *The Chinese Recorder* (May 1927): 309-318.

Marks, Robert B. *Rural Revolution in South China: Peasants and the Making of History in Haifeng County, 1570-1930.* Madison, WI: University of Wisconsin Press, 1984.

McCord, Edward A. *The Power of the Gun: The Emergence of Modern Chinese Warlordism.* Berkeley: University of California Press, 1993.

McDonald, Angus W., Jr. "Mao Tse-tung and the Hunan Self-Government Movement." *China Quarterly* 68 (1976): 751-777.

_____. *The Urban Origins of Rural Revolution: Elites and the Masses in Hunan Province, China, 1911-1927.* Berkeley: University of California Press, 1978.

Meisner, Maurice J. *Li Ta-chao and the Origins of Chinese Marxism.* Cambridge, MA: Harvard University Press, 1967.

"Merchants and the Conference." *Peking and Tientsin Times* (December 6, 1924).

Min Tu-ki. *National Polity and Local Power: The Transformation of Late Imperial China.* Edited by Philip A. Kuhn and Timothy Brook. Cambridge, MA: Council on East Asian Studies, 1989.

Munro, Donald J. *The Concept of Man in Early China.* Stanford: Stanford University Press, 1969.

Munro-Faure, p. H. "The Kiukiang Incident of 1927." *Journal of the Hong Kong Branch of the Royal Asiatic Society* 29 (1989): 61-76.

"Ninety-two Outrages against Foreigners in China." *North China Daily Mail* (January 15, 1924).

North China Herald. Weekly supplement to the North China Daily News. Shanghai.

North China Daily News. Shanghai.

North China Daily Mail. Shanghai.

North, Robert C. *Moscow and Chinese Communists.* Stanford: Stanford

University Press, 1953.

Peake, Cyrus H. *Nationalism and Education in Modern China.* New York: Columbia University Press, 1932.

Peking and Tientsin Times. Tianjin.

Powell, J. B. "Nationalists Take Over Shanghai—The Present Situation." *CWR* 40 (April 2, 1927): 121-123.

"President Sun's Manifesto to the People of Kwangtung." *Canton Gazette* (September 13, 1924).

Rea, Kenneth W., ed. *Canton in Revolution: The Collected Papers of Earl Swisher, 1925-1928.* Boulder, CO: Westview Press, 1977.

"Resolutions on the Peasant Movement." In *Missionaries of Revolution*, eds. C. Martin Wilbur and Julie Lienying How, 745-749. Cambridge MA: Harvard University Press, 1989.

"Resolutions on the Student Movement." In *Documents on Communism, Nationalism, and Soviet Advisers in China, 1918-1927: Papers Seized in the 1927 Peking Raid*, eds. C. Martin Wilbur and Julie Lienying How, 311-312. New York: Columbia University Press, 1956.

Robinson, Joan. *The Cultural Revolution in China.* Baltimore, MD: Pelican Books, 1969.

Roosevelt, Nicholas. "Russia and Great Britain in China." *CWR* 38 (October 30, 1926): 234-238.

Saich, Tony. *The Origins of the First United Front in China: The Role of Sneevliet (Alias Maring).* New York: E. J. Brill, 1991.

Schiffrin, Harold Z. *Sun Yat-sen: Reluctant Revolutionary.* Boston: Little, Brown & Co., 1980.

Schwartz, Bruno. "The Siege of Wuhan: From Day to Day." *CWR* 38 (September 18, 1926): 74-77.

Shanghai Times. Shanghai.

Sharman, Lyon. *Sun Yat-sen: His Life and Its Meaning, A Critical Biography.* Stanford: Stanford University Press, 1934.

Shieh, Milton J. T. *The Kuomintang: Selected Historical Documents, 1894-1969.* New York: St. Johns University Press, 1970.

Snow, Helen F. *The Chinese Communists: Sketches and Autobiographies of the Old Guard.* Westport, CN: Greenwood Publishing Co., 1972.

South China Weekly Review. Shantou.

South China Morning Post. Hong Kong.

Stremsky, Richard. *The Shaping of British Policy During the Nationalist Revolution in China.* Taipei: Soochow University, Department of Political Science Publication Series, 1979.

"Sun and the Treaties." *Peking and Tientsin Times* (December 10, 1924).

"Sun Beats Us." *Peking and Tientsin Times* (December 10, 1924).

Sun Yat-sen [孫中山]. "The Doctrine of Sun Yat-sen: To Act is Easy, to Know is Difficult." In *Prescriptions for Saving China: Selected Writings of Sun Yat-sen*, eds. Julie Lee Wei, Ramon H. Myers, and Donald G. Gillin, trans. by Julie Lee Wei, E-su Zen, and Linda Chao, 199-222. Stanford: Hoover Institution Press, 1994.

_____. "The Foundation for Building the Republic of China." In *Prescriptions for Saving China: Selected Writings of Sun Yat-sen*, eds. Julie Lee Wei, Ramon H. Myers, and Donald G. Gillin, trans. by Julie Lee Wei, E-su Zen, and Linda Chao, 246-251. Stanford: Hoover Institution Press, 1994.

_____. "The Means of Introducing Local Self-Government." In *Prescriptions for Saving China: Selected Writings of Sun Yat-sen*, eds. Julie Lee Wei, Ramon H. Myers, and Donald G. Gillin, trans. by Julie Lee Wei, E-su Zen, and Linda Chao, 240-246. Stanford: Hoover Institution Press, 1994.

_____. *Memoirs of a Chinese Revolutionary: A Programme of National Reconstruction for China*. Reprint edition. Taipei: Sino-American Publishing Co., 1953.

_____. *San Min Chu I: The Three Principles of the People*. Translated by Frank W. Price. Shanghai: China Committee, Institute of Pacific Relations, 1927.

"Sun Yat-sen Ill." *Peking and Tientsin Times* (December 8, 1924).

"Sun Yat-sen's Little Programme." *Peking and Tientsin Times* (December 8, 1924).

"Sun Yat-sen's Son in Shanghai." *North China Daily News* (September 29, 1924).

Sutton, Donald S. *Provincial Militarism and the Chinese Republic: The Yunnan Army, 1905-25*. Ann Arbor, MI: University of Michigan Press, 1980.

T'ang Leang-lin. *The Inner History of the Chinese Revolution*. London: G. Routledge & Sons, Ltd., 1930.

Trani, Eugene P. "Woodrow Wilson, China, and the Missionaries, 1913-1921." *Journal of Presbyterian History* 49:4 (Winter 1971): 328-351.

Tsin, Michael. *Nation, Governance, and Modernity in China: Canton, 1900-1927*. Stanford: Stanford University Press, 1999.

Tso, S. K. Sheldon. *The Labor Movement in China*. Shanghai: 1928.

"Two Farcical Events." *Hong Kong Telegraph* (January 27, 1923).

United States Department of State. "Records of the Department of State Relating to the Internal Affairs of China, 1910-1929." National Archives Microfilm Publications, no. 329. Washington DC: The National Archives, 1960. [Abbreviated *USDS*.]

Varg, Paul A. *Missionaries, Chinese, and Diplomats: The American Protestant Missionary Movement in China, 1890-1952*. Princeton, NJ: Princeton University Press, 1958.

_____. "A Survey of Changing Mission Goals and Methods." In *Christian Missions in China: Evangelists of What?*, ed. Jessie Lutz, 1-10. Boston: D. C. Heath and Company, 1965.

Vishnyakova-Akimova, Vera Vladimirovna. *Two Years in Revolutionary China, 1925-1927*. Translated by Steven I. Levine. Cambridge, MA: East Asian Research Center, Harvard University, 1971.

Wasserstrom, Jeffrey N. *Student Protests in Twentieth-Century China: The View from Shanghai*. Stanford: Stanford University Press, 1991.

Wei, Julie Lee, Ramon H. Myers, and Donald G. Gillin, eds. *Prescriptions for Saving China: Selected Writings of Sun Yat-sen*. Translated by Julie Lee Wei, E-su Zen, and Linda Chao. Stanford: Hoover Institution Press, 1994.

Welsh, Frank. *A Borrowed Place: The History of Hong Kong*. New York: Kodansha International, 1993.

Wilbur, C. Martin. "Military Separatism and the Process of Reunification under the Nationalist Regime." In *China in Crisis*, eds. Ho Ping-ti and Tang Tsou, 203-263. Chicago: Chicago University Press, 1968.

_____. *The Nationalist Revolution in China, 1923-1928*. Cambridge, MA: Cambridge University Press, 1983.

_____. *Sun Yat-sen: Frustrated Patriot*. New York: Columbia University Press, 1976.

Wilbur, C. Martin, and Julie Lien-ying How, eds. *Documents on Communism, Nationalism, and Soviet Advisers in China, 1918-1927: Papers Seized in the 1927 Peking Raid*. New York: Columbia University Press, 1956.

_____. *Missionaries of Revolution: Soviet Advisers and Nationalist China, 1920-1927*. Cambridge, MA: Harvard University Press, 1989.

Wong, Hin. "British Ask Intervention Against Bolsheviks." *CWR* 34 (September 12, 1925): 35.

_____. "Co-operation, or Non-Intervention, Wanted." *CWR* 32 (May 30, 1925): 362-366.

_____. "Farmers and Workers in Canton." *CWR* 32 (May 16, 1925): 301.

_____. "The Passing of the Kuomintang in South China." *CWR* 32 (March 21, 1925): 72-76.

_____. "There is no Anti-Americanism in South China!" *CWR* 37 (August 28, 1926): 319-320.

"World Brotherhood." *Chinese Recorder* 70:4 (April 1939): 214.

Yeh, Wen-hsin. *The Alienated Academy: Culture and Politics in Republican*

China, 1919-1937. Cambridge, MA: Harvard University Asia Center, 1990.

Yip Ka-che. *Religion, Nationalism, and Chinese Students: The Anti-Christian Movement of 1922-1927.* Bellingham, WA: Center for East Asian Studies, Western Washington University, c.1980.

Young, Ernest P. *The Presidency of Yuan Shi-k'ai: Liberalism and Dictatorship in Early Republican China.* Ann Arbor, MI: University of Michigan Press, 1977.

Yuan Zheng. "The 'Partification' of Education: A Pivotal Turn in Modern Chinese Education, 1924-1929." *Twentieth-Century China* 25:2 (April 2000): 33-53.

Index

schools and colleges, 10, 22, 158
Provincial Federationists, 45
provincialist(s), 15, 24, 26, 28-29, 31-32,
34, 76, 87-88, 103, 284; forces, 107;
identities, 109; leaders, 24, 108;
organizations, 26, 70, 89; resistance to
the GMD, 71, 89-90, 107; thinkers, 24;
views, 23, 108
Pukou, 225

Q

Qianshan, 144, 150
Qiaokou, 116
Qin dynasty, 73
Qing dynasty, 5, 13-15, 20, 121-22
Qingdao, 157, 180

R

Red Cross, 181
Red Flags, 27
Red International of Labor Unions, 251
Renji (Yan Chai) Street Church, 230
Republic of China (ROC), 3, 7, 13-19, 24,
29, 49, 73, 128, 254, 288-89
Republican Daily *(Minguo ribao)*, 48,
111, 114, 116, 263
Revolutionary Alliance (Tongmenghui),
15, 27, 162
Revolutionary Party (Gemingdang),
15-16; regime, 16-17
Revolutionary Youth *(Geming qingnian)*,
116
Roots, Logan, 11
Russell, Bertrand, 29
Russia, 30-31, 68, 177, 231, 253, 269,
Also see Soviet Union; GMD ties, 31,
217
Russian: agents, 30; educators, 20;
embassy, 11; government, 30; imports,
80; influence, 285; institutions, 123;
language, 131; servants, 174; ships, 78
Russian College, 131
Russian Communist Party, 37

S

S.S. Longshan, 264
S.S. Yick, 146
Saich, Anthony, 8
Sanshui, 81
Schurman, Jacob Gould, 29, 31, 68, 94
Seamen's Strike, 63-66, 68, 88, 93-94,
100-01, 146, 288; GMD advantage
from, 168; impact, 64
Seamen's Union, 63, 101, 177, 267
Second Eastern Expedition, 138, 146
Second National Conference of Chinese
Labor, 57
Second Revolution, 15
Second United Front, 8
Shaanxi, 132
Shaji: Incident, 136, 148, 157, 161-62,
187, 217, 247; Street, 263
Shamian, 87, 91-93, 96, 107, 137-38,
145-47, 150, 164, 186, 188, 244, 247,
263; banks, 81, 93, 107, 145; bridges,
189; concessions. *See* foreign:
concessions (Shamian); localist ties to,
150; residents, 146, 187
Shandong, 27, 221; troops, 222, 260
Shandong Christian University, 105, 121,
124
Shanghai, 1-2, 16-17, 27, 32, 37, 47,
49-50, 66, 73-75, 109, 112, 116, 118,
121, 125, 136, 156-62, 170, 180-81,
199, 205, 215, 217-18, 225, 228, 234,
236, 239-40, 243, 250-51, 255, 258-64,
268, 271-72, 279; concessions. *See*
foreign: concessions (Shanghai);
interventionists, 242; newspapers, 48,
83, 87, 109, 116; police, 243; schools,
11, 119, 280
Shanghai Christian Student Union, 162
Shanghai Incident. *See* May Thirtieth
Incident
Shanghai Provisional Municipal
Government, 262
Shanghai Student Federation, 59, 73
Shanghai Student Union, 162
Shanghai University, 114, 116, 119, 269
Shanghai-Hangzhou Railroad, 260
Shanghai-Nanjing Railway, 260

CORNELL EAST ASIA SERIES

Order online: www.einaudi.cornell.edu/eastasia/CEASbooks, or contact Cornell East Asia Series Distribution Center, 95 Brown Road, Box 1004, Ithaca, NY 14850, USA; toll-free: 1-877-865-2432, fax 607-255-7534, ceas@cornell.edu